D1557060

THE VOICE OF THE TAMBARAN

THE VOICE OF THE TAMBARAN

Truth and Illusion in Ilahita Arapesh Religion

DONALD F. TUZIN

UNIVERSITY OF CALIFORNIA PRESS

Berkeley | Los Angeles | London

University of California Press
Berkeley and Los Angeles, California

University of California Press, Ltd.
London, England

© 1980 by
The Regents of the University of California

Printed in the United States of America

Library of Congress Cataloging in Publication Data

Tuzin, Donald F
  The voice of the Tambaran.

  1. Arapesh tribe—Religion. I. Title.
BL2630.A72T89   299'.92   79-64661
ISBN 0-520-03964-5

---

1 2 3 4 5 6 7 8 9

In memory of my father

Then said Jesus unto him, Except ye
see signs and wonders, ye will not believe.

JOHN 4:48

Contents

Illustrations

Preface

THIS book is about a secret men's cult among the Ilahita Arapesh, a horticultural people inhabiting a portion of the nonriverine hinterland of the East Sepik region, New Guinea. The cult is known as the "Tambaran." Taken from the Pidgin English 'tambaran,' this name has been assimilated both to native usage and to the English technical vocabulary of the Sepik region. Its range of meanings is very wide; and, at least among the Ilahita Arapesh, there is *no* equivalent vernacular term for the cult in its holistic aspect. In this study the upper-case "Tambaran," when used to denote the cult as a religious institution, invites comparison with our phrase "the Church," even to the extent that the sometime feminine symbolism of the Roman Catholic church finds its counterpart in the masculine personification of the Tambaran. In addition, however, 'tambaran' is the generic term for the spirits, individual and collective, who are venerated within the cult. Ritual initiation grades and sacred paraphernalia are also 'tambaran,' and there are a host of metaphorical referents as well. Indeed, broadly speaking, this study is about the meanings of the Tambaran and the metaphors that arise from it. My intention is to show that, beyond the ideas and artifacts of the men's cult, beyond even the wider domain of supernaturalism, the Tambaran signifies tradition itself; it is the personified mystique of a total way of life.

By this, I mean that the Tambaran constitutes a symbolic system which, by formulating and integrating images of personal and collective identity, creates for the individual-in-society a source of highest meaning that is mystically true and compelling. This raises a number of analytic problems and opportunities for the anthropological student of religion. To begin with, an empirical validation of this admittedly rather grand assertion requires a detailed examination of cult ideas and practices, with special attention to those elements expressive of individual and group identity. The initiation sequence covers the life span from early childhood to old age. For the Arapesh male, the sequence is a path leading to the heights of ritually ordained knowledge, power and authority; for the analytic observer, it is a rich panorama of cultural themes rendered symbolically and intertwined with the ceaseless fluctuations of life in society. The book's format roughly parallels the initiation sequence, with occasional topical digressions and a two-chapter exploration of Tambaran symbolism as embodied in religious art and architecture. The ninth chapter examines the implications of cult ideology for social control and integration, as a prelude to assessing, in the penultimate chapter, the role of Tambaran ethics in Arapesh society and culture, and also the relevance of this study to broader issues attending the anthropology of religious change.

Another question immediately presents itself: How can the Tambaran's supreme cultural significance be reconciled with the fact that women and children are rigidly excluded from cult secrets and are, furthermore, victims in body and mind of terrorism systematically applied by men acting in the name of the Tambaran? Do Arapesh men and women inhabit different cultural worlds? The cultural schism is actually more apparent than real; but an understanding of why this is so requires analysis of the politics of ritual secrecy and of the nuances of belief which not only divide men from women, but also some men from other men. Hence, these and various subordinate issues will command increasing attention as the study develops.

The Tambaran Cult exists in varying forms throughout the cultures of the Sepik River basin. Forty years ago, Margaret Mead sketched the general beliefs and practices of Sepik-area religions, recommending "tamberan" as a generic term "in the hope that it may be adopted into the vocabulary for this area, as it is already in widespread use as an equivalent for the various native terms" (1938:169). "There is," she rightly averred, "in this area no other socio-religious trait which has anything like the universality or importance of the tamberan cult" (p. 171). Since that time, despite numerous references and some lengthier discussions, there has not appeared a full-scale description of the cult in a particular setting. The following study is offered in service of this ethnographic need. In addition, treatment is given to the social and cultural mechanisms through which the Tambaran has spread across the region. As Boas (1911) and Herskovits (1948) understood long ago, for diffusion to occur it is not enough that peoples be brought within reach of one another, nor even that social interaction exist between them; there must also be a way in which meanings originating in one cultural-symbolic system can be translated (or transliterated) into terms consistent with meanings already inherent in the importing system. The practice of the Arapesh in imposing their own mythological understandings on imported ritual and artistic elements is an instance of this general process and will be analyzed accordingly.

I have used mythology in this study as a means of illuminating the Tambaran, not as a source of additional analytic problems in its own right. Cult myths are presented as overtures to the chapters whose moods and themes they most directly express. Except for a few places in which the analysis calls for closer scrutiny of some mythically constituted symbol, the stories will be dealt with only in this limited way. The story of Nambweapa'w is appropriately placed at the beginning of chapter 1; for, as the epic creation myth of the Arapesh, its paradigmatic themes and images reverberate through the entire ethnography.

Although I have sought to contain this study within itself, a good deal of relevant historical and sociological background is covered in a previous volume (Tuzin 1976) which was partly intended as a preamble. From time to time, elements from the earlier work will be reintroduced in support of the current discussion; here I will merely sketch the general relationship between the two studies.

In Ilahita village, the site of my research, public life is organized largely according to an elaborate system of dual social structures which crosscut the community at several levels and involve all adult males (and, by implication, their dependents) in a comprehensive web of reciprocity. These relationships do not, as in many other moiety systems, involve marriage exchange; rather, they embody alternating ties of cooperation and competition that are activated in a variety of secular and religious contexts. Recruitment to the groups comprising these structures is determined by the interconnected criteria of descent, residence and ritual status.

The thesis of the first study was that the successful integration of Ilahita village, with nearly 1,500 inhabitants, is achieved through the conventions prescribed within the dual organization. Accordingly, emphasis was placed on the development and functional properties of this system in relation to the problems of settlement size and density.

In this volume we return to the dual organization, not as the prime object of analysis, but as the framework for Tambaran ideology and practice. The dual structures, whose social functions are now a matter of record, are imbued with ritual significance. The system as a whole is, in fact, suffused with religious meaning. To the list of motives underlying conformity to the system's prescriptions, some of which are pragmatically based, we now add the actors' perception of religious necessity and their submission, more or less, to Tambaran symbolism. In short, this study complements its predecessor by applying the dimension of cultural meaning to that of social utility.

Orthographic Note

AS in the earlier volume, the convention used here for distinguishing vernacular terms from Pidgin English is to place the former in italic print and the latter in single quotation marks. Arapesh proper nouns are capitalized and not in italic. In addition, I have taken the liberty of treating a small number of Pidgin English terms (e.g. 'tambaran') as having passed into the technical vocabulary of the Melanesian ethnographic literature. The terms are defined upon their first appearance in the text, and are thereafter used as English words. They are also entered into the Glossary (Appendix A).

For the spelling of Pidgin English words, my authority is Francis Mihalic's dictionary and grammar of Melanesian Pidgin (1971). In Arapesh orthography I have used a simple phonetic rendering, but I should note that an x in final position (a noun-class plural suffix) is sounded as a lenis voiceless velar fricative, while the feminine singular suffix, 'w, is a labialized glottal stop. The phoneme ng is sounded as in the English "finger." Nearly all Arapesh words are stressed on the penultimate syllable. For a discussion of the taxonomic relationships of this language, see Tuzin (1976: 18–19). See also Fortune (1942) for an analysis of Mountain Arapesh, a language grammatically and phonologically similar to that spoken by the Ilahita Arapesh.

A Note on Ritual Secrecy

IN deference to the wishes of my Ilahita hosts, I am obliged to refrain from publishing photographs depicting certain ritual scenes and paraphernalia. Strictures of secrecy do not apply to verbal descriptions, but there is no question that words alone are poor witnesses to the rich forms and textures of the Tambaran. Inquiries regarding access to unpublished photographs may be addressed to the author at: Department of Anthropology, University of California, La Jolla, California 92093.

Acknowledgments

THIS book is a sequel to an earlier work which dealt with social organization among the Ilahita Arapesh (Tuzin 1976). Both studies arose from a common body of ethnographic materials, and thus my agreeable duty is to remember again those agencies and persons that variously contributed to the original research project, extending my thanks to include those who have assisted in the present effort.

Field research was conducted during three visits totaling twenty-one months in the period 1969–1972 under support of a scholarship in the Department of Anthropology of the Research School of Pacific Studies, Australian National University. I am obliged to that institution for its generous funding, to the Wenner-Gren Foundation for Anthropological Research for a supplemental grant-in-aid, to the University of California at San Diego for financial assistance during the final stages of writing and production, and to the Editorial Committee of the University of California for subventions to defray the costs of publishing this and the preceding volume.

In what was then the Territory of Papua New Guinea, officers of the Department of District Administration were most helpful in providing occasional transport, supplies, general information and access to patrol reports and court records. Assistant District Commissioner Mike Neal must be acknowledged in this regard, and in particular I wish to thank Bob and Carol Lachal for their abiding support and hospitality. Field staff of the South Sea Evangelical Mission were equally munificent. I am indebted to Keith and Mabs Duncan, Helga Weber, Ursula Geffke and especially Liesbeth Schrader—a saintly lady of long-standing residence in Ilahita, who welcomed me to the village and introduced me to its people and culture. Of the villagers themselves, I cannot convey adequately their unwavering kindness and tolerance toward me. In the limited space I can mention only a few of my attentive hosts: Councillor Kunai, Gidion, Supalo, Saowen, Moses, Kwamwi, Ongota, Behinguf and Ribeka. My only chance of repaying them resides in the hope that their descendants will find value in this record.

During early studies at the University of London, my interest in Sepik cultures was stimulated by the late Phyllis Kaberry, while Anthony Forge did me the momentous favor of recommending Ilahita as a likely research base. Reo Fortune (University of Cambridge) subsequently oriented me to the Arapesh language. The late Margaret Mead, whose classic writings on the Mountain Arapesh were (and are) an inspiration for me, displayed a gracious interest in the project from its start. During many exchanges, culminating in a memorable visit she made to us in Ilahita itself, she offered valuable insights which have found their way into these pages. My greatest intellectual debt, however, is owed to Derek Freeman. As my doctoral supervisor, his scrupulous concern addressed all aspects of the research. Accordingly, many of the thoughts contained herein were conceived under the influence of his friendship, advice and gentle criticism.

For their helpful criticisms on portions of this study while it was in progress, I am grateful to F. G. Bailey, Michael E. Meeker, Melford E. Spiro and Jehanne Teilhet. My special thanks are given to Gilbert H. Herdt, David K. Jordan, Richard Scaglion and Marc J. Swartz, all of whom read and criticized the complete manuscript. While they share in whatever credit may accrue to the final work, the defects thereof are entirely my own doing.

I take this opportunity, also, to express my gratitude to Phyllis Killen and Jesse Phillips of the editorial staff of the University of California Press, whose skill and diplomacy were at all times reassuring. I commend with thanks Tirzo

Gonzalez, who prepared the series of spirit-house drawings; Jennifer Kotter, who photographically reproduced these drawings; Adrienne Morgan, who drafted the maps and diagrams contained in the volume; and June Wilkins and David Marlowe, who typed the final manuscript.

To my wife Beverly, I owe more than can be told.

1. Introduction

In the beginning there was no village of Ilahita and there were no people in the world. There was just one man. We do not remember the name of this man, but one day he was walking along and he heard a commotion start up in a nearby pond. It sounded like women's voices, laughing and shouting, and the man was instantly intrigued. Early the following morning he went and hid in the bushes near the edge of the pond and watched what happened.

Soon a group of cassowaries came down to the water and, as he watched, the leader of the group took off her skin entirely and jumped into the water to bathe. The rest of them took off their skins as well and piled them on top of the leader's skin. But when they were without their skins they no longer looked like cassowaries: they looked like human women. The man had never seen anything like this before, and he lusted.

Later in the afternoon the cassowaries were still there, playing and splashing. The man crept stealthfully to the pile of skins and pulled the bottom one out from under the others. It belonged to the leader of the group, the one he particularly liked. He folded the skin tightly into a small bundle and put it into a short bamboo tube which he placed in his shoulder basket. Then he sat down and waited.

As dusk approached, the cassowary-women came out of the water and began putting their skins back on. But the leader of the group could not find her skin, though everyone searched carefully. Finally she suggested that the others go ahead and she would continue looking; perhaps she would sleep here and they could rejoin her the following day. When the man heard the sound of the group die away completely in the distance, he stepped out of hiding and said to the woman, "What are you looking for at this hour?" "Just something that belongs to me," she replied with downcast eyes. She lied and said she was looking for a bit of food she had dropped.

Then the man remarked that it was almost dark and that soon she would not be able to see well enough to continue searching. He suggested that she go home with him to spend the night. "What will happen if I go with you?" she asked. "You can stay with me and cook my food and help me in my gardens," he said. This sounded all right to the cassowary-woman and so she went along with him.

When they arrived at the man's house they ate and slept. In the morning when they got up the cassowary-woman asked the man where she could defecate. He showed her the place and, while she was out of sight, fetched a sharpened piece of white quartz and buried it (with the point sticking out) in the base of a tree near his house. This tree was a pandanus palm which has edible fruit and red, fuzzy leaves.

The cassowary-woman returned and the man told her to clean herself against the base of this tree. But when she went to rub herself the stone pierced her groin and formed her vulva. (This was necessary because cassowaries do not have vulvas.) The woman was very alarmed at the flow of blood and she asked the man if he could show her a house where she could go to sleep; she had started her first menstruation. After several days her vulva had healed and the blood had stopped. She bathed and came back and now the two people were married: they slept together and had sexual intercourse. She was a good wife to the man.

Over the years they had many children, males and females alternately. When they finally had their last child—a male—the two of them were quite old. The last child was still very young, so his parents typically alternated work patterns: when the father took the older children to work, the mother (her name was Nambweapa'w) would attend the youngest child, and vice versa.

One day when Nambweapa'w took the older children to the garden the youngest child cried and cried for its mother, and nothing the father did would appease it. Finally, in frustration, the father took the old bamboo tube containing his wife's cassowary skin out of the roof thatch. Donning the skin, he appeared to the child and pretended that he was going to eat him. Terrified, the child cried out for its father. Then the father ran behind the house, took off the skin, and rushed back to the boy. After the boy told him about the terrible monster, the father warned that his cries had attracted the beast. This way he succeeded in tricking the child into silence. He did this several times and then, one day, the child saw what his father was up to and where he had rehidden the bamboo tube.

The following day the father went off with the older children, leaving his wife and the child at home. The boy watched as his mother peeled yams and put them into the water to make soup. Then she began scraping coconut meat to add to the soup. The child begged for a piece of coconut and Nambweapa'w became annoyed. "You're always crying for coconut. Be quiet and let me get on with cooking soup for everyone." The child slyly replied that if she gave him some coconut he would tell her a secret about her husband.

Nambweapa'w was curious, so she gave the child some coconut. When he had finished he demanded more, and she gave him another helping. Then the child demanded that they wait so that he could have some of the soup before telling his mother the secret. So the mother stoked the fire and hastily finished it. Finally, the child went into the house and fetched the bamboo tube and gave it to his mother. She opened it and there she saw her casso-wary skin which she had lost so many years before. Then she realized that her husband had been deceiving her all along.

She pulled out the skin and filled the tube with yam scrapings and peels. Then she ordered the child to replace the tube where he had found it, warn-ing that if he ever told his father about this, he (the father) would surely kill him.

Later the husband returned with the other children and Nambweapa'w told them to eat while she disposed of some yam scrapings. She took these and the cassowary skin and, when she was out of sight, she put on the skin. As a cassowary, she returned and made threatening gestures to everyone be-fore running away to the gardens. All the children were very frightened, but their father knew what was happening. "There's no reason to be afraid. That is no cassowary. It is your mother. Now go after her and bring her back." So the children ran after her, but Nambweapa'w was too quick, and she escaped them. She stood on a hill and called to them: "All right, I am your mother who bore you, and I am leaving you now. You must all look after your little brother. Look at this row of tulip trees I have planted. When the nuts on them are ripe, all the girls must go up and fill their netbags with the nuts. Then you boys must take your sisters and come in search of me. Bring a conch shell and blow it as you walk along and call my name. You will have to sleep in the tall grass. If I hear you calling, I will come to you."

With that, Nambweapa'w turned and disappeared into the forest. Only the father remained to look after all the children, and everyone cried at the loss of Nambweapa'w.

When the brothers noticed that the nuts of the tulip were ripening they reminded their sisters of the words of their mother. The girls filled their bags to overflowing with nuts. Then the brothers fetched their spears and took their sisters off in search of their mother. They came to a tree which their mother had told them about, climbed it, and blew the conch in the direction of the grass fields—where their mother had told them she would be. The sisters climbed one tree and the brothers climbed another. The youngest brother was the first to go up the tree, and the rest of the boys arranged themselves in birth-order down the tree trunk, with the oldest at the very bottom. Their father was with them, but he was too old to get into the tree.

It was the eldest son who first called for his mother. As he called her name he threw a blade of grass in the direction of his call, as his mother had earlier instructed them to do. Because he was near the base of the trunk, the object landed only a short distance away. Then the next eldest tried, and so on; each time the grass flew a little farther. When the youngest, who was at the top of the tree, threw a blade of grass the wind carried it far away to where Nambweapa'w was sitting making vegetal salt. The blade landed nearby, in a ground-crab hole.

Nambweapa'w saw this and then heard her youngest child calling for her with the conch shell from far away. She started off in the direction of the sound, following the trail of grass which the children had thrown. She found her way to the tree where all her sons were perched, told them to come down, and asked them where their sisters were. "Oh, they are in another tree," they replied. So the mother went and told the daughters to come down as well. When they had all gathered, Nambweapa'w told the sons to collect their spears and the daughters their netbags and to come with her to her home far away.

The sons picked up all their spears, but when they were finished there was still one left—their father's. Before they had climbed into the tree they had hidden the old man at its base, covering him with a broad leaf. Nambweapa'w saw the spear and asked, "Whose spear is this? I think it looks like the one that belongs to your old father. Where is he? Show me." But the children were afraid for their father, and it was only after she threatened to kill them with her own spear that they showed her where they had hidden him.

Nambweapa'w removed the leaf and, with one thrust, crushed her husband's skull with his spear. All the children wailed at this, but she silenced them by saying that if they cried for him she would kill them too. The children were very frightened of her, and when she started off they followed meekly behind.

They walked deep into the great forest and, near nightfall, Nambweapa'w spat, causing a heavy rain to begin falling. They had actually arrived at her home, but the children did not realize it. Their mother sent the boys into a wild palm to sleep protected from the rain, and the girls she sent into a wild banana plant. They slept and in the middle of the night some of the boys turned over against the side of the tree—but it was not the side of a tree any longer. It was the inside wall of a great spirit house. (The walls of the spirit houses are today made from the wood of this palm.) The girls also turned over in the night and found, not the wild banana plant in which they had fallen asleep, but a menstrual house whose walls were made from sago bark. Both the boys and girls stoked the fires of their separate houses and marveled at how their surroundings had changed. Then they straightened their beds and went back to sleep.

In the morning when the cock crowed they looked out of their houses and beheld that they were in the middle of a large village that had materialized during the night. The previous evening they had gone to sleep in the middle of a big forest, but now an entire village had sprung up. They knew that their mother had caused all this, and now they were even more frightened of her powers.

Their mother told them to eat first and then she would show them around the village. And what a beautiful village it was! Many flowers and gaily colored crotons, and chickens and dogs. The houses were well and newly built, and all the storehouses were filled with yams.

(Ending A)

The children and their mother stayed on in the village, and each young man took the sister following him in birth order as his wife—all except the youngest, who had no younger sister, and was too young to marry anyway. They had a very easy life because the mother's magic was turned to helping them with their gardening. Thus, when a couple went out to clear a new garden, they had only to cut one tree; they would go home, return the next day and find that the entire garden had cleared itself. If they wanted to plant some vegetables, they would only plant one, and the next day the entire garden would be planted—in nice neat rows. When it came time to harvest, they would dig only one yam or taro, or cut only one stalk of sugar cane, and the next day all the harvested food would appear magically in neat piles at the edge of the garden. This was how they lived. All was provided by their mother. They were, however, forbidden to eat one kind of food, which occasionally grew up by itself in their gardens. This was the aerial tuber of a particular kind of yam.

This went on for some years, until the older children became impatient at being denied the forbidden kind of yam. So, disregarding their mother's warning, they picked some of these tubers and ate them. Only the youngest child remained obedient to his mother's wishes. When the mother found out what they had done she was very angry, but she did not let them know it. Instead, she punished them in another way. She told her youngest son, who was by now a grown man, that she had observed a tree kangaroo return daily to a particular tree; she was sure that if he stationed himself there with a spear he would be able to kill the animal. He said he would go there that evening. As the time drew near, the mother transformed herself into a tree kangaroo, and she herself went to the tree she had described to the son. Sure enough, the son was waiting and when she appeared he stabbed her in the chest. As he did so, she cried out in her own voice that she was his mother, why was he killing her so? Horrified, the young man ran to help his mother by pulling the spear, but she told him to wait until she had spoken. "After this, if a man falls from a tall tree, he will die; if a man is bitten by certain kinds of snakes, he will die; if a man catches certain kinds of diseases, he will die; if a man is victimized by a powerful sorcerer, he also will die. Hereafter, there will be much pain in childbirth, and both men and women will have to work hard to grow their food. The magic is finished." With that, she told her son to remove the spear, and when he did, she died.

The young man returned to his older siblings, grieved by his mother's death and very angry at the others for having been the cause of it. He scolded them severely for having originally broken the mother's taboo, the result of which was that they would hereafter be denied all the advantages of her magic. Such was his fury, in fact, that it caused a great swell of water to rise up and swirl around him, lifting him and the log on which he was standing and carrying him far away—to America, as we now know. The coming of the white man is the return of our little brother, clever and willing to show us all the things we lost long ago.

(Ending B)

After the children had looked around the village their mother proceeded to divide everything among them—houses, gardens and all other possessions. She also paired them off into married couples: the eldest boy married his sister who had been born just after him, and so on. Their mother forced them to do this. But when they came to the youngest son, he was left without a wife. He had been born last. "All right, all you other men have sisters of your own to marry. As for your youngest brother, he has no one to marry, and therefore I myself will hold him and look after him." This is what Nambweapa'w said.

They all settled down in the village, and their mother provided everyone with yam soup, coconuts, tulip leaves, and taro. But to the youngest child, she gave very special food. Unknown to the others, the youngest received various kinds of meat, and tinned fish, onions, tomatoes—all good food. Meanwhile, the others thought he was eating the same kinds of food they were.

After a long time Nambweapa'w became concerned. "It would not be good if they all stayed in this one place, for that way their descendants would all speak the same language. What can I do to produce the different languages?" Then she had an idea. She told all her sons that they must climb up her betelnut palm and fetch her some of the fruits. The youngest was to go up the tree first, followed by the rest in ascending order of birth. The eldest was near the base of the palm.

When they were all in the tree their mother spat on the base of it. The youngest son picked a spray of nuts from the top of the tree and handed it down to his brothers, who continued passing it until it reached the eldest son, who handed it to Nambweapa'w. Then Nambweapa'w told them to come back down to the ground. There were insects of a certain type living in the base of the palm, and when the big brother slid down they bit him. Because of this he came down speaking the language of Ilahita. The second one down was also bitten, and he spoke the Bumbita language. As they came down each was bitten and each spoke a different language—Wam, Urat, Wosera, Sepik, Tolai, the Papuan languages. All the languages of the world were formed this way. Finally the last brother came down, was bitten and he spoke English. Everyone marveled at the strange sound of this language, and no one could understand one word of it. They could understand a little of what each other said, but the language of their littlest brother was completely strange to them.[1]

And so all the brothers and their sister-wives lived on and had many children and gradually became dispersed throughout the land. All except the youngest who had no wife. He stayed with his mother and was cared for by her. Then one day Nambweapa'w told the boy to make a strong, sharp spear and temper it well in the fire so that he could shoot a tree kangaroo which she had been seeing in the area. When he had prepared the spear as instructed, he was sent to watch for the tree kangaroo at the base of a particular tree where she always spied it. She would go first to collect water nearby, and he was to follow and wait near the tree. When he had killed it, Nambweapa'w would eat it.

But instead of going to collect water, the mother, as soon as she was out of sight of her son, turned herself into a tree kangaroo and returned to feed in the tree that her son was watching. She deliberately exposed a vulnerable part of her body toward where her son was standing. The boy took careful aim and the spear pierced his mother, turning her instantly back into her human form. She cried: "Child, why did you shoot me? I am your mother." But the boy knew better. He knew that his mother had tricked him and had turned herself into a tree kangaroo, and that she herself was to blame. He ran to her side and started to pull out the spear shaft, but she stopped him, saying, "Wait. Don't pull it out until I have told you what I must say. After I have spoken you can pull out the spear and then I will die." So the mother pronounced these instructions.

"When I have died you must cut down this tree and cover my body with

---

1. In the alternative version of the story (see above) this linguistic division occurs when the children descend from the tree they had climbed earlier in order to make contact with their mother in her hiding-place in the grassfields. The storyteller does not seem to notice that this implies the siblings are speaking different languages for the entire second half of the story.

it. Ask your brothers to help, and if they agree, then later they will share in whatever good comes up here. If they are too lazy, or if they are cross with you, then you do it yourself and afterward they will be sorry."

"Later you will see all sorts of food grow up from this place where I am buried. All of this you may eat, except a red fruit which will grow straight out of my heart. This will be taboo to you. You will see it: the leaf is brilliant red and black. This you must not eat."

When the mother had finished speaking, her son pulled out the spear and she died. The boy ran back to his brothers and explained how their mother had tricked him into killing her. Then he asked them to help him cut down the tree to cover over her body. But they were all cross and said that this was his affair alone for shooting their mother. They would not help him. So the boy worked by himself for many months to cut down all the trees. After a time his next elder brother took pity on him, and the two of them worked together. When the sun had dried the underbrush and logs, they burned the area and then left it.

When they returned to the spot the following year, about the same time that their mother had died, they found that an enormous amount of food had grown up in the garden. Everything was there: yams, taro, sugar cane, greens of all kinds, even meat. Pig meat, cassowary, tree kangaroo, opossum, bandicoot, rat—all the kinds of game we know. This is how we came to have all these kinds of food.

Now, when I tell this story I cannot help thinking about the patrol officers' mark.[2] *When I see the cassowary and tree kangaroo I wonder if the Australians have the same story of Nambweapa'w. Perhaps they do.*

WITHIN hours of my arrival in Ilahita, after hearing the story of Nambweapa'w, I was taken by a few of the villagers to a large, spring-fed pool situated in a grove of trees a few meters downhill from one of the ceremonial hamlets. By night the place would no doubt be alive with buzzing and croaking, but at our midday visit the pool reposed in deep, uncanny stillness. In hushed tones brought on by the infectious tranquility, my companions told me that this was the very pool in which Nambweapa'w and

---

2. This is the Great Seal of Australia, on which is embossed a kangaroo and an emu. For a more comprehensive introduction to Arapesh culture and history, along with a description of field work conditions, see the opening chapters of the previous volume (Tuzin 1976).

the other cassowary-women were bathing when First Man spied them. Ilahita, they proudly confided, was the seat of all human creation—theirs and mine. On our way back up the hill, one of my female guides wondered aloud how they would accommodate the throngs of international tourists who would surely flock to Ilahita once they learned that Creation had begun here.

The story of Nambweapa'w holds a highly privileged place in Ilahita self-consciousness. By far, it is their favorite, most widely known and often repeated story—the ultimate, in their judgment, of narrative excellence. Although the creation it describes is universal, the story belongs to Ilahita alone; the anticipated tourists would be coming not only to commemorate their Primal Mother, but also to pay homage to Ilahita, the First Born, custodian of Nambweapa'w's sacred tradition.

A comprehensive analysis and interpretation of the story of Nambweapa'w would take us very far off the track of this study. Moreover, as a source of insight into the Tambaran, the story's manifest content is sufficiently illuminating. Briefly stated, Nambweapa'w contributes in three sorts of ways to the story of the Tambaran. First, "she" appears by name in a number of ritual contexts, enhancing their significance by a kind of symbolic cross-referencing to the primordial ground of Arapesh being and identity. Secondly, many of the existential themes dwelt upon by the Tambaran are traceable to prototypes found in the story of Nambweapa'w. Thus, time and again the analysis will return to issues of sexual antagonism, aggression, power, retribution, metamorphosis, dependency, tricks and illusions, and the prepotencies of old age—issues which comprise the dramatic structure of this story. Finally, as we have just seen, Nambweapa'w crystallizes for the Arapesh a sense of themselves in relation to (and in mythic priority over) a larger humanity. The Tambaran, largely by virtue of its participation in the same array of existential themes, likewise serves as a summary symbol of Arapesh cultural identity. When the two images are brought together under ritual auspices, the complex wedding of male and female, past and present, creation and destruction—all

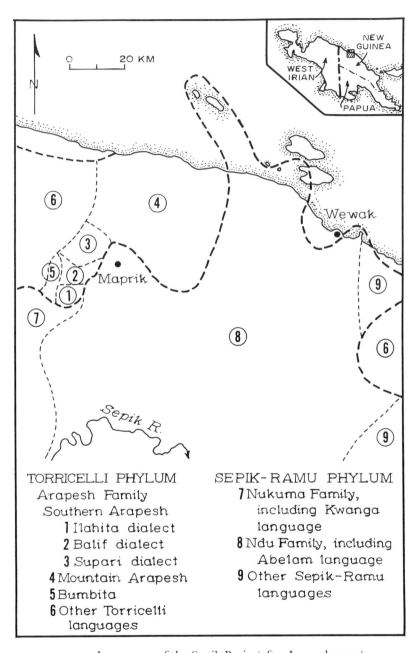

MAP 1. Languages of the Sepik Basin (after Laycock 1973)

raised to mythic proportions—yields a transcendent meaning of supreme cultural value. Nambweapa'w and the Tambaran may be independent symbolic foci, but in the final analysis they are not culturally complete without one another.

THE SETTING

The Ilahita Arapesh are a culturally and linguistically distinct population inhabiting seven villages in a region of gently rolling hills marking the transition between the coastal Torricelli Mountains and the broad, grassy plain that rises north from the Sepik River. Maprik, the subdistrict administrative headquarters, lies east-northeast at a distance of some 25 kilometers. The evidence is that the Ilahita Arapesh and their cousins the Mountain Arapesh (Mead 1938) once occupied a continuous, sparsely settled territory stretching along an east-west axis across the upper plains and lower foothills. During the last century, and continuing into the early decades of this century, the Arapesh were encroached upon by warlike peoples migrating northward in a predatory expansion from the environs of the Sepik River. The easternmost Arapesh withdrew higher into the inhospitable recesses of the Torricelli Mountains, while in the west the refugees—no longer in communication with the "Mountain Arapesh"—gathered defensively into villages large enough to prevent further serious intrusions. As a result the Ilahita Arapesh, descendants of the westerly contingent, are today bounded on the north and west by closely related Arapesh-speaking groups, and on the east and south by the Abelam and Kwanga, respectively, both of which are descended from yesterday's invaders. Across the latter boundaries, the Ilahita have acquired a number of important cultural traits, including elements of Tambaran ideology and organization.

Arapesh villages are dense, sedentary habitats strung out along the ridgetops of the hilly terrain. Their surroundings are taken up with gardens in various stages of use or reforestation, sago groves in the valley floors, and ancient forests in the more distant parts. Yams (*Dioscorea* spp.) are by far the

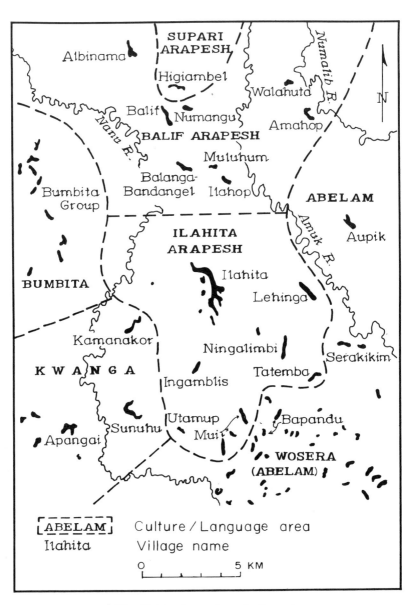

MAP 2. The Ilahita Arapesh and adjacent groups

most important staple, both nutritionally and ritually (Tuzin 1972). Men's reputations, individually and collectively, depend greatly on their prowess as yam growers, and the display and competitive exchange of these tubers play a large part in the political life of the society. These prestige considerations apply both to short yams (measured in quantity) and to the giant yams (*D. alata*) which can reach lengths of over three meters and weights which tax the strength of two strong men. Sago, taro and banana follow yam in approximately that order of dietary emphasis and ritual importance. Breadfruit, papaya, greens of many types, and a wide range of other lowland tropical cultigens are also eaten. Meat is a rare delicacy, consumed almost exclusively by men on ceremonial occasions, even though the flesh of game animals (pig, cassowary, cuscus, bandicoot, opossum, wallaby) is highly prized by the villagers. Correspondingly, hunting is a rather intermittent, unreliable food-getting activity. Spears, nets, lairs and clubs are the primary weapons of the hunt.

The specific location of this study is Ilahita village, a sprawling community of 1,490 residents from which the collection of seven "Ilahita Arapesh" villages takes its name. Traditionally, relations among these villages were organized around two relatively stable alliance blocs, the dominant one being led by Ilahita itself. Old friendships and animosities persist to the present day and are expressed through a variety of institutions that have emerged since the Australians enforced peace in the early 1950s. However, even in the days of chronic hostilities, truces were regularly called for the purpose of cooperation in ritual enterprises. Next to warfare itself, ritual reciprocity was—and to a considerable extent continues to be—the chief mechanism of areal integration and the basis of perceived cultural identity. On the other hand, it would be an exaggeration to claim that this network of cooperation disqualifies the individual village as the ritual unit. The Tambaran Cult is very much a village entity and, in principle, can be sustained without outside help. Nevertheless, the technical and political factors favoring intervillage cooperation do lend to the Tambaran a regional character as well.

1. Giant "male" yams are decorated and proudly displayed by the men of
one of Ilahita's wards. Note the pubic triangle painted on the "two-legged"
yam that is first in line.

2. A multi-appendaged "female" yam, decorated with mask, shells, yellow-colored leaves and feathers, and two new netbags on "her" back.

Residential organization in Arapesh villages operates at two levels, which I have called "wards" and "hamlets." Ila-hita, by virtue of its unusually large size, contains six wards in comparison with the more common pattern of two or (less commonly) four wards in the other villages. Each ward is named and residentially contained. Unified by closely over-lapping ties of kinship and neighborhood, ward residents

3. One of several yam displays at Lawank's funeral. The corpse is decorated so as to signify his fame as a short-yam grower. The bundle of rods rising from the center of the yam heap consists of markers commemorating recent, particularly successful harvests.

recognize a community of interest and identity which frequently involves them in political contests with members of other wards. Marriage predominantly occurs within rather than between wards, reflecting at the local level a preference for *village* endogamy, the frequency of which exceeds 90 percent of extant unions. The wards of Ilahita are Balanga (pop.

309), Bwi'ingili (172), Hengwanif (148), Ilifalemb (213), Ililip (487), Nangup (161).[3]

Each ward is divided into a large number of named domestic precincts comprising a circle or haphazard clustering of yam-storage and dwelling houses. In all, there are more than ninety of these "hamlets" in the village. Typically, a hamlet is occupied by one or more descent units consisting of agnatically related males, their wives, children, parents, and perhaps a small number of nonagnatic kin or friends who are there at the discretion of the primary owners.

SEX AND DOMESTICITY

Weather permitting, most domestic living goes on in the clearing in front of the nuclear-family dwelling, and in general the hamlet has an air of casual intimacy marked by informal exchanges of food, services and conversation. Men in their prime, especially those with nubile daughters, often sleep and take their meals in their yam house, lest the intense femininity of the dwelling house jeopardize their spiritual well-being and spoil the success of magical endeavors. The other deviation from the nuclear-family residence pattern concerns the habit of adolescents from neighboring hamlets of banding together to build a dormitory for themselves. Youths and maidens establish separate sleeping quarters— but this segregation does not survive very long after dark. Girls' houses are the scene of night-long courting parties during which, apart from some harmless fondling, the main activity appears to be giggling. Heavy petting and intercourse are avoided for fear of the damage they would do to the male's future marriage or yam-growing prospects (Tuzin 1978b).[4]

3. For continuing reference, ward names and other technical and vernacular terms are included in a glossary at the end of this volume (Appendix A).

In this brief review I am omitting discussion of outlying camps and colonies spawned by the village in both recent and remote times. Although they figure prominently in the story of Ilahita population dynamics (Tuzin 1976: 174,199), in ritual terms they are undifferentiated from the main village.

4. Young married women sometimes retreat to a girls' house during their menstrual period; but this is as much to enjoy a reunion with their younger girl-friends as it is to avoid contaminating their marriage dwelling.

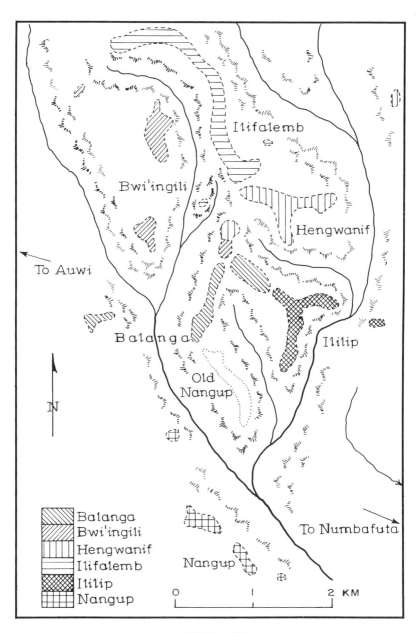

To Auwi

Ilifalemb

Bwi'ingili

Hengwanif

N

Balanga

Ililip

Old
Nangup

To Numbafuta

Balanga
Bwi'ingili
Hengwanif
Ilifalemb
Ililip
Nangup

Nangup

0   1   2 KM

MAP 3. Ilahita village

The overdetermined male bias of Arapesh religious culture begins, in a mythic sense, with the story of Nambweapa'w, in which First Man is credited with inventing the first marriage as well as with creating the first vulva and the first menstruation. Indeed, it is a phallocentric belief (the women know better) that the resumption of menstruation following the postpartum lactation interval is the direct result of the lifting of the taboo on coitus and the penetration of the vagina by the penis: a re-creation of the primal wounding. Be that as it may, today's Arapesh males gladly join in the celebration of a girl's first menses and wedding, granting that at these times the girl is very special and ought to be recognized as such. Since the rest of this study is given over so heavily to the actions and concerns of Arapesh males, a moment's pause on the distaff side of ceremonialism would not seem likely to upset the balance given by this culture.

A girl's first menstrual flow is followed immediately by a month's seclusion in a house in her father's hamlet, attended by a number of girl friends of her own age. Word of the event is sent about to friends and family, who respond with visits to the hamlet and gifts of meat and other delicacies, so that she will be well rounded and beautiful at the time of her debut. During this interval, modesty demands that the girl not be seen by males. By night, she and her friends go abroad and collect firewood, stacking it in a pile which by the end of the month will have grown to immense size. The purpose of this lavish display is to broadcast to passers-by that the girl now entering womanhood will make a fine wife, for gathering firewood is one of the archetypal female roles in this society.

As the girl begins her second period, a time is appointed a few days hence for her ceremonial debut. While her parents make final arrangements for the feast, her mother's brother(s) and father's sister(s) gather the materials they will use to adorn her. On the morning in question, the girl is bathed by her female cross-kinsmen; her scalp is shaved, leaving only a strip of hair down the middle; and her skin is rubbed to a golden tone with the juice and oil of turmeric. Her costume, its parts bespelled with beauty magic, consist of shell neck-

4. A stack of firewood collected by a girl and her close friends during the seclusion period following her first menses. It is a sign to passers-by that the girl now entering nubility will make a fine wife.

laces and pendants, leaves and feathers of (symbolically feminine) yellow, and two new netbags stretched on light frames and hung on her back. In the early afternoon, her cross-kinsmen lead her into the clearing and display her to the crowd of assembled well-wishers. Typically, she is joined by a few little girls of her group, who beg their mothers to let them be decorated and stand in the line. The older girl's manner seems sullen and withdrawn; this results from the wish to appear dignified, the subdued body conditions required by the beauty magic and, not least, a certain amount of embarrassment over the admiring words and glances. No mistake about it, however, she will long remember this day when all eyes were on her.[5] After 5 to 10 minutes the display ends, and the celebration feast begins.

The Arapesh traditionally practiced infant betrothal, and so it happened that a girl went from her debut directly to the house of her new husband and the life of a married woman.[6] The wedding itself is a simple affair, consisting of a feast between the two contracting families. Afterward, the newlyweds retire to the seclusion of their nuptial house for a three-day honeymoon. Serenaded by ribald wisecracks from their friends, who make a point of being around the hamlet during this period, the couple emerge only to answer nature's call, at which time they must hold their hands over each other's genital region.

One of the most interesting and touching features of the marriage rite occurs at the end of the honeymoon seclusion. The young couple descend to a nearby stream to bathe, and then, for the first and last time in her presence, the new husband lets blood from his penis (by means described in chapter 3). They begin by making a small dam of twigs and debris, creating a pool into which the blood is directed. After the operation, they swish away the dam and send the blood on its way, praying to the ancestral spirits of the stream to bless their union with love and fruitfulness.

This raises a very important point. The display of tenderness just witnessed is entirely consistent with Arapesh con-

5. In neighboring Ningalimbi village, a variation was observed in which about ten nubile girls were displayed collectively. They had experienced first menses at various times during the previous year, but had deferred their seclusion and debut in order to participate in a large-scale puberty ceremony. My Ilahita companions stated that this procedure was occasionally followed in their village, though nothing of the sort occurred while I was in the field.
6. In recent years, the marriage age of girls has drifted upward as they have begun resisting family pressures to marry someone not of their own choosing. This in turn has put strains on the politically ramified institution of sister-exchange marriage. See Tuzin (1976: 100ff.).

5. Friends and kinsmen turn out to celebrate the sexual florescence of the decorated girl on the left. The little girls in line with her have successfully begged their parents to let them be decorated and join in the display.

ceptions of how husbands and wives ought to treat one another. There are many other conventional expressions of marital felicity, and a short visit to the village is enough to persuade one that relations between spouses, and between parents and children, are generally quite warm and affectionate. And yet, the image portrayed in the following chapters is one of unmitigated hostility on the part of men toward their wives and children, an attitude marked by repeated, ritually ordained acts of terrorism against these cult outsiders. At the heart of the matter is a contradiction between the canons of ritual and domestic conduct, one which expresses itself, among other ways, in the uneasiness which men, by their own report, occasionally feel when carrying out deeds required by the Tambaran. This moral uncertainty interacts, in turn, with recurrent moments of religious skepticism, in which men verge close on the overt realization that the compelling truth of the Tambaran is, when all is said and done, an illusion created by themselves. These matters will be discussed in due course; for the present, what must be stressed is that this study addresses only a segment of the ideas and experiences making up Arapesh cultural life. If the topic chosen were "domestic relations," the feeling tone of the picture would be much different, perhaps, but equally incomplete in its own right.

VILLAGE ORGANIZATION AND DESCENT STRUCTURES

The ritual correlates of the residence structures discussed earlier will be examined in proper context later in the chapter. For now, it should be mentioned that the village is divided into moieties comprised of wards, while the wards are, in turn, divided into *sub-moieties* comprised of hamlets. I have called the latter "sub-moieties" to emphasize their localization in the wards; however, as the generic sub-moiety division is repeated in each ward, they also form, in aggregate, a dual structure as inclusive as the village-wide moieties. In each ward, the two sub-moieties converge on a large, communally owned hamlet which is the spiritual heart of the ward and the site of most collective activities, including, of course, ritual.

Descent structures are the other major component of village organization. They occupy three levels of inclusiveness. In the village there are 39 totemic *patriclans*, localized within the wards. Different clans of the same name may occur in different wards, but never in different moieties. All but a few of the tiniest clans are subdivided into *sub-clans*, of which there are always two: the Sahopwasinguf ("line of the elder brothers") and the Owapwasinguf ("line of the younger brothers"). Like the sub-moieties, the aggregate of sub-clans of like status form a village-wide dual division that is manifest on ritual occasions. Sub-clans are also the largest exogamous unit in the society, and there is nothing to prevent clansmen of opposite sub-clans from intermarrying. The preferred and statistically prevalent marriage form is based on simultaneous or deferred sister exchange, and there is some evidence that complementary sub-clans were formerly joined in prescriptive marriage alliance.

Sub-clans are comprised of an indeterminate number of patrilineal segments. These units are genealogically shallow, their origins being no more removed than the parental or grandparental generation of the oldest living members. Accordingly, while it is proper to speak of the sub-clans as units of descent, their constituents are more accurately regarded as units of patrifiliation. Patrilineal segments tend to be identified by the name of their ancestral hamlet, or, alternatively, by the name of their oldest or most important male. An informal (and, as far as can be determined, functionally insignificant) hierarchy exists among fellow patrilines, based on real or presumed precedence in the sub-clan genealogy.

Residence and descent structures form, so to speak, the "outer shell" of ritual organization. Or, perhaps a better analogy would be that of a cell membrane; for these structures not only contain the Tambaran, they also bring it into dynamic relationship with the vicissitudes of secular society. They do this in conjunction with an additional series of dual structures—initiation classes, sub-classes, age-sets—which are defined in purely ritual terms, but which are also highly implicated in the structures we have been discussing. More about this presently.

THE CULT OF THE TAMBARAN

In its most abstract aspect the Tambaran stands for the totality of Arapesh tradition; which is to say, it signifies a unitary and unifying dimension informing all categories of the cultural heritage. Superficially, this phenomenon resembles the ethnographically familiar practice whereby some element—perhaps a textile pattern or a way of dressing the hair—is symbolically upgraded to serve as an emblem, an expressive form (Langer 1953), of cultural identity. No matter that the item is inherently trivial, its importance lies in what it *signifies*. Likewise, it is an open question whether by its form the marker reveals anything interesting or important about the content of the culture. With the Tambaran, however, we have a case in which the marker is neither trivial nor arbitrary, denoting in its primary sense an institution— the men's cult—which integrates a major share of culturally expressive ideas, images and experiences. Thus, a closer parallel might be "The Chosen People" as an epithet used by the ancient Hebrews to signify a cultural distinctiveness divinely mandated. In both instances the symbolic linkage of cultural identity with specifically religious imagery is diagnostic of a way of life that is, or is at least perceived by the actors to be, suffused with religious meaning. Far from being arbitrary, the form of the marker is intensely motivated.

With this as a guiding perspective, the following chapters relate how the Tambaran creates a wide range of beliefs and activities, as it were, for the purpose of feeding off them. Just as men and women perform cult-related activities "because the Tambaran ordains them," so the putative reality of the Tambaran (and the cultural consciousness signified by it) is sustained by these very acts. It is important to realize that ritual acts are in turn enmeshed in the mundane aspects of everyday social life; by this means, the latter participate in the aura of the Tambaran, while the former monitor and respond to changing circumstances and thus maintain the Tambaran's relevance to the pragmatic sphere. In fine, the men's cult is a crucial mediator between the outer limits of ideas and actions, of reality and experience, as defined by Arapesh culture.

The scope of mediation does not end here. Oblivious to the anthropologically pampered dichotomy of Nature/Culture, cult ideology boldly extends its sovereignty to existential areas that may be influenced by human intervention but which ultimately obey laws of their own. Birth, death, fertility, sexuality, growth—these are the biological mysteries of which the cult claims privileged knowledge and control; its authority rests in part on the urgency of these matters in the thoughts and emotions of the people. Adherence to cult doctrine is enforced by the exigencies of a ritually defined dominance hierarchy, the structure of which expresses the Tambaran's preference for men over women and age over youth. The perquisites of this arrangement are part of the reason why high-ranking members promote cult orthodoxy, while the materially unrewarding status of women and junior males is held constant by real and imagined punishments held in store for rebels and apostates. The order is stabilized by the fact that its parts are defined according to differential access to ritual secrets bearing on the mysteries mentioned above—and there is no power quite so unassailable as that enjoyed by those who hold the secrets of existence itself.

These general remarks give notice that the Tambaran Cult presides over the organization of Arapesh society and culture. The details of its office occupy many pages. But before turning to these, let me review some technical matters pertaining to the cult as a whole.

TAMBARAN GRADES

The cult contains a fixed sequence of five grades corresponding with successive life stages and personified with a spirit figure or "tambaran." Thus: (1) *Falanga*, early childhood; (2) *Lefin*, late childhood; (3) *Maolimu*, adolescence; (4) *Nggwal Bunafunei*, adulthood; (5) *Nggwal Walipeine*, old age. Advancement is achieved as a member of a ritual subclass into which one is born (see below). With the exception of those who die prematurely, every male passes through all the grades. Women are rigidly excluded from membership per se; however, it must be said that, in addition to producing and preparing food for the cult feasts and providing men with the leisure time needed to pursue cult activities, women perform the residual but essential roles of outsider and spectator—without which a good deal of what goes on within the cult would be meaningless.

The complexity and duration of initiation ceremonies vary from grade to grade, but the minimal feature shared by all is an ordeal followed by the novices being shown the secret paraphernalia (flutes, drums, paintings, statues, bullroarers, etc.) associated with the tambaran to which they aspire. Also, initiations are typically divided into two phases coordinated with the wet and dry horticultural seasons. Thus the first phase generally occurs during *wafita* (c. June–September), the dry period prior to planting, and the second phase follows the next year during *ambal* (c. March–June), the end of the wet season and the time for harvesting yams.[7] The ritual off-season (October–February) is a time when food is not in feastly abundance, when the gardens require considerable attention, when rainy weather keeps men close to home and hearth. In spare moments men often work individually or in small groups to produce artwork or other paraphernalia for the forthcoming ritual season. Ceremonial events may occur, but these would be small-scaled responses to some immediate and unscheduled public need. In general, the Tambaran is quiescent during these months.

Candidates for admission to a cult grade do not pay their initiators, but they are expected to feed them—often on a grand scale and for long periods—with yams and meat. If the novices are children or adolescents, their fathers finance the initiation on their behalf. Such provisioning is also perceived as requital for the last time the initiation in question took place, when ritual roles were reversed. Although my descriptions do not dwell on the economic aspect, it should be understood that nearly every ceremonial event is attended by food offerings; indeed, it would not be inaccurate to epitomize the cult as an immense framework for the reciprocation of goods and services.

CULT ORGANIZATION

The Tambaran Cult operates through an elaborate, multi-layered dual organization (Tuzin 1976). For present purposes the most important structural opposition occurs between what I have called "initiation classes," the Arapesh names of which are Sahopwas and Owapwas—"older broth-

7. Characterizing these periods as "wet" and "dry" for ritual purposes slightly distorts the meteorological facts. Measured by actual rainfall patterns the dry season is approximately May–September while the wet season is approximately October–April (Arnold 1968:51). Thus, part of the Arapesh "wet" season occurs during months that are objectively "dry," although the vegetation is still lush and the dryness not very noticeable, compared with the droughtlike conditions of June–September. What we have, then, is a *relative* contrast exaggerated to express the complementary ritual phases.

ers" and "younger brothers," respectively. These are the groups that initiate one another. Although membership in a particular class is fixed by patrifiliation, the names and implied super/subordinate statuses reverse themselves at a particular point in the cult cycle; Ego's class may be Sahopwas today, but thirty years hence it will be Owapwas.

This gross opposition is refined through a multitude of initiation partnerships between minimal agnatic units of rarely more than two degrees' breadth. Thus, Ego is born into a partnership which he shares with his father, brother(s), and perhaps father's brother(s) and the son(s) of father's brother(s). These males belong to Ego's sub-clan—the exogamous unit in this society—while their partners belong to the opposite sub-clan. That is to say, the partnerships and the initiation-class opposition are coincident with sub-clan complementarity. The term applied to one's particular initiation partner(s) is *ombaf* (pl. *ombif*).[8] The way the system works is that Ego is initiated by his father's junior *ombaf*, who was himself initiated by Ego's father. Ego, in turn, initiates this man's son—and so on, the grades descending back and forth down the generations of partners.

In most cases the age span of a sibling group is narrow enough to allow brothers to advance together through the cult grades. Their father(s), however, would be further along in the hierarchy, implying the existence of a generational, sub-class division within the initiation class. For want of an indigenous term I have called these Sahopwas Seniors and Juniors and Owapwas Seniors and Juniors, respectively. Figure 1 illustrates these sub-classes and also the reciprocating pattern of initiation that obtains between the classes as a whole.

As a further refinement each sub-class is divided into two age-sets (Balangaisi, Owangufwisi) reflecting sub-generational differences among the members: Balangaisi is the line of (actual) older brothers, Owangufwisi the line of (actual) younger brothers. In practice the Balangaisi are subjected to

8. Although in succeeding chapters I have tried to be sparing in my use of Arapesh terms, the reader may occasionally find it helpful to refer to the glossary of terms appended to this volume.

Sahopwas   Owapwas

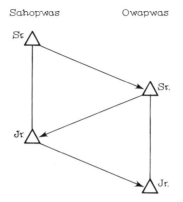

FIGURE 1. Cult initiation structure

a greater initiation ordeal than are their younger brothers—
until the final grade, when this situation is reversed and
when, also, the age-set distinction assumes an organizing
saliency for the first (and last) time.

The preceding entities—initiation classes, sub-classes, age-
sets, sub-clans and partnerships—form an integrated system
of dual structures which is the organizational core of cult
ceremonialism. All of the structures are localized within the
patriclan, but it must be emphasized that class, sub-class and
age-set divisions also crosscut the clan system at the village
level, and that members of these generic groups work and
perform together in cult activities.

This system is in turn integrated with two higher-level dual
structures which, though important in their own right, play
a relatively minor role in cult organization. The great totemic
moieties mentioned earlier (Laongol, Bandangel) arrange
the village wards into two competing halves. In simple terms,
the competition is specified according to the initiation couplets discussed earlier; that is, each couplet recognizes another couplet in the opposite moiety as its conventional and
hereditary "enemy" (*nautamana*). Inter-moiety relations was
a topic appropriate to the previous study (Tuzin 1976), and,
as will be seen in due course, its relevance to the Tambaran
is chiefly restricted to the higher grades of the cult.

The final element in this baroque organization is the structured opposition between what I have generically termed "sub-moieties." Each ward is divided into two residential sections named Afa'afa'w and Ondondof. Their chief function is the organizing of pig hunts when pork is needed for a Tambaran feast. Each sub-moiety owns a hunting reserve and a magical concoction which putatively controls the pigs within that stretch of forest. The sub-moieties' ceremonial role is twofold. First, Afa'afa'w males immediately precede those of Ondondof during the actual induction. Accordingly, the Arapesh gloss of these terms is "those who go first" and "those who come behind," respectively. Second, the spirit house associated with each grade is divided longitudinally by an imaginary line corresponding to that which defines sub-moiety (and sexual) complementarity. The right side is Afa'afa'w and "male," the left side Ondondof and "female." In Arapesh villages other than Ilahita, there is no independent structure equivalent to these sub-moieties, and the functions just described are elsewhere assimilated to the moieties (Tuzin 1976:297).[9]

TAMBARAN CYCLE

Viewed from the egocentric perspective there is nothing at all complicated about the cycle of initiations: the individual simply enters the lowest grade (Falanga) and progresses upward through the hierarchy until death or final retirement at extreme old age removes him from the cult. The inevitable complexities begin when we attempt to comprehend the sociocentric character of the system, for then we must contend with the fact of multiple groups ritually exchanging multiple tambarans.

Figure 2 illustrates the intricacies of the cycle by showing how the distribution of tambarans among the several subclasses alters slightly with each initiation. The chart should be read as *columns* from left to right; in effect, what is shown

9. For a more detailed summary of the Ilahita dual organization see Tuzin (1976: 211–232). A comprehensive diagram is to be found on pp. 298–299 in that volume.

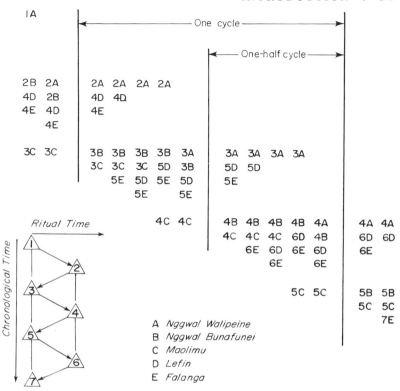

FIGURE 2. The Tambaran cycle

is a *single* column—a tambaran distribution—transforming with each downward step through time. With the help of the legend, we read in the third column (the one beginning a new cycle) that Nggwal Walipeine, Lefin and Falanga are held by one initiation class—the first named by the Senior sub-class, the other two by the Junior sub-class—while Nggwal Bunafunei and Maolimu are held by the opposite class. The fourth column shows that Falanga has been passed to a newly created sub-class "5" entering the cult at the bottom.

Continuing in this way we cross the vertical line and discover that the configuration is identical to the one just described—re-created, as it were, one half-generation later.

This is not the point of inertia, however, since the distribution from the initiation-class standpoint is the opposite of the original one; the sub-sequence beginning here is a mirror image of that contained in columns 3–7. A full cycle is completed only at the next vertical line, after which the original configuration is repeated one generation later.

It can be seen that a particular half-cycle ends at the time Nggwal Bunafunei is passed between classes. This is the moment when the Sahopwas and Owapwas names and statuses are reversed between classes (see above), while each re-reversal marks the end of a complete cycle. Sahopwas status is defined by current possession of Nggwal Bunafunei. Thus, in the first half-cycle those in the even-numbered class are Sahopwas, those in the odd-numbered class are Owapwas; in the second half-cycle the Owapwas are even-numbered, the Sahopwas are odd-numbered—and so on.

A final complication, mercifully omitted from figure 2, is that induction ceremonies admitting boys into the lowest grades of Falanga and Lefin occur with greater frequency than the half-generational intervals indicated in the figure. As we will see later, these initiations are closely coordinated with the novices' age and maturational standing. Their magical purpose is to insure various aspects of masculine growth —a purpose which would be soundly defeated if the ages of Falanga or Lefin novices ranged from four to twenty-five! Accordingly, what are shown schematically as single transmissions of Falanga and Lefin from one class to the other are, in fact, several transmissions occurring at three-to-five-year intervals until the pool of initiates is large enough and old enough to warrant admission to Maolimu. This detail does not affect the formal properties of the system, nor will it enter into later discussions.

Needless to say, the actors do not have to understand the initiation sequence *as a system* in order to operate it in a regular and efficient manner. Indications are that in Arapesh perceptions the overall cyclical aspect resolves itself into a multitude of reciprocal actions: "We initiated them, now they must initiate our sons!" The system, so to speak, takes care

of itself, unfolding as the reciprocity principle regularly con-
joins with the knowledge of which initiation is triggered step
by step through the sequence. Depending on the availability
of feast foods, the vicissitudes of community politics and the
distractions of military pursuits, the entire cycle occupies
about fifty years—an interval roughly corresponding with
the life expectancy of an Arapesh male, providing he survives childhood. For him, as for us, the experience begins
with Falanga.

2. Falanga:
Conditioning the
Ritual Allegiance

*Long ago there was no such thing as the Falanga tambaran, and it was
a woman who discovered how to make the basketry mask that goes with this
tambaran. It was named Kwaluwi, and she made it in her menstrual house
out of finely woven rattan fiber. After decorating it with painted designs,
leaves and orange fruits, she hid it in the forest near where the women of
the village fetched their water each day.*

*When all the women went to draw water, this woman quickly sneaked
into the forest, put on the mask and decorations, and then appeared before
them. The women had never seen anything like this, and when the tambaran chased them they were very frightened and fled into the forest. Then the
woman took off the mask, concealed it again, and then came to the women
to ask what they were crying about. They described the monster and how it
had chased them, but the woman accused them of lying. After many recur-
rences of this the men decided, having been told about it by their wives, to
find out what was going on.*

*One man was chosen to hide in the undercover and see what happened.
He saw how the Falanga woman tricked the others. Later he approached
the woman, told her that he had seen all that had happened, and demanded
that she teach all the men how to make the decorations. Fearing that she
would be killed, she agreed. But when all the men had learned how to do it,
they realized that they knew something the women did not. To protect their
secret they killed the woman.*

*So now the men hold the secret of the Falanga tambaran. They kept all
the masks in one house, but not long ago one moiety became angry with the*

other moiety, and they burned down the house. All the masks were destroyed,
but if you stay long enough you will see us make new ones. The water hole
where all this happened no longer contains water, but if you look carefully
at the place called Wafitaningen, you will see that it was once a spring.

L O N G ago, Malinowski set forth the proposition that in
nonliterate societies myths of origin often function as
"charters"—sacred mandates—for currently existing
social and material relationships. The story just told operates
in this fashion, for it is the men's way of explaining how Falanga came to be, and why it is that its custodianship persists
today as a prerogative of males. And yet, paradoxically, the
content of the story nullifies any justification for ritual pri-
macy which the men may seek in telling it. It was a *woman*
who created Falanga, by first weaving the mask that is central
to this tambaran. The act took place in her menstrual house
—proof enough that it was not merely some nameless ances-
tress, but femininity itself which was implicated in Falanga's
primordial beginnings. The men, discovering the truth about
Falanga, violently usurp its illusions, thereafter (and to this
day) turning them to the purpose of concealing Falanga's
true nature and origins from its rightful owners. This is why
the story must remain a closely guarded male secret.

Secrecy, deception, violence, culpability, the spiritualism
of artistry—these are themes to be remembered; for the
story of Falanga is to a considerable extent paradigmatic of
the Tambaran Cult as a whole. Not only are the themes the
"raw material," so to speak, of Arapesh religious culture;
their recombination in ritual settings endlessly re-creates the
paradox of reality and illusion which, by all indications, continually fascinates the Arapesh collective imagination. It is a
play which, even in its comic moments, is performed with
high seriousness.

The depth of commitment to this paradox is no better evi-
denced than by the fact that the story of Falanga, and others
like it in the cult repertoire, continues to be told. If the deed

it recalls is so potentially damaging to the men's position, would it not make better sense to terminate this masculine conspiracy by letting the secret die with the last man who knew it? In other words, why preserve this incriminating "charter"? Having put this question to many informants, I am convinced that they regard the prospect as unthinkable, in a quite literal sense. For them, it is tantamount to asking, Why preserve religion? The answer, which can only be proposed by an outsider to the belief system, is that the symbolic figures of Arapesh myth and ritual give urgent expression to deeply interwoven elements of personal and cultural identity, some of which are undoubtedly ego-dystonic. Such elements do not yield to precise definition; for actor and observer alike, they emerge as *qualities*—understood, not known, or apprehended, not comprehended—from the many redundancies of the symbolic system. The enculturative process through which these meanings are developed in and by individuals begins very early in life. This is why the Tambaran takes an interest in little children.

THE INITIATION

Falanga is a young boy's point of entry into the Tambaran Cult. It is the first and most junior tambaran; it is also the only one that is entirely ward-based. Because, however, the ceremonies require participation by the brothers of the novices' mothers, as well as by certain helpers who must be outsiders, it necessarily happens that men from different wards or even different villages are in attendance. It is also true that the several wards coordinate their separate Falanga activities to the extent of having all the initiations within the same year —in quick succession during the post-harvest ritual season. This is because Lefin, the next tambaran, presents itself immediately the following year and involves all wards acting in concert.[1] Hence, it is desirable to have all the candidates ad-

---

1. At the very close of fieldwork, I was startled to learn that Falanga and Lefin are sometimes conceived as complementary phases of a *single* tambaran, comparable to the respective sub-phases of later tambarans. This is because they occur in adjacent years (as do sub-phases) and the growth functions they are

vance to this threshold at approximately the same time. Furthermore, children from different wards interact during family gatherings, and it would be difficult to keep the secrets from spreading to uninitiated cousins.

The novices are children—boys—preferably about five but ranging up to ten years of age. The general purpose of the initiation, it is said, is to rid the male child's body of the polluting influences of his mother's milk. As soon as a boy is weaned[2] and has begun participation in a play group, he is deemed ready to be admitted to this grade. Falanga formalizes both sorts of development: the break in biological dependency, on the one hand, and its replacement by an orientation toward the wider society, on the other. Summarizing, so to speak, both parts of the transformation is the notion that Falanga sexually differentiates the boy: he becomes, by mystic and social decree, a novice male. Without this endorsement, there is no guarantee that future growth will lead him toward competent manhood as a warrior, magician, yam-grower or lover.

Wafitangai. This is the preparatory stage occurring late in the year after the gardens have been cleared and are ready for planting. The initiating group is the Owapwas Junior sub-class, those initiated are the sons of the Sahopwas Junior sub-class. During the night before the appointed day the initiators, unbeknown to the novices, stage a massive bandicoot

---

intended to serve are identical. Also, the fact that each takes its name from a variety of sago indicates a conceptual parity between them. Granting this element of pairing between Falanga and Lefin, I have chosen to treat them as separate tambarans, since this is by far the most conventional way of conceiving them. The point is academic, except that the very fact of the ambiguity testifies to the inherent messiness of cultural ideas and the high tolerance for inexactness that is implied on the part of the actors.

2. According to mission baby-clinic records, the average age of weaning is 36 months, ranging upward to 52 months. Weaning is a prerequisite to Falanga initiation for three reasons: (1) it permits the boy to be physically separated from his mother for relatively long periods; (2) it minimizes the chance of recontamination for a boy who might otherwise be tempted to return to the breast after initiation; and (3) because the urine and feces of a suckling child, being constituted of breast milk, are thought to carry polluting female essences, initiators would be put at risk while handling unweaned novices who are prone to fear-inspired incontinence during these initiation rituals.

hunt. Then, in the early morning, they blow a conch signal toward the ward, asking, in imitation of vocal intonation, "Where are you?" The novices' fathers feign puzzlement as they gather their sons in the main ceremonial hamlet. Once everyone is there, the initiators enter wearing Falanga decorations and carrying the bandicoots. As the novices watch, the Sahopwas group circles the clearing counterclockwise and then leaves, proceeding to the small Falanga spirit house in a nearby hamlet.

The novices are taken by their fathers to the Falanga hamlet in groups based on sub-moiety membership, Afa'afa'w conventionally preceding Ondondof. On finding it empty, the fathers remark that they are being tricked by the initiators, who, they speculate, have run to hide in the forest. Just then a rumble is heard from within the spirit house, caused by a low trill sounded on a slit-gong. At this signal all the initiators begin blowing small flutes (*embin* and *efi'w*) in such a way that the sound is relayed back and forth inside the house.[3] Then they burst from the house, blowing the flutes and carrying the bandicoots. Flutes and carcasses are presented to the novices, who reciprocate in the customary manner by giving their initiators sprouted coconuts. The initiators leave to fetch long yams—a singularly masculine food —which they roast whole and give to the novices. These, along with coconut meat and drinking water, are consumed throughout the night. At dawn the initiators assemble large decorated pots of yam soup, to which have been added pieces of bandicoot flesh.[4]

At this feast, the novices divide themselves into Balangaisi (elder brothers) and Owangufwisi (younger brothers) agesets. While the latter are taken to another hamlet to eat their soup, the Balangaisi remain in the Falanga hamlet to eat soup which has been magically treated. After eating, the older novices are told that the magic will strike them with

3. This back-and-forth pattern will be seen twice again during the Maolimu initiation.
4. The bandicoot meat is referred to metaphorically as *angwalef*, which is the bark from a species of tree. The women, who have prepared the soup, are told that the novices are fed pieces of *angwalef*.

sickness if they do not properly observe taboos on cold water, bathing and yam soup during the following fortnight. No such taboos apply to the Owangufwisi age-set. Thus is established a pattern which persists during nearly the entire initiation series: the ordeals and taboos are more vigorous for the line of the elder brothers.

After about two weeks the Balangaisi novices are ritually fed yam soup, thereby lifting the taboo on this particular item. This, too, is a characteristic cult practice: an everyday item of diet or behavior is withdrawn and then restored under ritual auspices, thus imbuing its future enjoyment with the sacred significance befitting male activities. The boys are now allowed to bathe, but are restricted to drinking only warm water during the succeeding five or six months while the yams are growing. During this period, also, the novices may eat only the basic staples (yam, taro, sago, pitpit [*Saccharum edule*]) and must avoid anything regarded as a delicacy, especially meat.

Ambalingai. This stage opens once the yam harvest is under way the following year. During the preceding month 'singsing'[5] are held by both initiation classes to the exclusion of all females and of male children who have not yet attained Falanga. The sequence begins with a pig feast referred to as "lizard," the metaphor having to do with the fastening of the lizard-skin drum heads in preparation for the festivities. After a month of almost nightly singsings, the first of the new yams are given to the novices. Then the initiators hunt for a pig,[6] which they carry to a section of stream bank designated traditionally as the site of Falanga initiations for that

5. I am using the Pidgin English term here in preference to approximately equivalent English words such as "festival" or "dance." (For grammatical convenience I treat it as if it were an English word.) Among the Ilahita, singsings may be either sacred or mundane, public or restricted, and typically involve singing, dancing and feasting from dusk until first cock's crow the following morning. Mead (1938:217) reports that the Mountain Arapesh use magical techniques to prolong the night of merriment; their Ilahita cousins resort to similar measures to hasten the dawn.

6. This pig is called *mefilen*, which is the word for the stick placed as a brace behind the yam vine, when it is severed prior to harvest. Both the hunt and the vine cutting are seen as prefatory to the big event.

ward. It overlooks a part of the stream course supposedly inhabited by the dead of one of the ward's clans. They cook and eat the pig, clear the undergrowth for the forthcoming ceremony and hold an all-night singsing by the water's edge. Following this, singsings are held every night in the village for two weeks.[7] At the end of this period another pig is eaten, this time referred to as *hangato'w* ("broom"), the significance being that the initiation site is now cleared.

A couple of weeks later the initiators let blood from their own penes and apply black paint to their entire bodies. Singsings continue every night, during which the fathers of the novices prepare yam soup laced with beauty magic for the initiators. After several more weeks the initiators set about refurbishing or preparing anew the *hangahiwa* (sing. *hangamu'w*). These are full-body costumes of the sort whose origins are enshrined in the sacred story which began this chapter. They consist of a woven vegetable-fiber helmet mask surmounting a surface of coiled fibers made to simulate the figure's broad "shoulders." The mask is coated with a thin clay wash and then painted with rich earth tones of red, yellow, black and white. Around its neck and covering the area of the shoulders is a long coiled strand of large, bright orange fruits called *su'witix* (sing. *su'witip*). The body of the wearer is entirely concealed beneath an encircling curtain of bright yellow sago fibers[8] fastened around the rim of the chest, back and shoulders and reaching to the ground. He moves with a long, loping gait which sends waves of motion down the costume. Except for the swish of his movement, he remains utterly silent. In all, the effect is extraordinarily dramatic: if ever one wanted to fashion a hobgoblin out of local materials, this would be it.

Women are told that the *hangahiwa* are materialized spirits

---

7. The calendar of events is not kept strictly and should be regarded here as a rough approximation. The most common cause for delay is that it often takes the men several days to capture a pig. In general, the *sequence* of ritual events is taken more seriously than their timing.

8. These sago fibers (*maolihiwa*, sing. *maolimu*) are collected from the central growing point of the palm. Note that the third Tambaran grade, entry to which corresponds roughly with the onset of puberty, is called Maolimu.

6. *Hangamu'w* with crimped-leaf homicide badges.

rather than men merely disguised as such. When summoned to the cult ceremonials, they are said to come dancing out of the clan water shrines, where they normally reside with other cult beings, ancestral spirits and *maolinipunemb*.[9] On days when the ground is soft the wearer goes so far as to strap coconut husks to his feet, lest his human footprints give him away.

Renewing the masks involves minor patching and repainting, which is done in the small Falanga spirit house in the ward. Each sub-moiety works on its own collection of masks, with Afa'afa'w sitting on the right side of the house and Ondondof on the left. *Hangahiwa wandafunei*—those which have a history of violence (see below)—are painted on the first day, the harmless and/or "female" masks (*hangahiwa tangel*) on the second. Then the masks are taken down to the stream site where the fruits, leaves, fibers and other decorations are affixed. Men of other wards and villages assist, and these outsiders are asked to wear the masks during the ceremony that afternoon so that female onlookers will not notice the absence of their menfolk and suspect they are under the costumes. Those who oblige are rewarded by the initiators with long yams and sprouted coconuts—the standard ritual remuneration—and later each receives another long yam from a father of one of the novices.

In the afternoon each initiator leads his *hangamu'w* up into the Falanga hamlet, passing through a double line of the novices' fathers. After the *hangahiwa* have been paraded before all the spectators, females and uninitiated boys are sent away, worried over what might happen to the novices in the hands of these monsters. The novices' worst fears are realized as they and their fathers are forced into a tiny cluster in the center of the clearing, while the *hangahiwa* prance menacingly around them, lunging with their spears and beating at the novices with (very light) sticks. The boys scream convulsively, cling to their fathers, lose bladder control. As one cult member put it, they are so frightened their penes

9. *Maolinipunemb* (sing. *maolinimuna*; P.E., 'masalai') is the generic term covering a diverse array of non-human sentient beings: nature spirits (anthropo- or zoomorphic), bush demons, imps and ogres.

shrink. At the peak of emotional intensity the *hangahiwa* plunge into the group and, at a signal, suddenly transfer the masks to the astonished novices. Whimpering continues momentarily from the younger members, but in general the crying quickly gives way to relief that the nightmare is ended and mounting excitement over the realization that the masks are now theirs. While they are getting used to this idea, their initiators go down to the stream to wash off the black paint which has incrusted them these many weeks. A celebratory singsing is held that night.

Early next morning the initiators return to the stream site and decorate themselves in preparation for the final ceremony. They arrange themselves in a line reaching from the stream to the village, singing and drumming as the anxious novices are passed hand to hand down the hill. At the water's edge the youths are divided into the two age-sets. As the Owangufwisi look on, three or four men attired hideously as pigs (and called *mbongof*, "pigs") advance on the Balangaisi youths and lacerate their penes with bamboo razors. These instruments are called *falanga*, which is also the thorny wild sago palm from which the grade takes its name. The metaphor here is that the boys are forced (by the Tambaran) to climb one of these palms and slide down its trunk, ripping their bellies open on the vicious spikes. This is what the women are told.

The blood from the Balangaisi genitals is caught on leaves (type unspecified) which their fathers place under the bark of certain large trees (*bangwan*) growing near the stream. With this mystical metonymy, together with the association alleged between these trees and the spirits of the dead, the novice is ordained to grow as strong and as large as the tree. When the penile attack on the Balangaisi is accomplished, the "pigs" turn on the Owangufwisi and rub their penes and scrota vigorously with stinging nettles. Then both age-sets are hurled headlong into the stream, which is heavily strewn with stinging nettles (*apa'wis*). It is customary, in this final ordeal, for the boys to be joined in the water by their mother's brothers, whose avuncular concern impels them to share the suffering and, if possible, lift their nephew clear of the water.[10] This is prescribed irrespective of the MB's initiation-class affiliation; inasmuch as ward members are densely interrelated by ties of agnation and affinity, it happens that a good many of the men present immerse themselves.

After the ordeal, the "pigs" lead the novices back to the village and hide them in the Falanga spirit house so that the women will not see their genital wounds. The rest of the initiators remove their regalia and go home. Those who are married instruct their wives to prepare steamed yams—a delicacy reserved for ceremonial occasions—which are fed to the novices. After one or two weeks, when the sores have healed, the boys resume normal activities. Approximately one month later they return to the spirit house, there to remain for an additional month.[11] During this time their yam soup is prepared by prepubescent daughters of the older initiates, and, if there are too few of them, by young daughters of other men of the initiating class. The soup is charmed with beauty magic in anticipation of the final coming-out, for which the novices are decorated lavishly and publicly displayed as the new possessors of the Falanga tambaran. This is an important, happy event and draws people from miles around, especially if they are kinsmen of the celebrants.

While on the subject of food, there is another Falanga element which must be recorded; indeed, in the opinion of at least one informant, it is the most important part of this tambaran. At a point during their seclusion the novices are invited to partake of the flesh of a python (*doa*), steam-baked with a mixture of edible greens. Most people are disgusted at the prospect of eating snake meat—all the more so in the case of python, which is thought to contain an evil spiritual

10. In this, as in later ritual contexts, it is seen that the mother's brother exercises a special protective and supportive role vis-à-vis his novice nephew. In the previous volume I discussed at some length the MB/ZS relationship (1976:151ff.), which is not only very positive, but is, in comparison with most other kinship sectors, remarkably untrammeled by structural or emotional contradictions.

   It must be said that the Arapesh use stinging nettles in a wide range of routine medical and magical procedures. Thus inured, the mothers' brother—if not the novices themselves—finds this ordeal not nearly as awful as would, for example, the present author.

11. Living "in the spirit house" means simply that they live in the Falanga hamlet which is, for that period, taboo to women. During this period, one or more *hangahiwa* are at large in the village.

substance known as *maulas*.[12] The boys are not forced to eat it; but for those who can overcome their fear and loathing, the strength they ingest enables them to become superior yam growers when they grow up.[13] If, on the other hand, a boy cannot bring himself to do this he may postpone the python feast until later in life. Specially ambitious men are known to eat python fairly regularly—in order to keep their "strength" up.

The fact that Falanga is the most junior tambaran should not distract us from the important developmental implications of its timing in the life of the individual. Granted, little substantive knowledge is gained through the experience: to the young mind the initiation is by all indications a mass of inchoate, mostly terrifying sensations. Even to those precocious enough to comprehend it, the ideological rationale is somewhat academic when measured against the immediacy of the ordeals and celebrations. The extensive preparatory activities could have educational value, but they are closed to the novices until years later, at the next Falanga induction, when they themselves are among the initiators. If, however, initiations are more properly judged by their broader socializing functions, then the power of Falanga is discovered in the traumatic imprinting of future role expectations. By this criterion, Falanga must surely be ranked on a par with the other tambarans.

Falanga introduces the Arapesh boy to the world of men and of spirits. Barely weaned, he is violently scourged of his mother's influence and is apprenticed to the life that will be his. Thenceforward he carries the responsibility of the Tambaran, adopting a role which according to his mentors must be his constant study. Material and emotional comfort at this tender age requires continuing traffic with women; but within these limits the boy is urged to minimize female contacts

12. Interestingly, *maulas* is also the term used in reference to the collective dead, in which sense there is no evil connotation. The coincidence is probably related to the general ancestral significance attached to the supernatural giant pythons which are believed to co-reside with the dead in the clan water shrines. See Tuzin (1977).

13. For a brief discussion of Arapesh food taboos, with particular reference to pork-related customs, see Tuzin (1978b).

for the sake of his masculine vigor and proper growth. Most painfully perhaps, his mother is no longer the complete confidant and reference figure she once was. For, more than anything else, Falanga teaches the boy that a secret divides him from some persons as profoundly as it unites him with others. It is a sad lesson, one he must never forget.

Falanga introduces the novice to three curious customs: the ritually hygienic practice of penis incising; the "breaking of the plank" singing; and the mysterious antics of the *hangamu'w* masks. The first of these figures more prominently in the conduct of the next tambaran (Lefin) and can await further comment until that time. The latter two will be mentioned hereafter only in passing, and therefore it is worth pausing to consider them in more detail before moving on to Lefin.

"BREAKING OF THE PLANK"

In the foregoing description, I did not mention a curious singing held on the two consecutive nights prior to the coming-out of the Falanga novices. It is called the "breaking of the plank" and to my knowledge is not found anywhere outside the seven Ilahita Arapesh villages.[14] A large log, about five meters in length and nearly a meter in diameter, is cut and roughly planed along one side. The dancers form themselves into two groups, one of which lines itself along the log. Singing, they rush back and forth across the clearing, carrying the heavy object as they go. When the song is ended they drop the log and belabor it for about thirty seconds with sticks. Then, in the manner of a sea-chantey or other work

14. The single exception which I know of is the nearby Abelam village of Serakikim, where, in fact, I first saw it performed. Residents of that place claimed to have borrowed the singsing from their Arapesh neighbors. One informant traced its origins to Arapesh-speaking villages northward from Ilahita, but my data neither confirm nor deny this claim.

The name I have given to this singsing is an adaptation of the Pidgin English phrase which I heard most often in reference to it: 'brukim plang,' meaning "to strike the plank, or to break the plank in two." Although somewhat more cumbersome than its Arapesh counterpart (*nda' lawank*), the English phrase does have the virtue of being more recognizable to the average reader when it reappears in later contexts.

song, the leader wails the beginning of another verse; the others join in, hoist the log and repeat the sequence. Meanwhile the other group stands with interlinked arms off to one side. As the log-bearers rush back and forth, the second line moves in synchrony singing the high harmony of the song. On secular occasions men carry the log while the women perform the less arduous office of the second line. A sexual hilarity prevails, and the women especially are bold and brazen in their burlesque; this, I might add, stands in odd combination with the keening, dirge-like quality of the song itself. When, as we shall see later, the same dance occurs in secret Tambaran conclaves, the second part is performed by male transvestites who greatly amuse themselves and everyone else by their ribald impersonation.[15] As with all other singsings the "breaking of the plank" continues inexorably, exhaustingly, until dawn.

HANGAMU'W

A survey of the village's ritual inventory turned up 214 of these masks—many of them physically extant, others temporarily defunct but scheduled for restoration in due course. They are individually named and belong to specific initiation partnerships within the larger class opposition of Sahopwas-Owapwas. As I have discussed elsewhere (1976:225–227), these partnerships are corporate entities, consisting of paired patrilines belonging to complementary sub-clans. The patri-

15. Since the Arapesh traditionally went nude, transvestism was necessarily rather token and did nothing to conceal the sex of the imposter. The same is true today. A male transvestite hangs a netbag down his back (female style) and decorates himself with symbolically feminine yellow paint, leaves and feathers. Female transvestites affect an exaggeratedly jaunty swagger, sling a netbag over their shoulder and brandish a spear. It should be added that ritual transvestism, to the best of my knowledge, carries no homosexual connotations. Homosexuality itself is very rare and strongly disapproved among the Ilahita, and there is no institution sanctioning homosexual liaisons at any stage in life.

The dance pattern described in the text may be altered slightly in the case of an all-male performance. Instead of a dancing line, the group carrying and beating on the log is surrounded by a moving circle of dancers with spears over their shoulders. During the beating phase the circle marches around, punctuating their steps with a falsetto "wau ... wau ... wau." During the singing-and-carrying phase the outer circle speeds up to a trot, quickening their monotonous chant accordingly. In this version "women" join in either group.

line, in turn, is a narrow agnatic grouping rarely extending beyond the first degree of collaterality. The *hangahiwa* personify and also personalize the partnership. Thus, within the general partnership, individuals are paired under the emblem of (among other paraphernalia) a jointly owned *hangamu'w*. Obviously, numerical symmetry is rarely exact, but the system survives by permitting individuals to have more than one partner—and, accordingly, more than one *hangamu'w*. Similarly, masks may be created, temporarily loaned out, or allowed to die according to the vicissitudes of ritual-group memberships. Considering that the survey revealed a ratio of adult males to masks of 477/214 (not far off the expected 2/1), and allowing also that a number of *hangahiwa* were probably overlooked during the search, we may judge that the system works reasonably well on average to provide each man and his *ombaf* (initiation partner) with a mask of their own.[16]

Consistent with their nominal identities the *hangahiwa* have individual characters and life-histories (see below). They are also gendered. Of the 214 recorded, 176 were "male" and 38 were "female." The female *hangamu'w*[17] carries an unsharpened stick and in general people are not frightened of her. Likewise, a large percentage of male *hangahiwa* have a reputation of being harmless, even though they carry spears and are capable of turning nasty without notice. These benign creatures, when they are at large in the village, move about begging small gifts of food, salt, tobacco or betelnut. They cannot speak, but indicate their wishes with various conventional gestures, such as holding a small coconut-shell cup on the end of their spear point as a sign that they would like to have some soup. The man who is ap-

16. One might ask why I am counting adult males in this exercise rather than the youthful Falanga initiates, who are the official custodians of the *hangahiwa*. In fact, Falanga's control over the masks is nominal: in practice, they are worn and used by older males of the class currently in possession of the Falanga tambaran. With effective ownership residing in the initiation class as a whole, the *hangahiwa* are able to play a role in the initiation activities of *all* Tambaran grades.

17. Note that, in terms of the noun-class system embodied in the Arapesh language, the term *hangamu'w* is connotatively strongly feminine.

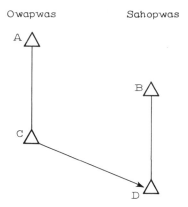

FIGURE 3. *Hangamu'w* relations

proached (or the husband of a woman who is approached) cheerfully carries the desired item to the Falanga spirit house in the ward where it is deposited along with other booty, to be enjoyed by the wearer and by certain others of appropriate ritual standing (Webster 1968:113).[18]

For example, in figure 3, Person D is the one to have received the *hangamu'w* at the current initiation, that is, from his senior *ombaf*, C. Person B is known as the "papa" of the *hangamu'w*; it is to him that most requests for food and other goodies are addressed by this *hangamu'w*—regardless of who happens to be wearing it. The wearer may consume some of the goods, but the bulk of them are taken by A and C in payment for having given D the mask in the first place. The commodities are identified by being placed alongside the mask that collected them. In all, the institution has a character not unlike Halloween trick-or-treating in the United States, and the autumnal colors of red, brown and orange in the costume add to the verisimilitude. The difference is that the tricks *hangahiwa* play can be rather grisly.

Margaret Mead refers to the Mountain Arapesh 'tumbuan'

18. As noted earlier, the *hangahiwa* roam about only during specific ritual seasons, so it should not be supposed that their begging is a chronic drain on community resources. Even during the right season, these odd mendicants are active only intermittently.

as "gay and laughter-giving" (1934:245).[19] As we have just seen, the same is true in Ilahita; but there is also a more sinister side to the institution. About ten percent of the male masks are infamous, having to their bloody credit one or more ritually licensed *laf* murders. Their regalia include homicide badges: crimped leaves (*Cordyline terminalis*) and certain bones of their successive victims displayed in the following manner:

#1 Victim: the skull hung from the neck of the *hangamu'w*
#2 Victim: a radius bone mounted in the left earlobe
#3 Victim: a radius bone mounted in the right earlobe
#4 Victim: a humerus bone mounted in the septum
#5 Victim: a knotted rope draped on the neck which records this and all subsequent kills[20]

These *hangahiwa wandafunei* (the latter term being an adjective meaning "violent" or "hot-blooded" in a ritually powerful sense) are universally feared, and nothing can vacate a hamlet so quickly as one of these spooks materializing out of the gloom of the surrounding jungle. The reason why even men flee before it is that the spirits of its victims have putatively impregnated the mask. Thus, when an ordinary man dons one of these costumes he feels the "heaviness" of the mask, and the indwelling spirit(s) transform him into a compulsive killer; his own child or brother would not be spared if he came upon them. To this extent, the men are not entirely deceiving the women when they tell them that the *han-*

19. In addition to their presence among the Mountain Arapesh, basketry helmet masks of the general sort we are describing are found among the Abelam and, indeed, throughout the area of the Bismarck Archipelago. The Pidgin English name for them, 'tumbuan,' is taken from the Tolai of New Britain, where the *tubuan* are powerful female entities in the *dukduk* cult (Powell 1884; Churchill 1890; Epstein 1969). Among the Lakalai, also of New Britain, these creatures are part of the Valuku secret society (Valentine 1961), while in New Ireland they are found in association with *malanggan* rites (Powdermaker 1933). The *lewa* masked dancers of Wogeo (Hogbin 1970) clearly belong to this series, as does a cognate form on Manam (Wedgwood 1933/34).
20. Pax Australiana has outlawed ritual murder and has also discouraged both exhumation practices and the ceremonial use of human bones. Nowadays, *hangahiwa* with homicidal reputations must be content to use crimped cordyline leaves and a dagger of cassowary bone through their nasal septum as badges, although one occasionally still sees crania and long bones brought out from hiding for this purpose.

gahiwa are spirits incarnate.[21] Traditionally, *hangahiwa wandafunei* sought out victims who were alone in their garden or on the forest paths at dusk.[22] Pigs, dogs and chickens were also fair game. After spearing the victim, the offending *hangamu'w* would escape back to its spirit house. The wearer would replace it with the other costumes and emerge without fear of detection—in time to join the general alarm aroused by the discovery of the body.

Alternatively, the killer might have cut the trappings off the mask and fled with it to a nearby enemy village. The nature of his mission would have assured him safe passage into their territory, where he would make contact with someone —a kinsman, perhaps, or other acquaintance—who would offer to take custody of the mask, since what the *hangamu'w* had done was surely a favor to the enemy. The killer was allowed to return home, his secret secure. The mask remained with the enemy either until it killed again and fled to yet another village (or possibly back to its home village), or until it was repatriated at the request of the true owner. In the latter event a payment of yams and pork was given as a kind of ransom to those who returned it.

By means of such truce events, then, the Tambaran sponsored intermittent interaction between otherwise implacable enemies (Tuzin 1976)—nervous gatherings, to be sure, but not devoid of the possibility of productive talks concerning

21. Lucien Lévy-Bruhl (1935) could have had the Arapesh in mind when he wrote the following: "As long as the actors and dancers wear these masks, and from the mere fact that they cover their faces, they are not only the representatives of the dead and the ancestors whom these masks portray: for the time being, they actually *become* these dead and these ancestors. . . . To put on a mask, with these people, is not, as it is with us, a mere disguise behind which the individual remains himself. It is to undergo a real transformation." (Pp. 123–124.)

Such beliefs, taken at face value, do indeed support Lévy-Bruhl's claim that the "primitive" mode of thought is radically distinctive. The problem is not that simple, however. In later chapters we shall discover unexpected subtleties in the Arapesh "theory of signs," in comparison with which Lévy-Bruhl's formulation —especially his willingness to take these beliefs "at face value"—can only be called "primitive."

22. Someone being pursued could take refuge in a house and wait there to be rescued. One incident is recalled when a pregnant woman of Ilifalemb managed to reach the safety of her house. But then she made the mistake of peeking out too soon: the *hangamu'w* had been waiting quietly outside, and despatched the unfortunate lady with a single thrust through the belly.

matters of mutual or common interest.[23] Indeed, it could be said that the paths trod by these *hangahiwa* described a gruesome alliance of enemies, predicated on the institution of ritual murder.[24] During the 1950s the Australian authorities moved vigorously to suppress this and other forms of ritually ordained killing, and for at least a decade prior to field work *hangahiwa* terrorism had stopped short of actual homicide. Nevertheless, the institution remains vital because of the lively and continuing fear, especially among non-initiates, that one of these masks might revert to its true, bloodthirsty nature. Enemies still lend each other masks occasionally, and convene a feast at the time one is returned; but under the altered circumstances of pacification this aspect of the institution is probably not as compelling or dramatic as it once was.

Speaking, then, in the "ethnographic present," murders committed by the *hangahiwa* are regarded as quasi-legitimate acts performed for the glory and satisfaction of the village Tambaran.[25] Indeed, the family of the victim is obliged to

23. Among other New Guinea groups, including the Iatmul (Bateson 1936), it was apparently common for enemies to use feasts and the like as enticements leading to ambush. When I discussed this with Arapesh informants, they indicated that these *hangahiwa* feasts were risky affairs because of the high probability that a fight would break out. Premeditated betrayal, on the contrary, was out of the question: the offenders' own Tambaran would have wrought terrible vengeance on them for having thus abused his name. Even in the case of a spontaneous outbreak, the combatants were inviting supernatural reprisal, and the knowledge of this went far in keeping tempers under control.

24. In principle, this network could be quite extensive. The history of one of these killer masks—as told to me by its owner—involved a lurid odyssey of no fewer than nine murders and five other villages, one of which was Abelam. Interestingly, when I sought to corroborate the story, a second informant dismissed the earlier account with a snort: the mask had killed only *one* person, he sneered, and this was when it accidentally knocked someone off a cliff during a ceremony. Some masks do indeed have rich and bloody histories, he added, but certainly not this one! Further inquiry showed that the tendency to take perverse pride in the exploits of one's *hangamu'w*, even to the point of making boastful exaggerations, is not unusual.

25. As noted earlier, although *hangahiwa* are revealed in connection with Falanga, they associate as independent ritual entities with all cult grades. *Laf* murders committed by them or anyone else are, however, credited exclusively to the senior tambaran, Nggwal.

I qualify the legitimacy of these homicides to the extent that, if, for example, a family member of the victim happened upon the scene in time to catch the *hangamu'w* he would be justified in taking revenge right then and there. It is only after a clean getaway, when the identity of the (human) assailant is unknown or open to question, that the deed becomes fully legitimate under the terms of Tambaran ideology. Furthermore, even today, when the mischief is relatively

exhume the skull and other bones and hand them over to the owner of the appropriate *hangamu'w* for inclusion in its regalia. If the mask has fled to an enemy village, the trophies are sent there. The aggrieved are formally denied redress, and in any case the identity of the man who actually wore the mask, which need not have been the owner himself, normally remains concealed.[26]

Informants describe cases in which, in their frustration and desire for revenge, the family of the deceased attempts to ensorcel the owner of the *hangamu'w* that has been linked with the killing. They realize he is probably innocent—no one is foolish enough to use his own mask in a murder plot—but he is the only person they can single out for blame. The informants noted that this enabled a man to dispose of two enemies at once: he uses the *hangamu'w* of one enemy to kill another enemy in the presence of a witness, knowing that the family of the victim may retaliate with sorcery against the owner of the mask.

In principle, *hangamu'w* murder is supposed to be a form of execution of persons who have offended against the Tambaran in some way.[27] In practice, it is known that some men use the masks to carry out their infamies—either in the form of random slaughter or in targeting their enemies—under the masquerade of Tambaran justice. Nevertheless, given the general belief in Tambaran spirits and their sanguinary appetites, villagers have little option but to recall the death of innocents with resignation, noting that in the old days life with the Tambaran was sometimes very harsh and tragic.[28]

---

trivial, the wearer (if his identity is discovered) is not necessarily immune from censure. In one case a Balanga *hangamu'w* had terrorized a woman of Nangup and had stolen her knife when she fled. The wearer was revealed to be a notorious ne'er-do-well, whereupon the men of Balanga severely reprimanded the young man—not because of the substance of the deed, but because it was *he* who had done it.

26. Moreover, because the deed is done under Tambaran auspices the mystery will not yield either to divination or to the form of retaliatory sorcery which recruits the ghost of the victim to be his own avenger.

27. There are other forms of ritual homicide (*laf*) which will be discussed in later chapters. See also Tuzin (1976:47,51).

28. The last ritual murder, which did not involve an *hangamu'w*, occurred in Ilahita

When their season is over, the *hangahiwa* are disposed of in such a way as to indicate to non-initiates that they have returned to the sacred pools of their owners. The costumes are dismantled and the masks are stored in the rafters and secret confines of yam houses where women may not go. The orange fruits and yellow *maolihiwa* are hung high in treetops near the streams, so that when the women see them the next morning they will know that the *hangahiwa* have doffed their skins and returned to the world of the spirits.

---

around 1958. A middle-aged woman was garrotted at her doorstep by persons unknown for having seated herself too near a spot where men were performing secret Tambaran rites. There was consensus among the men that she would have to be killed, but the actual executioners remained—in the nature of *laf* homicides—anonymous. Simbiaken, her husband, was absent from the village that day and was not party to her murder. See Tuzin (1976:127ff.) for a case study featuring Simbiaken.

3. Lefin:

Pangs of a New Identity

It was the woman who, long ago, made the first bullroarer (walop), which was named Mimi'unemb. One day she was chopping up an ambop tree for firewood. One of the chips flew into the air, making the sound "Brrrrr." She liked the loud sound, so she threw the piece of wood into the air several times to hear it cry out again. Then she got the idea of attaching a line to the object and twirling it continuously in the air. This produced a very big sound, bigger even than the voice of a man.

All the other villagers heard the sound and wondered what could be making it. Sometimes they heard the sound rush toward them, and they ran away in great fright. One day some of the men stayed for a moment to see what was making the noise. When they saw that it was only a woman they were angry and said that it was not right for a woman to be able to frighten the men. They demanded that she teach them how to twirl the object, and when she did so they promptly killed her. That way none of the other women would ever know the secret now held by the men.

IF you were to ask a cult member to name the distinctive features of the Falanga tambaran, chances are he would mention (1) the emphasis on bandicoot meat and (2) the stinging-nettle ordeal. He might also include the revelation of the *hangahiwa*, even though these masks are found in association with all cult grades and are, so to speak, paraphernalia without portfolio. Falanga is the baby tambaran. Its secrets are few and innocuous, and the men openly admit that the women probably know much of what goes on in the rites.[1] Regardless of whether its secrets are open or closed, Falanga's contribution to male character formation is that it gives young boys *something of their own*—a thing which the adult community conspicuously values, a thing for which they are responsible. Surely, no cultural strategem could be better designed to turn these boys into serious little men, loyal to their sex and proud of the fact that a small part of ritual heritage depends on them.

These socializing functions pertain as well to Lefin,[2] but the list of special attributes is longer corresponding with the increased range and severity of ritual experiences. Here, we first encounter the idea of the Tambaran being directly personified: in the imaginary form of a dwarf with bright red hair and beard who leads an elusive existence in the forest during intervals between Lefin ceremonials.[3] The dwarf has, however, two giant features which metaphorize the central secrets of Lefin. The sound of the bullroarer portrays the enormous voice of this tambaran; also, his great teeth and mouth are allegedly the implements with which drums and slit-gongs are carved. In addition to revealing the truth about bullroarers and carving techniques, admission to this grade involves another assault on the novices' genitals—this one more traumatic than that experienced in Falanga.

The ritual significance of the bullroarer, and its association with the little big-man of the forest, illuminates the central meaning of the story which opened this chapter. Although "Mimi'unemb" repeats several elements portrayed in its Falanga predecessor, it is distinguishable by its more exclusive and overt concern with *power*. To see why this is so, we need a bit of background information.

In most of its guises the awesome might of the Tambaran

---

1. This raises the subject of the nature and function of ritual secrecy, about which I shall have something to say in a later chapter.
2. The word *lefin* is the generic term for sago as food (pl. *lefis*).
3. Whether genetic or due to protein deficiency, red hair color is not uncommon in Ilahita, though it is invariably dull in shade rather than bright. Beards are thought to be grown only at the expense of sexual body energies, and therefore one tends to see them on men past their sexual prime. Sporting a beard is also a gesture of self-importance.

is generally perceived to be a potentiality: either it is a passive spiritual force which can be called upon by magical entreaty; or, if it should exercise itself spontaneously, though the effects may be observable the precise nature of the causal movement remains an impenetrable mystery. By contrast, the *active* aspect of Tambaran power, to the extent it can be known, is conceived by men to reside in its voice. Like Yahweh of the ancient Hebrews, the Tambaran *speaks* creation; *speaks* destruction; *speaks* existence itself.[4] And yet, paradoxically, despite its omnicompetence the Tambaran cannot speak unaided. Secret sound-making devices such as bullroarers and flutes are not mere imitations of its voice, they *are* its voice, the concrete instrument of Tambaran power. This is why operating these devices in a ritual setting is a supremely sacred act. It is a moment when the power of the Tambaran is made manifest (created, in fact) through the agency of men, who, by the same token, become godlike by virtue of the power they momentarily command. Indeed, in the Voice of the Tambaran, men and their spirits (both those dwelling within them and those dwelling outside in the form of supernatural beings) are rendered indivisible; hence the choice of this image as the title metaphor of a study dealing with Arapesh religious culture.

This explains why the feminine discovery and use of Mimi'unemb—the voice of Lefin, a sound "bigger even than the voice of a man"—should have excited intolerable fear and envy on the part of the men, and a murderous desire by them to have possession of it. At stake was the sovereignty of males—and with it the very basis of masculine self-identity. But it is not enough merely to have achieved power or identity, nor even to have achieved them under mythic auspices; the problem of acquisition, once surmounted, instantly re-

---

4. Accordingly, however diminutive his stature, the voice of the dwarf Lefin makes him the "big-man" he proclaims himself to be. (See text below.) Arapesh informants are amused and attracted by the image of a man "little-yet-big"—an image which, after all, governs the tambaran of *little* children to whom is vouchsafed *big* power. Similarly, in a later chapter it will be seen that the oxymoronic figure of "old-yet-young" stands at the heart of Nggwal Walipeine symbolism. For another instance of such paradoxes, this time concerning flute size and amplitude, see Tuzin (1976:351n.).

generates itself as the problem of maintenance—a problem to which, as the following chapters will many times affirm, there can be no lasting resolution. Only by repeated assertions of power, sometimes in a violent mode, can the men preserve that sense of themselves from which all other meanings flow. This is the lesson of the Tambaran, begun in Falanga and continuing now in Lefin.

THE INITIATION

As in the case of Falanga, entry into Lefin is accomplished in two phases scheduled in successive years: *wafitenei* and *ambelinei*, the former preferably occurring the year after Falanga concludes. A month or two before the first activities begin, a small spirit house is erected in the village—indistinguishable in most respects from a normal dwelling house, except that the façade is enclosed by a blind of sago raffia and fronds instead of a proper wall.[5]

Wafitenei. After the gardens have been cleared and are ready for planting, the initiation class (Owapwas) catches a pig for the opening feast. The metaphor used for the pig is *angalaf*—literally, the broad, smooth leafstem of the sago palm. Some actual *angalaf* is also used: reduced to ashes, it is mixed with water and added to the novices' yam soup. The soup is also cooked with a bouquet garni consisting of bark scrapings, aromatic herbs and diced leaves, all of which are thought to have magical efficacy. Some of the pork is cut into small pieces which are tied on stakes overhanging the soup as it cooks; this is done so that something of the meat's spiritually strong essence can transmit itself to the novices' food. Along with the soup and roasted yams, this meat will be fed to the youths; the bulk of the meat, unadulterated soup and tubers are eaten by the older men present.

By eating the magical soup the novices take into themselves a substance which lodges permanently in their stom-

---

5. The same is true of the Falanga spirit house mentioned in the preceding chapter. During ceremonies the fronds are put to one side, leaving only a raffia curtain hanging over the portal. This enables figures to burst forth from within when the libretto calls for such drama.

achs and causes them to become sick if they should *ever* break a taboo.[6] The taboos immediately levied prohibit sexual contact, bathing, taking food from any woman other than a close kinswoman, drinking water and eating all but a few specified foods—yams (either roasted or in soup), taro and unblemished pitpit. A week later the novices are fed (nonmagical) yam soup, which lifts the taboo on bathing and also modifies the prohibition on water so as to deny the novice only *cold* water. (At this juncture the new yam gardens are planted.) The other food taboos remain in effect until after the yam harvest the following year—in particular, the short-yam harvest. Members of the initiating class display their crop in circular bins and pile quantities of the tabooed food on top of the uppermost layer. When this food, along with a few of the yams, is given to the novices, the taboos carried forward during the planting and growing season are finally removed. By this time, the second phase of Lefin is about to begin.

Ambelinei.   This phase consists of two ceremonial sequences staged in quick succession.[7] One features the revelation of the bullroarers and the secret carving implement, the other

6. Intermittent taboo periods occur frequently throughout a man's life, and always it is primarily the magic lingering from the Lefin initiation which acts as the enforcer of the rule; hence, the need to specify early on a ban on sex even though boys the age of Lefin novices are not likely to run afoul of this particular injunction—with or without the sanction of a taboo.

   As an example of the lasting effect of this magic, the case is recalled of Tatangafum, a man who died around 1960. Years before, when he was in his early twenties, newly married, he contracted a disease which wasted his lips, nose and palate. The resulting damage—including a cloven palate—interfered with eating, speaking, smoking and spitting. It was said at the time, and the victim himself concurred, that the condition had been brought about by his having violated a taboo and thereby activated the Lefin magic. He forced his young wife to leave him, saying she should not be married to one who is maimed and the butt of jokes. During the rest of his long and solitary life, Tatangafum grew to be admired as a yam producer and warrior—but his disfigurement was always there to remind people of what might happen if you ignored a taboo. Even now, years after Tatangafum's death, his story is told homiletically to young people.

7. As a general rule the scheduling of Tambaran ceremonies is necessarily contingent on a sufficiency of yams. If the current harvest is too meager, cult leaders would normally move to postpone the rites until the next year—lest it be said that they had dishonored their Tambaran with a low-budget production. This is another way of saying that the debt in yams carried over from the last Lefin initiation, when the class statuses of present-day groups were reversed, could not be satisfied without threatening basic subsistence or cutting into the seed yams set aside for the next planting. For the initiating class to offer anything less than full requital would be to dishonor their *ombif* and disgrace themselves.

is climaxed by the ordeal of penile incision. The latter experience is primarily associated with Lefin rather than with Falanga, under whose auspices it first occurs, because in the older Tambaran *both* age-sets are forced to submit to the trauma. This part of Lefin was not performed during my time in the field, so my description must rely on well-corroborated informants' accounts. The bullroarer segment was witnessed in Lehinga village when I accompanied a large band of Ilahitans who attended the enemy's initiation as invited (if not honored) guests.

On the afternoon before the Lehinga initiation a considerable number of men and boys gathered in Bafimbil, the ceremonial hamlet of Hengwanif ward, to enjoy a feast[8] and to prepare for the events of the next day. Their specific purpose was to refurbish their bullroarers and practice the techniques involved in using them. Bullroarers are simple but effective sound-making devices consisting of a length of wood twirled at the end of a line. The Ilahita version is carved either from 'limbum' (*Kentiopsis archontophoneix*) or from sago-palm wood. It has the shape of a double-edged blade, tapering to a point at both ends, and measuring fourteen to twenty centimeters in length and about seven centimeters at its widest point. The line, about two meters long, is made from the inner fibers of a type of tree bark known for its toughness and resembles in texture and appearance a leather thong. Its sound, as I said earlier, is the unearthly voice of the big-mouthed, red-haired dwarf Lefin. The twirler casts the bullroarer with added force at one part of the arc of revolution. In so doing he varies the pitch in such a way as to imitate the intonation pattern of the utterance "Ai tembi-tembinei . . . Ai tembi-tembinei," which may be translated as "I am a great, great man . . . I am a great, great man." In the nature of such illusions, upon being told what the words of Lefin's song were, I had no trouble whatever in "hearing" them. The effect is altogether remarkable in purely aural terms—all the more so when we add the context of religious mystery and terror.

8. The food is provided by adult members of the class that is to be initiated the next day, and consists of roasted yams, yam soup and sprouted coconuts.

The men and boys practiced not only the technique of twirling the bullroarer, but also the mock attack staged upon the person twirling it. As we shall see in later Tambaran transferals, the novice class—that is, the fathers rather than the novices themselves—succeed to the Tambaran by *seizing* it forcibly. Thus the initiator uses the bullroarer as a weapon to fend off members of the opposite class as they attempt to move in on him from all sides.[9] This continues until the man tires and lifts his throwing arm as a signal that the others may safely rush in under the flashing blade. They pinion his arms, take the bullroarer, and then vacate the clearing to let another initiator try his hand. This goes on until all the bull-roarers have been transferred.[10]

The affair just described continued, with intermittent bull-roarer performances, through the night and on until 10:30 the next morning. After the group had formed up to set off for Lehinga (about five kilometers to the east), they were addressed by Sala'apen, one of the two village councillors[11] and a resident of Hengwanif ward.[12] Alluding to a series of disputes with Lehinga during recent years, Sala'apen cautioned his audience against allowing their standing grievances to tempt them into doing real and malicious injury with the bullroarers. The truce of the Tambaran must be respected.

En route to Lehinga the party paused twice at streams in

9. The real danger here should not be underestimated. An "attacker" could mis-calculate and step within range of the bullroarer, but the greater worry is that the line might snap and send the blade flying into the encircling crowd. One fairly recent incident is recalled where this happened and an onlooker was killed instantly as the missile buried itself in his skull. The informant telling me this added that if the line broke on the upswing the bullroarer would fly very far—he indicated a location about three kilometers distant—before coming to rest. He claimed to be speaking factually, but I take this palpable exaggeration to be an instance of the mythical thinking that often accompanies Tambaran topics. Cf., for example, the same motif as it appears in the stories of Nambweapa'w and Ambupwiel, respectively.

10. Of course, the bullroarers in this case were not actually transferred, for this was only a practice session and not an initiation. At the same time, it was a proper Tambaran rite in the sense that Lefin was allegedly present and was given a feast.

11. Ilahita is large enough to entitle it to two representatives to the Greater Maprik Local Government Council. See Tuzin (1976:38ff.) for more on this subject.

12. As I have reported elsewhere (Tuzin 1976:58), Ilahita's external political relations tend to devolve on the ward that shares a boundary with the other village in question. Thus, Hengwanif, being the easternmost ward, is the one most immediately involved with Lehinga in matters of war and ritual.

order to decorate themselves for the occasion. The theme was ferocity, the treatments were various. Bluish-gray sediment was scooped from the bottom of pools as paint for circles, lines, dots or total coverings on the body. Earth colors of red, green and brown were also applied to skin and hair; likewise, black, greasy paint. Other elements included cordyline leaves tucked in armbands and legbands, flowers and cassowary feathers in the hair, sundry objects (stems, sticks, rolled cordyline leaves) in the nasal septum—and so on.

On reaching the outskirts of the village, the main body of Ilahitans waited while a couple of leaders went in to inform the Lehingans of their arrival. They returned with a man of the place who guided the entire group along a path which brought them to a place of concealment adjacent to the ceremonial clearing. The Lehinga cult leaders were notified that everything was ready and the initiation could begin.

The scene opened with the young novices—about twenty-five in all—being brought by their mothers' brothers into the clearing. Some were led by the hand, others were young enough to be carried in the uncle's arms; many of them were already crying, all were visibly frightened. Waiting for them in the clearing was a force of fierce-looking strangers brandishing spears—members of the initiating class from Ningalimbi village who, like the Ilahitans, were there to add numbers and frightfulness to the Lehinga spectacle.[13] A mock attack was unleashed on the Lehingans, concluding with the beleaguered band being forced into a tight knot in the center of the clearing and encircled with a length of lawyer vine, thus being "captured." At this cue the rest of the Ningalimbi visitors started entering the clearing, bursting upon it in

13. Ningalimbi is also an enemy of Lehinga as well as being Ilahita's most loyal ally. According to an Hengwanif informant, Ilahita was dealt the honor of being the last to arrive not only because Ningalimbi was their ritual "child" and therefore junior to them (see Tuzin 1976:63), but, more importantly, because Ilahita is the "origin place" of Lefin and enjoys precedence in all matters concerned with this tambaran. When asked to corroborate this, a Lehinga informant confirmed the former reason but denied the latter, saying that no one knew the "origin place" of Lefin and that this was simply another example of Ilahita conceit. These sorts of claims of priority go on endlessly at virtually all levels of social structure—both between and within villages—over every matter that could conceivably involve an issue of priority. Needless to say, I gave up early on trying to decide which claimant was "right."

7. At the Lefin initiation, boys and their sponsors are "attacked" by decorated initiators before being shown the bullroarers.

groups of two to four. Throwing small coconuts or sticks ahead of themselves, they circled about in an aggressive manner swinging bullroarers, leafy branches or heavy ropes. Occasionally, one would enter carrying a coconut shell vessel and dash around the clearing throwing what was said to be "feces" on those sitting or standing around the perimeter of the clearing.[14] In each case the Ningalimbis were escorted by two Lehinga initiators who ran around the clearing ahead of them. Also, each entrance involved a mock attack and defense in which the initiator swinging the weapon eventually allowed himself to be captured by members of the novice class. The idea is that these displays illustrate to the new Lefin members, who were standing to one side with their mothers' brothers watching all of this, how the bullroarers are used in ritual. Each time a man was "captured," those who did it and those around gave off with victorious whoops.

14. The substance was, in fact, rancid, foul-smelling sago mash. As one who was sprayed, I can attest to the accuracy of the counterfeit.

8. Ritual "attackers" capture the bullroarer during the Lefin initiation.

With all the Ningalimbis now in the clearing, space was made for the Ilahitas to make their (equally dramatic) entry. It began with six Balanga men going through a series of aggressive maneuvers comparable to those just described. Instead of bullroarers and branches they fought with long, double-pointed sticks—only to be subdued in their turn. One of them, however, carried a length of bamboo (two meters) to which was lashed a steel adz blade. Around the blade, nearly obscuring it, were decorations of cordyline leaves and ritually significant grass (*walal*). As anticipated above, this is the instrument used to carve drums and slit-gongs and is, along with the bullroarers, one of the central secrets of Lefin.[15] With this initial foray completed, the rest of the Ila-

15. Formerly, of course, the adz blade would have been fashioned from stone. In general, cult leaders do not hesitate to introduce nontraditional items into the paraphernalia or ceremonies, if the result is to augment the power and illusion of the Tambaran. Even when there is no practical incentive, the Tambaran is tolerantly amused by the skillful incorporation of modern items and motifs into the ritual. This is consistent with the carnival aspect of the cult, which will become more pronounced in later grades.

hita force came in, swinging bullroarers and being captured in the manner described for Ningalimbi.

When the excitement of the foreign "attack" had abated, the novices were brought into the clearing, lined up, and given the bullroarers by the men who had seized them (i.e., older members of their own initiation class). Each boy received several.[16] Then food (long yams, short yams, yam soup and pork) was distributed among the visitors by the Lehinga initiators, who had received it from the fathers of the novices. Also, each of the initiators, individually and in his own right, gave to one of the visitors a sprouted coconut in special recognition of his having lent assistance. After the ensuing feast, speeches were exchanged on the eminently safe topic of how the local member of the House of Assembly[17] ought to desist in his efforts to outlaw Tambaran activities. Late in the afternoon both groups of visitors set off in time to reach home in the remaining light, leaving the Lehingas to their own feast and celebratory singing.[18] Throughout the proceedings, attitudes between hosts and visitors had been polite but restrained, with little or no fraternization.

A general comment before moving on to the closing subphase of Lefin. The foregoing illustrates well how the Tambaran Cult is the premier integrating mechanism of Arapesh *areal* culture (Schwartz 1963). We are dealing here with a strongly *village*-based system of social relations. As I explained at length in the previous study (Tuzin 1976), relationships predicated on kinship and economic exchange, which in many other parts of New Guinea underlie relatively enduring ties between localities, tend in the Arapesh case to be contained within the village and thereby to accentuate this

16. There is a trick involved even at this late stage. The boys are given plain bullroarers, and after a day or so of practicing they are dismayed at finding themselves unable to produce a very loud sound with them. This provokes teasing from the older men, who finally reveal that a bit of coconut husk tied to the base of the blade will achieve the desired effect. For this additional bit of knowledge the initiators are paid another one or two pigs.

17. This was the territorial legislative body. At the time the local member was Pita Lus (now Sir Pita Lus), a member of Lehinga village who occasionally excited the ire of his own elders with his modernistic advocacies.

18. This would be a bilateral exchange feast of yams and soup between the initiation classes with the novice class additionally providing pork.

regional atomism. War alliances, it is true, were durable, but these ties remained functionally specified and did not, by and large, lead to more broadly based interaction. War *antagonisms* were curiously more productive in this regard, since periods of active hostility alternated with periods of uneasy truce—the latter having been declared exclusively for the purposes of Tambaran cooperation.[19] The procedures of cult initiation require the presence of strangers—not only strangers, but *enemy* strangers—to lend verisimilitude to the mock attacks staged to terrorize the novices or to conceal from noninitiates the truth behind the illusions. The same cooperation occurs between allies, and the overall result is to intensify religious life by exposing the individual to many more ceremonies than he would otherwise experience. Such frequent—indeed, nearly incessant—reaffirmations of religious ideology surely augment an individual's attachment to these ideas and his convictions as to their immanent reality. All the more so when otherwise cruel and unrelenting enemies join in surrender to the Tambaran—an idea which, *in their act of submission*, is made to transcend them all. To my knowledge no other phenomenon projects a more crystalline expression of Arapesh culture writ large. As to the business of introducing a genuine enemy, armed to the teeth, into the heart of one's village—what other arrangement could rival this in the unique piquancy which it adds to the mystery and terror already surrounding the Tambaran? None that I can suggest.

PENIS CUTTING

The final sub-phase of Lefin does not require foreigners, perhaps because its climactic moment could little bear any more horror than it already has. This is the dramatically staged assault on the penes of the novices.

19. Of the few inter-village marriages, the majority occurred between enemies under circumstances of abduction or of unhappy daughters running away to people who would not send them home. The custom of infant betrothal virtually precludes matches between residentially remote partners, since in the minds of Arapesh fathers no tenuous political benefit could compensate for the effective loss of a daughter. See Tuzin (1976:chap. 5) for a discussion of these attitudes and corresponding social patterns.

One problem entailed in studying the literature of an ethnographic area such as New Guinea is that the reader risks being desensitized—losing his cultural distance and with it his "fresh eye." Penile incision is reported often in the New Guinea ethnography. The resulting contempt-bred-of-familiarity takes the form of coming to view this practice as "just another" customary observance, equivalent in most analytic respects to members of the culture brushing their teeth with coconut husks or marrying their cross-cousins. Nothing could be more damaging to the advance of cultural theory than to say that the quality of experience implicated in a given trait does not matter to our analysis. *We* might be bored by the subject of New Guinea penile incision, but we can be sure that the young boy whose penis is being slashed by a savagely attired adult under conditions calculated to inspire maximum horror will take a very lively interest in what is happening to him. One does not have to be a Freudian zealot to see that the special, subjective character of this experience, coming when it does in the life of the individual, could play a crucial role in instilling culturally approved attitudes and values on the part of impressionable novices. In this respect, then, we may say that culture is grounded in the experiences of individuals—even while affirming the obverse: that culture produces the very circumstances under which these experiences occur.[20] Forewarned, then, as to the culturally portentous significance of psychological trauma inflicted as a matter of convention, let us see what Lefin holds in store for his would-be protégés.

20. In a recent book, Marshall Sahlins (1976) strenuously advocates the exclusively a priori status of culture in relation to material conditions and experiences. It escapes me why Professor Sahlins insists on a relationship of unilateral causation between these two domains and why he dismisses all forms of materialism—however qualified—as mere throwbacks to the outmoded reductionism of nineteenth-century social philosophy. Since the eighteenth-century publication of Vico's *Scienza nuova*, and again in the writing of modern scholars (e.g., Hallowell 1955; Popper 1957; Spiro 1951), we have had repeated and persuasive arguments in favor of an *interactionist* perspective on culture and praxis. Sahlins, it seems, would have us ignore these contributions and indulge in that sterile narcissism toward which anthropology is fatally tempted, viz., the reifying error entailed in asserting the autonomy of culture. In a forthcoming review, Keesing (n.d.) has pinpointed the flaws in Sahlins's argument. For another criticism of this general position—one which is undiminished by the passage of time—see Sapir's answer (1917) to Kroeber's notion of the Superorganic.

The sequence begins with the capture of a pig, which is the signal to the initiating class that they should clear away the undergrowth at Alahimbil—the stream site which is the traditional scene of Lefin initiations.[21] An all-night singing and feast is then held, and the next day the initiators construct a shelter at Alahimbil. It is a roofless affair built over the water itself. Hefty logs are laid from one bank to the other as supports for a crude, palmwood floor. The walls are made from foliated branches of particular varieties of trees, bamboo and palm placed upright at close intervals. Each initiator cuts a piece of palmwood to serve as a seat in the house for his junior *ombaf*; these seats are lined along the two side walls.

The next job is to fashion two concealed chambers at the Alahimbil shelter: one is under the floor, that is, between the floor and the surface of the water; the other is a small room partitioned off from the main area of the interior. The lower chamber, hidden behind a blind of sago thatch, serves as a place of concealment for the pig-incisors. The inner sanctum on the main floor is walled by leaves from the growth point of various plants including pitpit, a decorative tree, and the black-leaved shrub known as *bombop*. This chamber and the activities associated with it are the province of pig magicians who have achieved the penultimate grade of the Tambaran, Nggwal Bunafunei. Here is housed a side-blown *kondo* flute, which the magicians play intermittently throughout the remaining period of initiation.[22] This instrument will be shown to the novices at a given point in the ceremony.

The final fixture consists of a stripped hardwood sapling (*amenumb*) which is anchored in the floor near the main door so as to extend out over the water at an angle of about thirty degrees. The *amenumb* is decorated along its length with various colorful leaves (cordylines, crotons, etc.), and its tip is hung with a flat, narrow, anthropomorphic sculpture known

21. The Arapesh hunt pigs with nets, making every effort to capture the beast without hurting it. Thus, in the present context, the pig can be kept alive for several days while the men undertake various tasks, such as clearing Alahimbil or performing a ceremony, before convening the feast.

22. *Kondo* flutes are also associated with Nggwal Bunafunei and will be encountered again in chap. 5 in connection with the ceremonialism of Nggwal spirit-house construction.

as *aminguf* ("bird").²³ Later when the platform is rocking under the weight of a crowd of dancing initiators, the *amenumb* will jerk up and down causing the *aminguf* to slap the water loudly and rhythmically.

The novices' departure for Alahimbil is preceded by two singsings held in the village on consecutive nights and featuring a number of initiators who are costumed for the occasion. During this prelude the two men nominated as incisors²⁴ sleep at Alahimbil and, along with helpers drawn from the ranks of current pig magicians, make final arrangements for the initiation. Apart from putting finishing touches on the shelter (see below), the men make the incising instrument by sharpening a piece of bamboo to a razor's edge and tempering it over a fire which, in addition to normal fuel, contains pig bristles and opossum hair. The incisors also disguise themselves to resemble pigs—except that Nature would scarcely recognize these balefully weird creatures as her own. Most of their skin is painted black, with white lines drawn on the cheeks. An opossum skin covers the forehead and beneath this hangs a mask of cordyline strands arranged in such a way that the man's upper face is obscured from view but his vision is fairly unaffected. Opossum pelts are also draped on his shoulders and down his back. A pig-tusk ornament hung from his nasal septum completes the disguise. When they hear the band of initiators and novices noisily approaching Alahimbil—early in the morning following the second singsing—these "pigs" repair to the chamber under the floor to await their call.

The boys are brought into the shelter by their *ombif*, who show them their seats and then stand aside to give them a clear view of Lefin's decor and paraphernalia. With the dark-

23. The *aminguf* sculpture is cryptically referred to as the "baby" of Nggwal—meaning, to those who know, that it is a miniature version of the giant statues carved to embody the spirit of Nggwal. As we have already seen and will see again, birds appear as auxiliary images in all grades, invariably characterized as the "children" and/or "messengers" of the Tambaran. This is consistent with the recurrence of birds in non-cult contexts: as augury figures in myths, and as familiars to sorcerers.
24. There is no special skill or qualification demanded of the incisors; they are simply two senior and generally respected men who are offered the job by informal acclamation.

ness of the enclosure, the half-light of early morning, and the gloom of the surrounding jungle, it takes the novices a few minutes to make out what it is they are supposed to admire. Eventually, they see that the side walls are covered with *maoli-hiwa* decked with long strings of *su'witix*, parrot and cockatoo feathers, and colorful leaves and flowers. The set of paraphernalia consists of *enip* flutes—long bamboo culms covered with large, circular 'pangal'[25] shields painted with geometric and quasi-anthropomorphic designs and fringed with white chicken feathers. These, along with the *kondo* flute which is also revealed at this time, number about ten objects in all. After being shown the technique the novices are invited to try their hand at playing the flutes, singly at first and then in groups of two. During their practice all the men in the crowded chamber sing and shout and stamp their feet in order to cover the sound of missed notes which women back in the village might detect and be led to suspect that the voice they hear is something less than divine.

Suddenly, the din ceases. A pig is being called: someone is emitting the distinctive, nasal grunt that a person uses in summoning a household pig home in the late afternoon. Then, from underneath the floor comes an answering grunt —deeper and throatier than the first. As the pig-incisor comes into view the shelter is again enveloped by a torrent of noise and activity: the decorated dancers, the flute players, the shouting and singing of everyone else combine with the heaving of the platform set up by rhythmic stamping and the syncopated slap of the *aminguf* to create a scene of total confusion. The object this time is to terrify the novices and to drown their screams from female ears—for the "pig" is now advancing to "bite" them.

The first pig is actually only a pretender. He goes down the line of boys slashing at their penes but deliberately miss-

25. 'Pangal' is a Pidgin English term referring to the midrib of a sago-palm frond. The narrower part distal to the trunk is used (after being split) as a light planking material for walls, floors and various other domestic purposes. At its base the midrib splays out and assumes a broad, flat form which makes it suitable for sitting, sleeping, and cooking mats. And, with their smooth, varnished-like surfaces, these stiff sheets are especially useful as a medium for so-called bark paintings.

ing them. Following immediately is the real incisor, who takes advantage of the novice's momentary puzzlement to deliver deep cutting strokes on their glans penis.[26] The blood flows prodigiously. The boys are quickly forced down into a prone position and are told to put their penes between the floor boards, letting the blood run into the water below. As one informant reported, there is such a volume of blood that the stream turns red. After this, the initiators treat the novices by magical techniques to speed the healing of the wounds. They also give them a small meal of boiled yams. When this is completed, the decorated initiators return to the village, remove their trappings, and return to Alahimbil in time for the final revelation late that afternoon.

Although the novices had been told that the paraphernalia displayed to them in the morning and the ordeal they were made to suffer *was* Lefin, they now discover that that was only a trick—or rather, those elements were only very secondary, second-rate "sago." The real Lefin, the choice sago, is revealed to be a number of sacred drums.[27] As night falls, a singsing starts up at Alahimbil featuring these drums, the *enip* flutes and conch shells. Boiled tubers are brought from the village. For an entire month the boys live and sleep at Alahimbil—cold and miserable, without the protection of a roof over their heads. Food is brought (by the initiators) from the village, and from time to time the all-night singsing is repeated. When the seclusion is ended, the boys are allowed to bathe, after which they are rubbed down with stinging nettles[28] and arrayed in decorative finery by their *ombif*— the same costumes, that is, that the initiators wore at the beginning of this sub-phase. That afternoon, they are led

26. While the pig is being called, the novices are told to masturbate to produce an erection and then hold their penes with the foreskin peeled back. Some turgor pressure is needed if the wound is to bleed sufficiently; but how, in the circumstances, the novices are able to comply with these instructions is a mystery to me. The younger or more frightened novices have their penes held by their mother's brother, who is standing by to give whatever comfort he can during the ordeal.

27. Note that the drums are the symbolic link between the two sub-phases of the Lefin Ambelinei, the first one having focused on the voice of that tambaran who allegedly carves drums and slit-gongs with his teeth.

28. This is not intended as an ordeal, but rather to refresh the novices and give an attractive luster to their skin.

back to the village by their *ombif* to be paraded under the admiring eyes of their mothers and sisters. They are guests of honor at the singsing held that night to welcome them home and rejoice over their progression toward manhood.

REMARKS

As with most (if not all) rituals the question of what Lefin means must be approached at more than one level. Ostensibly, the various ceremonies are designed (1) to transfer ritual knowledge and custodianship to the novices and (2) to complete the purgation of maternal influences through an operation more radical than that performed by Falanga. The lesson in penile bloodletting is the start of a lifelong regime of regular ritual cleansings; for, in years to come, the debilitating effects wrought by sexual contact must be routinely countered if the male is to succeed in the many tasks assigned to him by the culture. This raises a problem, however, to which I will return in a moment.

Another significance of this tambaran is revealed in an event which occurs a few days into the seclusion. When no one is looking, one of the initiators throws a stone into the water, creating an audible splash. He cries out in alarm, saying that the shell pendant which his friend had lent him has accidentally fallen into the water. The novices, he commands, must jump into the stream and help him find it. Unknown to the boys, as they are feeling around in the mud and silt for the nonexistent shell, they are contaminating themselves with the "oily essence" of their own penile blood, which supposedly has adhered to the bottom of the stream. The result is functionally equivalent to that of the magically adulterated soup they were duped into eating during the *wafitenei* phase; that is, to enforce under penalty of serious illness food and other taboos levied during the immediate growing season and at various intervals throughout their life. In the days that the blood essences have lain on the streambed they have mingled with the spiritual presences already there—the invisible potencies of ancestral shades, cult spirits, and *maolinipunemb* figures. In short, the blood which carried away pernicious feminine influences now comes back to the novices charged with superlatively *masculine* influences. The youths have met and interacted with the world of spirits by the medium of their own body essences, certifying in the act their office as complete males. This need to confront and be accepted by the spirits as a stage in male identity and character formation is the general reason why this part of Lefin, and the seclusion that follows, must take place at a *stream* site.

The final significance is not one which the Arapesh can talk about, but it should be obvious to the anthropological reader. One of the central themes of the Tambaran Cult is, as will emerge with increasing clarity over the course of this study, *dominance*—of spirits over mortals, of men over women, of older males over younger males. This pervasive, ritualized concern with aggressive power, so frequently reported in the New Guinea literature, invites qualification of the widespread notion that societies in this part of the world are "egalitarian." True, *within* sex categories there is equality of opportunity: accumulated wealth is not there to be passed on, and inherited prestige does not carry an individual very far in his own career. The Arapesh do not know about aristocrats and commoners, and in outlook they possess what might be called a "rugged individualism." And yet, the absence of these traits does not at all yield an "egalitarian" result in any meaningful sense. Rather, we see that patterns of authority and dominance are distributed in other ways: according to broad age and sex categories and a welter of ritual specialties and cult offices, some of which are held by virtue of hereditary appointment. These many statuses and attendant roles serve to structure a good deal of social life, rendering it predictable to the actors and continuingly viable in the face of pressures favoring disintegration. Such pressures stem from the very opposite of egalitarianism, if by that we mean an attitude of mind or quality of behavior. They are the forces of individuals who, seeking to dominate one another and in the absence of regulating or mediating structures, would part ways before submitting to arbitrary rule.

In the preceding study I considered at length the formal and informal structures which provide this regulative function and thereby underpin the solidarity of a large village. But I did not attend at all to the mechanisms by which acceptance of these structures and compliance with their prescriptive entailments comes about. Herein lies the lesson of Lefin and of nearly all other aspects of the Tambaran Cult. Conventional acts of terror against women occur throughout the canon of cult ideology, but in Lefin (especially in its dramatic final sub-phase) we see the act directed against helpless boys —novices who, in the normal course, will be tomorrow's senior cult leaders. Leave aside rationales of religious and pseudo-physiological necessity! However sincere the initiators may be in avowing that the ordeal they inflict is for the novice's own good and well-being, the act is objectively (and surely in the minds of the immediate victims as well) one of raw aggression and dominance assertion. Even without the element of castration fear, to a seven- or eight-year-old the event must seem life-threatening, convincing him in the most persuasive way possible that these existence-bestowing men and the rules they stand for are not to be taken lightly.

There is a problem lurking here. The ordeal we have been discussing is carefully and successfully designed to inspire maximum horror in its victims. How, then, do we reconcile this image with the prospect of these same individuals, ten or fifteen years hence, and for the rest of their sexually active lives, calmly and deliberately inflicting such genital wounds on themselves? It is all very well to speak of the need for "ritual hygiene," but this rationale must, it seems to me, be accompanied by a change in the affective content of the experience itself, if it is to be compelling enough to keep such an ostensibly self-punishing practice alive. The data confirm that such a change occurs, and with rather surprising results.

Observations of adult penile blood-letting are not easy to come by, not because the act is particularly secretive, but because it is regarded as a kind of "toilet function" which a man would not be inclined to broadcast in advance. Accordingly, when Kwambafum—a married man in his late twenties who had become a valuable informant on sexual matters—offered to take me along the next time he cleansed himself, I was eager, despite a certain vague apprehension, to accept.

The place chosen was a secluded part of a nearby stream, where the bed widens and the water ripples at ankle depth over a pebbly bottom. Kwambafum had brought a packet containing the necessary instruments, and he proceeded with the operation in the routine, business-like manner of one who had done this many times before. After stimulating an erection he inserted a green stem about eight centimeters long into his urethra and, with a shudder that ran visibly through his thighs and torso, yanked it out. Blood oozed from the urethral opening; within three or four repeats of this action, it was spurting in a fine spray to a distance of about two meters. The stem, as I had been shown before-hand, was covered with small barbs pointing slightly down-ward along its length. This meant that, while the stem could be easily inserted, on pulling it out the barbs caught and tore at the urethral lining. In all, Kwambafum used eight stems, inserting each of them until the barbs wore down, that is to say, five to ten times.

When the flow of blood had abated, Kwambafum set aside the remaining stems and produced from his packet a (metal) razor blade which had been broken obliquely so as to create a sharp point. After pausing briefly to recover his erection, he peeled back the foreskin and began vigorously jabbing at the glans penis. Apparently satisfied at having achieved four simultaneous sprays, he relaxed and waited a few moments for the flow to cease. Then he carefully washed the blood from his legs and hands, and concealed (against possible sorcerers) the bloodstained implements under the larger pebbles of the stream. The entire operation had lasted less than ten minutes.

Of the various noteworthy features of this performance, the one which most struck me, and for which I was least pre-pared, was the autoerotic component. Watching this, the realization dawned on me—and was later confirmed—that I was witnessing an act very close to masturbation.[29] From the start, quickly losing awareness of my presence, Kwambafum

---

29. In itself, urethral masturbation is fairly common in our own and other societies. The use of a barbed instrument, however, would probably send psychiatrists scurrying to their textbooks on sado-masochistic perversion.

adopted an expression of abstracted concentration, with sharper feelings occasionally flickering across his face. His thoughts were revealed when, afterward, I asked him how he had managed to sustain an erection during all this. "By thinking about things," he said. What sorts of things? "Things that I do when I am with a woman," he replied, thus affirming that erotic fantasy is the means by which the penis is maintained at the state of engorgement necessary for effective "cleansing."[30] He then went on to recommend, with a sly smile, that I try it myself: "I know it must look very painful to you, and it is true that the shock of the first stem makes your insides quiver. But after that the feeling is almost pleasurable, and you definitely feel better for having done it!"

The facts presented offer a clue as to why letting blood from the penis should be experienced as the sudden discharge of noxious, specifically feminine, substances.[31] If the climactic release of blood is emotionally equivalent to ejaculation, and if the thoughts leading up to this are fixed on erotic feminine images, then the postclimactic drop in intensity (and the corresponding sense of well-being) would be associated with the rapid dissipation of those images—discharged, by implication, with the blood itself. Experience would thus confirm that this operation has the specific and dramatic purgative effect ascribed to it.

More to the point of my analysis, however, the preceding episode suggests how the Lefin ordeal is implicated in the general acquisition of Arapesh male identity. The horrific character of the initiatory bloodletting, both as contrived and as experienced, is consistent with the novice's primary and still-pervasive identification with female figures. In a sense, the attack is directed against (and responded to by) "that which is feminine" in him. By eroticizing the act of penis incising, however, thereby converting something that is nightmarish into something that is "almost pleasurable," the youth,

---

30. To my lasting regret, I did not think to ask Kwambafum if he had ever experienced ejaculation during one of these operations.
31. The usual explanation given for why such acts produce a tonic effect is that they function as a counterirritant. While this is no doubt true, it does not account in the present case for why the *penis* is used, or why the offending substance is conceived to be feminine in nature.

as it were, traverses the boundary of sexual identity and assumes the position of his own master. Incising his own penis is an outward sign of his masculinity; taking pleasure in doing so is that sign's inward counterpart. Thus, although the men may quip that their periodic cleansings are the "male menstruation," it would be too simple to infer that this merely represents male envy of female sexual parts or functions (Bettelheim 1954). While cutting the penis is probably imitative of menstruation, and therefore a statement of the enviability of that function, the vaunting pride taken by the men in doing this to themselves proclaims the *transcendent* power of masculinity. In other words, women merely bleed; they are helpless creatures of their own sexuality, unable to govern or restrain their sexual energies. Men, on the other hand, because they create their own sexuality, retain the almighty power to control it and when necessary to direct its energies into the magic and ritual on which society depends. Letting blood from the penis, then, is proudly perceived by the men to be an act expressive of masculine autonomy and prowess, both in itself and in the face of dangerous, but controllable, influences from outside the community of males. What they do *not* perceive is that the menace "out there" comes, in large part, from within themselves.

Returning to the developmental question, I do not have the psycho-biographical data to say precisely when the shift in identity focus occurs; very likely, it is a process both gradual and subject to considerable individual variation. At the same time, there are indications that ritual terror has the effect of accelerating the process. Even in relatively mild initiations, I frequently observed a pattern of behavior which resembles the love-of-the-oppressor syndrome identified in the literature of social psychology (Bettelheim 1953; Lifton 1961). Under certain conditions the victim of extreme terror, by virtue of what may be called coerced regression, experiences love and gratitude toward, and deep identification with, his persecutors.[32] *During* the ordeal, of course, the

---

32. The same phenomenon has been reported in the attitude of airline passengers toward skyjackers, indicating that the conditions of terror do not have to be prolonged for this to occur.

novices' attitudes are at best highly labile; but immediately following it, the initiators drop their razors, spears, cudgels or what have you, and comfort the boys with lavish displays of tender emotion. What resentment the latter may have been harboring instantly dissipates, replaced by a palpable warmth and affection for the men who, moments before, had been seemingly bent on their destruction. As their confidence recovers itself, the novices become giddy with the realization that they have surmounted the ordeal. If there is an element of identification disclosed in this remarkable transformation—and I do not know what other interpretation to place on it—then the terror component may well be essential if the cult, and indeed the society itself, is to continue in its present form.[33] For, as I said earlier, these boys are the masters and theorists of tomorrow.

33. See Girard (1977) for a rich and provocative study of ritual violence, based on classical and modern ethnographical sources. One of the author's major interpretations, the subtleties of which cannot receive justice in this short space, is that ritual violence is both re-creative and expressive; that without these controlled, ritually sublimated displays, a primordial violence—historically derived, but also deeply rooted in social experience—could reemerge and tear the community apart. Although Girard's interpretation is strikingly consistent with many of the Arapesh data, especially the general relationship between Tambaran myth and ritual, the particularities of the case imply a wider range of dimensions as co-contributors to the problem of ritual violence in Ilahita.

4. Maolimu:
The Metamorphosis

THE DOGS AND THE MAOLIMU TAMBARAN

There was a time when men did not know about the Maolimu tambaran or how to work it. The dogs of the village were the ones who did it. They dug a deep hole in the base of a hill in the forest of Angawi (near Utamup village), and all the dogs went into the hole to perform their ceremonies. While the other dogs were in the hole, the dog leaders wandered about the forest in search of meat to feed those in the hole. When they caught a pig and brought it to the hole, they said they were bringing a "female" with which all the young male dogs could copulate. Meanwhile, all the villagers searched for their dogs, but were unable to find them.

One large dog was particularly good at catching pigs and cassowaries, and when his hunt succeeded he decorated himself with paint and sago-palm sprouts (maolihiwa). His owner noticed this and decided to follow the dog and see what happened. He watched while all the decorated dogs danced and sang in the forest in celebration of the Maolimu tambaran. The man heard them refer to the last pig as "breast milk," and all the other pigs as "females." He also saw the way they ritually beat on a log each time a pig was captured and brought to them.

But afterward, when the food taboos were in force, all the dogs were very hungry and desperate for something to eat. They had a meeting and decided that they should eat the feces which the villagers regularly threw into the bush near the village. "The people do not realize it," they said, "but this is good food they are throwing away." With that, the dogs presented the humans with a large clam shell to purchase the right to eat their feces. They had tabooed everything else; all that remained were feces. So today they eat feces and the men perform the Maolimu tambaran. Sometimes men are angry and disgusted at the dogs' filthy habits, and beat them for it. But they should remember that the dogs bought this right long ago for a clam shell. They may eat the feces.

T HE story of how the dogs once ruled Maolimu adds a
new symbolic twist to the contents and ritual correlates of its Falanga and Lefin congeners. The violence
of these preceding tambarans was aimed at severing the maternal bond and redeploying its emotional energies to serve
the novice's developing male identity. Absorbed with these
crucial but limited tasks, Falanga and Lefin gave no attention
to *reformulating* the boy's attitudes toward his mother and
other close female figures, except to imply that feminine influences are somehow inimical to masculine well-being. One
of the chief purposes of Maolimu is to finalize the transfer
of identification, to consolidate the gains achieved in Falanga
and Lefin, by systematically disparaging feminine nature in
its own right. It does this through a wonderfully redundant
array of images, beginning with the story of the dogs.

The message of the story reflects the predominant contemporary view of dogs—that they are despicable creatures.
They have not always been so: once upon a time, they hunted
pigs,[1] festooned themselves in decorative finery, danced and
sang their own rituals; indeed, the dogs once possessed the
Tambaran. But then, unable to withstand the rigors of ritual
food taboos, they surrendered all this.[2] And, for what? The
license to eat human feces! By an act of weakness, inspired by
tastes bestial and revolting, the dogs consigned themselves to
the loathsome existence that is now theirs.

Remembering the stories of Falanga and Lefin, one is compelled to the interpretation that the dogs in this tale are female surrogates. In a nutshell, the lesson of Maolimu is that
women, like dogs, are despicable creatures, unenviable and
unnecessary in every way. Interestingly, the substitution per-

---

1. Men say that dogs used to be much nobler and better treated than they are today,
because they were formerly valued as hunters. This is not very convincing, since
the importance and techniques of hunting—and, presumably, the canine role in
this pursuit—have remained unchanged, according to informants, since the
beginning of time.

2. Large shells (and especially shell rings) are ritual objects of great purity and
worth. Accordingly, the shell in the story may be taken as a token for the tambaran itself.

mits the transfer of ritual ownership to occur peaceably—by purchase, rather than by violent usurpation. In contrast with the violence of the preceding stories, which expressed the tenuous and vulnerable nature of male identity, *ab initio*, the altered mood of this story signifies that, once established, masculinity has nothing to fear from its feminine adversary; one who is despised cannot be seriously threatening. Behind the veil of the canine image, that is what the men of Maolimu appear to be telling themselves.

GENERAL FEATURES

Maolimu is third in the succession of tambarans. It is the grade which signifies among other things the Arapesh male's arrival at the threshold of social and physiological maturity. In addition to denoting this stage in the cult, the term itself occurs, to my knowledge, in four other contexts, any or all of which may be significant to an understanding of this tambaran.

1. The growing point of a sago palm. Second only to yams as an Arapesh staple food source, by its propagative habits the sago palm is also recognized as the model *par excellence* of natural fecundity.

2. Similarly, the growing point of the *bufwin* palm. This is an inedible, shrublike species which grows near the water and is associated with the spirits of the dead. In the story of Nambweapa'w the first spirit house is represented as a magically transformed *bufwin* palm.

3. A species of large fruit bat, commonly known in the literature as "flying fox."

4. In its plural form (*maolihiwa*), a particularly vicious type of destructive magic said to have originated in the Wosera, an area inhabited by Abelam speakers immediately to the southeast of Arapesh territory. The psychical powers imputed to the practitioner, and his ability to attack without recourse to the victim's exuviae, cause *maolihiwa* to resemble the classic anthropological description of witchcraft.

Of these, the connection with flying foxes is the most evident, both because of a mythic connection which I shall explain in due course, and because the Arapesh, when referring to this grade in Pidgin English, call it the 'blakbokis' ("flying fox") tambaran. Under this name the grade is found in all adjacent cultures; however, data on these cultures are too sparse to admit a judgment as to whether this nominal recurrence involves correspondences in ritual content as well.

The symbols of Maolimu are thoroughly and systematically addressed to the theme of flowering sexuality which one commonly associates with puberty rites. Also, it requires a prolonged seclusion in the forest, during which novices are given tuition in skills and conduct befitting adult males, clearly signifying the profound transition from boyhood to manhood. It further displays the well-defined stages of separation, liminality and reintegration which Van Gennep long ago described for rites of passage (1909). In other important respects it resembles rites which Hiatt (1971) has aptly termed "pseudo-procreative." Granting all this, it must be emphasized that puberty in the Maolimu context is preeminently a *socially* defined efflorescence. Admittedly, few anthropological readers would be startled by this insight—it was, after all, one of Van Gennep's main theses—but in the Arapesh case the social definition of maturity, at least as far as males are concerned, can be demonstrated with uncommon clarity. To begin with, the timing of the initiation is dependent not so much on the age of the novices as it is on the total initiation sequence, which prescribes that this tambaran follow in order the one preceding it and that a generally appropriate time interval be allowed. Accordingly, there is a considerable age spread among the novices: some are genuinely pubescent while others are men in their twenties with families of their own. Precocity or retardation in ritual sophistication entirely depends on where in the initiation cycle one happened to be born.[3]

There is a more trenchant reason why Maolimu is not profitably construed as a "puberty rite"—trenchant because

---

3. In the previous study I discussed two forms of ritual promotion (Tuzin 1976: 242,280). Both are structurally determined and do not contradict the point I am presently making.

its significance may well extend beyond the Arapesh case to touch an aspect of life-crisis ceremonials that seems often neglected by anthropologists (but see Turner 1967). By fixing attention on the passive novices—those whose "puberty" is being celebrated—we tend to overlook the culturally expressive gestures employed by those who are actively administering the initiation. As with all Tambaran inductions, and contrary to what is implied by the term "puberty rite," Maolimu is very much a production by and for the older men, while the novices typically occupy the role of mere spectators. Today's initiators were yesterday's novices, and it would accord with Arapesh perceptions of the matter to say that one's initiation is complete only when one has in turn performed as the initiator, thereby arriving at a richer and more meaningful position of ritual knowledge.[4] This diminishes, in the Arapesh case, the value of such notions as "puberty rite" and shifts the discussion to a level which contemplates Maolimu (or any other initiation ceremony) as expressing cultural values of broad significance to *all* participants. Furthermore, phrased in this way the problem of analysis potentially embraces the implied role of those who are systematically excluded from the proceedings. For, indeed, what are we to make of a culture whose central values are shared and articulated by only the male portion of the population? As the study develops it should become clear that this contradiction lies close to the heart of Arapesh ethos.

Maolimu is conducted in three stages: Wafita'wi, Ambeli'wi[5] and Tangawalei', the last of which involves the forest seclusion. In Maolimu, we see the organizational scale expand to the entire village, excepting the ritually autonomous ward of Ilifalemb (see below). Although each ward builds a

---

4. As we shall later see, this is especially true for the Nggwal tambaran, in which the vast bulk of ritual knowledge is contained in the activities *preparatory* to the initiation rite. Since the experience is educational for both novices and initiators, proper direction is necessarily provided by the fathers of the novices, who, as advisers to both groups and ultimate interpreters of custom, could rightly be considered the *real* initiators.

5. Note that these are lexical variants of the adjectival terms applied to Falanga and Lefin stages. According to Arapesh rules of inflection, suffixes are chiefly determined by the noun-class affiliation of the subject noun, the latter being in this instance the name given to the respective tambaran.

Maolimu spirit house in its ceremonial hamlet, these are small and have only limited purposes. The main seat of activities for this grade is the ceremonial hamlet of Bwi'ingili ward, also called Bwi'ingili.

WAFITA'WI

This stage commences when the yam vines are dry in the garden, about one month prior to harvest. Preparations, however, begin during the preceding season. At that time the men take advantage of a lull in gardening chores to build Maolimu spirit houses in the several wards, the largest being the main house in Bwi'ingili. Two ripe coconuts are hung in the Bwi'ingili house, one with a sprout emerging, one without. When the season turns, and the coconut produces a sprout of about finger length, with its first frondlet unfolding, all the men gather in their sub-moiety hunting teams (Tuzin 1976:222) and disperse in search of a pig. A blitz campaign of this sort usually succeeds in short order, and the resulting victim is eaten that very night amid much singing and merriment. The reason for the celebration, the women are told, is that "the girl has had her first period," this being an esoteric reference to the sprouting of the coconut.[6] In the morning the men blow Maolimu whistles in the spirit house, indicating that the tambaran (here personified as a young menstruating woman) is now in residence.[7] This establishes a connection with female fertility which is to become a pervasive, highly elaborated theme of the Maolimu grade.

For one month following the events just described, the initiating sub-class (Sahopwas Junior) sleeps in the ceremonial hamlet and is fed by members of their own group and also

6. Coconuts—the fruits themselves, not the trees—are consistently feminine in symbolism, with specific references to both vulva and breast. Thus, a little girl is teased by having her immature vulva likened to an unripe coconut, while in the story of Wilitin and Amilawen (Tuzin 1976:192) there is a direct symbolic correlation between the size of a coconut sprout and the breast development of a nubile girl.

7. The whistles are hollowed spheres varying in size from hard-shelled nuts four centimeters in diameter and larger, to full-sized coconut shells. Two holes are bored, one to blow across, the other to act as a thumb valve. The sound produced is a trill which very effectively imitates a bird call.

the fathers (Owapwas Senior) of the future novices. They are said to be caring for the "woman," feeding her by placing food in her mouth with a leaf holder. These men are called *awiawa'wi* ("young adolescent girls") after the group of female companions who commonly sleep with a girl when she is menstruating, especially for the first time.

At the end of this period the Sahopwas who have been living in the Bwi'ingili hamlet decorate themselves. The majority put on female clothing and ornaments and hold digging sticks. The others use male attire and carry their lime gourds with very long, serrated limesticks which are not used for any occasion other than this (cf. Bateson 1936:15). Both "sexes" arrange themselves along the two inside walls of the spirit house in pseudo-family groups: a man flanked by his two "wives." The initiates are made to enter the house in a line and walk down the center aisle between the decorated figures who make threatening gestures all the while. The men rasp their limesticks aggressively, while the "women" strike at the novices' penes with their digging sticks. Some men with sinister expressions are also present, apparently gloating over small bundles they are holding. The novices try to avoid looking at them, for they have been forewarned by their fathers that these unsavory characters are sorcerers from other villages, and that gazing at them would invite sorcery attacks on their (the novices') gardens in later years. To complete the ordeal, they also come upon a "corpse" stretched out across their path with men sitting around swishing flies off him. Pitpit moss has been smeared on his eyes, nose and ears to simulate maggots. Each novice is pushed down on top of the corpse as he attempts to step over the stretched-out man. Once all the novices are in the spirit house, the man is hoisted up and carried outside. A moment later, when the novices themselves reemerge, they find that the "corpse" has disappeared, and are told that if they reveal the secrets of what went on inside the house, their future will be that of a corpse's. Both "corpse" and "sorcerers," it should be noted, are played by volunteers from other villages—this to make the deception more believable—who are rewarded with pork during the feast held that night to conclude Wafita'wi.

AMBELI'WI

Just as the Wafita'wi stage is concerned with young, pubescent females, so the more advanced Ambeli'wi ceremony is called *hanga'wi*, "old woman." A couple of months following the Wafita'wi initiation, soon after the long yams are harvested, the initiating sub-class announces that the "old woman is menstruating."[8] The village women are instructed to stay away from Bwi'ingili hamlet, where, it is said, the Sahopwas will bring leaves for the old woman to sit on (to soak up the menstrual discharge) and cosmetic materials with which to blacken her teeth.[9] This is a veiled allusion to the leaf mats and earth colors (and, by implication, to the tubers themselves, the "old woman") that are used in the forthcoming long-yam display.

Two yams are placed on either side of the façade of the house. These are called *baiup*, which are the shell ornaments the old woman wears in her ears. Inside the house a longitudinal partition is erected and completely covered on the side of the outer sanctum with long yams. The tubers are painted with motifs of turtles, snakes and human genitals; this differs from the usual decorating of yams for formal display, in that no appliqué materials are used. The novices are formed into a line to be brought into the house, the order being a reflection of ritual categories: divided by sub-moieties, the hosts enter last and their moiety enemies (*nautamana*) enter first. Each sub-moiety is led by the heir to their pig magic. Considering, then, that the ceremony takes place in Bwi'ingili, the order would be:

(1) Hengwanif Afa'afa'w   (6) Nangup Ondondof
(2) Hengwanif Ondondof   (7) Ililip Afa'afa'w
(3) Balanga Afa'afa'w   (8) Ililip Ondondof
(4) Balanga Ondondof   (9) Bwi'ingili Afa'afa'w
(5) Nangup Afa'afa'w   (10) Bwi'ingili Ondondof

8. The correlation between long yams and the Ambeli'wi "old woman" has symbolic implications which become evident in the final Tangawalei' stage of Maolimu.
9. The reference here is to a traditional beauty aid used by Arapesh women. White teeth are considered unattractive. The men keep their teeth blackened by their

Note that groups 1–5 are members of the Laongol moiety and that 6–10 are of the Bandangel moiety. Also, each ward is led by its senior sub-moiety, Afa'afa'w; hence the significance of calling this sub-moiety "those who go first."

The novices are sent into the spirit house to look at the yam display. Behind the wall of yams, out of sight of the youths, a man paces back and forth blowing a Maolimu whistle. It is said this is the "old woman" who is carrying all the yams. At length, the man removes the large yam covering the opening to the inner sanctum and shows the whistle to the novices. This is the simple secret of Ambeli'wi. As usual, a singsing is held that night to mark the occasion.

TANGAWALEI'

The conclusion of Ambeli'wi signals to the Sahopwas initiators and their senior *ombif* (the novices' fathers) that it is time to begin work on the forest village of Wamwinipux in preparation for the Tangawalei' stage of Maolimu. The sacred precinct is built in the forest of Wamwinip, about midway between Bwi'ingili and the Ililip colony of Auwi (map 3). Once started, the construction must proceed with all haste until it is finished. Accordingly, several preliminary weeks are devoted to gathering building materials—posts, saplings, sago thatch and vine ropes—so that there need not be any interruptions once the building is actually under way. When all is in readiness the work starts. The pace is furious: the effect sought is to have Wamwinipux seemingly rise before one's eyes in the forest. Each day one or two houses are erected; and each night, after a brief rest and some refreshment, the laborers convene in Bwi'ingili for a celebratory singsing. The last two houses to go up are the towering *wangon* spirit sanctuaries belonging to Ililip and Balanga (see below). The women are told, in typically oblique fashion, that the task involves clearing the foliage off the tree branches and string-

---

constant betel chewing. Ilahita women, who with rare exception do not chew betel, achieve the same end by staining the enamel periodically with certain leaves. This practice appears to have been discontinued at the time research was conducted.

ing a latticework of lawyer vines between them. This is in preparation for the time when the novices are allegedly transformed into flying foxes, in which state they are said to spend the entire period of their seclusion. The reason for this bizarre metamorphosis is said to originate in the story of Ambupwiel, which goes as follows.

AMBUPWIEL

This is the story of a masalai woman who lived in a large tree in the forest. Her name was Ambupwiel and she had the power to grow plants overnight. One day a man took his wife and his tools and went into the forest to clear a garden. That afternoon, as soon as they had gone, Ambupwiel emerged from her tree and restored the forest to its original growth. The next day the man and his wife were amazed, and they labored again to cut down the forest and undergrowth. And again Ambupwiel restored it. This happened several times until the man decided he must stay behind in the garden to watch. He sent his wife and children down the path toward the village, telling her to rattle his limestick so that the mischievous person would think they were all leaving.

After the man had seen Ambupwiel put back the forest, he sprang on her and threatened to kill her. She pleaded for her life, promising the man that if he spared her and took her back to the village with him, she would make him a very nice netbag. The man agreed, and let Ambupwiel go back into the tree. Then he cut off the top and base of the tree and carried the middle section (containing Ambupwiel) back to the village. He hid it in the spirit house so that no one would discover her.

Ambupwiel made him the netbag and everyone admired it. Asked where he had gotten it, he claimed that he had made it himself. But his wife knew he was lying. Finally the men pressured him so much that he said, "If you want a netbag like this one, bring a supply of food to the spirit house and I will show you how to get one." That was how all the men found out about Ambupwiel, and they shared in the secret of her existence.

One day all the men went to hunt pigs, while the women remained in the village to gather fruit from the trees adjacent to the ceremonial clearing. When they threw down the fruit some of it rolled into the spirit house, where it was eaten by Ambupwiel. When the women could not find it, they were angry and decided to burn down the spirit house. The house burned completely and all the women ran down to the stream with their water containers, so that they could later deny any knowledge of the fire. Unknown to them, however, they had been seen burning the spirit house by an old masalai man who lived in a cockatoo hole in a nearby coconut palm.

While the spirit house was burning, a flame flew high into the air, over the forest, and came down straight into the netbag of the man who had originally brought Ambupwiel to the village. Fearing something might be wrong, the men dashed back to the village only to find their spirit house in ashes. Try as they might, they could not find out why it burned. All the women were too frightened to confess.

Then the masalai man came down out of the coconut palm and spoke to the men. "If you find some meat and give it to me, I will tell you how you can get away from all these women; for it was they who destroyed the spirit house." So the men did this, and the masalai man told them to assemble all the males in the village—infants and toddlers included—and all of them must smear ashes from the spirit house on their bodies. Then they should go stand at the edge of the forest. The masalai man told them to cut the leaves of a wild black taro and rub them on their groins and genitals. This turned all the males into flying foxes and they soared away over the forest. As the women watched, the great swarm of flying foxes circled and disappeared beyond the trees. They went south to the great grassfields.

After that, there were no longer any men in the village, and the women became very worried. Who would take care of them? When the masalai man heard this (from inside his hole), he came down and said, "If each of you will let me have intercourse with you, I will show you how you can follow your husbands and sons." So all the women had intercourse with the masalai, and when they had finished he told them what they must do with the ashes and the wild taro leaves. But the men had earlier used up most of the ashes, and the women were able to put only a small amount on their bodies. That is why men have beards and more body hair than women: they were able to cover their bodies more thoroughly with the magic ashes.

When the women all turned into flying foxes, they headed south and soon found their menfolk. The men were very angry to see them, saying, "Who do you think we were running away from? You alone. It was your own fault for burning down our spirit house, so we ran away from you." They sent the women back to the village. That is why today you can see the small flying foxes flapping around the village in the night. They are the women. The men are the enormous flying foxes which live in the grassfields and in the heart of the forest. They never come near the village. This is the story of how this came to be.

Here, then, is the mythological precedent for the radical change of state awaiting the Maolimu novices. Informants say directly that the ritual symbolically re-creates that magical, wistfully remembered episode when the women's misdeeds caused their menfolk to abandon them. However, before going into the details of Wamwinipux and the events leading up to the seclusion, a background note on flying foxes—especially the Arapesh notions attached to them—may help us to understand why this creature has been singled out for such privileged treatment.

A NOTE ON FLYING FOXES

My first night in Ilahita was very nearly sleepless, thanks to the excitement of the day and the fact that my new cot had irreparably collapsed the instant I reclined on it. To one un-accustomed to the tropics, the jungle night is crowded with more or less menacing sounds. One in particular I found impossible to identify: whatever it was, was certainly airborne, but knowing this only heightened the mystery of what might be producing the sound. An observation the next day at twi-light revealed that what I had been hearing was the noisy flight of giant fruit bats—flying foxes (*Pteropus* spp.)—that had descended on the village in droves to celebrate the ripen-ing of the breadfruit crop. As if by some error in Nature's Design, the ungainly flight of these creatures announces it-self with resounding slaps caused by the flapping together of their large leathery wings. With their curious habits, unlikely appearance and fiendish expression, they are precisely the kind of anomaly which ritual uses as its raw material.

The Arapesh admit to being baffled over the phenomenon of the flying fox; in respect of their noun-classification sys-tem, there is some evidence that "flyingness" is seen to be its most salient feature. At any rate, the perceived ambiguity of form perhaps helps to justify ascribing to this animal a num-ber of singular characteristics. It is said, for instance, that they have no stomachs, that they merely suck the juices out of the fruit without ingesting any of the solids.[10] That they feed by *sucking* provides a clue as to why there is a connection

---

10. This may accurately describe their feeding habits, since flying foxes typically leave behind under the tree a quantity of debris consisting of masticated fruit fibers. As to their lacking a stomach, this is an inference drawn from the rigid Arapesh distinction between the mechanisms of eating and drinking. Fluids they consider to be taken directly into body and blood stream without, that is, passing through the stomach or gut.

between flying foxes and various forms of sorcery. Just as the sorcerer qualifies himself by sucking the juices of a dead body, and attacks his victim by sucking out his soul-stuff, so the sorcerer-healer may choose to remove alien objects from a patient's body by sucking them out. The flying fox is claimed to be a favorite familiar of sorcerers, and the two words meaning "flying fox" (*maolihiwa* and *ufwial*) also apply to extraordinary and common sorcery, respectively.[11]

In terms of Maolimu symbolism the most prominent part of flying-fox lore concerns this animal's allegedly extravagant sexuality. The visually impressive genitals of the male suggest a corresponding prowess in their strength and frequency of use. Prepubescent children are warned against touching bats of any kind, lest this contact prevent the future growth of pubic hair. There is also the assumption that the foul odor of the males (emanating, in fact, from a sex gland) is further indicative of their lasciviousness.[12] Set in the context of Mailimu, the image surpasses mere sexuality. It becomes an unbounded bestiality, a primal lust, an apotheosis of lechery.

TANGAWALEI' RESUMED

The forest village, shown in figure 4, is a microcosm of the entire village and its dual structures.[13] It can be seen that the vertical diameter divides the circle into opposed moieties:

Informants also report that the flying fox, having eaten its fill, commonly carries one or two fruits home in its pouch. Apart from the general implausibility of such an idea, it should be said that these bats are placental mammals. Accordingly, they do not have pouches.

11. *Ufwial* (pl. *ufwiangof*) refers to the smaller, "female" variety found near the village. *Maolihiwa* (sing. *maolimu*) are the larger, "male" flying foxes which have shunned the village since mythical times (see above, "Ambupwiel").

12. The Arapesh prize the flesh of the large, forest variety, but consider those that come around the village to be unfit to eat. Similarly, because of the "unclean" influences of human habitation, papayas and bananas grown in the village are tolerated only as food for pets. I should add that, although I have been following Arapesh usage in referring to two varieties of flying fox—large, forest "males" as against small, village "females"—I would not be at all surprised to learn that the difference is purely a matter of cultural convention.

13. The last Maolimu Tangawalei' initiation was held in Ilahita about 1960. The Waminipux map (fig. 4) and the following description are reconstructions based on accounts given by ritually expert informants.

Laongol on the left and Bandangel on the right. The symmetry is marred only by Nangup's intrusiveness on the Laongol side. Informants admit that, for the sake of dual symmetry, this is unfortunate. But they add that it is more important that Nangup be represented as a unitary ward even though it is divided ritually. The clearing is dominated by two very large spirit houses, side by side, which belong to the senior sub-moieties (Afa'afa'w) of the two most important wards, Balanga and Ililip. A person entering the clearing from Ilahita would normally pass between these two *wangon*.

Opposite and facing the two *wangon* are two moderately sized spirit houses (*alambwin*) belonging to the Afa'afa'w sub-moieties of Bwi'ingili and Hengwanif wards. The rest of the circle is taken up with other *alambwin* and *gasala'akw* (smaller spirit houses) belonging to various sub-moieties, as shown.[14] The presence of small "menstrual houses" in the outer periphery of the circle completes the illusion of a typical village.[15] Each ward possesses one of these *kamba*, which is used as a "green room" by the ward's Sahopwas initiators when they decorate themselves from time to time during the period of seclusion.

When Wamwinipux is ready, the Sahopwas agree on a

14. Ilifalemb ward, with its separate ritual system, holds its Maolimu seclusions in a forest village of its own, known as Fafatuax. The large moiety *wangon* are located as in Wamwinipux, but all the other houses are *gasala'akw* and each belongs to a particular patriclan. These are grouped in the semicircle of the appropriate moiety. There is no suggestion of anything comparable to the Ilahita sub-moieties. Furthermore, this is the pattern of Maolimu ritual precincts throughout all the other Ilahita Arapesh villages—which likewise do not have sub-moieties. For more on the subject of Ilahita's singularity in having sub-moiety structures, and the structural-functional implications thereof, see Tuzin (1976: 294ff.).

15. The reader will recognize this as a possible example of what Lévi-Strauss has called "concentric dualism" (1963), in which the "center" is male and sacred, the "periphery" female and profane. In the actual residence situation, where the pattern is not so perfectly circular, the concentric feature is correspondingly less evident. Also, the reason given for the peripheral location of the menstrual houses (more accurately, girls' clubhouses; see chap. 1) is that the all-night courting parties held there will not disturb the rest of the community. However, this subtracts nothing from the structuralist possibilities of the Wamwinipux layout; and, although I have strong reservations (Tuzin 1976: chap. 12) about the ontological claims made by doctrinaire structuralism, I would not want to deny that there is something like a "concentric structure" manifest here. Indeed, the case will become stronger when we see that the superior Sahopwas are periodically associated with the "center," while the inferior Owapwas are relegated to the forest environs.

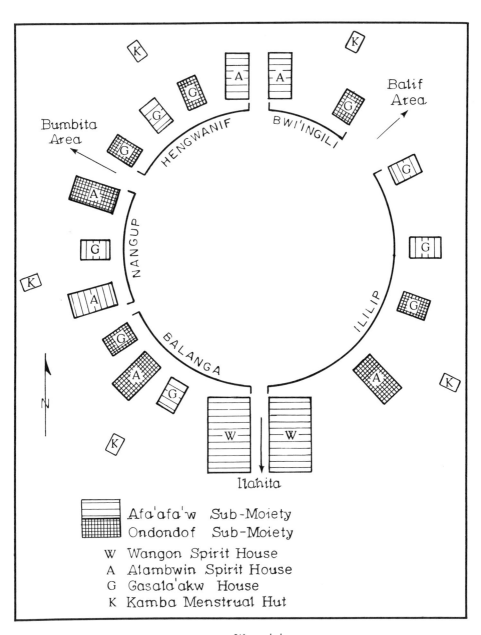

FIGURE 4. Wamwinipux

time one or two months hence for the ceremony which will bring the novices into seclusion. By then an entire year will have passed since the Wafita'wi stage, and a new harvest is at hand. The novices are told, quite without warning, that the next day they will be transformed into flying foxes to begin their life in the forest. In the early evening of that day the boys are brought individually to Bwi'ingili by their fathers. Women are not present. As they assemble they can hear the sound of the bird calls (actually Maolimu whistles) coming from the direction of Wamwinipux—of whose existence the boys are still unaware. The sound rushes back and forth, coaxing the boys to join the forest creatures. This is an illusion cleverly engineered by a long line of men (from Ilahita and assisting villages) stretching all the way from Wamwinipux to the outskirts of the village—a distance of nearly three kilometers. Each man has a whistle and the sound is relayed in rapid succession. The effect, I am assured, is quite remarkable and realistic.[16]

As the boys sit in the clearing wondering what will happen, a group of Sahopwas enter carrying bamboos of "enchanted" water, a type of grass (*maliwap*) and ashes. The ashes are rubbed on the foreheads of the novices, the grass is stuck in their hair. The latter is said to cause their characters to turn into that of flying foxes when they are later struck with stinging nettles. The bamboo tubes are held over their heads and broken, it being claimed they are thus "bathed" by the flying foxes.[17]

As soon as the Sahopwas have gone, the novices are savagely accosted by a group of men called *kwapeangax* who are made up to look like pigs—covered with greyish-white pond silt, their hair bristling with cassowary feathers, and their noses grotesquely drawn up and back by a string passed through the septum and tied behind the head. (These are

16. The whistles are pitched according to the age and standing of the men blowing them. Important men blow large, deep-throated coconut shells in imitation of the goura pigeon, while younger men blow small, shrill whistles copying the call of a sparrow-like bird. These "birds" are supposedly sent by the flying foxes to bring their foster sons to them.

17. There is a vague suggestion that the water in the tubes symbolizes the flying foxes' urine. This is in further aid of the symbolic metamorphosis.

men from other villages who will later be compensated with gifts of pork.) At the height of their mock attack a large force of Sahopwas arrives and, in a realistic-looking battle, drives off the hideous intruders. The latter then proceed to the nearest stream, where they bathe themselves and loosen the uncomfortable nose strings.

When this excitement dies down, the novices observe five men enter the clearing from the direction of Wamwinipux. They are decorated as females, one from each ward, and each carries a "baby" wrapped in banana leaves. The babies are actually small anthropomorphic figurines modeled in clay, and it is said that these "women" have just given birth to them. With great solemnity the Sahopwas "mothers" approach their individual junior *ombif* and hand them the babies. After a time the figurines are placed to one side and nothing more is done about them.[18]

Next the Sahopwas form a long double line leading up to and disappearing into the spirit house. Each man holds a long rod of pangal tipped with a thick wrapping of stinging nettles. The novices are forced to run this gauntlet, to be whipped by their initiators while their fathers stand by watching. The younger boys are carried on the shoulders of their mothers' brothers, who, as in prior initiation ordeals, submit themselves to the brunt of the attack. The last initiator in the line, waiting in the dimness of the empty spirit house, strikes each novice on the head with the clublike base of a shrub called *huininga*. This is wrapped in very potent red stinging nettles called *lefix*. The blow is powerful and some of the youths may be knocked unconscious.

Called back into the clearing, the novices notice that many of the Sahopwas have gone, leaving only the Owapwas Seniors, that is, the novices' fathers. Soon, however, the Sahopwas return from the nearby undercover, parading in single file and blowing the whistles and shells they had used earlier. These are given to the novices according to ceremonial partnerships, but the latter are told not to practice with them un-

18. These Maolimu transvestite parts are hereditary in one of the initiation partnerships within each ward. Transvestism occurring at later points in the Maolimu initiation is fully optative. The sex of the "babies" is unspecified.

til duly instructed. Then the youths are sent away, dispersing
to their homes in the village. A secret feast begins in Bwi'ingili. The yams and pork are supplied mostly by the Sahopwas, who compensate the outsiders who assisted that day
and, by so doing, secure their good will and cooperation for
activities to follow in the months ahead.[19]

That night the novices, under direction of their senior
ombif, begin singing in their separate wards. Starting at the
foot of the ward, the cohorts pass through each hamlet on
the way to Bwi'ingili. Their song is a mocking farewell to
their mothers and sisters, saying, "Look well at our faces, for
tomorrow you will not see them. We are going away now and
there will no longer be men here to copulate with you. You
must copulate with the village dogs!"[20] Each boy is escorted
by his *ombaf*, who is arrayed in a helmet mask and body costume of either the *kwambefowa* or *osaputa* type. Though the
outfit is an abbreviated *hangamu'w* in appearance, there is no
attempt to deceive; the women are aware that they are simply
costumed men who are taking their sons and brothers away
to join the flying foxes. In the song exchange the women reply with a standardized lament—having certain ribald pas-
sages of its own—before following in a group after the
youths. From every direction the bands, which have been
growing with each hamlet traversed, converge on the central
hub of Bwi'ingili to engage in an all-night singsing.

The affair begins with a group of Sahopwas men entering
the clearing. Each has between his legs a stick which is tipped
with a bright orange *su'witip* fruit. This represents what will

19. It should be noted that all feasts—certainly all ritual feasts—involve an exchange
of food. The host group fulfills its sponsorship role by giving long yams and
pork in addition to the more mundane short yams. Recipients of the feast
simultaneously provide short yams only. Also, a portion of the long yams and
pork channels back to the host group through the various ritual ties that link the
groups, but in such a way that no one ends up eating food which he or his
immediate ritual associates have initially provided. The upshot is that everyone
shares more or less equally in the feast. The groups involved in the present
case are the Ilahita Sahopwas (as hosts) and the Ilahita Owapwas (as guests),
with the outside villagers enjoying the general feast in exchange for only a token
number of short yams.

20. In addition to its relevance to the story of Ambupwiel, note that this song helps
to confirm my interpretation of the story of the dogs told at the beginning of
this chapter. Contemptuously telling the women to copulate with dogs, the lyric
implies that the two have a common nature.

happen to any woman with whom a novice copulates during the year-long sex taboo following his return from seclusion. The woman will be afflicted with *akutum*—described as a large growth or tumor on her vulva. It is reddish and visible from front and rear, more embarrassing than painful. The men also smear red betel juice down the backs of their legs to resemble the additional sores that go along with this condition. To complete the message, there is a leaf sponge for wiping up the discharge from the oozing *akutum* and a *lisiwa* leaf spray for shooing away the flies.

In all this there is a strong element of carnival, of festivity and teasing rather than malice or threat. But underlying it there is also a strain; for both the novices and their womenfolk are aware that the imminent separation is real, and neither knows what life in the forest will be like. Experience tells them that one or more of the novices will not return.[21]

At the end of the night, in the predawn darkness, the Sahopwas initiators drift unnoticed out of the village and proceed to Wamwinipux. The outsiders go there also and station themselves in the surrounding forest. When the first cock crows, signaling the end of the singsing, the novices are taken by their fathers to Wamwinipux. En route they are fed a tiny bit of pork. This is to turn their thoughts away from the women they are leaving behind and to prepare them emotionally for what is to come. The taste is given them "by Maolimu," and an important objective during the ensuing months is to train in them an insatiable craving for pig meat —without which they could not aspire to the Tambaran as whole men.

Fathers and sons enter the Wamwinipux clearing in full song, only to encounter a macabre tableau vivant. They circle

21. This is simply because, during an absence of several months, it is very probable that one or more of the youths will succumb to disease or serious accident. Such is the mortality rate even under normal conditions; the forest retreat is attended by somewhat higher risks involving climatic exposure and accidental injuries. When death occurs the funeral is held at Wamwinipux. By keeping the true circumstances hidden from the women—as they must in order to preserve the secret of Maolimu—the men use the tragedy to enhance the mystery and importance of this tambaran. Considering, however, that deaths in this age group are never assigned to natural causes, and that a Tambaran-related motive is presumed by all to underlie it, the men are not being totally dishonest in their representation to the women.

the clearing singing, but the occupants of the place seem not to notice them. A funeral is in progress with a pretended corpse laid out and men and "women" mourners gathered around. In the clearing one man is pretending to be a pig, another a chicken, another a pet cockatoo. Another is "weaving a netbag." The fathers of the boys feign puzzlement and ask where the "trees" are, for the novices still believe they are to be turned into flying foxes. No response. The intruders feel as if they are invisible and noiseless spectators in a village complete in its masculinity.

The fathers seat themselves and their sons under the porticoes of the several houses and watch the activity in the clearing. One initiator, who has been miming the motions of clearing grass, goes to throw away an invisible handful of cuttings. Having just disappeared from sight, he staggers back into the clearing, impaled with a spear through his chest. (The spear is actually only tucked under his arm—a schoolboy trick that may well be universal!) Instantly there is a massive attack on the camp. Armed and decorated warriors (the outsiders) pour into the clearing from all sides, terrifying the novices, who, in light of the abortive attack the previous day, are inclined to think this is genuine. After much confusion the outsiders sit down amiably alongside their erstwhile victims.[22] The pantomime ceases, though the men continue to refrain from speaking. There is no tobacco, no betelnut, no fire—the three elements that are unfailingly present at most such gatherings of men. The novices are led to notice this by their fathers, who also speculate with them as to how and what they will eat.

Two men of the Nangup Ondondof sub-moiety, the group charged with keeping the ritual fire, rise and walk over to the Nangup sector of the circle. One of them takes a faggot from its hiding place in the Nangup *kamba* and climbs up the Nangup *gasala'akw* by mounting the ridgepole from the rear. When he reaches the peak the other man, standing below in front of the house, blows a Maolimu whistle. The fire is thrown down to him, whereupon he ignites strips of dry

22. Cf. the mock attack staged against the mourners at nearly all funerals (Tuzin 1976: 256ff.).

coconut husk and distributes one to each of the houses. Meanwhile, the Sahopwas pig magicians have been decorating themselves in their separate *kamba* houses, and after the fire is distributed they enter the clearing in a single file, singing and displaying themselves.

Later that day a pig is cooked and pieces of pork are handed about to all present—especially to the outsiders, whose cooperation had lent so much authenticity to the "battle" sequences. More significantly, this is the official opening of the forest seclusion: the novices are permitted to practice blowing the whistles they have received from their *ombif*, and each of them is instructed to coat his skin with black soot as a sign that they have begun their lives as flying foxes (see "Ambupwiel"). It is imperative that no woman or other noninitiate see them in this state, the penalty being that any novice(s) thus seen must die by sorcery carried out by one of the cult members, who would consider Tambaran secrecy violated by the exposure.

Most importantly, this opening feast launches the serious meat-eating that is the focus of Maolimu and is designed to instill in the novices a lifelong craving for pork. For miles around no pig is safe. Day after day, month after month, Ilahita and outside hunters of the Sahopwas class bring pigs in repayment for the time before, when *they* lived as flying foxes in the forest and were fed royally by the fathers of today's novices. It is said that so much meat is brought that some of it rots for lack of attention—a waste that is unthinkable under more normal circumstances. Never again in their lives will these novices be so glutted on pork. The youths receive the meat from the hands of either their *ombif* or their mothers' brothers, signifying that in the liminal state they are now entering they must rely exclusively on the conventionally nurturant affections of their matrilateral kin and ritual partners.[23]

As each pig arrives in Wamwinipux a slit-gong is sounded to proclaim the event; and that night, amid the feasting, a

23. That both matrikin and *ombif* occupy this role tends to support the speculation (Tuzin 1976:246f.) that the dual organization was formerly structured by the kin relations generated by a bilateral cross-cousin marriage system.

breaking-of-the-plank ceremony is held. Also, while the pigs are being carried to the precinct, the hunters announce their passage by singing Maolimu songs and blowing whistles. This is primarily done to drive women and non-initiates from the vicinity, for they are not to know that this steady traffic consists merely of pigs. Instead, they are told that "women" are being brought to the forest for the purpose of copulating with their sons and brothers. This is consistent with the putative sexuality of flying foxes, and more specifically with the female symbolism of the earlier stages. Thus, a large pig is alluded to as an "old woman," and if a yam accompanies it, this is her "walking stick." Small pigs are "young women," and a small yam is referred to as the "bark string" she carries for netbag weaving.[24]

As implied earlier, the time for repaying all the pigs supplied by donors from Ilahita and elsewhere is after the next turn in the initiation cycle, when today's novices have become Sahopwas and are obliged to assist whenever Maolimu reappears to demand vast quantities of pork. Yams, however, are another matter; convention requires that these be returned with little delay and in a manner that is typically complicated. First, the yams given by a mother's brother are not subject to strict requital, but rather they signify a warm relationship which the sister's son will honor in the years ahead with periodic gifts of meat—primarily from smaller game such as bandicoot and opossum. Second, with regard to short and long yams given directly to the novice by his senior *ombaf* (i.e., the Sahopwas initiator), a careful record is kept of the size and quantity of tubers,[25] and a massive repayment in kind is made by the novice's father at the ceremony marking the end of Maolimu. Third, yams given by any party other than the mother's brother and *ombaf*—that is, for the most

24. Cf. "The Island of Women," a Mountain Arapesh story recorded by Margaret Mead, which tells of a place peopled only by women, who give birth exclusively to female offspring after having their vulvas "scratched" by their flying-fox husbands (Mead 1940:378ff.).

25. For long yams, a pole of corresponding length is used to which is attached a loop of rattan to indicate girth. Short yams are recorded with strips of coconut husk. At other times, as when a man wishes to place on record a particularly fine short-yam harvest, the measurements taken are the length and width of the space covered when the tubers are neatly lined in ranks inside the yam house.

part, outside villagers—are presented and repaid in the following way. When the donor first brings the gift to Wamwinipux he gives it to one of the Sahopwas initiators, who in turn feeds it to his junior *ombaf*. The next day the *ombaf* initiator returns an equivalence in yams to the outsider, plus a quantity of cooked yams and yam soup for immediate consumption. The uncooked yams, which comprise the larger portion, are taken home to be distributed among those who had participated in the hunt. Meanwhile, the *ombaf* has kept record markers of his expenditures to outside donors, and these along with records of his own contributions (see above) are given to the novice's father for eventual repayment. The point of all this is to channel food to the novice via his senior *ombaf* (except for direct gifts by mother's brothers), with the novice's father ultimately providing repayment.[26]

A final note before leaving the subject of these food exchanges. Readers familiar with the often competitive character of New Guinea ceremonial gift-giving will see in the foregoing ample opportunity for prestige jockeying. A group whose sons are being initiated stands to suffer great humiliation—perhaps even yam bankruptcy—if the gift is too large for them to repay with the year's harvest. While one would not wish to exaggerate the importance of this dimension, it is true that the most ostentatious gifts of yam and pig come from traditional enemy villages intent on embarrassing the recipients (Tuzin 1972). In this, as in so much else connected with the cult, the novices are reduced to being pawns in the serious games grown-ups play.

LIFE IN THE FOREST

Early one morning, several weeks into seclusion, the novices are awakened and told that they and their fathers must

---

26. Corresponding with the fact that the minimal ritual unit is a patrilineal segment, it should be understood that the liabilities incurred in Maolimu are usually of a collective nature. Depending on the age composition of a given unit, there is likely to be a ratio of fathers to sons sufficiently large to prevent the onus from falling too heavily on individuals. Furthermore, older novices typically contribute to the repayment with surplus produce from their own gardens, assuming that a wife or some other person farms them during their absence in the forest.

vacate Wamwinipux to give the Sahopwas privacy for doing important things. The Owapwas assemble at spots in the nearby forest according to ward membership, and each group sets about steam-baking yams (by a process known as 'mumu').[27] When the yams are cooked the fathers return with them to Wamwinipux while the novices reassemble at certain designated streams to renew their black body paint.[28] After this, they gather at some prearranged location to await being summoned back to Wamwinipux.

Meanwhile, back in Wamwinipux the Sahopwas, in addition to roasting a quantity of short yams, have been preparing a special concoction for the novices. Each sub-moiety prepares a waterproof tub made from the tough flower-sheath of the limbum palm. Each tub is filled with coconut water, and two or three orange fruits (*su'witix*) are added to float on the surface. The meat from the coconuts is scraped and set on top of the roasted yams that have been neatly lined up in front of each house. Contrary to usual practice, the carbon coating is left on the yams. Then the Sahopwas blow their Maolimu whistles to signal the youths to return.

Acting on their fathers' instruction, the novices enter Wamwinipux holding leaf blinders over their eyes. After encircling the clearing once, singing a song taught them earlier that day by their fathers, each youth goes and sits in front of his sub-moiety house. Their *ombif* and *olawa* give them the roasted yams and coconut meat, which is put to one side while their fathers reciprocate with mumued yams.[29] Then the novices are told to eat some of the blackened yam, after which they are instructed to gather at the tub of their sub-

27. This involves heating stones and then wrapping them in large bundles consisting of alternating layers of green leaves and unpeeled tubers. The moisture from the leaves steams the yams while slightly flavoring them. Mumued yams are a treat reserved for ceremonial feasting; pork, which is exclusively a ceremonial food, is always prepared in this way.

28. This time the basis for assembling appears arbitrary—or at least there are no apparent moiety criteria. Thus, Balanga and Nangup novices gather at Bawalef, Ililip and Hengwanif at Nangax, and Bwi'ingili alone at Lefufungel.

29. *Olawa* are secondary exchange partners who do not normally interact in the context of initiation per se (Tuzin 1976: 231–232). Corresponding with their differential importance, *ombif* partners both give and receive two yams during the Wamwinipux ceremony, while *olawa* partners exchange only one.

moiety and, using bamboo straws, to drink some of the "breast milk" of their new "mother." This continues—alternating bites of yam and sips of coconut water—until there is no more food remaining.

At this point the Sahopwas bring out the large number of coconut husks left over from the earlier preparations and line them up in front of their respective sub-moiety houses. After being shown what is intended, the youths take over, placing the husks in lines from their housefronts toward the two *wangon* houses dominating the head of the clearing. Laongol boys work on their side of the clearing, Bandangel boys on theirs. The term used for this exchange feast is *kwafamunana*—"she lights (the fire)"—and it is repeated in its entirety approximately every fortnight during the seclusion. As the lines of husks grow longer, eventually continuing out the passage between the *wangon*, they form a simulated set of strands reaching from each sub-moiety house and gathered into a tight bundle at the mouth of Wamwinipux.[30]

In native exegesis the strands metaphorically represent the lawyer vines which the novices use to go up into the trees as flying foxes; that coconut husks are the materials involved is appropriate, since the asocial character of the novices while in their transformed state is attributable to their regular suckling on the teat of their flying-fox mother—that is to say, sucking the coconut water through straws. At the end of the line of husks a cordyline is planted to signify that this is the spot where the boys actually go up into the forest canopy. When a man of the village leaves to go to Wamwinipux, he says to his wife, *Ai indindawa angal*, meaning, "I am going up (into the trees)"; and conversely, when he returns, *Kwani ai angal*, "I have come down."

One main objective of Maolimu is to transform the novices into whole men by severing once and for all the ties of sub-

30. There is some indication that this form—reminiscent, interestingly, of a maypole—has generalized fertility associations. Informants describe the propagating pattern of sago and taro in terms of the encirclement of the "mothers" by their offspring. The positioning of seed yams around a central support pole, with guidelines leading from plants to the top of the pole, similarly evokes for the Arapesh an image of natural fecundity.

stance and affection which bind them to women, especially their mothers. This is achieved less by formal instruction than by immersing them for a prolonged period in a totally masculine world, setting before them an uninterrupted example of male conduct. It is in the nature of *men* to crave pig flesh; the unremitting pork diet distills this essence by effecting a spiritual link between the novice's flesh and that of the pig itself. The new man not only likes pork, he *requires* it. By the same token, a filial bond between man and beast dissuades anyone from knowingly eating the flesh of a pig caught in his own sub-moiety's reserve, for, as informants express it, this would be tantamount to eating one's own child. Hence the need for exchange conventions which supply men periodically with their "essential" food and yet do not place them in violation of this sacred relationship. The parallel case of men's requirements in relation to sex is immediately obvious and is symbolically connected with (or embedded in) Maolimu through the notion that the pigs brought to Wamwinipux are "in reality" women carried there to satisfy a different appetite (Tuzin 1978b). More about this later in the chapter.

As noted above, Maolimu teaches by example. The skills which the novices acquire are ones they have had some knowledge of, all their lives. Maolimu, however, sanctions the use of these manly markers and gives the novices a chance to practice them without fear of appearing foolish in the eyes of women. For example, the youths are taught the art and technique of formal speechmaking. Arapesh oratory is a highly stylized affair, with the speaker pacing briskly back and forth in front of his audience while using a combination of vocal, facial and body gestures to drive home his argument.[31] A man who has not been through Maolimu is

---

31.Speeches tend to have a pervasively angry tone—understandably enough, since the occasion usually involves airing grievances or debating matters of public concern. To my mind, the most curious gesture used is a kind of guttural bark, a prolonged sound resembling that of a man exaggeratedly clearing his throat. This signal punctuates the speech at frequent intervals, reminding all within earshot that they should be paying attention. A less forceful version of the same vocalization is used to call pigs home from the bush in the evening—in imitation of the pig's rhythm of grunting.

barred from using these techniques, and without them no one will suffer any compunction to listen. In addition they are taught many songs and dances, including the female parts for them. Boys who show promise at playing the female role are further coached and eventually join the merry gang of regular ceremonial bawds.

To implant securely the instruction received here, and ensure that the good conduct of the boys will attend them for the rest of their lives, a magical procedure is used. A number of sprouted coconuts (*sumbamu'w*), one for each novice, are placed on a low platform at the back of the main spirit house of each sub-moiety. Each is stabbed with a dagger carved from the femur of a pig or cassowary. For as long as the daggers remain buried in the coconuts (i.e., the entire seclusion), whatever behavior the boys manifest will become their life-long character.[32] A youth who steals during this period will become an inveterate thief. One who carelessly puts his finger in the hole of his Maolimu whistle will always be a womanizer, the hole being likened to a vagina. Similarly, there is a strict prohibition against entering any house in Wamwinipux other than one's own; in a densely settled society, trespass is a serious offense. Thus in this precinct, a microcosm of the entire village, a novice would have to be a fool or a moron if he failed to exercise good conduct in the time of Maolimu.

Let it not be thought that the serious socialization function of Maolimu must be clothed in solemnity. Far from it: Maolimu is fun-loving, and in keeping with the bacchanalian tone of the feast the Sahopwas delight in staging ribald and clownish stunts for the amusement of themselves and the novices. Mock marriages are arranged between suitors and "women." Inevitably, this leads to infidelity and accusations of adultery, ending in an hilarious scene where the cuckold and his rival pull the strumpet back and forth between them.

At the same time, mirthful tomfoolery of this sort should not obscure the essential—and analytically weighty—signifi-

---

32. The heirs to the pig magic of the sub-moiety must sleep in these houses close to the coconuts. The magic emanating from these strengthens both their supernatural power over pigs and their responsibility in exercising it later in life.

cance of this curious little village in the forest. In a society of men, women are not missed. Men may with ease perform both sides of the division of labor, and surrogate women (i.e., pigs) are available in profusion. If women are absolutely needed to partner a marriage or to sing the high harmony of a song, a man simply plays the part. Life is good away from women and in the company of men; conduct is exemplary, discord nonexistent, meat so plentiful as to be beyond appetite. Moreover, it is this uncorrupted male existence which, in the logic of the pierced coconuts, stamps itself indelibly on the imaginations of the novices.

Women are the bane of a peaceful society, and as long as men never compromise their masculine unity, they will hold the secret to a paradisiacal world devoid of women and full of life's pleasures.[33] Indeed, in this Elysium women are not required to produce babies, for men will have taken over this role as well—as symbolized in the curious baby presentation staged before the boys leave for the forest.[34] A man's supreme loyalty must therefore be given to his sex group and to the important secrets they guard. No devotion to family may override this, and a man must be prepared to sacrifice —if necessary, by his own hand—his mother, wife or child at the behest of the Tambaran. The discipline is harsh and exacting, but in the ideology of the cult humankind depends on it.

CONCLUDING CEREMONIES

Ceremonial events and revelations occur more or less continuously during the long seclusion, to the point where a routine of sorts is established. With each pig caught, the songs and whistles of the hunters tell the women back in the village that another female is being brought to the forest hangout, and so it goes day after day. Then, as the season turns and

---

33. One missionary, although not fully informed about what goes on during the seclusion, remarked to me that the most striking change evident in the Maolimu novices when they returned was the utter and cruel contempt they showed toward women, especially their mothers.

34. The same arrogation is expressed in the story of Olafen. See chap. 6.

the time of planting approaches, plans are laid for the boys to cease their flying-fox ways and return to the village. The ritual pace quickens, and in the final days of the seclusion several sequences occur which culminate the initiation experience.

The festivities begin with each of the two initiation classes going out separately in search of a large pig. Assuming all goes according to plan, the two pigs are carried back to Wamwinipux around midday. The novices are told to remove themselves to the forest, while the older men set about making preparations for that evening's singsing. The pigs are singed to death in the customary way;[35] but instead of being butchered they are propped into a sitting position in the dance clearing and are decorated. The Afa'afa'w men take the larger of the two beasts and deck it in the ceremonial costume of an Arapesh male. A large netbag is slung over its shoulder, filled with the small cowrie shells (*galawis*) that rattle when a man walks. A tall headdress is attached to the back of the head, with yellow cockatoo feathers, cassowary quills and hornbill feathers stuck in at appropriate spots. The front of the head has an arrangement of cassowary and chicken feathers, dogs' teeth, a hibiscus blossom, and even a spot of red *ambon* paint on the forehead—to ensure magically that the pig's beauty will dazzle the onlookers. To complete the imitation, there are anklets, arm rings, a shell chest ornament and face paint. A red hibiscus blossom is inserted by its stem into the urethra of the boar (or over the genital area if the pig is not of the sex intended), and then he is placed in a suggestive pose—legs spread, forelegs supported on the bent elbows—facing the female pig about four meters away.

"She" is also placed in an alluring posture, with a red hibiscus blossom between her legs. Her costume includes two net-

---

35. Singeing a pig to death is one of the most dreadful and startling practices that I encountered in the field. The pig is trussed on a pole and hung over a stack of dry palm fronds, which are then lit. The terrible screams trail off after a minute or so into a spasmodic gurgling, which is the beast choking on the blood of its hemorrhage. When the singeing is completed (with hand-held torches), it is butchered and mumued. The men deny that they are being cruel; they are simply indifferent to the pig's agonies. When asked why they do such a thing—and in the case of a pig raised in the village, it is always someone's erstwhile pet—they just laugh and say that the pig's cries attract other pigs to the vicinity of the village, where they, too, can be caught.

bags worn on her back, together with the predominantly yellow leaves and feathers and shell materials befitting a maiden of beauty and virtue. In this grotesque posture, the pigs will be silent, sightless observers of a special breaking-of-the-plank dance to be held that evening. Meanwhile, however, they and the plank are concealed under a cover of palm fronds and breadfruit leaves.

When all is in readiness, the novices are brought into the clearing with their eyes shielded. They are shown a series of small yam piles arranged in a line. From each pile protrudes a stick about one meter high on which is fastened coconut meat and cooked pork. Each initiator takes his junior partner to the pile he has prepared for him, inviting him to eat while he (the initiator) has a light meal of the mumued yams which the Owapwas had previously cooked in the forest.[36] When both parties have eaten, the Sahopwas volunteer to clear away the leaves and other debris which had been strewn about before the novices arrived. In the process they remove the covering from the pigs, piling it and the other rubbish on the still hidden plank. Some of the men get heavy sticks as if to shift the debris; but instead of doing this, they beat on the plank and begin to dance. While most of the Sahopwas attend to the plank, a few others go into their houses and return in female attire with netbags slung on their backs, and ask if they may also join the dance. As the novices look on, the men and "women" continue the dance, while entertainment is heightened by intermittent comic skits on sexual themes. This is the first time the novices have seen the breaking-of-the-plank dance performed with transvestite males. Eventually, the novices join the dance, and those who had previously shown promise in women's roles act accordingly. The pigs are rotated slightly to afford them a better view of the proceedings—before being butchered and eaten.[37] The following night, the breaking-of-the-plank is repeated, this time without pigs.

36. They explain their light eating by saying that it would not be good for women to see their swollen bellies.
37. Each initiation class eats the pig that the other class has supplied. Volunteers from other villages, who are also invited to this affair, are supplied pork and other food by both classes.

These two breaking-of-the-plank singsings signify that the seclusion is ending. The novices are about to conclude their pseudo-sexual frenzy, are beginning their retransformation: they are no longer copulating, nor are they suckling from their flying-fox mothers. The rite has two magical intentions: first, to ensure that the boys will grow up to be fine yam growers; and, second, to stimulate pig fertility so that the devastated porcine population will be restored in time for the next Maolimu appearance a half-generation away, and also for the advent of Nggwal in the more immediate future. The pigs' costumes signify that the novices are hereafter entitled to wear certain body ornaments belonging to Maolimu.

On the afternoon following the second breaking-of-the-plank ceremony all the men gather in Wamwinipux. After the usual round of speechmaking, the novices and their fathers are sent to spend the night in the forest.[38] With their departure and the onset of true darkness, Nggwal "appears" in Wamwinipux. The Sahopwas remove their secret drums and flutes from hiding, and all through the night the novices hear songs of warning from Nggwal that he is the next tambaran they must face. Some of the fathers wander over to join the chorus, but for the most part they do not participate.

The next morning is taken up with the Owapwas mumuing yams in the forest, while the Sahopwas remain in Wamwinipux to fashion the paraphernalia that will figure in that day's ceremony. These include a large structure built to resemble a cassowary. It is formed with sticks and limbum sheets, a long neck, bivalvar shells to simulate the wattles, and various leaves and grasses to achieve the effect of feathers and quills. The costume, which is designed to be worn over a man's body, is said to have originated in the northern (Balif Arapesh) villages of Amahop and Muluhum.[39]

In addition, six men dress themselves up as flying foxes. A

---

38. By now, it might be added, there are rude camps established to which the Owapwas retire when privacy is required in Wamwinipux.

39. The cassowary effigy is a ritual element found throughout the cultures of the Torricelli and Prince Alexander mountains, from the Mountain Arapesh in the east (Mead 1938:170) to the Umeda near the West Irian border (Gell 1975). Among the Mountain Arapesh the cassowary is the ritual incisor, whereas, as we have seen, in Ilahita the surgeon is dressed as a pig. Among the tribes of the Middle Sepik, the incisor is typically a "crocodile."

single white cockatoo feather is stuck in the hair behind the center of the hairline; there is a strip of white paint across the forehead, white hash marks on the shoulders, and a white circle around the navel. Three *bundufum* (ovulum) shells are hung around the neck, and each "flying fox" carries a light pitpit spear. They dance in pairs, holding hands, with each partner carrying his spear in the off-side hand.

Finally, several of the outside villagers contribute to the ceremony by taking on the appearance of ghosts (*gamba*).[40] They paint their faces black and tie small clam shells to their fingertips to accentuate the threatening, clawing gestures they will make toward the novices.

When everything is in order, and the weirdly decorated figures have concealed themselves in various houses on the clearing, the Owapwas are summoned back to Wamwinipux. They enter carrying the cooked yams only to find the place seemingly deserted. By now old hands at this type of ruse, the novices freely permit their fathers to guide them into a small cluster in the center of the clearing. Suddenly, the three pairs of flying foxes rush into the clearing from their hiding place in one of the "green rooms." Moving with a stylized battle prance, they circle the clearing, lunging and jabbing at each house in turn. Then they return to one of the houses and beat with their spears on the panels covering the entrance. Out rush the ghosts to terrify the seated novices with their clawing and snarling. Then they move to one side, while the flying foxes dance to another house to summon from it the cassowary. This figure likewise dances around the novices, making threatening gestures before retiring to remove his costume.

These creatures set the scene and excite the imagination for the most important revelation of all. The flying foxes distract attention from the disrobing cassowary as they dance to the large Balanga Laongol house. As before, they beat on the panel with their spears. But, this time, instead of costumed figures, the voice of Maolimu issues forth from within the

40. The association of outsiders and "ghosts" is hinted at in the mock attack conventionally performed upon Arapesh mourners at a funeral (Tuzin 1976: 256,260).

THE METAMORPHOSIS / *111*

house. At length, once the effect is fully registered on the novices, the panel opens and out come the Sahopwas men of that sub-moiety—decorated in moiety designs and playing *bowas* flutes.[41] After parading around the clearing, they move to one side while the flying foxes turn next to the Ililip Mausimbilinga house. The same sequence occurs, and so on all around the clearing in the following order. (Note that the Bwi'ingili house is the last to be opened, in honor of their being the primary hosts of Maolimu.)

Hengwanif Afa'afa'w'	*bowas*
Nangup Afa'afa'w	*ambon meingafo*
Balanga Ondondof	*bowas*
Ililip Ondondof	*bowas*
Hengwanif Ondondof	*bowas*
Nangup Ondondof	*hawafiwa meingafo*
Bwi'ingili Afa'afa'w	*ambon meingafo*
Bwi'ingili Ondondof	*kwalelimel meingafo*

The vernacular term following each sub-moiety name refers to the specific flute used by that group. They differ in name only and are indistinguishable in appearance—being, merely, an unadorned length of bamboo.

After a feast consisting of mumued yams (supplied by the Owapwas) and roasted yams and pork (supplied by the Sahopwas), a singsing begins in which, among other things, the novices are able to practice playing their newly acquired flutes. All the *bowas* flutes are playing together in the clearing, and a group of transvestite males, arms interlinked, sing the high female part. After a while a plank is brought, whereupon the "women" desert the flute singing to "break the plank." They are, in turn, followed by most of the men, leaving only a few to continue with the flutes. Just as this arrangement gets settled, the *meingafo* flutes emerge from the Nangup and Bwi'ingili houses; and, as before, the "women" display their fickle nature by deserting to these—tak-

41. These are unvalved, end-blown instruments made of bamboo culms about one meter long. Inasmuch as the sound is produced by blowing with pursed lips over an ellipsoid hole cut in the end, it would more accurately be described as a "trumpet." Here, I have chosen to apply the generic term "flute" to these, as well as to panpipes, side-blown flutes and the giant pipes of Nggwal. For a discussion of the *meingafo* music associated with Maolimu see Tuzin (1976:351ff.).

ing about half of the men with them. By now, there are three singsings proceeding simultaneously in the clearing of Wamwinipux. At nightfall the men remove their costumes and decorations and continue with the flutes and plank until dawn.

Next morning, while the novices and their fathers are sleeping off the night's revelry, their Sahopwas partners go off in search of a variety of odd and unlikely items. They gather breadfruits of the type in which only the large seeds (not the flesh) are edible. They also collect a quantity of plaintains and sprouted coconuts, the latter from yam houses in the village where they had been stored. In addition, some less savory things are assembled: rotted wood from a large tree (unspecified), sticks and wattle from a bush turkey's nest, and pig and cassowary feces. These revolting materials are bundled into a limbum wrapper along with the ripe and rotted fruit of the wild *mambafip* tree—a product whose juice is tasty and sweet, but whose smell is reminiscent of feces. In another bundle are placed trochus-shell arm rings (*alihif*), large cowries (*masilif*) and *bundufum* shells, larger arm rings (*pipingil*) and bailer shells (*kafia*).[42]

On the following morning, each of the three bundles (food, "feces" and shells) is divided into two smaller bundles, and the resulting three-bundle sets are taken to different streams. The older men among the Sahopwas, especially those with a reputation for sexual and dietary abstemiousness, take the set containing the prized arm rings and bailer shells to Balal stream. The younger initiators take the lesser shells to Mafata stream. Both sets contain food and feces bundles.

At each stream site, the same procedure is followed. The breadfruit and plantains are cooked by the water's edge. The coconut is opened, and its heart and meat are cut into small pieces and sprinkled on the water. The breadfruit seeds and cooked plantains are also thrown in the water. Then the feces and shell bundles are placed side by side in the water a little

42. Shell treasures of these sorts were traded into the area from the northeast. The Ilahita themselves did not gather them and, in fact, had no knowledge of their true origin.

way upstream. Finally, bright orange *su'witix* are floated in the area of the food.[43]

Corresponding with the division between greater and lesser shell bundles, the Maolimu novices are arranged into their age-set groupings of Balangaisi and Owangufwisi and are taken to Balal and Mafata, respectively. Upon arriving, they are shown the food floating on the stream and are told to eat it, alternating bites with sips of water. They are, of course, unaware of the shell and feces bundles whose influence, from a few meters upstream, is magically tainting in various ways what they are eating.

When there is no food left, a signal is passed to some Sahopwas men who start up a Nggwal song in the forest nearby. While the novices scurry back to Wamwinipux, their initiators recover the bundles and follow them there. After hiding the shells (for these are the province of Nggwal and are not to be seen by the Maolimu novices), they put the feces bundles in the middle of the clearing and tell the novices to unwrap them. It is explained that these materials had also been in the water, that the novices had been tricked into eating them, and that if they violate certain taboos during the following year the substance now in their stomachs would permanently ruin their capacity to grow good yam crops.[44] The taboos include avoiding the food varieties that were floating in the water, as well as certain greens, sugar cane, banana, sago and meat. They are further warned—as a lifelong regimen—to avoid "eating about" and thereby risking contact with women who are menstruating or are otherwise unclean. Thus, they are advised to take food only from a pre-pubertal sister, their wife (if and when they marry) and their mother (for as long as they remain single). Once they marry, they must no longer receive cooked food from their mother.[45]

43. *Kumbamana laf* is the name given to all these materials. Women know the term but not what it signifies.
44. Though eating feces is generally thought to have a detrimental effect on one's physical well-being, the special connection here with yam growing is achieved by the power of Nggwal which inheres in the greater shell bundle.
45. In other words, men take food from women whom they *know* are safe. Normally, these would be females from their own households. The interesting implication is that a man can no longer fully trust his mother once he is married.

With these warnings solemnly conveyed, the boys are shown the lesser shell bundle while the feces bundles are thrown away.

THE RETURN TO NORMAL LIFE

With months of feasting, camaraderie, serious instruction and ritual revelations behind them, all that remains of Maolimu is for the novices to stage a reentry into human society. In keeping with the Tambaran's passion for trickery, no effort is spared in projecting the illusion that an authentic retransformation is taking place.

Soon after the events previously described, the novices are sent out during the afternoon to make what mayhem they can in the forest between Wamwinip and the main village. Their mission is to break down a large number of trees: smaller trees and saplings can be dispatched by climbing them and bending them to the ground, larger ones by attaching a rope and pulling them over with several hands tugging. The object is to be noisy and messy: the women in the village will hear the racket, and the following day will see for themselves that their brothers and sons are finally "coming down from the trees." The following night the boys move right up to the edge of the village. While some are breaking limbs and smaller trees, others are scattering about bits of coconut, breadfruit, 'tulip' (*Gnetum gnemon*), and birds' feathers. Still others are standing by with large, elephant-ear taro leaves, flapping them together to counterfeit the audible flight of the flying foxes.

On the following day, the boys make their appearance in the village. As the women look on, the new men are lead into Bwi'ingili by their senior *ombif*, the men who initiated them and who, so it is said, supplied them with women and other requisites during their long sojourn in the trees. The boys are wearing the *kwambefowa* and *osaputa* costumes which their partners had worn when they led them to Bwi'ingili that last night before the retreat to Wamwinipux. On their legs the women spy flecks of blacking—bits of flying-fox skin to "prove" that the retransformation is only just being completed. The boys, of course, do not speak, for this is a human skill they have long since abandoned and forgotten.

The day after they arrive back, the unwashed initiates are decorated and displayed. That night and the next, there is a breaking-of-the-plank dance in Bwi'ingili. On the morning of the third day the initiates are bathed and decorated in all Maolimu's finery. In the afternoon they are displayed, and this is followed by a drum singsing in which the boys (now fully "human" again) freely express their joy at having returned home.

During these first three days back in the village, the initiates stay close to Bwi'ingili, maintaining an attitude of silence and general nonresponsiveness whenever they encounter a woman. When they are fed soup for the first time, they pretend to retch and vomit at the taste. Then they disappear to eat, instead, in the Maolimu house, where, the women are told, their flying-fox mother continues to suckle them during the recovery period. (Whistles are sounded within in aid of this deception.) After a day or two, small heaps of "flying-fox vomit" are discovered around the village—an inscrutable mixture containing cooked and mashed tree-seeds, fruit and greens. This is a sign that the boys are truly losing their flying-fox ways; correspondingly, they are able to withstand increasing portions of human food. On the second day, the first haltering words of human speech are uttered; and by the night of the drum singsing their verbal capacity is fully restored. The restoration is complete.

What was it like to be a flying fox? They do not remember: they were flying foxes, then.

5. Nggwal's House:
The Architecture of
Village Spirituality

NGWANGWA'UM

There was once a tambaran who lived in the top of a tall tree in the village. This tambaran had the power to distort men's thinking, and drive them mad; he also killed many children. When children were left behind in the village during the day, the tambaran would hear them cry and carry them up to his tree-house to eat them. When he was finished, the tambaran would throw the bones to the ground.

This went on for many years until one day a man decided that he would try to kill the tambaran. He hollowed out a log and prepared a stone blade and a sharpened sago spike. Then he lay in the log and covered himself with a slab of wood which he held tightly in place from the inside. This way, from the outside, one could not see that the log was hollow or that it was in two pieces.

When all was ready and everyone had gone to his garden, the man carried his log to the base of the big tree and climbed inside it. Then he cried like an infant who had been left behind by its mother. The tambaran climbed down and searched about for the crying child. When the tambaran re-ascended his tree in angry bewilderment, the man again imitated the cry of a child. The tambaran came down and, not finding any child, picked up the log and took it back up the tree with him. The man in the log waited quietly until the middle of the night before peeking out. There he saw the tambaran lying sound asleep nearby. With the stone and the spike the man quickly cut off the tambaran's head. Then he shouted to all the villagers below that he had killed the tambaran. He threw down the head and body for the people to chop up and burn.

But the instant the body of the tambaran landed on the ground, all the tall trees standing near the tambaran's home tree moved far away from it.

At the same time, the tree in which the man was standing grew very tall and very fat. The men below tried but could not reach him with ropes or ladders. He was trapped at the top of the tree. Finally he told them that they should give up: there was no escape for him. For months he lived at the top of the tree, until feathers began to grow on his body. He told all the people below that he was turning into a bird. "Soon I will be entirely a bird and I will no longer be able to talk with you." So, knowing that soon he would be unable to talk, the man issued those below with instructions. "When you hear me cry 'Ngwa, ngwa, ngwa, ngwa . . .' you will know that it is time to harvest your yams. But when you hear me sing 'Owa, owa, owa, owa . . .' you must not dig your yams because the time is not right."

With that the man turned into a bird. This bird we call ngwangwa'um, *and you can hear it call out in the night. Sometimes it calls "Ngwa, ngwa, ngwa, ngwa"* [verb root, "to eat"], *and other times it calls "Owa, owa, owa, owa"* ["No"], *and we know what he is telling us. This bird lives inside the big holes in the tops of great trees.*

THIS story signals a departure in mood and expressive content from all that has gone before. We are entering the domain of Nggwal, the tambaran whose symbolic grandeur is unsurpassed in Arapesh imagination. Identity remains an existential issue; but instead of the prefigurative gender orientations enjoined by the symbols of the lower grades, we find in Nggwal an image of masculinity in full season, its mature powers invested in the manly arts of politics, war and procreation. Furthermore, and more importantly for the direction this study is taking, Nggwal metaphysically unites elements of personal identity with the spiritual qualities of social groups, extending, finally, to the collectivity itself. In this way a higher-order meaning is crystallized; building on the expressive achievements of Falanga, Lefin, and Maolimu, the Tambaran becomes, in Nggwal, a mature image of Arapesh *cultural identity*.

"Ngwangwa'um" is a commentary on some of the more primitive elements in this scheme of symbolic relationships. If the nameless tambaran depicted in the story is a cannibal ogre, it is because perverse violence of this kind is a potentiality of masculine character. Ritual combats this violence, subdues it, with a controlled violence of its own. The result is that chaotic, destructive energies are converted into the powers of creation, as signified by the story's reference to yam harvests. The cost of this victory—the hero's lonely fate, his sacrifice—is that man becomes akin to that which he has conquered. His clever *vocal impersonation* of a helpless child eventuates in man—the child who is not eaten, but is carried aloft—becoming forever the child of the Tambaran. By a double identification, man is both himself—a childish creature dependent on the Tambaran—and his own familiar— the little bird who lives in the tops of great trees and whose benign augury is a reassuring sign that man is in touch with the Tambaran.

The key image, then, in "Ngwangwa'um" is that of "child": man as child, bird as child; indeed, as will be seen in certain ritual contexts, Tambaran as child. The lesson to be developed in later chapters is that power presupposes dependency. As a creator, the Tambaran has absolute power over man, the object of creation; but as an *idea*, the Tambaran is absolutely dependent on those who nourish that idea, exalting it as a creational entity outside themselves. Interestingly, this paradox is closely analogous to (and is perhaps rooted in) certain other power relations in the society, namely, between men and women, and between older men and younger men. Like the Tambaran, men (or "older men," as the case may be) survive in their own esteem by sustaining the illusion that their power is real, absolute and self-sufficient.

The secondary image of "Ngwangwa'um" is that of "tree." We are told that the tambaran inhabits the top of a tall tree, a tree made *supernaturally* tall when the hero conquers the ogrous aspect of the Tambaran, thereby becoming himself the beneficent aspect. Today, the Tambaran dwells in a great and lofty house, which is the subject of this chapter. And yet, by its form and decorations this man-made structure distinctly recalls the mythic former residence.

THE SPIRIT HOUSE AS AN OBJECT OF STUDY

The tribes of lowland New Guinea offer many fine examples of architectural excellence. In particular, there are dramatically large and impressive spirit houses found in varying forms in the Papuan Gulf area (Firth 1936) and in the Sepik River region (Bateson 1936; Forge 1966; Newton 1971). Apart from their aesthetic qualities—which are certainly arresting enough in their own right—these structures are anthropologically inviting in at least three ways. First, students of material culture cannot but admire the engineering ingenuity displayed in raising a house of enormous proportions with the available materials and technology. Not only do these builders achieve the desired *size*, but, what is equally impressive, they do so without compromising aesthetic integrity; without, that is, cluttering the interior with support posts, buttressing the exterior with visual impedimenta, or resorting to other means which disclose a philistine interest in size for its own sake.

In the absence of draft animals and artificially driven mechanical devices, the only remaining energy source is human muscle. Large numbers of individuals are needed in the construction task; and this implies not only the aggregation itself, but also a form of social organization capable of mobilizing such numbers in respect of a shared objective. Both features—large scale and a correspondingly elaborate social organization—are relatively uncommon in New Guinea, and are, in fact, distinctive attributes of the cultures possessing these giant spirit houses.

The third point of anthropological interest scarcely needs to be said. In their size and manner of execution, these houses serve no practical purpose. Therefore, in considering why these people put themselves to so much trouble in erecting them, we may be fairly sure that the structures embody a mode of *cultural* expression in which symbols of transcendent importance to the populace are materially formulated (Bateson 1936:124; Forge 1966:27). It is, of course, true that these architectural enterprises fulfill important social functions in providing a focus around which groups of otherwise divergent interest may coordinate themselves. But the *mystification* involved in assigning supernatural significance to these activities has an equal claim to analytic absorption. The issue here, age-old for anthropology, is the nature of the relationship between cultural ideas and social activities. Among the Ilahita Arapesh, the spirit house is a prime mediator of this relationship—a fact attested in the statement of a man who was gloating over a handsome spirit house recently completed. Although Ilahita's traditional success in war is objectively attributable to this village's superior numbers, the man waved this explanation aside with a sweeping gesture in the direction of the house: "It is because of the power and support of our spirits. The magnificence of the house proves that they are with us!" And, in a way, allowing for the religious idiom, he was right.

Spirit houses among the Ilahita Arapesh are a stylistic variant of a form which has reached its apogee among the neighboring Abelam.[1] Both consist of ground-level houses with tall triangular façades. From the apex the ridgepole—usually formed of a single timber—slopes down, nearly reaching the ground at the rear of the structure. In all, it is an exaggerated version of the domestic house and, like that, is covered on the two sides with sago thatch. The peak of the house is finished with a conical covering made of woven vegetable materials. What gives the edifice visual power and intensity is a skillfully restrained use of the cantilevering principle: the leading edges of the side walls angle forward; the peak overhangs the space immediately in front of the house; and the spirit figures painted on the façade appear to gaze down upon the clearing.[2] Seen from the air the impression given is that of

1. The Abelam house is, in turn, genetically related to varying forms found among the Iatmul (Bateson 1936) and other tribes of the Middle Sepik and its tributaries (Newton 1971). Thurnwald (1916) charmingly refers to the Banaro versions as "goblin halls." For a comparative analysis of Abelam and Iatmul spirit-house symbolism see Forge (1966). See also Mead (1938:187ff.) for a wider-ranging comparison—in particular, her photograph of a gigantic Mundugumor bark painting (p. 188) which, as she notes, resembles the detached façade of an Abelam or Plains Arapesh spirit house.
2. The peaked spirit houses of the Papuan Gulf area (Firth 1936) are impressive in many ways, but their exaggerated use of the cantilevering principle on the façade rather defeats the aesthetic purpose by bringing the peak so far forward as to require visible and unsightly vertical supports. The feelings wrought by the Abelam and Arapesh counterparts are, in contrast, restraint and self-support. In saying this, I am representing the Arapesh "aesthetic position," as inferred from a large number of highly consistent (though never fully systematized) expressions of value and taste by and among informants.

some bird-of-prey brooding over a clutch of fledglings—an image protective and yet menacing.

Apart from some variance in artistic appointments—a topic for later consideration—the major difference in design between Abelam and Arapesh spirit houses is in their vertical scale. The Abelam have pushed their houses to astonishing heights of 25 to 30 meters, with a correspondingly marked foreshortening; in exchange for the added external impressiveness there is, at least in comparison with the Arapesh houses, a radical loss of usable interior space. One steps into the gloom to discover a chamber surprisingly small in its floor-level dimensions, while overhead the walls converge indistinctly in a darkness relieved only by the few sunbeams that find their way through chinks in the thatch.

The Arapesh spirit houses have a façade only 15–18 meters high—still impressive, but nothing like the Abelam skyscrapers—with a somewhat squatter triangularity; and the ridgepole slopes gently rather than steeply, terminating high enough off the ground to form the apex of a triangle of no mean size at the rear of the house. The result is a comparatively great depth, width and perceived *massiveness*, a cathedral-like effect in which the interior dimensions have a majesty all their own.

My object in this chapter is to discuss the spirit house in Ilahita village from the technical, social and cultural points of view outlined earlier. Though the first of these would seem susceptible to straightforward descriptive treatment, on the assumption that the house's *merely* technical aspect is fully subsumed by its physical parts, there is much more to it than that. The spirit house is not simply an oversized domestic house, however similar in proportions the two might be. Rather, there are two size-related technical features which distinguish its construction and form the basis for cultural elaboration. First, the scale of the enterprise, in particular the length and girth of the timbers that have to be hoisted into place, requires techniques beyond what anyone would use in erecting a domestic house. Second, even with scores (sometimes hundreds) of men working together, the project must be advanced by stages, each of which becomes the occasion for elaborate feasting and other activities having magico-religious significance. Thus it happens that aspects of social organization and cultural ideology carry over and inform the very procedures by which the house is created. In addition, of course, these contributing elements find their full significance in the relationship they hold with the congeries of like elements which ultimately subsumes all of Arapesh religious life.

All this reminds us of a truism that is often overlooked by modern social and cultural anthropologists who sometimes look down their noses at the seemingly humdrum and vacuous nature of so-called material culture and, indeed, of artistic productions. It is that these artifactual activities are fully as much a part of social life and expressive of cultural understandings as anything else, and that they thereby offer theoretical possibilities that do not deserve to be ignored.[3] All the more so when the artifact in question possesses aesthetic grandeur and sacred significance, and is born over thousands of man-days of carefully coordinated labor.

This brings me to why I have devoted an entire chapter to a seemingly arcane topic which merely preludes the ritual sequence of Nggwal. The preceding paragraphs should dispel any notion that serious attention to the spirit house implies a throwback to an outmoded theoretical era when anthropology was dominated by "idiographic" or museum considerations. As to its being a prelude, it took me some time to rid myself of Judaeo-Christian preconceptions as to what a ritual *is*—that it is not the substance of an activity

3. Malinowski understood this. In *Argonauts of the Western Pacific* (1961, orig. 1922), he devoted considerable space to the subject of Trobriand canoes and sailing, arguing that even the extensive economic and sociological features of this topic do not touch "the most vital reality of a native canoe. . . . For a craft, whether of bark or wood, iron or steel, lives in the life of its sailors, and it is more to a sailor than a mere bit of shaped matter. To the native, not less than to the white seaman, a craft is surrounded by an atmosphere of romance, built up of tradition and of personal experience. It is an object of cult and admiration, a living thing, possessing its own individuality" (p. 105).

For a recent study which shares Malinowski's appreciation of the cultural significance of canoes, but which approaches the subject from the perspective of the modern anthropology of symbolism, see Munn (1977).

which defines it thus, but rather the significance that attaches to it—and to realize, thereby, that the ritual according to Nggwal truly began even before the men went out to cut the first timbers.

THE SOCIAL IMPETUS

For well over a year pressure had been mounting to stage a Nggwal initiation. The ritual elders—men of the Owapwas Senior sub-class—were angry and exasperated at the blasé reluctance which their junior *ombif* expressed over repaying the ritual debt engendered on the occasion of their own induction. More and more, the oratory of public gatherings shifted from unifying denunciations of enemy villages or other outsiders to disruptive harangues by the elders over the feckless conduct of their partners. "Years ago, your fathers showed us Nggwal; and we repaid them by showing you. Now it is time for you to do the same by showing our sons!" References were made to the likelihood of supernatural displeasure; there were even veiled threats that some Owapwas sorcerer might be riled enough to take matters into his own hands. To no avail. Indeed, so unpromising was the deadlock that when neighboring Ningalimbi held a Nggwal initiation, some of the Owapwas decided to take their sons there for induction, both as an insult to the Sahopwas[4] and from sincere worry that ritual life in Ilahita was in the process of collapse.

What we see in this confrontation is an example of how contact with another culture can generate unprecedented situations which subvert and eventually bring to ruin traditional institutions. The Sahopwas were men in their prime, and they had a great deal on their minds besides the Tambaran. Cash-cropping occupied much of their time, as did

---

4. Note that we are speaking here of a dispute between ritual *classes*; there were some individuals among the Sahopwas who agreed with the Owapwas complaint. The Owapwas who stormed off to Ningalimbi did so with the compliance of their own particular partners, who played their part, as custom demands, in the Ningalimbi ceremonies. I should also mention that these tended to be men who already had friends or kinsmen in Ningalimbi.

other 'bisnis' affairs and local government council activities. Assuredly, most older members of the cohort trafficked little in this nontraditional sphere and were sentimentally more aligned with their senior partners. But they were a minority whose interests were overruled by younger men whose gaze was ambitiously fixed on the future. Because their values were reforming themselves in a new direction, the sting of their elders' insults was losing its venom: the degree of symbolic sharing upon which truly effective abuse depends was year by year diminishing. Ironically, the Sahopwas' prophecy that the cult was expiring, because of which it was pointless to proceed with the next initiation, was entirely self-fulfilling. Their own *actions* would decide the future of the Tambaran *idea*; and although most of the Owapwas orators seemed to understand this, the Sahopwas preferred to cast themselves as merely responding to a set of circumstances beyond their control.[5] Here and in other contexts the Tambaran is the vehicle by which issues of major public concern, issues central to the life of the society, are formulated and operated upon. In this case it was no accident that generational disagreements over the vitality of the Tambaran Cult corresponded with the palpable (but unmentionable) erosion of elderly authority in the modernizing context. And yet, as it happened, a combination of fortuities proved that there was still life in the system—more than anyone appears to have suspected.

First, the weather intervened on the side of the Tambaran. The year 1969/70 witnessed what can only be called a season inversion: unseasonable rains during the normally dry months of April–September carried over into the period when gardens are cleared and burned, disrupting these activities and causing delay in the plantings. Then, just about the time the seed yams were safely underground, the sky cleared and perversely remained so for nearly the entire growth season. The resulting harvest was so poor that fami-

---

5. I cannot resist mentioning that the Sahopwas perception of the problem is a splendid instance of the strongly apprehended, *but illusory*, ontological reality of ideas. It is perhaps fitting that the present example is drawn from Arapesh religious life, where such expressiveness is both necessary and highly elaborated.

lies were forced to consume part of the yams normally set aside as the basis for the following year's crop. This alarming misfortune was generally taken as a sign that the Tambaran spirits were displeased over the neglect shown them in recent years—an interpretation naturally favored and promoted by the cult seniors.[6] Their subsistence threatened, even the younger men could not ignore the warning that they should return to their senses and give up those vain pursuits which only muddled and corrupted their values.

Second, the cause of modernization received a major setback about this time. In January 1970, after many months of planning and waiting, the village took possession of a new, four-wheel-drive truck. This was to be the vehicle that would carry Ilahita into a new age of prosperity and fame; nothing traditional could compete with the excited anticipation of its coming. I have described elsewhere (1976:41f.) how, instead of what was expected, the truck became the focus of fearful and prolonged contention among various segments of the community. Here, it is enough to report that a considerable number of men felt they had been duped by a few unscrupulous villagers, suffering an angry disillusionment which (temporarily at least) turned them against any enterprise having modernistic overtones.

The low price they felt they had received for their coffee crop the previous September did not help either.

Finally, there was the galling fact that Ningalimbi had already embarked upon the construction of a large spirit house, in anticipation of a Nggwal initiation the following year. Galling, not because Ilahita had anything against Ningalimbi, but, on the contrary, because the other village was its ritual "child" (Tuzin 1976:63) and the "mother" village should be expected to take the lead in such matters. Also, even though some Ilahitans actually assisted in the project, they envied the regional acclaim and cultural focality which the Ningalimbis enjoyed for having launched the Tambaran initiation. While Ilahita had been dithering around over the

---

6. The two scapegoats were modern politico-economic activities and conversions to Christianity.

truck and other futile schemes, Ningalimbi had been culti-
vating distinction in a field of traditionally paramount importance. This put the final bloom on a situation already ripe for
a shift of sentiment favoring the Owapwas Seniors' demand
for a Nggwal initiation in Ilahita.

The Sahopwas resistance finally broke on a day in Decem-
ber 1970.[7] A feast had been held in Elaf (Ililip's ceremonial
hamlet), after which occurred the usual speechmaking with
the (by now) tedious theme of Sahopwas ritual malfeasance.
Among the orators, Asao went so far as to denounce the
Sahopwas for behaving like women; worse, he sneered, their
feces were fastened up inside them ("Umba mei akwa-
hipipa!"), meaning they were impotent, they had no power,
they were not productive. Asao's challenge could only be answered by meeting it head-on. Three leaders among the Sahopwas leapt forward and vowed to demonstrate their manliness by taking their men and cutting posts for the largest
spirit house the village had ever seen. It must be said that
these three were flamboyantly overreaching themselves in
promising this: the other Sahopwas were in no sense "their
men," nor did they possess any warrant to commit everyone
to such a huge undertaking. But, such is the nature of political action in this place—the informal mix of antecedent circumstance, force of personality, symbolic focus, and momentary group disposition—that their indignation did in
fact communicate itself to their group as a whole. Scorning
any assistance from their Owapwas accusers, the Sahopwas
agreed on a time a few days hence when they would cut the
posts.

At this juncture let me recite briefly the lesson which the
foregoing exemplifies about the nature and workings of the
Tambaran Cult. Like all supernatural agents, especially those
connected with nonliterate cultures, the Tambaran's existence is exceedingly precarious. Let there be a break in the
oral tradition—or, indeed, in the ceremonial tradition
through which the ideas are materialized—and it would be

---

7. This was while I was on leave for some months in Australia. The following incidents were related to me upon my return the following March.

difficult to conceive how the Tambaran could be reconstituted in anything like its present form.[8] This is why the Tambaran emerges as a somewhat nervous deity—jealous, insecure, constantly seeking for opportunities to demonstrate its indispensability and thereby ward off the human realization of its nonexistence. Regular social patterns and events furnish ample "evidence" of this reality; but even when something as traditionally unprecedented as a motor vehicle or missionary program of conversion appears, the Tambaran, largely by virtue of its monopoly on the physical and emotional requirements of existence, is well able to respond and turn them to its own advantage.

There is, however, a further point of paramount importance. The distinction just implied between "regular" social phenomena and unprecedented ones associated with culture contact must be treated cautiously in this context, lest we mislead ourselves into thinking that the former agents were utterly reliable, nonproblematic contextual factors. As I tried at length to show in the previous study, and will repeat here, this is a wholly unwarranted assumption, one that can yield only a very wooden picture of the functional interplay of

8. With the exception of truly isolated communities, where such a break in tradition could spell an absolute loss of cultural material, victims of such calamity are commonly able to turn to neighbors in recouping a large part of their heritage. That culture tends in this way to be distributed and integrated is a thesis of an important article by Schwartz (1963).

Significantly, however, native conceptualization appears oblivious of the safety features of areal integration—first, because the village cult is viewed as quite special and in important details unduplicated elsewhere; and, secondly, a break in oral tradition is contemplated as a general catastrophe—perhaps of cosmic scale—in which all villages would be affected. With regard to the latter eschatology, it is interesting to note a parallel instance in Arapesh flood myths. Though arising locally, the Flood is portrayed as universal; and yet, at a later point in the stories, the protagonist survivor comes upon a village (presumably one of many) that has escaped the Flood. The contradiction implied by something being simultaneously universal and also strictly local is invisible to the storyteller, who is unaware that his tale formulates a crucial paradox in Arapesh religious culture: that supernatural forces and events are at once universal and provincial. Far from conceiving these as local manifestations of something that is universal— one way of resolving the paradox—the Arapesh appear to be egocentrically expanding their local ideology to the scale of the cosmos. A moment's thought will reveal that such hubris informs all cosmological systems, which, in the absence of perceived universal *adherence*, must violate cognitive consistency; hence the proverbial intolerance of the "true believer" toward infidel and apostate.

ideas and activities in the traditional milieu. My contrary contention is that the Tambaran has always, as it were, had to
fight for its life. All evidence suggests that the inertia of the
system tends against undertaking anything so vast as a Tambaran initiation; and if the most recent example of this resistance had certain novel features, these belonged to the
province of content and did not impinge on the stereotypi-
cally Arapesh form of events leading up to the final angry
capitulation. My point is that cumulative stresses—some
structurally predicated, others unpredictable—are both signified and resolved by the Tambaran. And yet, because of
their internal perspective, the actors are unable to recognize
the considerable extent to which Tambaran ideology depends on these stresses. Instead, the perception is that the
Tambaran requires this or that; servicing these requirements
generates a sense of well being that is taken as a sign of Tambaran immanence and benevolence. To the outsider, this
positive result merely signifies the alleviation of behavioral
tensions. In their own ways, however, both parties would
agree that such processes are crucial in maintaining accord
between the expediency of actual behavior and the eternal
verities which stand for the actors' collective interest.

THE NGGWAL SANCTION

Earlier, it was implied that work on the spirit house began
as an immediate Sahopwas response to the intolerable nag-
ging of their senior initiation partners. The actual procedure
proved to be more complicated, in a manner illustrating the
ritually embedded character of this building project. Just as
the Sahopwas were agreeing upon a date for cutting the
house posts, objections were heard from three old patriarchs
who had remained silent during the preceding speeches.
These were the few remaining members of the group that
had initiated today's Owapwas Seniors; although they had
retired from ritual and public affairs, their opinions nonetheless carried authority. Events, they charged, were about
to be initiated out of the proper sequence. Before the posts
were cut, it was necessary to summon Nggwal to the village.

Only Nggwal might initiate the building of his house, and without his blessing nothing could be achieved—not even something so relatively minor as cutting the posts and dragging them to the village. Nggwal must speak; he must be fed.

Thus apprised, the Sahopwas suspended the plans just laid and began instead to prepare for Nggwal's coming. Word was circulated to all cult members in the village. Drums and flutes were readied and the night was set.

Nggwal is said to reside normally with the other clan beings and the spirits of the dead in the clan water shrines. The choreography of his coming is calculated to give expression both to his multiple clan manifestations and to his unified presence as exalted in these great village convocations. By prearrangement at about midnight before the day appointed, clansmen renowned for their bellowing voices make their way to their respective water shrines. They and their attendants carry the large bamboo pipe and accompanying drum which together transform the singer's voice into the voice of Nggwal. That is to say, the vocalist sings mightily into one end of the pipe, while the other end is placed in the drum. The effect is to amplify and distort the human voice, giving it an eerie, preternatural quality—especially when heard from a distance.[9]

One of the men starts the singing, signaling the others to join in from their dispersed locations. After about ten minutes of this, all parties begin to move up the ridge spurs and into the sleeping village, converging on their destination in Elaf. The singer carries one end of the pipe, continuing his song while another man walks ahead holding the drum in place at the other end. A second helper carries a sprouted

9. A lifetime of shouting messages between distant ridgetops has given Arapesh males' voices an amplitude and projective quality that we in our society rarely encounter outside the opera house. This is just as well; for, in order to produce the right sound out of this pipe-and-drum combination, one must, in the words of one informant, "fill the bamboo with sound." With a pipe approximately three meters long and five centimeters in diameter, this is no minor feat. Upon hearing the puny and pathetic result of the anthropologist's attempt—self-justified by a youth spent whispering around library stacks rather than hollering from one county to another—those present had the grace to emphasize technique and the need for practice, rather than the requirement of essential manliness that was stressed on earlier occasions.

coconut, and with it thumps the ground loudly and rhythmically as they advance, simulating to the (by now awake and
alarmed) womenfolk the ominous tread of a monster passing
in the night.

Here, then, is the symbolic figure seen earlier in the context of Maolimu: the many strands of ritual structure converging on a central point of unity. More specifically (in the
present case, though implicit also in Maolimu) the movement
is characterized by the actors as the coming-together of enemy nggwals (*nautamana*), advancing on one another from
opposite directions—opposite moieties, opposite wards—to
unite finally in their song contest.[10] The song is led by its
primary owner, but all who wish to join him contribute their
voices and pipes to the grand chorus, audible for miles
around. The singing continues until the first cock's crow,
when the men lay aside the pipes and, bone weary and painfully hoarse, find a comfortable spot where they can sleep
undisturbed until about mid-morning. Later that afternoon,
the Sahopwas of each ward collectively present to their Owapwas partners a pig and an ample quantity of yams as basis for
a feast held immediately in Elaf. This presentation formally
initiates the season of Nggwal, a ritual time lasting three or
more years and punctuated by a series of feasts and ceremonies enormously expensive in manpower and resources.
Feast yams are provided by both initiation classes in the context of bilateral exchanges between *ombif*, but pigs are the
sole responsibility of Owapwas. During the early months of
spirit-house construction, twenty-eight pigs were delivered
and eaten in the name of Nggwal.[11] The meat is said to
strengthen the Sahopwas in their physical exertions, at once

10. I call them "contests" because enemy nggwals alternate songs with an air of
rowdy rivalry. Both sides typically claim victory, and the atmosphere throughout
is bawdy and good-natured.

11. The record is kept by placing the poles on which the pigs were trussed in a line
along the path entering Elaf. It is worth noting that the actual burden of providing the pigs falls mainly on the *sons* of these Owapwas, men in their early
prime who will be the novices in the forthcoming initiation. Added to the practical advantage of assigning the task to a group whose members are younger and
more numerous, there is the inglorious fact that their ritual ignorance makes
them highly vulnerable to whatever coercion cult members (their fathers and senior *ombif*) apply to them in furtherance of the mysterious purposes of Nggwal.

satisfying the debt brought forward from the last time a Nggwal spirit house was built—then, by today's Owapwas as nourished by the *fathers* of today's Sahopwas.[12]

A CONSTRUCTED REALITY IN THE LITERAL SENSE

The above-ground possibilities of an edifice depend heavily, of course, on the depth and solidity of the foundation. The Arapesh are aware that unless the four foundation posts of the spirit house are made of the strongest available wood and are planted deeply and firmly, the first sizable wind is liable to push over the top-heavy structure. Fortunately, Nature assists by providing a clayey soil; barring a severe earthquake, a post which is sunk deep and secured at its base with stones will not shift. A problem remains, however: with the available tools, how does one dig a narrow shaft which descends vertically as much as three meters? The diameter should be only sufficient to admit the post, otherwise the loosened backfill encircling it would have a destabilizing effect. As the hole proceeds downward beyond arm's length, it is a simple matter to continue loosening the soil with a long pointed stick; but how is this soil to be excavated?

The problem is solved simply but ingeniously by taking a bamboo culm of moderate diameter, splintering one end, and then reinforcing the splintered part with a rope-cuff tied around it about one-third meter back from that end. This places a tension on the splintered ends forming the mouth

12. Nggwal normally insists on being fed *wild* pigs, the relatively fatty flesh of village pigs being not to his liking. In the present case, however, Owapwas hunters repeatedly returned empty-handed and were forced to resort to village pigs. The Sahopwas accepted these as being better than nothing, but grumbled audibly that only wild pigs would constitute genuine repayment. This tendency of finding fault with the other's contribution to an exchange—sometimes justifiably, oftentimes not—is so characteristic of the Arapesh way of doing things that I am inclined to treat it as a latently central component of exchange convention. At best, the transaction proceeds without comment. Actual praise for the generosity of one's partner is withheld until that final transaction when one delivers a eulogy at his funeral.

The gain arising from such ingratitude is obvious. By remarking publicly on the inadequacy, one carries forward an advantage in future dealings with the partner. Death, of course, drastically modifies the relationship; for the survivor there is nothing to be lost—and everything to be gained—by flattering the ghost of the deceased.

of the tube, such that when this end is plunged into the loosened, somewhat gluey soil, it grips and holds the equivalent of a large handful of backfill, which is then easily conveyed to the surface. Using these devices a couple of men can excavate a hole quickly and without forcing its diameter beyond what is strictly necessary.

In referring to this technique, either among themselves or when talking to non-initiates, the men say, "Ifelemb nosaf nowafa etap"—meaning, "The ant-lions are digging into the ground."[13] In this, as in all cult contexts, assigning a metaphor is a way of attaching a special significance to an act beyond its mundane apparency. The digging technique demands a metaphor. Why? Because it is *remarkable*: it operates in a context outside ordinary daily life; furthermore, it presupposes a cleverness, a measure of creative inspiration, far superior to that which today's Arapesh male feels himself capable of. A kind of wonderment attaches to those elements of technology invented in the forgotten past—to such an extent that informants reject the suggestion that these skills, however marvelous, must have been devised by someone at some point in time. Instead, they aver that such wisdom belongs to tradition: just as no one ever thought up a myth, so no ancestor in particular ever invented a technique. Legends and myths may tell of ancestors (generalized or specified) *finding* something of cultural worth or being given it by beneficent spirit figures, but the idea that someone like themselves spontaneously *invented* it requires a degree of hubris that to them is unthinkable.

After excavating the four corner holes, the men dig a shallow slipway about two meters long leading from the mouth of each one so as to facilitate placement of the massive, forked post. The timber is laid down with its base in the slipway and its pointed end over the hole. While three or four men hold a wooden barrier[14] to prevent the base of the post from slip-

13. Ant-lions are small, carnivorous insects who trap their prey in funnel-shaped holes located in sandy spots sheltered from the rain. Perhaps because their holes are often noticed in and around caverns, rock shelters and other such formations, the Arapesh consider ant-lions to be responsible for echoes.

14. This consists of a piece cut out of the flat, heavy, extremely dense buttress root of a giant fig tree. Alternatively, a fragment of an old slit-gong might be used.

9. Levering the spirit-house post into its hole.

ping forward, with possible serious injury to those lifting
the upper end, the post is levered into the hole. One body of
workers mans the forked end, pushing upward with outstretched arms and sturdy poles while, on the other side of
the hole, a second group heaves on a line attached to the top
of the post. Tension and excitement run high; for, during
that dangerous moment when the post is angled at about sixty degrees to the ground, it is under minimum control and
could easily lurch sideways, crushing anyone standing beneath it. If anyone panicked, the result could be disastrous.
Laying into the effort, the men sing and shout to steel their
nerves, quicken their muscles and coordinate their actions.
Amid what seems to be organized chaos, the huge timber angles lazily upward until, with a ground-shaking thud, it drops
into the hole.[15] A great cheer goes up. Poles are lashed to the

15. Although Arapesh men tell their women that the post is held firm by a tambaran
    spirit residing in the hole, among themselves they acknowledge that the indwell-
    ing protective spirit is an amalgam of the tambaran and the spirit of the sculptor
    who carved an anthropomorphic figure in deep relief on the post itself. Others

post as capstan bars for auguring it more deeply; stones are dropped into the hole for added support, and the backfill is replaced.

All during the preceding sequence, a curious flute recital has been proceeding off to one side. The base of a large *bowan* flute is laid in the opening of a slit-gong. Giant taro leaves are then used to cover the slit along its entire length. The flautist sings a rhythmic tattoo into the pipe, producing a somewhat muffled, deeply sonorous tone—in specific imitation of the drumming call of a cassowary. The object in doing this is to recruit the magic of Nambweapa'w in aid of the work effort and also to re-create the central episode of the story of Kamba'wa (chap. 7), where the boys sang into a tube whose base had accidentally penetrated a submerged log—thereby discovering Nggwal.

The next step is to connect front and rear posts on each side with heavy poles resting in the forks and later to become supports for the side walls. Flushed with victory over the earlier, more difficult tasks, the workers lift these lateral members into place quite handily. Then they retire to their feast, content with a job well done.

The following task dwarfs all others in complexity and risk. As in the solution to the hole-digging problem, the technique by which the ridgepole is raised is a closely guarded secret; the men delight in presenting its accomplishment to the women as proof positive that Nggwal directly aids them in constructing the house. Similarly, I would invite the reader to consider how, with only bush materials and without benefit of winches, cranes or other such devices, a timber weighing as much as a ton could be positioned at a height of

---

maintain that it is the great sky masalai, Wale, who inhabits the post. Both schools agree, however, that the spirit in question is very powerful: for example, during a lengthy delay between the cutting and carving of the posts and the actual onset of construction, it was pointed out that the posts must not be allowed to start rotting, lest the spirit take offense and deliver sickness or some other calamity on the community. No such danger exists if the posts, as structural members, rot naturally along with the house itself.

For more on the subject of post spirits, see the story of Olafen at the beginning of the next chapter; cf. the notion of ancestral spirits residing temporarily in ground-crab holes (Tuzin 1977:212).

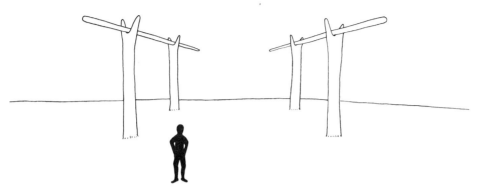

FIGURE 5. The spirit house. Front elevation showing posts and lateral supports.

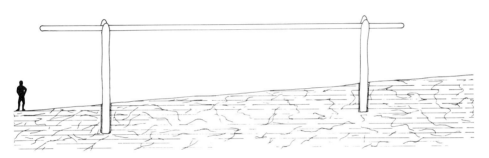

FIGURE 6. The spirit house. Side elevation showing posts and lateral supports.

15–20 meters and roughly parallel to the ground. This is how it is done.

A number of tall breadfruit timbers are sunk, at about three-meter intervals, in a row down the center of the floor area. The tops of these are then joined by a line of horizontally placed betelnut trunks, which, though small in diameter, are flexible and have remarkable tensile strength. The ridgepole is dragged to the foot of the breadfruit trees. Lawyer vines are tied to it, and their ends are carried up and over the horizontal betelnut fulcrum. When all is ready, crews of men grasp the end of each vine, and, again amid a cacophony of songs and shouts, slowly hoist the massive ridgepole into

10. Hoisting the massive spirit-house ridgepole.

place, just below the line of betelnut trunks. There, men clinging to the breadfruit masts lash it to these uprights with lawyer vines, where it remains suspended until the next stage of construction when it can be more solidly secured.[16]

Let me interrupt myself at this point to fill in some ethnographic details. First, erecting the scaffolding of breadfruit trunks involves the same technique as that used in sinking the house-posts. On the occasion which I witnessed, as the first of these timbers was being levered into place, a commotion arose on the opposite side of the clearing. Whooping and crowing, a number of older men (Owapwas Seniors) burst into the clearing, carrying long bamboo poles, each pole with a bundle of some kind attached to the end. While the Sahopwas struggled to hoist the trunk, the men wielding these poles danced about, touching the bundles to it at various points along its length. This was repeated for each of the masts. Afterward, the bundles were unwrapped and their contents revealed to the Sahopwas workers. In addition to a bunch of aromatic, magically significant leaves, each contained a long bone—the humerus of an ancestor, which, it was explained, mobilized the strength of the dead in this, a task which mere mortals could not hope to accomplish unaided. The bones were used again when the ridgepole was hoisted.[17]

A second detail is the metaphorical operation performed on the central secret of this phase of construction: the use of lawyer vines drawn over a fulcrum. The idiom is that "birds" have helped the men raise the ridgepole—small birds, of the varieties *solopoank*, *asofowank* and *kumbanga*.

16. From boyhood, Arapesh males are skilled and fearless tree-climbers, and, in hunting, will not hesitate to pursue arboreal prey into their own habitat. Indeed, when the rare fall does occur, sorcery is immediately assigned as the cause; for it is inconceivable to these people that anyone (except, perhaps, clumsy Europeans) could accidentally fall out of a tree. Qualities of strength, courage and good balance are essential at several points in the construction, when the men are required to do heavy work at lofty heights.

17. Suspecting that the bone was not human, I inquired and learned that it was in fact a cassowary femur. My informant explained that this was an allowable substitution, in that human bones were difficult to come by since the Australian administration had outlawed traditional exhumation practices. I failed to ask why the bones had not been brought out earlier to aid in hoisting the house posts.

11. Kwamwi displays the bone which magically assisted the workers in hoisting the heavy timbers during spirit-house construction.

Further, there is the significance attached to the ridgepole itself. Like the two lateral supports, the ridgepole is the straight, stripped trunk of *Vitex confossus*—a very hard, rot-resistant wood also used for slit-gongs.[18] After being felled the log is pierced at its base, and a vine rope is attached so

18. The ridgepole used in the Ilahita Nggwal house measured 27.1 meters in length, with a base girth of slightly under one meter. The lateral members measured 24.4 meters and 23.5 meters respectively.

that a line of men can drag it back to the village. For weeks or even months the poles lie in the center of the ceremonial hamlet, until the time has come to put them in place. During this period the men are rather nervous about these poles: children are warned not to play or make loud noises in their vicinity, and women are careful not to touch or step over them; similarly, a man who has recently had sexual inter-course, or whose wife is either menstruating or pregnant, takes extra care in staying away from the poles. It is claimed that if any of these taboos are broken, the poles will be so heavy that the men will not be able to lift them. The effective agent here is feminine sexuality—emanating directly from females, from children by virtue of their closeness to their mothers, and from men in the above-mentioned categories for obvious reasons. Hoisting the ridgepole signifies that the cult members have triumphed over these fulsome influences and have attained to that purity of masculine prowess which is the essence of Nggwal (cf. Bateson 1936:163). For this reason, early morning is invariably chosen as the best time to attempt this risky procedure, since the men feel they are strongest and most potent at that time of day (cf. Forge 1966:26).

But, sometimes, even the most scrupulous observance of these ritual precautions is not enough. On the occasion wit-nessed in Ilahita, the ridgepole had been hauled about half-way up when suddenly the vine ropes ominously began snap-ping. Apart from the imminent physical danger, a falling pole would have signified that Nggwal was withholding sup-port for the endeavor—a bad omen indeed for the forth-coming ceremonial activities. As an emergency measure, the pole was quickly lashed where it hung, while the men with-drew to consider how to interpret and rectify the problem. It was decided that someone in the work force was, perhaps unconsciously, harboring ill will toward the operation. In Nggwal ideology, the necessary supernatural assistance is contingent on total unity of intention among the workers. Ferreting out the source of negativism would, it was agreed, involve lengthy and perhaps futile hearings. So, as a short-cut remedy, it was decided that a pig feast held then and

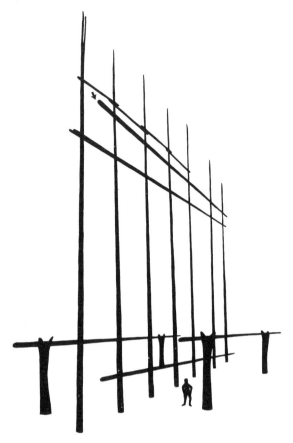

FIGURE 7. The spirit house. Front elevation showing breadfruit supports, betelnut fulcrum, ridgepole (arrow), and horizontal scaffoldings.

there would enhance *everyone's* morale, thus removing the difficulty—from whomever it sprang. A collection was taken up to purchase a village pig. The feast was convened forthwith; and, when the men resumed their work later that afternoon, the ridgepole was lifted the remaining distance easily and without mishap.

These incidents—analytically very opportune—reveal the heart of Nggwal as a focus of social ideology, as a metaphysical construct signifying the spiritual bond of the village collective. In ritual, as in war, nothing short of complete unanimity of purpose and harmony of action will enable men to achieve the great works of which men in groups are capable. The genius of the system is that the authority dictating this necessity is not perceived as a matter of mundane consensus; it does not reside among the men themselves, where negotiated values become compromised values; it is projected outward as a personified dogma, as the will of Nggwal. This is why when the informant quoted earlier averred that the Ilahitans won wars and erected memorable spirit houses because of the power of their spirits, he was essentially correct.

SOCIOLOGICAL EXCURSUS

The preceding incident offers an occasion to examine how, in the immediate context, the Tambaran reacts creatively upon the very society from which it derives ideological sustenance. As much as the spirit house monopolizes public attention and focuses community pride, the fact remains that during the months of construction life does go on. Men may have it in their power to postpone or stifle their arguments

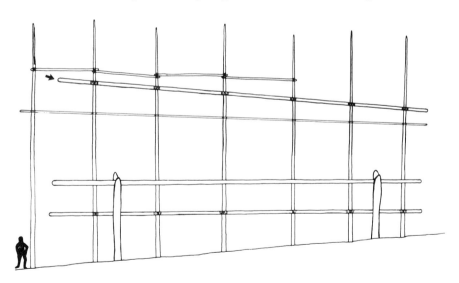

FIGURE 8. The spirit house. Side elevation showing breadfruit supports, betelnut fulcrum, ridgepole (arrow), and horizontal scaffoldings.

out of respect for the Tambaran, but Death is not so accom-
modating, nor are the forces which govern the natural order.
Faced with his own impotence in such realms, cultural man
strives to make them his own through the act of signification.
Among the Arapesh, this is a very general phenomenon:
death does not strike randomly, but because some sorcerer
ordained it; unseasonable rains do not fall for no reason, but
because some magician is out to inconvenience his fellows.
This view of causality is certainly well known in the anthropological literature and is aided little by yet another ethnographic instance. The Arapesh case is, however, of special
interest because of the change that overcomes native epistemology with the advent of the Tambaran. Transcending the
congeries of conventional causes and effects, uniting the normally fractionated field of diverse events, there looms the
all-consuming significance of the Tambaran. A *grand cause*
arises to which all lesser causes are referred and in terms of
which they achieve more momentous meaning. The result is
a mutual augmentation of belief and experience: experience
is enriched under the embrace of a unifying purpose, while
the Tambaran is strengthened by the abnormally comprehensive jurisdiction claimed by the cult leaders. When the
ritual season ends, and Nggwal is chased back to his watery
lair, life returns to its petty causes—and well it may, for in
the meantime a rejuvenation has occurred in the community's relationship to its own most fundamental ideas.

As always, the point is best grounded in some concrete
cases. The following should illustrate how the Tambaran
manages to orient experience along a track leading, with un-
erring directness, to its own aggrandizement.

Case 1. The event of death is highly unnerving to cult members
for reasons having largely to do with the automatic presumption of
sorcery—at any rate, in cases where the deceased is neither very
young nor very old. First, it is the surest possible sign that the community harmony essential to all cult endeavors is seriously imper-
fect. And, second, if Nggwal has not moved to stay the sorcerer's
hand or to nullify his magic, this can only mean that he (Nggwal
himself) does not wish to see the cult activities go ahead. In other
words, although ambient sorcery beliefs intensify the significance

of nearly all deaths beyond what they would imply within a natural-istic system of causation, in proximity with Nggwal ideology death is further transformed into an *omen*. During the years-long season of Nggwal the question ceases to be "Who did it?" and becomes "What does it mean?"—thus projecting the inquiry onto a level of cultural self-scrutiny that is, in principle, unlimited. In a later chapter, it will be seen that this tendency toward augmentation is capable of spilling over into the interpretation of "out of season" deaths. For the present, however, the object is to show that a death in the village can easily disrupt the scheduling of Tambaran events.

Silembin's death, for example, occurring during the planning stage of the spirit house, nearly forced cancellation of the entire project. He was a young family man living in the Ililip colony of Numbafuta: bright, promising and extremely popular. The cir-cumstances surrounding his death were rather mysterious. By his own report, he had been working in his garden when suddenly the urge came over him to climb a nearby tree. Part way up he became dizzy, saw flashes of light and fell, landing on his back against a buttress root. Silembin felt sure that he was being attacked by a sor-cerer. Otherwise, why would he have thought to climb a tree in the first place, much less have fallen out of it? Strong confirmation came from the doctor on duty at the Maprik hospital, who upon examining Silembin was unable to get clear X-ray pictures of his injured back; that they persisted in being dark and fuzzy proved to the Ilahita onlookers that some sinister force was operating on Silembin's insides. (Later, in the post-mortem analysis, it would also be noted that the victim had dropped from a height of only about three meters. Who dies from something so minor, unless sorcery is at work?) Silembin lingered for about a month and then died.

Among the bereaved none was more devastated than Supalo, Silembin's mother's brother. Toward the end, the dying man had dreams in which he saw certain men of Ililip, Balanga and Bwi'ing-ili coming to take him away. On hearing this at the time, Supalo vowed publicly that if Silembin died he would employ retaliatory sorcery against these villains. As it happened, Supalo did eventually *accuse* these individuals, but there is no evidence that he actually resorted to punitive sorcery. Nevertheless, the others would not let Supalo forget that he had made the threat and for a long time af-terward acrimony—sometimes flaring toward violence—prevailed between the principals and their supporters, subverting efforts by the wider community to unite and move ahead with the spirit-house project.

The problem was one of motive. Silembin had been everyone's friend, and even Supalo grudgingly conceded that the men he was accusing had not been enemies of the deceased. Then, soon after the funeral, a leading man of Ningalimbi passed on a bit of news which instantly wrapped up all aspects of the case. He had "heard" that Lehinga village had induced an Ilahita man to betray his fellows. In exchange for meat, cash and other valuables, Mangas had allegedly provided these traditional enemies with exuviae and birth names belonging to all (or at least a great many) members of the Owapwas initiation class. In due course the black magic was activated, and Silembin (an Owapwas Junior) was the unlucky victim.

It was an inspired solution. Mangas was the ideal suspect for several reasons. First, he was a prominent member of the Sahopwas class and had been among the most angry defenders of his group against Owapwas taunts during the weeks leading up to the decision to build the spirit house. That he might betray the other class to the enemy—either by his own initiative or by inducement—was both understandable and not entirely blameworthy.[19] Second, Mangas lived in and presided over the outlying Ililip camp of Ambitemba (Tuzin 1976:201). The present accusation confirmed the long-held view that Mangas must be using nefarious means toward his ambitious ends, or else he would not require that amount of privacy.[20] Third, Mangas fancied himself something of a village diplomat, often boasting that he was known all around the area and that he was even well received in Lehinga. Finally, although Mangas generally stayed nonaligned in village politics, preferring to remain a power unto himself, in the dispute surrounding the decline and death of Silembin he was inclined to take sides against Supalo. Indeed Kwaliapuna, one of the three men whom Supalo had specifically accused, lived with Mangas in Ambitemba and was his good friend.

Mangas's expected denial was not believed, but even by that time the matter had become somewhat academic. Not only did the Nggwal sanction discourage anyone from taking overt revenge, but also the mere fact of having found a scapegoat went far to cool the passions in the case. If the act was nothing more than wicked, then supernatural punishment or retaliatory sorcery would, in the fullness of time, find its mark. Meanwhile, relieved by the broken deadlock, the community could resume plans for the spirit house.

19. A degree of legitimacy accompanies all Tambaran-related murders, bringing them under the rubric of *laf* homicide. Although the assassin's personal motives may be reprehensible, the involvement of ritually defined actors stamps the deed with the warrant of the Tambaran itself. This subject will be explored more fully in chapter 9.

20. Mangas gave as his own reason for establishing Ambitemba the fact that he was a yam magician. For long periods his magic had to be protected from a multitude of polluting influences in the village, not to mention the nullifyingly noisy antics of children. Altogether, the peace and quiet of Ambitemba made better sense, even though it caused occasional mutterings against him.

Some analytic observations. The final explanation for Silembin's death was persuasive because it pronounced that the attack had been impersonal: the victim's misfortune was to belong to a ritual corporation that had come under mystical assault, and therefore his innocence and universal popularity were beside the point. Moreover, the case exemplifies the expansion of significance that typically occurs whenever the Tambaran is implicated: the individual tragedy first triggers social discord in the form of sorcery accusations and counter-accusations; then, as if by the action of a safety valve, the invocation of the Tambaran accelerates the issue to the *total* community level, trivializing the previous contention, diffusing blame throughout adult male society and, withal, reaffirming the moral transcendence of cult ideology. In the matter of Mangas's role, although he persisted in denying the conspiracy part of the accusation, even threatening to withdraw support from the Tambaran if the talk continued, in a more profound sense he conceded privately that he might be guilty. He had been, after all, very angry at the Owapwas class, and he was a regular practitioner of (licit) magic. Perhaps, he speculated, his mood somehow grafted itself onto his magic, turning it, without his knowledge or specific intent, into a power for destruction. The possibility grieved him, for he too had been very fond of Silembin.

Case 2. Despite the apparent closure of the Silembin case, another death a couple of months later revived some of the earlier antagonisms and once again delayed progress on the spirit house. This time, the deceased was Suna, a Balanga man of early middle age. He died after a short illness, whose visible symptoms were a numbness in his left leg and a stiffness in his jaw which prevented him from opening his mouth to eat. Before dying, Suna had named Sahaefen of Bwi'ingili as the culprit, since he had received from that man a gift of (poisoned?) cassowary meat about ten days before he was afflicted.[21] Suna's friends and family, however, charged that he had been stricken by revenge sorcery enacted by Supalo and one of his supporters in connection with Silembin's death.

21. The motive was reasoned to be that Sahaefen was acting to protect the interests of his MBS, who had been absent for a long time at the plantation. Suna had been trying to talk the absentee's wife into marrying him, defying the threats of her father-in-law (Sahaefen's MB) that there would be trouble if he did not desist.

Both of the accused pleaded innocent and demonstrated their good faith by coming to lay hands on Suna—to no avail.[22] After the funeral Kwaliapuna, still smarting from the treatment he had received during the Silembin inquiry, reported to Suna's survivors that Atupwin and Baimanuwi (both of Ililip) had spied members of Supalo's faction working sorcery against the deceased. This testimony was promptly discredited when the two so-called eyewitnesses refused to corroborate Kwaliapuna's account. Nonetheless, Suna's friends remained convinced that someone in Ililip had done the deed, and for a time their attitude threatened further delay on the spirit house.

The air of suspicion was (at least temporarily) dispelled during a feast held about one month later in honor of Suna and another Balanga man who died about this time. During the speeches the peace-making initiative was taken by Owap, a much revered elder of Hengwanif. The mourning period for Suna was now ended, he declared, and (addressing Balanga and Ililip) everyone should now bury their disagreements and join in rapidly building the spirit house. This evoked general assent. But then Owap changed topics and began to lambast the Sahopwas class for not yet returning yams to them in conjunction with the forthcoming Nggwal initiation. Although they (the Sahopwas) had more or less satisfied their obligation in pigs, the yams had yet to be paid. The storm of protest which greeted this rebuke had the effect of undoing much of the good Owap had wrought in the earlier part of his speech.

Kafia spoke next and managed to save the occasion. As the clansman closest to Suna, and the one most anguished at his passing, Kafia carried maximum authority when he, echoing Owap, vowed that this feast would finish the mourning. "After this, if it rains— next week, next month, whenever—you cannot blame us [the Owapwi clan], for our hearts are no longer heavy with feelings of revenge. You will have to find someone else to blame." The way to cooperation was again open.

Case 3. Kafia's reference to rain was largely figurative; he was including in the metaphor any future misfortune which might be construed as the fruit of Owapwi vengeance. Still, it is nothing short of ironic that, before the season was out, untimely rains had created yet another obstacle to building progress. It was the stage

---

22. This is a standard procedure used when someone is ill and the evidence—divinatory or circumstantial—points responsibility in a specific direction. It consists simply of the accused treating the victim with stinging nettles and blowing on the affected part. Because most attacks occur inadvertently—a love charm or garden spell gone haywire, or any of myriad other causes—the matter is usually disposed of quite amicably. Rarely, the accused refuses to attend, in which case he reveals himself as the villain he is.

just before thatching, at a time of the year normally very dry. Beyond imposing annoying delays, the rains were repeatedly soaking the exposed frame, causing deterioration of some of the flimsier parts. Someone, it appeared, was intent on destroying the entire project; otherwise, why did it so often happen that Ililip would be drenched while the adjacent wards of Balanga and Hengwanif would be left untouched?

Unlike death and other personalized mishaps, rain cannot be deciphered by any known divination technique. Furthermore, it is thought that rain can also be caused by nonhuman agents (especially masalai), whose purposes are beyond divining anyway. Against these imponderables the Arapesh response is to proceed as if the cause were human: through public discussion the men seek to discover a possible underlying motive, and, having done so, they move to rectify whatever inimical elements exist in the situation as interpreted. Failing any clear determination or immediate improvement, rain magicians are enlisted to combat the problem on a mystical plane.

This time, it was Mangas who took it upon himself to harangue both his own and the other moiety, demanding that the saboteur reveal himself and let his grievance be known. Supalo joined him, and the two speakers reviewed all recent disputes, challenging the principals each in turn to deny culpability in the present instance. After all had sworn innocence, and the discussion had gone on for a while, Dongwande, an important Sahopwas man from Hengwanif, strode to the center of the clearing and planted a stake to which he tied a wild taro leaf (*aolaf*). This symbolized and directed that the community was and/or should be united in their efforts; that their "bellies were cold" and no ill will existed. By implication, then, the fault lay with some nonhuman agency.

Materials (feathers, leaves and bamboo) were gathered and placed in a small heap in the clearing. Seven magicians, representing four of the six wards, arranged themselves in a semicircle facing the pile.[23] Each held the dried base of a coconut frond. Muttering secret chants under their breath, each individually directed the magic to stop the rain and then raised the frond slowly over his head. When the last one had done this, they cried out in concert and slapped the fronds on the ground. Then they quickly swept up the magic materials and dropped them into a fire that had been prepared a few steps away. The smoke rising was lemon-scented. As one magician explained it, when the four birds whose feather types were in the fire next cried out, the sound would stop the rain

23. Specifically, the mélange consisted of: a lemon leaf (*nifinga*), a black cordyline leaf (*owa*), a white cockatoo feather (*sangalif*), a red parrot feather (*ambon*), a yellow parrot feather (*afo'w*), a black feather from a small, sun-loving bird also renowned for not bathing (*tangili'w*), and, finally, five short lengths of bamboo.

12. The eight rain magicians of the village mutter their individual spells before slapping their pangal paddles on the ground. The magical materials are shown at left of center in the picture.

from falling. For whatever reason, the sky did indeed clear later that day, and work on the house was able to continue.

Case 4. Not every incident has to be as profound as death or as prevalent as rain for the Tambaran to become implicated. About a week before the rain business just described, a fight nearly broke out in Elaf between young men of Balanga and Ililip. Bun (Balanga) was incensed by the news that lewd comments and gestures had been made to his wife and sister by two Ililip youths who happened upon them in the gardens. He sent word that the two had better watch out; and they responded with a challenge to fight in Elaf.

The two sides (the principals and their supporters) were in the process of squaring off when two Balanga men realized what was happening and jumped up. Angrily they separated the fighters, saying that if the boys (they used a word that emphasized juvenile worthlessness) wanted to fight over girls they would have to do so elsewhere, away from the eyes of Nggwal and the older men. The boys were totally cowed by the reproving onslaught that followed immediately. One Hengwanif man was especially irate: "Women are only something to copulate with. They are nothing! The Tambaran stands above everything, and you children must not interfere with the work of all these men for the sake of your petty squabbling!" The other older men chimed their agreement.

When matters had cooled, Behinguf (Balanga) took the contrite youths to one side and counseled them. "There must be peace during Tambaran times, otherwise one or more wards may withdraw their support and the Tambaran could not go ahead. If every time the village gets together to work on the Tambaran, the young men start fighting, then some of the big-men will refuse to participate because of the trouble it causes, and then what would we do?"[24]

Case 5. The final example is in itself trivial, but it illustrates a dimension of Tambaran law which is implicit in all that has been said so far. A few days after the house had been completed, and the sacred hamlet was no longer off limits to non-initiates, some adolescents got together in the evening to amuse themselves with a guitar-and-ukelele singsing. At about 2200 hours Kumbwiata, a cult leader from Bwi'ingili, arrived and called for silence. He announced that if they wanted to sing like that (i.e., in a modern fashion) they would have to go somewhere else. "Nggwal is in Elaf now, and the big-men are completely in charge. This is something very important, something that belongs to your elders. This is Nggwal!" Obediently, the young people repaired to Hengwanif for their song-fest.

The interesting point about this last case—typical of many that could have been cited—was the arbitrary quality of Kumbwiata's command. There is nothing in the "rules" prohibiting such singsings; moreover, Kumbwiata had not been the first cult member to stroll through the hamlet that evening. Witnessing the encounter, my clear impression was that Kumbwiata was simply annoyed at the noisy, faintly insolent antics of the youngsters. Under ordinary circumstances, he would have appeared foolish and undignified in voicing his objection to this clatter—unless, of course, it had been incon-

24. A case reported in the previous volume (1976:101–102), entitled "Sister-Exchange Default," also occurred during the building of the spirit house and was likewise turned into an occasion for expounding Tambaran values. In that instance a taro-leaf marker was erected by cult leaders as a warning that dissension over women would not be tolerated in the presence of the Tambaran.

veniencing him in some definite way. With Nggwal present, however, he was able to make his point without, as it were, taking responsibility for it.

By this, I do not mean to imply that Kumbwiata plotted this petty subterfuge or in any way abused his power. On the contrary, there is every indication that he was reacting to an intuitive feeling of what was appropriate and responsible in the circumstances. But, where, one might ask, is the dividing line between the will of Kumbwiata and the will of the Tambaran? The answer—usually unthinkable to the Arapesh—is, of course, that there is no line. Citing the authority of Nggwal, both to himself and to the teen-agers, was Kumbwiata's way of objectifying his eminently *subjective* feelings. Not only did his will prevail, he also emerged from the incident feeling *virtuous*. We see here the grass roots of Durkheim's "collective conscience," for the identical process of "objectification through exteriorization" occurs at the group level—as, for example, when a degree of legitimacy was granted to the sorcerer who attacked the Owapwas class for failing to honor their initiation partners. As long as the line is held between the affairs of men and the meanings of the "other reality," the Tambaran will continue to serve the Arapesh by giving expression and coherence to their deepest cultural intentions; hence, the mutual augmentation of belief and experience referred to at the beginning of this section.

CONSTRUCTION RESUMED

The next step of construction is technically rather straightforward and is, probably for this reason, unencumbered by ritual precautions and procedures. It consists of lashing a multitude of slender poles at short intervals between ridgepole and lateral members, reaching to the ground, to serve as rafters for the eventual thatch walls.[25] These are then interconnected with a series of horizontal poles, which both

25. Informants pointed out that the Abelam use bamboo for these rafters instead of the lighter, more perishable saplings employed here. This is because they build their spirit houses with the intention that they will stand for a long time, whereas the Arapesh lose interest in the house once Nggwal has left it.

13. Lashing the horizontal rafters of the spirit-house frame.

strengthen the walls and provide a scaffold for further work on the sides and top of the house. Later, three heavier poles will be lashed obliquely to each wall as additional support. The resulting frame is sturdy enough to permit the bread-fruit trunks, which heretofore had been supporting the ridgepole, to be removed, leaving the interior completely open and giving the structure a pleasing, free-floating archi-tectural character.[26] Also, taking away the temporary sup-ports subtly alters the line of structural tensity. With the center columns in place, the edifice had a bolt-upright pos-ture, rather like someone trussed up and artificially erect. Now, with the terrific weight of the ridgepole being borne entirely by the rafters, the latter bow very slightly. The house takes on a faintly "hunched" appearance, enhancing the

26. As a matter of convention rather than of structural necessity, the center sup-ports are not removed until after the house is thatched. This is a dangerous, ritually important operation which requires a pig offering by the Owapwas to the Sahopwas. Note that a pig was given in the opposite direction at the time they were installed.

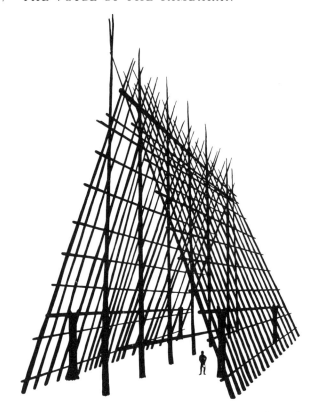

FIGURE 9. The spirit house. Front elevation showing horizontal and vertical rafters.

enigma of weightlessness and converting what was a static
image of mere support into one of dynamic *self*-support.
This effect combines with the cantilevered "head" of the
house (see below) to produce a figure brooding and yet tense
—as if crouched ready to spring.

With the basic frame completed, a structural detail is
added whose significance I was not able to comprehend fully.
The experienced men build a conical form just above and
jutting forward from the front apex of the house. Later, this
will be the frame for a handsome woven crown. For now it is
rudely covered over by a layer of thatch. A rough but adequate floor is added to the base of the cone, forming a peaked
chamber just large enough to hold two men. This is called

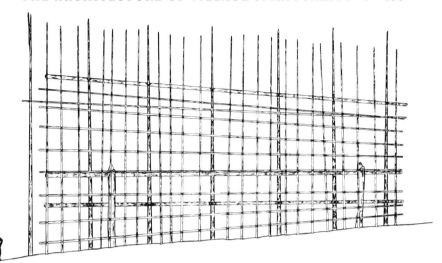

FIGURE 10. The spirit house. Side elevation showing horizontal and vertical rafters.

kamba, the same term used for menstrual houses and the "green rooms" used during the Maolimu seclusion. The term could be reasonably glossed as "hidden chamber" or "secret chamber." A side-blown *kondo* flute is installed, available to any initiate who chooses to make the harrowing ascent to the summit of the house and play its repetitive song. A sprouted coconut is also placed in the chamber. The flute is the voice of the infant Nggwal, crying alternatively for pig flesh (specifically, the liver—*hu'up*), water and women. The cry is sounded intermittently during lulls in construction; on days when work or feasting is in progress it becomes continuous and insistent, urging the men to hasten their efforts.[27]

Kondo is also the name given to a type of bird, whose call the flute is said to represent. Informants claim with all apparent sincerity that in addition to the *kondo* flute housed in the tiny garret there is also a caged *kondo* bird. Yet, although I

27. For most of the time between placing the house posts and thatching the walls, the hamlet is off limits to anyone who has not "seen" Nggwal. Ceremonial hamlets are typically situated on prominences, so that activities occurring there cannot be observed from lower, surrounding hamlets. Accordingly, for months during the period being described here, women and non-initiates routinely use paths which wind below and around the hamlet in going about their daily affairs.

occasionally heard (or thought I heard) a faint chirp coming from the direction of the house peak, at no time was I ever shown the creature—nor, despite considerable searching, was I ever able to locate it. The same informants—who had previously demonstrated their reliability on countless occasions—aver that the *kondo* bird, after being dramatically removed from the house (see below), is delivered to the most senior men, who eat it in a small but solemn feast.

The point may well be academic. Either the informants were correct, and it was a case of the bird and the ethnographer somehow failing to cross paths; or, for reasons I was never able to fathom, they were departing from their usual openness and attempting to persuade me of something which was patently and demonstrably untrue. Or, as a third and more intriguing possibility, this may be another instance of the men believing and yet not believing; of couching the layers of their ideas in a series of metaphors which is so involuted as to call into question the very fact of what is palpably "real." Schizophrenic madness plays with reality in *analogous* fashion; and although the conceptual relationship between psychic structures and cultural structures is far from being specified, or even agreed to exist, it has been known for a long time that the shared understandings which comprise culture construct a reality which is highly persuasive (if not downright coercive) to the psyches of its members. This being so, the human condition necessarily includes an element of cognitive dissonance—especially visible from a perspective lying outside the culture. The implied methodology is saved from arrant relativism by affirming the value of a fixed analytic viewpoint. Insofar as a people's ontological sensibilities are normally focused in the domain of religious understandings, it follows that the *anthropology* of religion is a matter of systematizing this alternate reality and studying its ramified effects in any and all areas of mental and social life. Whatever may be the "true" status of the *kondo* "bird," the case offers an opportunity to enunciate a methodological principle which in my estimation is generally valid in the analysis of Arapesh religion.

About the time the rafters are added, a sturdy latticework

scaffolding is erected across the front of the house. This facilitates movement between the ground and the *kamba* chamber and later, after thatching, will give the workers a perch from which to apply a colorful dressing to the leading edges of the house walls. Also, when the time comes, it will provide a means whereby a large number of men can carry aloft the woven cover for the house crown.

First, however, certain details must be fashioned. A rattan chain is suspended from the inside of the crown reaching about halfway down the façade. This is called *maolenif*, from the stem *maol*, meaning "mouth." The chain ends in a wound bundle of rattan called *ba'om*, which is pierced by two pointed sticks at right angles to one another. Each is tipped at both ends by a bright orange fruit (*su'witip*). According to informants, the *maolenif* represents a particular kind of hawk (*komon*) which figures in both mythic and totemic contexts and is especially known for its savagery and appetite for meat. This symbolism no doubt explains why, while the house is being built, the *ba'om* is draped with a long rope knotted at close intervals along its entire length, which is the record of all pig kills achieved by the Sahopwas class and thereby credited to the Tambaran.[28] On another occasion I was told that the *maolenif* is the "nose" of the spirit house, a point I shall return to in a moment.

On each side of the façade, starting about halfway down from the apex, a shorter rattan chain is hung, terminating in a bird's nest (*waola*). An orange *su'witip* (the "egg") is pinned inside so as to be visible from below.

Finally, a line of "flying-fox wing bones" is fastened down each leading edge of the house façade. These consist of

28. At the Ningalimbi spirit house, I was told by the men of that village that the knots stood for enemies killed during former days of warfare. My Ilahita companions privately informed me that this was a lie, that the knots were merely pig counters. Whatever the truth of the matter—and I am inclined to believe my Ilahita confidants—the notion that there is a symbolic link between warfare and the men's cult is probably borrowed from the Abelam, among whom the Tambaran demands, among other things, that the testicles of slain enemies be pounded to pulps in the ritual hamlet (Forge 1966:27). For the Arapesh, the Tambaran is *the* patron of village warfare, as well as being bloodthirsty in various other ways; but when I told some Ilahita men what the Abelam did to enemy privates, they were aghast with horror and disgust.

forked sticks about one meter long, each of which is crossed with a shorter stick lashed to it with a pleasing design of rattan. The forked ends protrude some distance out from the walls, supporting the forward edge of the thatch.

SPIRIT-HOUSE SYMBOLISM

The preceding details invite consideration of what the general symbolism of the spirit house might be. My Ilahita informants, whose understanding of symbolic expression was well developed and who were fully articulate in discussing the particulars just described, flatly denied that the house as a whole had any representational significance. Forge (1966: 26) reports that Abelam construe their spirit houses as symbolically feminine, with the dark interior likened to "her" belly,[29] but nothing comparable appears to exist in the Arapesh case. We have had mention of the *maolenif* being a "nose"—a fact which, together with later elements reminiscent of "ears," suggests that the façade represents a face. Indeed, the initiation procedure requires the novices to crawl through a portal ("mouth"?) in the center of the façade to be "eaten" by Nggwal. One reliable informant found this line of interpretation to be quite ingenious—but wrong. Finally, we have the aggregate of details associated with birds or bats: *kondo*, *komon* pendant, *waola* nests, flying-fox wing bones. Clearly, the juxtaposition of these items can be accounted for if the spirit house symbolically represents a *tree*.

Other data support this interpretation: for example, the ceremonial hamlet in Ningalimbi village is dominated by a gigantic fig tree which can be seen from miles around.[30] When I remarked to my hosts how unfortunate it was that their spirit house was dwarfed by the lordly tree, they replied

29. Cf., however, Kaberry's note (1941:246n.) that the Abelam word *mbia* means both "belly" and "womb." As we shall see later, the Arapesh refer to the inner sanctum as Nggwal's "netbag"—an object which, in both Arapesh and Pidgin English usage, evokes associations with the *womb*. It seems possible that a genetic link exists with Abelam spirit-house symbolism—one which, as if by error of translation, involves iconographic alteration and a development of this symbolism along lines which no longer have anything to do with femininity. And yet, as we shall see, the *fertility* connotations have been preserved.
30. A couple of the ceremonial hamlets in Ilahita also boast giant fig trees, but Elaf itself does not.

quite to the contrary: the tree added to the splendor of their house. "When people from far away see the tree silhouetted on the distant ridge, they will exclaim, 'Ah, see the Tambaran in Ningalimbi!'" The decorations applied to the house when it is finally finished are suggestive along these same lines. Thus, in addition to the leaves and blossoms attached to the crown (see below), two fronds from a fan palm are stuck in each side (the "ears" mentioned earlier) and *kwambefowa* arrangements are elevated on tall masts flanking each side of the façade. *Kwambefowa* (sing. *kwambeno'w*) are decorations concocted of *su'witix* fruits and the yellow, raffia-like fibers of a sago sprout—reminiscent, that is, of *hangahiwa* costumes. Indeed, capitalizing on this resemblance, men are fond of teasing and frightening children by telling them that the "*hangamu'w*" is going to get them. As we saw in an earlier chapter, *hangahiwa* costumes are discarded in treetops—as a sign to non-initiates that the spirit portion of the monster has returned to the water shrine—and the corpses of persons who die in old age are disposed of in the same way.[31] If a man clears a garden containing a tall tree, he typically hangs a *kwambeno'w* at the top of it—to celebrate its size and to associate his works with its magnificence. As additional support, we may recall the story of Ngwangwa'um cited at the start of this chapter, where the tambaran ogre preyed on children from his lair at the top of the tree.

The symbolic value of trees for the Arapesh is confirmed in an array of other cultural contexts. When a great man dies, it is said that a mighty tree has fallen in the forest, dragging down a multitude of lesser trees and leaving a void where there was once fullness.[32] The terms given to the

---

31. Cf. the statement of one knowledgeable individual that, in the very beginning, the Tambaran was a ghost (*kamba*). Although, to me, the cult seemed rampant with ancestral significances, this is the closest any informant ever came to confirming this understanding of it. Among the Abelam (Forge 1966) and the Iatmul (Bateson 1936), the ancestral significance of the men's cult is quite explicit.

32. The smaller trees are pulled down because a web of vines connects them with the giant. In the metaphor the vines refer to the plenitude of political and kinship links enjoyed by an important man. Also, women are archetypically the "vines" of the social forest, crawling mindlessly about the stately trees (men), binding them into a network where—for better or worse—each part is implicated in all the rest.

ritual age-sets, Balangaisi and Owangufwisi, are derived from the head and base, respectively, of the sago palm—a tree which, as we have seen in earlier chapters, looms large as a ritual symbol. In the story of Nambweapa'w, it may be recalled, the treelike shrub in which the sons slept sheltered from the rain was magically transformed during the night into a spirit house. Many other examples could be given. What do they add up to? I have no very satisfactory answer, except to say that the tree image appears to envelop a series of existential virtues: strength, solidity, endurance, spirituality and (in certain of its forms) fecundity—all of which may be applicable both to individuals and to corporate groups. Insofar as the spirit house, as a material expression of the Tambaran, connotes these same qualities, it is perhaps not surprising that an arboreal element should be detectable in its symbolic status. Such an interpretation is, furthermore, consistent with the once greater emphasis on hunting and gathering which is presumed to have existed in the remote history of Arapesh life and subsistence.[33]

FINISHING TOUCHES

Of the many building procedures in raising the spirit house none is so sheerly enjoyable as thatching. It is the most festive part of *any* house-building project; for it is relatively unskilled, light work which permits the thatchers to chat and sing merrily as the walls go up with astonishing speed. All the more so in the case of the spirit house, where, in marked

33. This remains the condition of linguistically related cultures living farther west in the Torricelli Mountains (e.g., Lewis 1975; William Mitchell, personal communication). In an impressive piece of anthropological detective work, Alfred Gell (1975) has traced detailed symbolic connections between trees and ceremonial headdresses in Umeda, a village in the Bewani Mountains—a range contiguous with the western Torricellis—near the frontier with West Irian. Gell's illustrations reveal a striking morphological resemblance between Arapesh spirit houses and Umeda headdresses (e.g., Gell 1975:187)—or, at the very least, the crown portion of the former. Given the ease with which cultural traits appear able to move through this general area, it would not be too bold, I think, to speculate that we are dealing here with symbolic transforms (tree, house, headdress) related to one another at deep cultural and temporal levels. However, more ethnographic coverage of the Torricelli area is needed before comparative tidbits such as this can be theoretically (or even ethnologically) ennobled.

contrast with some of the earlier tasks, thatching is not particularly dangerous.

For days preceding the event, virtually every able-bodied person in the village is out gathering the thousands of sago fronds and miles of lashing ropes which go into covering the house.[34] Great heaps of these materials form around the perimeter of the clearing, where, in the afternoon preceding the appointed day, a general feast is held to celebrate the work accomplished. As night falls the women and non-initiates are sent away so that the men may convene a private feast of pork in honor of Nggwal. This is accompanied by speechmaking which carries on into the small hours of morning. At first light, work begins.[35]

The labor force is divided into four teams, manned according to degrees of physical fitness. (1) The oldest men work pulling sago fronds out of the heaps and splitting them along the center spine. These are dragged over to the house by (2) somewhat younger men who use forked sticks to lift them up to (3) men in their prime who are perched on bread-fruit poles planted at intervals along the outside walls of the house. Swaying with great dexterity and economy of movement, these men then pass the fronds (again, using forked poles) over to (4) the youngest, least experienced men, who sit in rows on the house frame, lashing the fronds into place as quickly as they receive them. The technique consists simply of binding reverse overlays, at intervals of about five centimeters, starting from the bottom.[36] The scene is splendid:

34. Unlike the actual construction phases, there is nothing secret about the procurement of building materials. Women and children are called into service; indeed, among the latter, there is inter-ward competition to see which group of youngsters can collect the most fronds. The same applies to the earlier gathering of rafter poles, where lines of children scarcely older than toddlers proudly drag gaily decorated saplings to the hamlet, there to receive the lavish praise of the men.

35. On the occasion witnessed the night was clear, and a brilliant full moon bathed the precinct in a silver glow. At about 0300 the younger men succumbed to eager friskiness and impulsively started to thatch. Thereupon, their elders restrained them by gently remonstrating that crawling around on the scaffolds at night was too dangerous—however bright the moon.

36. The ridge of the house is prepared in advance by covering it with overlapping squares of woven thatch. These are tied down over the upper layers of side thatch, thereby waterproofing the top part of the house.

14. The men work with maximum speed and coordination in thatching the spirit house.

with figures rushing madly about shouting and gesticulating it could be the maelstrom of a pitched battle—except that jollity and rollicking fun are written on everyone's face. As the older men chant their Tambaran songs, the younger men up on the house bellow bawdier lyrics, such as "Don't give us food cooked by old women, give us food cooked by young women!" And, behind and over it all is the incessant, haunting tattoo of the *kondo* flute.

On the occasion witnessed, the left side (Ondondof) was assaulted first, taking one hour to be covered. Immediately, the men turned to the Afa'afa'w side and, their coordination now perfected, completed it in the astonishingly brief space of thirty-five minutes! By 0730, the skeleton was fully cloaked in a rust-colored mantle of thatch. Vastly pleased with their effort, the workers retired to rest and refresh themselves in preparation for the busy day that was already beginning.

At about 0900 the men reassemble in Elaf. The plaited crown cover (*kimbinip*) is removed from its hiding place in one of the hamlet's auxiliary houses and is laid flat in the center of the clearing.[37] While some men grate turmeric roots on the prickly back of a sago spathe, others take the oily rubbings and apply them to the fabric, giving it a decorative yellow burnish. Meanwhile, a prominent man among the Owapwas Seniors summons together all the Sahopwas Owangufwisi (the line of younger brothers). After cutting a pole which measures equal to the length of the plaiting, he leads the way down to the water named Alahimbil to show them one of the last Nggwal secrets yet remaining for them. This consists merely of preparing a woven panel which will later be used to finish the irregular bottom edges of the crown once it is mounted on the house.[38] Then they are shown how to decorate their chests, backs and legs with Nggwal designs drawn in greyish pond silt and varying according to the wearer's moiety affiliation.[39]

At about noon, the Sahopwas Owangufwisi return in a long line to Elaf, carrying on a pole the mat they have just woven. Singing, they enter the clearing and circle around the *kimbinip* before placing their load to one side of it. A moment later a signal is given and several men seize the *kimbinip* and

37. The *kimbinip*, prepared earlier for this occasion, is fashioned according to a technique which is a cult secret. Sahopwas men are taught it by Owapwas Seniors in the course of actually making the house crown. Green sago frondlets form the warp, strips of bamboo skin the weft. The ingenious part is the use of a wallaby (*meho'w*) femur as an instrument for weaving. When split, the inner surface of the bone reveals a broad, flat trough, which enables the weaver to grip the bamboo strip as it is pulled through the tiny slits in the warp fibers.

   Traditionally, spirit-house construction was the only context in which the *kimbinip* was used. In recent years, some men have taken to copying the stilted dwelling houses native to coastal groups. Their roofs involve weaving the thatch in a way not dissimilar from the *kimbinip*, and occasionally the builder uses a plaiting identical to it as a wall covering. For this reason, cult leaders have declared that men who have not seen Nggwal are prohibited from using these techniques—unless they are willing to forfeit a pig and a quantity of yams paid to the cult members in the name of Nggwal. Here, again, we witness the Tambaran extending its sway over new areas of cultural experience, turning them to its own advantage.

38. Although the activities at Alahimbil are simple and innocuous, the ritual significance is that the Sahopwas Owangufwisi are said to have gone to fetch Nggwal, to bring him to "cover up" his house; hence, the need for going *to the water* to execute a task which could as easily be done in the village. While they are absent from the clearing their older brothers, the Sahopwas Balangaisi, are told informally what is transpiring at Alahimbil.

39. Traditionally, the decorations would have included an elaborate coiffure, but this was dispensed with in the present instance.

FIGURE 11. The spirit house. Front elevation, thatched and decorated.

carry it quickly up the front scaffold to the house peak, where men are waiting to wrap and secure it around a tightly bound thatch cone. When this is in place a finial is added consisting of an inverted earthenware pot, on top of which is affixed an inverted, painted metal pot which, in turn, forms the pedestal for a carved hornbill effigy. All the while, the *kondo* flute continues, as the men on the ground chant a rhythmic "u-u-u-u-u-u." Finally, when the finial is positioned, the recently woven panel is quickly taken up the scaffolding and tied around the base of the crown. Then the decorations are applied: a strand of large orange fruits (*su'witix*) around the base of the finial, red and yellow blossoms and brightly col-

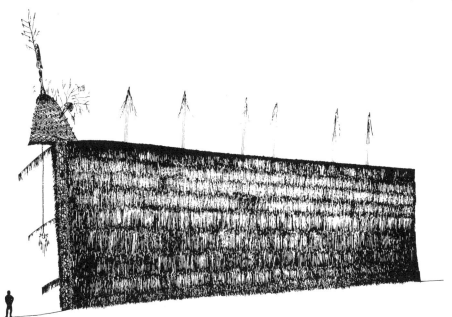

FIGURE 12. The spirit house. Side elevation, thatched and decorated.

ored leaves in a pattern over the crown, and a frond from the fan palm stuck in each side as if to resemble "ears." Then a gracefully executed design is fashioned down the forward parts of the two walls, extending some distance along the ground on each side. The decorative belt is formed by geometrically arranged leaves and other natural substances in brilliant colors of red, yellow, green, black and white. To complete the picture, *kwambefowa* arrangements (see above) are hung on the top of the two front breadfruit poles used that morning during the thatching operation. In all, it is a grand sight.[40]

During the decorating, a feast has been in progress down in the clearing. Yam soup and roasted yams are exchanged bilaterally between Sahopwas and Owapwas. Each recipient

40. All the decorative materials are assembled in Elaf on the previous day. *Kokolalo'w* whistles are blown to drive women from the path of men bearing leaves, flowers and other gay articles—the metaphor being that Nggwal has seconded the birds of the forest to trim his house.

15. The spirit house at Ningalimbi on the day it is
thatched and decorated. During the subsequent rainy
season, the façade will be erected.

eats a small portion and then gives the remainder to someone
of his own initiation class visiting from another village. Two
pigs are also cooked: large chunks of pork are handed to
representatives of each group present, who then cut them
into smaller pieces for general distribution.[41] With the feast

41. In this as in other sections of this volume I am giving scant attention to the sub-
    ject of ceremonial food exchanges, for the reason that an adequate treatment
    would produce mind-dulling repetition and little ethnographic reward. Suffice

consumed and all traces of it removed, word is sent for the women to come. Immediately, as if awaiting their cue, they file in, heavily burdened by baskets of yams which they empty in a huge heap in the center of the clearing. Then they step to one side to admire and, in hushed tones, exclaim upon the beauty of the spirit house.

After the full effect has had time to register, a commotion breaks out in the clearing. Twenty or so of the younger men charge noisily around the yam pile. After several revolutions, a great collective whoop is sounded and they all scamper madly up the scaffolding, racing to "kill" the *kondo* bird. As the first man reaches the hidden chamber, the flute—whose song has been going non-stop since the previous day—falls silent. Everyone clusters around the house crown and, in the confusion, the flautist returns unnoticed to the ground with the others.

This dramatic event formally concludes the ritual sub-phase of house construction. Its mystical auspices no longer necessary, the *kondo*—the infant Nggwal—is violently and ungratefully destroyed.[42] All that remains—apart from painting the carved house posts[43] and dismantling the scaffolding—is the celebratory feasting and singing. Those who participated in the thatching arrange themselves in lines along the inside walls of the spirit house, according to which side they worked on. Yams are brought from the central pile and are placed in small heaps in front of each man; bowls of

---

it to say that virtually every time the men come together in the name of the Tambaran there is a food exchange and feast. Yams, sago, coconuts and meat are the primary foods, and the transaction is typically a complicated assortment of intra- and inter-moiety transfers. Yams are the one seasonal item on the list, which is why Tambaran activities are scheduled during the time when they are in abundance, that is, between this year's harvest and the clearing of next year's gardens.

42. We see this pattern again at the conclusion of the overall ritual sequence, when the once terrifying Nggwal is ignominiously "chased" out of the village and back to his watery lair. The notion is that the ritual transfers Nggwal's enormous potency to the body collective, leaving the spirit a shriveled, pathetic object of human contempt. There is in the universe a quantum of spiritual energy; and, accordingly, the power of men may wax in proportion as the power of Nggwal wanes. A close parallel exists in the mortal sphere in the zero-sum relationship between youth and age. More about this in chap. 8.

43. Sub-moieties paint each others' posts. Following the way they were carved, the larger, more important front posts are painted as Afa'afa'w male and Ondondof female, with rear posts reversing the sexes.

yam soup are also presented.[44] Yams and soup are then distributed to the women, who take home whatever they cannot eat. Around 1800 the feast winds down and some of the older people begin to move off in order to arrive home before nightfall. Others leave to rest and refresh themselves for the slit-gong singsing scheduled to begin at twilight. All through the night the songs and chants roll on with loud joyfulness. The gong is large, and its thunder carries to listeners for many miles around the news that Nggwal now has a home in Ilahita.

AFTERMATH

The slit-gong singsing occurred on the night of 14–15 September 1971, two months to the day after the house posts had been set in place.[45] As the decorations wilted and the thatch turned from rich russet to weathered grey, the men put aside their ceremonialism and turned to the serious business of clearing and planting the next year's gardens. Elaf continued to be the preferred meeting place; for, with the house located there, the hamlet was no longer merely a constituent of Ililip ward; it belonged, in a sense, to everyone. Rarely did it happen that there was not someone present,

---

44. This feast is sponsored by the Sahopwas class, whose responsibility it is to finance the house construction and feed the workers. Having just devoured a considerable feast, the recipients have little appetite; but they stoically force down a few more mouthfuls, lest the women suspect that they and not Nggwal had enjoyed the earlier repast.

   At one point I was surprised to see one of the Sahopwas hosts remove from his netbag a piece of pork left over from the preceding feast and give it to old Nango'atom, who promptly set about eating it right there in full view of the women. Thinking this to be highly irregular, I inquired and learned that Nango'atom was entitled to the meat since he had worked splitting fronds that morning. As to his eating it in public: his age permits him to do this without shame or embarrassment, since it is generally known that Nggwal sometimes shares his pork with the oldest, most honored men.

45. The house measured 22 m. in length, with front and rear heights of 13 m. and 9 m., respectively. The width at the front was 13 m., narrowing to eight meters at the rear. Though doubtless unintentional, the exact equivalence of the base and height of the triangular façade produced a form which, given the nature of the materials, possessed maximum structural stability.

   Taking into account all aspects of the project—including materials gathering and feasting, as well as actual construction—a conservative estimate of the time invested in the house would be 10,000 man-days.

contemplating the house and tending the small, smoking fires which supposedly season and temper the lashings.[46] This is perhaps the place to mention, if it is not already obvious, that the Arapesh spirit house is emphatically not a men's residence as it is in many parts of Melanesia, although ceremonial obligations do require the men to live in the *hamlet* for occasionally long intervals. The hearths must not be used for cooking; food cooked here would cause those who ate it to sicken. The only exception to this interdiction occurs when the men of the cult avail themselves of their secret privilege of eating (i.e., "feeding to Nggwal") the first yams of the new harvest season.

Being something of a cultural spectacle, the house attracted visitors from all over the Arapesh and surrounding language regions. While the male strangers strode casually into the house to inspect the details of construction, their womenfolk held back warily, fearful of the aura of the Tambaran. Children were kept at a safe distance by anxious mothers, who knew from a lifetime's warnings that a child was a delectable morsel in Nggwal's eyes. That *this* Nggwal had such predilections was established early on—when, during the feast on the day following thatching, an eight-year-old boy inexplicably fainted away. Swooning, no doubt, from overexcitement and fatigue, the boy was speedily revived with no apparent ill effects. But, under the circumstances, the event's mystic significance was plain: there was now a powerful Presence in the village. This was Nggwal's politely ominous way of announcing himself.

---

46. During the planting season the front and rear of the house remain open. Each sub-moiety maintains a hearth, located on its side of the house just under the shelter of the overhanging façade. Idlers generally sit next to the hearth of their own sub-moiety.

   This is not the only time seating arrangements are made to reflect ritual categories. Whenever handiwork activity is going on in the clearing—sewing thatch for the house ridge, stringing decorative materials, etc.—the men of Ililip (if that is the only ward present) divide themselves by sub-moiety, according to a line which cuts the clearing diagonally. When men from all parts of Ilahita are present (e.g., during a feast), the division is ritually upgraded to demarcate the opposed moieties: Laongol wards sit on the erstwhile Afa'afa'w side, while Bandangel wards (including, now, *both* sub-moieties of Ililip) sit on the Ondondof side. This is the pattern in all Tambaran events.

6. Divine Artistry:
The Power and Aesthetics
of Self-Creation

OLAFEN

Long ago, our women did not know how to deliver babies in the normal way. No one knew that babies could be born through the vagina. Instead, husbands waited until their wives reached term, then they cut open their bellies and removed the infant. The mother of course died, and her body was sent to the husband's ritual exchange partner to be eaten. No one was happy with this arrangement, but it was the only way we knew.

One day, a man whose wife was nearing term left her in the village while he went with everyone else to the gardens. Soon after they had gone the woman began to feel labor pains, and eventually she cried out in agony. Now, next to the woman's house was a spirit house belonging to the men's cult. Olafen, a spirit who lived in one of the carved house-posts [olaf], heard her cry and came out to investigate. As he emerged from the post there sounded a noise like thunder.

The spirit knocked on the door, but the woman had heard the thunder and was too frightened to open it. Finally her pain overcame her fear and she unbarred the door. The spirit entered, took pity and showed her how to sit and move her muscles so as to give birth to the baby. When she had delivered, he instructed her to tell her husband all that had happened, adding that he must gather pork and yams and place them at the foot of the house-post, in payment for what had been done. Then the spirit went back into his post, again making a sound like thunder.

Later that day, as the villagers were returning home, the man of the story heard a baby crying from within his house. Furious that someone else had cut open his wife in his absence, he burst open the door, only to behold the mother and infant sitting peacefully inside. The man was amazed and de-

*lighted. "How did you find out how to do this?" he asked. At first she lied
and said that she had thought of it herself. But then she remembered the
spirit's instructions. Fearing what might happen if she disobeyed them, she
told her husband the whole truth. He gratefully did what was required. As
time went on, all the women learned of the new birth technique, and so that
is the way we do it now.*

(At this point the storyteller parenthetically added that it was
actually the husband's own spirit in the house post, *for he was the
one who had carved it.*)

T HE subject of art and its ritual significance is large
and prominent enough to warrant special treatment.
Nothing argues this more succinctly than the story of
Olafen. Thanks to the storyteller's adventitious remark at the
end, we are informed that the creational spirit of the Tambaran is none other than the spirit of man—projected outward-
ly, sculpted, and vitalized through the magic of art. In other
words, the role of man as creator vis-à-vis the Tambaran—a
notion introduced in the last chapter—is graphically enacted
by the self-expressive creation of religious art.

More specifically, the mythic event of the story marks the
transition from a bestial, precultural existence when, by consequence of a perverse child-bearing technique men can-
nibalized their wives (cf. "Ngwangwa'um," chap. 5), to the
current state of benign reproduction. Reaffirming the predominant theme of Maolimu, the event implicitly arrogates
to men the procreative powers of women. Art and ritual are
the means by which they accomplish this.

RELIGIOUS ART AS A CULTURAL EXPRESSION

Apart from its aesthetic virtues, the art of the Tambaran
Cult holds interest for this study because of its iconographic
features and because the enormous scale and constancy of
art production engenders a situation redolent with sociological and political possibilities. These two factors unite with the
aesthetic form to yield a figure which forcefully expresses
the mutual reliance of mythic and mundane spheres. The

preceding analysis of spirit-house construction has given us a foretaste of how this fertile intermingling of ideas and actions occurs; the case of art restates this mutuality with even greater clarity and specificity.

The approach adopted is generally consistent with that proposed by Anthony Forge, an ethnographer of the neighboring Abelam. In his Curl Lecture "Art and Environment in the Sepik" (1966) Forge compares certain artistic conventions in Abelam and Iatmul cultures and concludes that, despite environmentally related differences in outward form, the "messages" they "transmit" are quite similar.

> These "messages" I believe to be statements about the nature of man and his culture, statements that may not be totally conscious in either the creators or the beholders of the art—who do these things because they are correct—but which are relevant to and essential for the existing social structure. I also hope I have shown that at least in Abelam society these statements are not usually made, *and possibly even cannot be made*, by other means of communication. [P. 30, my emphasis]

Of course, the ability of the ethnographer to enter into the actors' perceptions is severely limited, and so the abstracted code becomes veridical only in proportion to its internal logic, its conformity with other manifest features of the culture, and its utility when applied to interpretative problems which were hitherto invisible or intractable.

One intention of the present study is to try to indicate the analytic value of examining the culturally expressive function of these artistic objects.[1] But, contrary to what is implied in the passage quoted above, such functions, while perhaps especially evident in the artistic and ritual spheres, are distributed throughout the cultural inventory. Shifting attention from the categorical to the *dimensional* permits an open-ended inquiry into the full range of cultural meaning. It also enables us to understand how meanings can be redefined when the objects in which they are invested migrate from one

---

1. I have elsewhere (1977) discussed the epistemological mischief resulting from symbolic forms being treated as *communicating* entities, that is, when the locus of action is removed from the percipient and applied to the object itself (e.g., Leach 1976).

cultural setting to another—a process I shall term the "naturalization of meaning" to emphasize the symbolic molding that must occur during authentic cultural borrowing. In this light, Forge's report of what art means to the Abelam is highly relevant to the subject of this chapter.

In many institutional respects, including settlement and subsistence patterns, the Arapesh and Abelam are nearly identical. And yet these similarities belie important differences in ethos. Not only are there distinctions in fundamental meaning-sets—to use Forge's phrasing, in the ascribed nature of man and his culture—but, more to the point of his argument, the respective channels differ as well. There are indications that Arapesh apprehension of visual art qualitatively differs from that of the Abelam. Most of what the Arapesh produce is based on design elements imported from their Middle Sepik neighbors, the Abelam and Kwanga. While not lacking enthusiasm in their artistic endeavors, their pieces convey (to me) an inhibited woodenness in comparison with the bold, often luridly imaginative flourishes of the Abelam artist. Holding this subjective posture for a moment, we are able to elicit rather provocative implications from Forge's analysis. For, if we assume (as I think we must) that Abelam art achieves subliminal "communication" through its ability to excite unconscious or preconscious materials in the mind of the beholder, and further (as seems likely) that this function is somehow correspondent with the aesthetic vigor of the medium,[2] then we are left to choose between two odd and equally repellent conclusions regarding the Arapesh and their art: either their culture is so relatively meaning*less* that their ontological needs are handled adequately by an inferior artistic tradition; or, they are so labile emotionally that the slightest stimulus evokes aesthetic arousal. Happily, there is a third alternative to which I will return in a moment.

---

2. Although I am uneasy about making aesthetic judgments cross-culturally, and have reservations about the existence of a "universal aesthetic," it is nonetheless difficult to resist the idea that "better art communicates better." On the other hand, as we shall see below, there is no justification for restricting such ontological messages to visual or conventionally artistic channels.

The Arapesh artistic "disadvantage" goes beyond the matter of originality and technical proficiency. Oddly enough, they and other neighbors of the Abelam have steadily borrowed artistic elements without understanding what they mean, even at the most superficial level. Forge (1973) has ably characterized the situation as seen from the Abelam side (though I cannot agree with him that Ilahita is a "confederation of villages").

The evidence for the Abelam being the exporters rather than the importers of style can be summarized thus: the process is still going on; the names attached to art objects are Abelam ones even though such names have no meaning in the language of the neighbours; the styles tend to be unskilfully used and their component elements misunderstood within about five miles of the Abelam border while they often peter out altogether within ten to fifteen miles. The process is mainly but not exclusively one way; the huge southern Arapesh confederation of villages, Ilahita, . . . has elaborated an individual style of figure painting on the flat which is called *ŋwal* (that is an Abelam word without Arapesh etymology) which is now being re-imported into some parts of the Abelam territory. [Pp. 174–175]

If one assumes, as I did initially, that the *meaning* of art is the same in both cultures, then the Arapesh iconography would certainly seem disorganized and unsophisticated in comparison with that of the Abelam exporters. The question, however, is whether the modifications undergone by these elements as they migrate represent random distortions, or whether, in fact, they are the result of systematic reinterpretations. Granting that some amount of actual distortion probably occurs, it must be stressed that the two most obvious barriers—language and ritual secrecy—do not present serious impediments to the transmission of meaning. Traditional occurrences of bilingualism, intermarriage, and the integration of cult activities across cultural boundaries clearly diminish such obstacles. Rather, the major factor in this transmission seems to be the intervention of fully elaborated, distinctively Arapesh meanings and expressive modes, symbolic devices which function quite as effectively for them as art does for the Abelam. The imported elements, detached

from their original (and now irrelevant) meanings, are rein-
terpreted iconically to serve the predominantly *mythological*
style of Arapesh cultural expression. That the modification
has a creative component is implied by Forge's report (above)
that some Abelam groups are reimporting styles of figure
painting from Ilahita.

The reference to mythology pinpoints another significant
difference between the two cultures: whereas the Arapesh
have evolved a large and wonderfully evocative myth corpus,
practically to the exclusion of an indigenous visual art tradition, the Abelam have exercised themselves with reverse
emphases. Forge echoes an earlier ethnographer (Kaberry
1941:359) in remarking that among the Abelam "there is
hardly any mythology at all" (1966:24).[3] Correspondingly,
in contrast with the Arapesh, among whom artistic elements
function through intermediate mythical referents, Abelam
art occurs as "expressions directly related to the culture"
(ibid.).

The obvious conclusion is that art and mythology, at least
in their traditional emphases in these cultures, provide alternative vehicles for the expression of existential meanings.
Middle Sepik religious art was successfully adopted by the
Arapesh, but only after it had been naturalized to the mythic
environment.[4] The measure of its adaptive success is the

3. On the basis of recent ethnographic research among the Western Abelam,
   Richard Scaglion informs me (personal communication) that Kaberry and Forge
   may have overstated the degree to which the Abelam lack a mythological tradition. I am not in a position to resolve this discrepancy; but, as Scaglion also suggests, a possible explanation is that the particular Abelam group which he
   studied lives relatively closer to Arapesh territory and could have been influenced from that direction. A comparison of Arapesh and Western Abelam myth
   corpora would be needed to test this hypothesis. In any event, the issue does
   not seriously affect my argument.
4. Nggwal is also a creature of Middle Sepik culture, and in the next chapter I shall
   deal with further historical and cultural aspects of the naturalization process.
      While Arapesh culture has been vastly enriched by exposure to Middle Sepik
   invaders (Tuzin 1976), the Abelam appear to be notably uninterested in anything the Arapesh have to offer. This one-sidedness in the balance of trade may
   be a manifestation of the Arapesh heritage as an "importing culture" (Mead
   1938), but it may also reflect the more widespread tendency for conquering
   peoples to export their culture to those with whom they come in contact. See,
   however, n.3, above.

breadth and depth of the expressive niche art has carved for itself in Arapesh culture.

ART AND PARAPHERNALIA

The preceding chapter brought the spirit house to completion on the eve of the season for clearing and planting the new yam gardens. Once this intensive work is over and the rains are established,[5] the men seal off the ceremonial hamlet and begin the prolonged task of manufacturing artistic goods and paraphernalia for the upcoming initiation. The decorative house façade is assembled and the paintings and statues representing individual nggwal spirits are fashioned by Sahopwas initiators for eventual transfer to their junior *ombif*. Many years have passed since the last initiation, and thus the great majority of objects must be made anew. Paintings are highly perishable, and only the most spiritually potent statues are allowed to survive in hiding through the entire interval. The crosspiece of the façade is carved from a hardwood species and, protected from the elements, has endured a succession of initiations reaching back beyond memory.

Unlike the construction of the house, which requires collective effort at every stage, most of the artistic work is done by individuals or small groups under the direction of master artists. Each ward has two or three master artists. They are men of high rank in the cult who, having shown early promise of talent, industry and spiritual power, were apprenticed in their younger years to older kinsmen-artists. The personal qualities underlying career eligibility combine with attributes

5. There are periods during this season when the rains fall more or less incessantly for days on end. Usually, however, the rain begins in the late afternoon (about 1600) and carries on into the night, with a bright morning sun following. Accordingly, daytime activities around the village are little affected by the rains. On the other hand, nonessential travel outside the village is minimized since the slippery paths are difficult and sometimes dangerous to navigate. And, without the attractions of harvest festivals and cult ceremonials, there are few reasons to travel abroad anyway.

I might mention that during the rainy season the staple food is yams, giving way increasingly to sago as the stocks of tubers from the previous harvest run out.

of the role itself to produce a variable of key importance at certain moments in social and political process. Before taking up this subject, however, it pays to examine the art itself and the part played by master artists in producing it.

Paintings. Reserving the details of Nggwal's ideological character for the next chapter, the object here is to extend the study of Nggwal's *material* expressions—shifting, that is, from the collective symbolism embodied in the spirit house to the individualist refinements captured in the art of the cult. Nggwal is, in one aspect, an abstract religious idea; but, like the collectivity it exalts, the abstraction is made manifest at the individual level. Thus, the idea of Nggwal is resolved into forty-three individual, named nggwal spirits which are transferred at regular intervals between client sub-clans. Within the sub-clan, each individual's relationship with his nggwal is personified in a painting.

Upon entry into the grade of Nggwal Bunafunei each novice is given a painting of "his" nggwal by his senior *ombaf* (i.e., his initiator). The work is executed on the smooth, varnished-like surface of a piece of pangal (the splayed midrib of a sago-palm frond) measuring about one meter long and forty centimeters wide. Traditionally, the paints were natural earth colors (varieties of red and yellow ochre, primarily), vegetal juices, charcoal, and a pure white made from pulverized limonite. Today, these colors are still used in abundance, but are supplemented by highly saturated store-bought paints; lurid shades of fire-engine red, electric royal blue, and equally shocking pink are infecting the artist's palette with increasing frequency. The subjects are handled in one of two ways. Most commonly, the artist paints a full-body portrait of an anthropomorphic figure arrayed in ceremonial attire. The body is large and elongated with a pointed abdomen; the head, round and enlarged by encircling white designs representing shell necklaces, has tiny, narrowly spaced eyes with no nose or mouth; the headdress rises to a point in sympathy with the abdomen. Arms and legs are diminutive and spindly, flexed at elbow and knee and crowded into the narrow side margins of the panel. The remaining space contains simply drawn totemic birds (hornbills, parrots, cockatoos) flanking the headdress and geometric shapes in the lower corners. The sex of the figure is somewhat ambiguous: the black triangle on the lower abdomen implies femininity,[6] while the headdress, shell-and-tusk chest ornament and other trappings are exclusively male. Apart from differences in technical quality and some freedom in color selection, these portraits vary only in minor details—reflecting, it would appear, the artist's whimsy rather than an inviolable set of motifs associated with particular nggwals. The artist may declare that *this* portrait *is* Sowambon or Wanimbea or some other named nggwal; but on closer questioning it transpires that this is so because he, the artist, has *made* it so. The exactness of the identity is, in other words, the artist's creative prerogative.[7] This is an important point when set against the artist's expressive role (see below).

The other type of painting admits a greater degree of virtuosity. Abandoning the anthropomorphic pretense, the artist combines various geometric shapes which are repeated in bands across the panel. The predominant motif is a horizontal zigzag, which, with the help of pictures intermediate between anthropomorphic and geometric types and a slight bit of imagination on the part of the viewer, reveals itself as an adaptation of the angles created by the flexed limbs of the anthropomorphic figure.[8] Any nggwal may be portrayed

6. It may also suggest an unspecified pubic region; for, although Arapesh sculptors represent the penis realistically on statues, they apparently do not attempt to portray the male member in paintings.

7. Many men can successfully guess which nggwal is represented in a particular painting, but the trick relies on extra-artistic clues, such as where it is placed among other paintings, who the artist is likely to have been, and so on.

8. Anthony Forge, whose knowledge of Sepik art is probably unexcelled among anthropologists, informs me (personal communication) that the painting styles he observed firsthand in Ilahita are highly distinctive. Regrettably, time and circumstance did not permit me to follow this up systematically in cross-village or cross-cultural terms. My impression, based on sketchy evidence, is that geometric emphases increase as one moves south, that is, toward the presumptive source of Nggwal's ideational and material elements (see chap. 7). This would be consistent with the greater tolerance and skill (relative to the Arapesh) which the Kwanga, Abelam and other Ndu-speaking peoples have for artistic abstractness. In contrast, the Arapesh display an indomitable—though not always achieved—commitment to artistic realism.

So as not to leave a false impression, however, I should mention one incident in this fashion, and the same artistic prerogatives apply here as in the previous type.

Custom requires that the initiator be *personally* involved in the creation of the painting he subsequently presents to his junior *ombaf*. The reason is that, as we glimpsed in the myth related at the start of this chapter, the act of artistic creation is simultaneously a magical act of *self*-creation. The artist is thought to invest the work with his own spirit, the part of him whose uniqueness is qualified only to the extent it is shared by lineal kinsmen and, in the act of ritual transmission, his initiation partners. Without his personal involvement, then, the spiritual significance of the initiation rite would be utterly lost.

One could not ask for a more striking metaphor, as regards Tambaran metaphysics, than the image of divine artistry. Arapesh art is imputed to be the materialization of the artist's own spirit. As such, it is readily transmissible, at least under appropriate ritual circumstances. The initiation event repeats on the ritual plane the creational significance of its prototype—the physico-spiritual act of procreation; hence, as will be seen in the next chapter, the prevalence of a corresponding primordial symbolism attending the Nggwal initiation, in terms of which man arrogates to himself mastery of the highest powers known or imagined.

Nor is Nggwal exempt from man's sovereignty. Just as the painting is vitalized by the artist's indwelling spirit, so it is also host to the spirit of the nggwal therein represented. Both spirits are manifested through their material expressions, without which their very existence is problematic. Moreover, their intermingling in the artistic mode reveals an important (but unspoken) truth about Arapesh religious ideology—namely, that the mystic relationship between man and Nggwal goes beyond mutual dependency and arrives at

---

in which I asked an Ilahita artist to verbalize his criticism of a mask from the Middle Sepik area. The piece—quite splendid, I thought—featured two through-cut crescents above and below each eye. My informant scoffed at the arrant idiocy of the artist: "Who ever heard of a man with five eyes on each side?" When I pointed out that one of his own masks showed *three* eyes on each side, he suddenly became bored with the conversation.

the deeper symbolic level of mutual identity.[9] Ultimately, however, it is man and not Nggwal who makes the art, conducts the rituals and tells the stories in which this identity is exercised. Whether or not the Arapesh, as participants in their own culture, are able to recognize it, the implication is clear enough to the observer: it is that the act of creation is indeed godlike; only it is *man* and not God who does the creating. Collective enterprises aside, the beliefs surrounding the manufacture and transmission of cult art provide the Arapesh individual with an occasion for religious expression that is personal, intimate, and superlatively ego-syntonic. As long as this condition persists, Nggwal's future is secure.

Assuming the validity of this analysis, how can it be reconciled with the fact that most men are unable to execute, let alone design, the art upon which so much depends? This is where the master artist comes in. From time to time during the rainy season, each master artist lets it be known among the men of his community that he will be available on a certain day to lend assistance to those interested in working on their paintings. On the appointed day, men bring blank pangal flats and meet in the ceremonial hamlet of their ward. Typically, such a gathering involves one or two master artists and perhaps a dozen or more laymen. Entering an enclosure where such work is in progress, one may see as many as ten paintings in various stages of completion. The studio has an air of quiet concentration, with occasionally someone getting up to stretch or to light his smoke. The men work mostly on their own paintings while the artist in charge continually moves among them, giving advice and in general facilitating their efforts. His role in large part consists of designing the figure and outlining it in charcoal, leaving to those of lesser skill the job of filling in large color areas. He also provides knowledge and a steady hand for the execution of tricky details. His payment is slight—a shilling or two, perhaps, or some meat the next time his client traps an animal; honor and prestige are the real recompense.

In sum, art is more than a pretty embellishment of prior

9. See the storyteller's exegesis following the story of Olafen above.

16. In quiet seclusion, some men work on their spirit paintings for the forthcoming Nggwal Bunafunei initiation.

and somehow more profound religious ideas; it is the material evidence that these ideas exist at all. The master artist is a creature of this requirement, performing as a kind of cultural or ideological "midwife." With his help the lay individual delivers an expressive form which unites the intimacies of his inner being with an idea that is ultimately coterminous with cultural selfhood. Moreover, by taking a hand in all the work produced under his guidance the master artist achieves a spiritual involvement above that of ordinary men and accordingly rife with political implications.

Between the collectivity signified by the spirit house and, at the opposite pole, the individual personified in the making and transmitting of religious objets d'art, the intervening symbolic space is, so to speak, spanned by the remarkably expressive manner in which the paintings are displayed. The completed spirit house is divided into an inner and an outer sanctum by an interior wall running along the longitudinal axis and intersecting the outer wall a meter or so below the line of the ridgepole. That is to say, the wall conceals a sizable chamber on the left (or Ondondof, "female") side of the interior, wherein the sacred flutes and drums are stored during the time Nggwal is actively resident in the village (chap. 7). The wall itself, as viewed from the outer sanctum, is a gallery composed of all the cult paintings, arranged so as to represent the entire descent structure of the village. Thus the painted panels are placed in columns reflecting the age hierarchy of living males of the patrilineal segment. Columns group themselves according to segmentary proximity and so on until every cult member and every autonomous descent group is represented on the mammoth chart. The technical problem is that the wall must not have any chinks, which means that the panels must first be hung as blanks. After they have been shuffled about and made to dovetail perfectly in the space to be filled, they are marked, taken down, painted and then remounted! The task is hideously complicated and time consuming, reminding us again of the value of the master artists' executive function during this period.

By its design the gallery wall elevates the symbolic office of these paintings to a higher level. Here, in a graphic rendition of the conceptual realm, the individual spirit is socially ennobled by virtue of its placement in a mosaic which orders while pictorializing the collective spirituality of the village. In the logic of the Tambaran, therefore, the men are quite correct when they proudly proclaim that Nggwal—the image par excellence of the village collectivity—dwells in his house. Had the scheme been designed by Durkheim himself, it could not have expressed better the mirror which religious ideology holds up to the social order.

Statuary. The mystic properties of graphic art apply similarly to the sculpted medium, only modified according to a symbolism directed immediately above the individual level. The parties to an initiation transaction are the respective (and always two) sub-clans comprising the patriclan associated with the nggwal in question. Individual partnerships, as we have seen, are operationalized through the sacred paintings;

statues, on the other hand, are passed between initiation partners qua sub-clans. The initiating sub-clan is the unit that commissions a master artist to carve an effigy of their nggwal, which is duly presented to their junior *ombif* in the opposite sub-clan. In category terms, then, statue is to painting as sub-clan is to individual member.

In a village as large as Ilahita, there may be sixty or more nggwal statues at a single initiation.[10] Each is a fully painted, polymorphous figure two to three meters in height. Compared with the bold, sometimes exaggerated, sculptedness of Middle Sepik figures, these statues reflect a timid, not entirely successful, attempt to adapt a two-dimensional form to a three-dimensional medium. The face, for example, has at most a low-relief nose as a sculpted feature, with eyes and mouth merely painted on a smoothly rounded surface. Similarly, there is a general definition of body and headdress parts, while details are rendered in paint. None the less, viewed in the half-light of the spirit house the tall, colorful figures amply achieve the desired effect of power and dignity.

Nggwals may be shown as either sex, though the decorative furnishings are invariably masculine. Females are so indicated with a simple slit for the vulva; on males the penis is pendulous, but with a prominent glans penis implying full or partial tumescence.

The sculptor applies his ingenuity to filling the unused wooden space around the figure's head and feet with birds and other animals. The most common device is to carve two birds of the same species (hornbill, cockatoo, parrot, etc.) above the nggwal's head, either facing each other or facing forward. Alternatively, depending on the natural curvatures of the log, the artist may decide to carve some kind of terrestrial creature above the nggwal's head—most commonly, a pig, wallaby, opossum, lizard or snake. As in the case of graphic designs, the choice is limited only by the artist's fancy

---

10. There are, however, considerably fewer clans. The reason for the discrepancy is that (1) a few sub-clan pairs share two cult spirits, and (2) some individuals consider themselves important enough to commission a statue in their own right. Both situations signal an incipient sub-clan segmentation. See text, below.

182 / THE VOICE OF THE TAMBARAN

and technical skill, rather than by any specifications of the nggwal being portrayed. Some of the species occur as totems in clan ideology (Tuzin 1976:347–349), but their role in this context is to signify Nggwal's benign oversight of the natural order. His fructifying influence was most explicitly revealed in one particularly handsome specimen, in which a mother pig was carved above the nggwal's head, looking down at her piglet, who was placed between the figure's legs—nursing from the penis. The interposition of Nggwal between mother and child as the ultimate nurturant source, the implied equation of semen and breast milk which arrogates to the masculine principle functions and prepotencies naturally associated with femininity—these are typical of the existential themes articulated by the Tambaran, which are expressed with greatest clarity in the art and ideology of Nggwal.

The singular abilities of the master artists are especially highlighted in the production of statuary. The carvers' studio is no place for amateurs, for mistakes would be too costly. The work is done in the nearby forest, handy to the wood source and secluded enough to prevent casual trespass and discovery by women and non-initiates. Also, placing it there rather than in the village obviates the necessity of having to dispose of massive quantities of wood chips and other debris, thereby inviting awkward questions. During leisure intervals throughout the rainy months the carvers, often accompanied by apprentice-helpers, retire to their secret quarters to work on the giant figures. When the sculpting is completed, a feast is called and all the cult members come to view the new carvings and congratulate the artists on their undeniable power.[11] Later the pieces are painted and their backs are hollowed out to reduce the weight to be transported (singly, on litters) to the village. In these tasks the rank-and-file are able to perform the necessary act of participation, this time as members of their sub-clan rather than as individuals.

11. Interestingly, this feast has the distinction of being the only occasion, other than desperate famine, on which the Arapesh eat dog meat. Dogs are normally loathed for their filthy eating habits, even though the dogs' right to eat feces was purchased in mythical times (chap. 4). Informants could not explain why an exception to the usual dietary aversion was made in this case.

In due course the statues are installed in the spirit house in a line along the right (Afa'afa'w, "male") side of the interior, facing the gallery wall. Another line of statues is laid at their feet in reclining position. While in the house, the effigies are thought to attract to themselves the full spirituality of the nggwal they represent. Some—the aesthetically more pleasing ones—are more powerful than others, but all are vitalized. Thus, if a man wishes to fortify magic designed for some purpose (gardening, hunting, war, love, etc.) he takes his bundle of cryptic materials to the spirit house, rubs it on the effigy of his nggwal, and beseeches the indwelling presence to aid his enterprise. As one informant put it, "Nggwal opens the road for all lesser magic." Whether physically embodied in these statues or invisibly immanent during the years intervening between initiations, Nggwal's presence makes the difference between efficacious magic and arrant hocus-pocus.

The house façade.   The spirit houses of the Abelam are undoubtedly one of the great cultural landmarks of New Guinea. Their dramatic proportions are vastly augmented by huge faces which dominate the painted façade, surveying their dominion with wide, staring eyes. The Arapesh counterpart has taken these imposing faces and reduced them to rows of small figures painted after the fashion described earlier. In some villages the rows climax at the apex of the triangular façade with a single nggwal painting—said to be, in some inexplicable way, the paramount Tambaran spirit of the village. In other places, Ilahita included, the rows continue upward to a line somewhat below the apex. The Ilahita house featured four rows, whose upwardly decreasing length was offset to some degree by the diminishing size of the figures.

Even the most knowledgeable informants were vague and inconsistent on the subject of what these rows of figures are all about. Some claimed that the figures in the lowest, most representational row were ancestor spirits; the next highest were nggwal spirits, after which came "more important" nggwal spirits, and so forth. Others maintained that they were *all* nggwal spirits, ranked according to relative impor-

17. Spirit-house façade, western Abelam. Comparing this with plates 18 and 21, note here the distinct treatment of spirit paintings and the use of faces rather than parent-child effigies on the crosspiece below.

18. The spirit house of Nggwal Walipeine, Ilahita village.

19. The Roman Catholic Church at Ariseli, in the Torricelli Mountains northwest of Ilahita. Inside, the Stations of the Cross are strikingly rendered in Tambaran motifs.

tance. The problem was that no agreement could be elicited as to which nggwals occupied a given row; each informant was inclined to regard *his* nggwal as among the more important ones.

The case is instructive in the following ways. First, it is quite likely that prior to my coming no one had ever asked these men to explicate the ranks in a systematic way. To the extent that a sense of spirit hierarchy exists, each man may freely believe that his nggwal is high in the ranking. Second, this interpretation is consistent with the fact that these nggwals are not individually identified, not even by the artists who paint them. Indeed, this is as it must be, for the façade paintings are in full view of women and non-initiates, who are categorically prohibited from "seeing Nggwal." What results is a doubt over whether these paintings, though identical to those inside the spirit house, represent nggwal spirits at all. Third, these issues aside, the clear consensus is that the figures ascend in some sort of hierarchy. The precedent for this perception is, of course, the interior gallery wall, in which those nggwals at the heads of the *columns* are identified with the oldest living members of the associated patrilineal segments. Explicitly, then, the ranks on the gallery wall correspond with generational or sub-generational differences

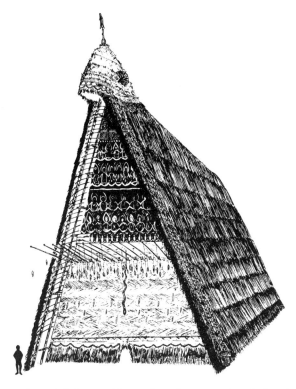

FIGURE 13. The spirit house. Front elevation, completed showing façade.

among the living. Likewise, the smallest, most simplified figures of the top rank of the façade show a predominance of white coloration in their headdresses—which, as we shall see when we come to Nggwal Walipeine, is strongly associated with old age.

Now, taking the interior as a clue to the exterior, it appears that the vertical, individuated emphasis of the former has been transposed into a horizontal, category emphasis in the latter; a concrete, highly specified ordering has been converted into a generalized ordering of existential planes. The apparent contradictions among informants' statements are thus resolved by a thoroughgoing concordance between: young/old, ancestor/nggwal, lesser nggwal/greater nggwal. The senior member of the synoptic set (old/nggwal/greater nggwal) verges on the summit of the peaked house, the abode of *kondo*, the abstract and summary idea of Nggwal.

In fine, it does not matter that the symbolism of this portion of the façade is neither understood nor agreed upon by the actors; whichever line of interpretation one takes, it leads ineluctably upward through an existential hierarchy culminating in Nggwal. This theme will be repeated often in the chapters to come. Its manifestation in this context is especially interesting for it dictates on grounds of structural "necessity" a conception that is not realized empirically—namely, the existence of (much less the relationship *between*) "lesser nggwals" and "greater nggwals." More precisely, the conception may be said to *exist*, but only in the special sense that it is an object of private conviction that one's own nggwal is "greater" in relation to other nggwals. Nor could such a conviction ever be tested publicly in a systematic comparison of nggwal statuses; for to do so would inflict intolerable stress on the egalitarian ideology that binds all men of Nggwal. From time to time, perhaps, one or another nggwal may rise to prominence, but in the end all must be accepted (publicly if not privately) as equal.[12]

---

12. In the next chapter I shall discuss the special historical priority of the nggwal Kamba'wa. However, insofar as Kamba'wa's arrival in Ilahita stimulated the other men to satisfy their envy by creating nggwals of their own, the case tends to confirm the present analysis.

The paintings I have been discussing occupy only the top half of the spirit-house façade. The lower portion is covered with a woven wall leaning inward to where its upper edge is dressed with a carved wooden crosspiece spanning the width of the façade. At ground-level center, a small portal leads into the house which must be traversed on hands and knees. At a height of about four meters a row of giant *kwongwof* (pl. *kwongwalef*) spears, decorated with cordyline homicide badges, protrudes ominously from inside the house. These belong to individual nggwals who, with the aid of an ingenious staging device, brandish them in concert during the initiation ceremony (chap. 7). When the spears are in place, Nggwal is said to be in residence. Above the spears the remaining wall space (measuring between one and two meters) is hung with carved snakes interspersed with wood carvings of giant shell rings, both of which are associated in other contexts with ancestral spirits.[13] Finally, we reach mid-height of the façade, demarcated by an impressive carved crosspiece. Each end is shaped and painted as a large adult figure lying on its side, one male and the other female. Stretching between them is a tightly spaced row of eighteen (in the case of Ilahita's spirit house) alternately sexed children. The explicit association is with the primordial Motherhood of Nambweapa'w.[14] Her wooden paramour, however, is not the feckless deceiver of the myth, but rather the culture-hero Baingap, protagonist of a different story, whose bestowal of staple foods is second in importance only to Nambweapa'w's gift of life itself.

The mid-height location of the crosspiece organizes the façade visually and conceptually in terms of the existential

13. See chap. 8 for more on the associations of *maulas* spirits. It should be noted that the only snakes they inhabit are pythons. The snakes on the façade are technically unspecified; however, I feel justified in presuming that they are (or could be) pythons since this is the only type of snake that figures in totemic and other areas of cult ideology.

14. To anyone critical enough to protest that Nambweapa'w had an *odd* number of children, I can only say that I (and my informants) agree. Perhaps it is a case of the Arapesh abhorrence of asymmetry winning out over mythical authenticity. On the other hand, the discrepancy may be a reminder of the special role of the youngest son—the odd man out—in the story. In all significant respects— historical, behavioral, temperamental, textual, indeed national!—he was never a member of his sibling group.

20. *Kwongwof* spears on the spirit-house façade, Ningalimbi.

hierarchy discussed earlier. Granting the uncertainties cloud-
ing an exact iconography of the upper portion, considered in
juxtaposition with the lower half its general significance is
clearly that of a superior sacred realm in harmony with an
inferior mundane world: above, the ethereal, unmoving purity of cult and ancestral spirits; below, the busy, textured
activities of men. And, what better intermediary than the
mythic, existentially ambiguous image of Nambweapa'w?

The problem with an absolute division is that the whole
point of Tambaran ideology is that creatures of the lower
part are imbued with meanings of the upper part. There is
evidence of spiritual "leakage" into the lower part, however,
in the special value assigned to otherwise mundane objects—
snakes and shell rings. The mystic quality of art is such that
the upper paintings are self-referential; they do not merely
represent Nggwal, they *are* Nggwal, they partake directly of
the same essence. By contrast, the objects below are doubly
remote from their symbolic referent. First, these effigies *rep-*

21. Nambweapa'w crosspiece on the spirit-house façade, Ningalimbi.

resent actual snakes and shell rings. For anyone to assert here
a relation of identity would be plainly psychotic, for who in
their right mind does not know the difference between the
object and a carving of the object? Not so with the sacred
paintings: since the spirit referent itself is a product of imagination, it is no more or less valid (or imaginative, or psychotic) to claim an identity between the painting and the spirit.
Second, and at a further symbolic remove, actual snakes and
shell rings are indeed prone to being *possessed by* ancestral
spirits; but in that event their outward appearance is unaffected, host and spirit remain conceptually independent, and
thus again the relationship is one of representation rather
than identity.

Similarly, the *kwongwof* spears, when they are jerking up
and down, are a sign of Nggwal's gigantic "physical" presence inside the spirit house. They are contiguous with him,
certifying the belief that on ritual occasions Nggwal assumes
material form and enters into the society of men. In his de-

scent through the mythic barrier and into the lower part of the house, Nggwal becomes, so to speak, manlike in appearance and temperament.

In sum, the configuration of icons on the spirit-house façade serves as a sign and reminder that the activities of men are ultimately meaningful only by reference to the timeless ideals of the Tambaran. The final irony is that these relata—men and the Tambaran—are, according to evidence already presented and yet to come, identical. The spirit exalted is none other than the spirit of man in a collective setting. The art, architecture and ritual of the Tambaran thus serve as a grand, unifying expression of the nature of man, his place in the social order, and the cultural meaning of his acts. Lest this statement be taken as contradictory of my earlier point that imported religious art is rendered meaningful by being filtered through a mythological medium, I would only aver that the positioning of, and necessity for, the Nambweapa'w crosspiece is intelligible as a defense of this thesis. Nor should it be thought that this places too great a symbolic burden on what is, after all, a single component in a complex façade. The focal role of the crosspiece obviates this objection; for it is Nambweapa'w who provides the key to the symbolism of the façade as a whole. The mediating office of Nambweapa'w is manifest again in a final detail added to the house just before the induction ceremony: on the left of the façade a rounded shape is fashioned from sago fibers (*maolihiwa*) and equipped with a carved and painted "bird's head." The object is called "Nambweapa'w" and is said to be an effigy of the Primal Mother *and*, at the same time, the left foot of Nggwal as it protrudes through the lower façade. Nggwal keeps his "male" right foot inside the house and uses it to crush the heads of novices as they crawl through the door.

As to the interior statues and gallery wall, these do indeed express aspects of individual and group identity in the absence of mythic intermediaries, to which extent they must be accepted as authentic symbolic forms in a purely artistic mode. And yet, however important their expressive functions may be in some respects, what is missing is an *organic*

22. Representation of "Nambweap'w," also referred to as the "left foot of Nggwal" as it protrudes from the spirit-house façade.

integration leading to ultimate meaning, such as that conferred by Nambweapa'w on the façade. To understand the *general* significance of the spirit-house interior, we must turn to the contents and significances of the inner sanctum; when we do (chap. 7) the characterizations encountered will again rely on mythic rather than artistic images.

To complete this section I should note that the façade is erected when all or most of the statues and paintings are ready to be placed inside the house. The hamlet is sealed off, and in a few days of intense effort supervised by the master artists the work is done. The climax of this phase occurs when the *kwongwof* spears are ceremonially mounted on the façade. The important part of this event, which has been described elsewhere (Tuzin 1976:280–285), is that the older age-set (Balangaisi) of the Sahopwas initiators is in effect promoted (along with a few selected Owangufwisi, thereafter called Umbaisi) to a ritual position approaching that of its senior initiation partners.[15] In the light of the symbolism discussed earlier, it is significant that the separation of age-sets is marked by a mock attack staged on the Owangufwisi by the Balangaisi who are armed with the *kwongwalef*! The implication is that the latter are asserting a closer (and now categorically distinct) identification with Nggwal in comparison with their subordinate younger brothers. After the assault the Owangufwisi install the spears, and the feast begins.[16] With Nggwal in his house all that remains between now and the initiation is the yam harvest.

THE MASTER ARTIST

Throughout most of traditional New Guinea, leaders are proverbially measured by diffuse qualities of character and personality. Prestige by ascription is extremely rare. The social and political role of the Arapesh master artist[17] is therefore ethnographically striking, in that it amounts to an occupational category whose members routinely exercise *generalized* authority in the community. This situation reflects all that we have been saying about the special place which art holds in religious life and ideology, as well as the executive stature of the artists stemming from the long production periods during which the community depends upon them for instruction and guidance. If, as is commonly assumed (Geertz 1973), sacred symbols hypostasize the central values of a culture, then one implication of this might be that those empowered to create and manipulate these symbols are in a sense larger than life. And it is the ardent study of politicians the world over to appear "larger than life," for such reputation affords those opportunities and immunities in respect of convention which leaders require to mold public opinion.

15. This is in preparation for a more complete assimilation occurring in the context of Nggwal Walipeine (chap. 8).
16. The techniques for piercing the woven front wall and rigging the spears on the inside are secrets revealed at this time by the Owapwas Seniors, in respect of which the Sahopwas provide the feast.
17. Most of the material comprising the remainder of this chapter appeared as part of a published symposium devoted to the subject of Sepik politics (Tuzin 1978a).

In what remains of this chapter the object is to interrelate action and expression in the cult by examining further the focal role of the master artist. This is the context in which art has made singular inroads into the heart of Arapesh life. Mythology may have expressive strengths of its own, but art vastly excels it in political significance by virtue of its lively association with social *action*. The religious involvement of Arapesh art confers on the genre a sacredness of which the artist (qua politician) partakes. The role of the artist becomes tinged with a priestly aura, and the sociology of art in this culture develops largely as a study in practical politics. In a world where power over symbols is interwoven with power over men, symbol-mongers and power-mongers are one and the same. Moreover, the importation of religious art on a grand scale has qualitatively altered Arapesh political culture by creating a new context of collective action along with a new avenue in which talented individuals may pursue greatness in their society.

Let me begin by entering caveats to some of the points just made.

First, in implying that the status of master artist is "ascribed," I do not mean that there is no achievement involved in becoming an artistic pundit; rather, that the status, once achieved, has ascribed to it various prerogatives ranging far beyond artistic matters per se. This raises the question of how individuals are recruited to this status, to which some attention ought to be paid.

I noted earlier that a promising young man is apprenticed to an older kinsman-artist. In principle, the teacher may be one of a number of relatives: a man of Ego's personal kindred, one who has married into this group, or a man of the group into which Ego himself has married. The only practical constraint is that Ego and his teacher, for the sake of convenience, ought to reside in the same ward. And, given the high rates of ward endogamy (Tuzin 1976:93), it is possible for Ego in most cases to trace—by whatever remote links—a consanguineal or affinal relationship with nearly every male living in his ward. The important point is that the kinship tie is invoked as the justification for the master-apprentice arrangement.

Obversely, a master artist commonly has only one apprentice in his lifetime, who becomes thereby heir to these special skills and magical procedures. One might suppose that in this strongly patrilineal society the artist's own son would be the obvious successor. But lineal succession is not possible since the son is a generation behind his father in *ritual* terms; while the artist-father is still alive and active, the son would be ritually too junior to see (let alone work on) the paraphernalia that are the objects in question.[18] The resulting discretionary element in recruitment ensures that men with proper talent and motivation have the opportunity to advance themselves to this status. Also, it gives the master artist flexibility in choosing a protégé who will be of maximum use to him politically in the years to come.

The second caveat is that artistic excellence is not the only path to political prominence. There are "big-men" whose reputations are founded on rhetorical ability, bombast and wittiness as social entrepreneurs. And although Ilahita big-men are pale versions of their Highlands counterparts, it is true that no complete political study can ignore them. On the other hand, it is also true that a disproportionate number of big-men are, in fact, master artists—a coincidence which, I suggest, is no *mere* coincidence. Authority is further distributed to men who officiate in specific aspects of the cult, primarily as keepers of certain paraphernalia. These incumbents, however, are named according to clan and initiation-class affiliation. More heraldic than executive, their hereditary privileges do not reach beyond their limited functions and constituencies. Successful hunting and gardening magicians may exercise somewhat broader authority, but they are likewise recruited from within the descent structure. Apart from the master artists, the only occupation tran-

---

18. The only exception—and it is an important one—occurs when an Umbaisi ritual promotee (Tuzin 1976:242) comes within range of his father's artistic talents. Indeed, this possibility casts a new light on the basis of selection for Umbaisi promotion, inasmuch as a disproportionate number of those chosen turn out to be sons of artists.

scending descent and ritual categories is that of healer-sorcerers.[19] Now, as it happens, all but a few of the master artists are also renowned sorcerers, and they are *all* respected healers. This is not surprising, since the mystic powers of artistic creation, as perceived in this society, are not dissimilar from those which magically confer life and death. But this coincidence aside, the sorcerer-healer in his role is a solitary worker, inconspicuous in the political sphere; his skills inspire fear, admiration, or personal indebtedness, not followings. The only exception is when these adepts perform collectively as war sorcerers, but here again their authority remains circumscribed.

Against these other functionaries the master artists rise above specific structures and situations and perform tasks of administration which are larger and more finely coordinated than any others in the society.[20] To this they apply themselves with all the domineering impatience of true maestros. In short, art may not be the only political career, but it aspires to a level of importance superior to that of any available alternative.

It could be argued that men of such driving ambition would have become leaders *anyway*, that the fact of their being artists is a secondary cause of their fame. This is undoubtedly true. But I would offer that in this culture such men are attracted to art precisely because it provides what no other pursuit can to quite the same degree: the opportunity to play among—manipulate, exploit, indeed *create*—the images and ideas upon which community well-being is thought to depend. Achieving mastery over this realm requires a comparable mastery over oneself. The rigors to which the artist ambitiously submits himself—sexual and

19. I am speaking here of the more advanced sorts of lethal sorcery, such as *maolihiwa* (chap. 4). The techniques are taught by established practitioners to men who have mastered the mystic arts of healing and who desire to extend their proven powers into the more dangerous and demanding field of sorcery.

20. It is possible that in former times secular war leaders were recruited at large in the community. My data are deficient on this point, but it is fairly certain that war leaders did not automatically accede to *generalized* authority in the village and were, on the contrary, regarded ambivalently on account of their violent characters.

dietary avoidances and other purifying regimes which, as one artist put it, enhance and focus his personal "power"— ostensibly ensure that his hand will be steady and the design exact. But in the process he also attains that complete confidence in himself which is the primary character trait of a New Guinea leader. His evidence is the work of art he produces and the magical potency it is presumed to contain, by virtue of which it is also judged to be aesthetically pleasing.

Finally, it should be remembered that, for reasons already reviewed, *all* men must participate in the manufacture of religious art, even though few deserve to be called artists. Accordingly, the artist's audience is very well situated to appreciate his special talent, since each is periodically reminded of his own relative inadequacy in this regard.

Normally, when we speak of "art symbolism," we have in mind the semantic element: what the figure explicitly represents or unconsciously expresses. Most of this chapter has been spent detailing the meaning of Arapesh art in these terms. Having become established as an independent mode of expression, art (with its custodians) has the power to react upon the very structures and activities from which it is ultimately derived. Herein lies the connection with politics and social process.

To illustrate: it is customary for a village planning a Nggwal initiation to send out solicitation gifts of pork to nearby villages, inviting them to contribute (give or lend) statues and paintings of their own to the forthcoming ceremony. This adds to the magnificence of the occasion; it also provides an excuse for interaction, an opportunity to air and resolve differences, reaffirm alliances and so forth. It is, incidentally, the prime mechanism for the diffusion of art styles and ritual details across potentially large areas. Although master artists may not be among those actually sponsoring a given invitation, they usually figure prominently in the ensuing discussions, since the focus tends initially to be on the art pieces themselves. And as the presence of art more or less defines the occasion, artists often emerge as masters of protocol as well. When, for instance, Ilahita received a statue it had solicited from a distant Abelam village, everything seemed to be going smoothly.[21] The foreigners had arrived the previous evening in a hamlet on the outskirts of the main village, announcing their presence with a cult song. Middle-aged Dongwande had previously been nominated to receive the statue on behalf of Ilahita, and so, on the following morning, he supervised a large official reception in the ceremonial hamlet of Nggwal. At the entrance to the hamlet he placed a large wild taro leaf (*bondaf*), covering its base partially with grass (*walal*). Then he himself lay down in a supine position across the path, so that the entering foreigners would step over him before coming to the *bondaf-walal* arrangement.

All this proceeded according to plan. The last visitor had entered the hamlet; the statue had been placed for viewing. At this point Kwamwi, a master artist and senior *ombaf* of Dongwande, entered the scene. Departing from his usual easygoing manner, Kwamwi began vigorously berating the Ilahitans, Dongwande in particular. A *bondaf* leaf is to be used, he said, only if the hosts have a pig ready to be given in exchange for the statue. As no pig was immediately available, the Ilahitans were making fools of themselves by the inappropriate way they were handling this reception. Dongwande sat quietly, his eyes narrowed and lips drawn tight. The other Ilahitans gave signs of being embarrassed at the show of their ineptitude, while the visitors tried awkwardly to pacify Kwamwi by saying there would always be time,

---

21. In traditional times, donations of this sort could only have come from Ilahita's immediate neighbors. Pax Australiana has all but obliterated the barriers of xenophobia and warfare that previously restricted spheres of interaction. In the case being described the deal was made between one of Ilahita's elected councillors and an Abelam councillor with whom he served.

Interestingly, it is my impression that the post-contact situation has diminished rather than enhanced the rate of artistic diffusion. Ilahita leaders consider objects imported from distant points to be more glamorous and exciting than those originating closer to home. In addition, to have such pieces testifies to the fame of one's village throughout the land. But by the same token these objects differ so radically from the indigenous art that local artists are neither able nor inclined to imitate them. They are treated as curiosities having little relevance to what is important or meaningful. In the present example the Abelam statue was rather abstract, and beyond showing the visitors the courtesy of admiring it, it was clear that the Ilahita artists could not make sense of the piece. Eventually, it ended up relatively unnoticed in a dark corner of the spirit house.

The point of the example is that diffusion succeeds best when the addition it makes to preexisting forms is incremental.

later, for a pig. After some further angry exchanges among the Ilahitans, the leader of the Abelam party proposed that some yams, tobacco and betelnut would serve adequately as payment for the statue. Kwamwi grudgingly acquiesced, but not before he had advised his fellow villagers to consult him on all future occasions, lest they shame themselves once again.

In another case, several of the Ilahita carvers had prepared a number of statues for presentation to Ningalimbi, Ilahita's closest neighbor and staunchest ally, on the eve of a Nggwal initiation ceremony. Disagreement arose as to whether the statues should be carried from the carving site back to the main village for painting and decorating or to Numbafuta, a colonial outlier located midway between Ilahita and Ningalimbi. Proponents of the latter alternative pointed out the considerable extra effort entailed in carrying them back to Ilahita, inasmuch as they now lay at a spot quite close to Numbafuta. The opposition, led by three master artists, contended that the few men who knew the secret of decorating the statues lived in the main village. For teaching purposes, it would be far more convenient to have the pieces transported there.

At first glance, this does not seem to be an issue worth arguing about. However, owing to the general spiritual and ritual significance attached to these art works, it matters a great deal where they are stored, even temporarily. Numbafuta spokesmen were, in effect, challenging the ritual priority of the main village in arguing that, "for the sake of convenience," the statues should be delivered to their place. In the end the will of the master artists, all of whom resided in the main village, prevailed; a constitutional crisis of sorts had been averted.

It goes without saying that the factors associated with art and the artist's status are, in the above cases, only two strands in a complicated political skein. In emphasizing them, my point is that the religious significance of art, the prominence of religion in collective life and the administrative role of the artist in these mass endeavors provide the artist with an authority base that is readily generalized. Two further political implications arise from this. The obvious one is that a master artist, disgruntled over the drift of public policy in some matter, can impose his will by threatening to withhold support for an upcoming ceremony, thereby blocking the intentions of a great many people. It is not a threat to be made or taken lightly, and the artist who applies it without good reason is squandering his political capital. Nevertheless, the possibility does exist and on several occasions was seen to affect the mechanics of decision making. The rare case is when the artist takes his reputation and popularity in hand and stands alone against public opinion, risking the serious displeasure of the wider community and also of his own following of kinsmen, neighbors and friends who depend upon him to provide artistic direction. More commonly the context is factionalism: the following connive in or indeed instigate the artist's bravado by way of expressing their collective threat of boycotting a forthcoming ceremony. In both cases, but especially the second, the majority party is motivated to seek accommodation because of the maxim that the magic underlying these ceremonies cannot work if there is any ill will present in the community (chap. 5).

The other implication concerns the master artist as symbol-monger in relation to social process. Although artists usually regard each other with friendly colleaguality, it is also true that their circle comprises an elite political arena. The more or less latent competition erupts when they find themselves champions of opposed factions and also when the legitimacy of a new art motif is under discussion, even though it may be a minute new element or a minimal rearrangement of familiar patterns. In the light of all that has been said, it should come as no surprise that the most important critics an artist faces are his fellow artists. Applying conservative standards, they are the ones who judge whether a created or introduced form is aesthetically *acceptable*. But there is much more to it than mere artistry, for what is at stake is orthodoxy of a higher order. The religious significance of art implies that the creation of a new motif (or the rearranging of patterns in a new way) is tantamount to the creation of a new spirit entity. The occasion for this is invariably the assertion of sociopolitical autonomy by the individual or group commissioning the piece. Little wonder that critical taste tends to be conservative. For the creation of a new form—a new name, a new spirit—is potentially the creation of a new group and the dissolution of a former social bond. By the time this stage is reached, political relations within the group have deteriorated to such an extent that its members can no longer work together. Through the idiom of art[22] the dissident element (usually the genealogically inferior members of the sub-clan) seeks public approval or acquiescence in the bid for mystical autonomy. Failure means that the malcontents must either abandon their efforts or, as a theoretical but practically impossible alternative, pursue their fortunes outside the village. Their success, on the other hand, symbolized by the critical consent of the master artists, implies that members of the community are resigned to the inevitability of the split and have reordered political and ritual relations in anticipation of this eventuality. At the moment of consummation the artist presides over and gives expression to the process of social segmentation, and the new status quo is duly enshrined on the gallery wall.

OBJECTS AND IDEAS: SOME FINAL REMARKS

This chapter and the one preceding it are a background to the next grade of the Tambaran Cult, Nggwal Bunafunei. If at times the discussion strayed beyond what seems strictly

22. I emphasize the *idiom* of art rather than the art itself. In most cases, if the degree of artistic innovation (objectively speaking) were taken as a measure of the social event signified, it would be difficult indeed to reconcile the subtlety (perhaps even nonexistence) of the former with the importance of the latter. What matters is that the artist ordains that the painting or statue *is* the new nggwal; therefore, as a matter of subjective fact, the piece must also be "new."

Of course, events such as clan or sub-clan segmentation are exceedingly rare, whereas artistic experimentation is relatively constant and usually entails minor alterations that go unnoticed. My point is, first, that major artistic deviations are by definition important political gestures, since they are incompatible with any preexisting spirit figures; and, second, that if a social or political crisis happens to be brewing, then even the most minute deviation is liable to be seized upon as

necessary for this purpose, I hope it is clear by now that a comprehensive anthropology of the cult must include its material, as well as its performative, intellectual, and sociological aspects. My approach has been to identify a ritual "thing" not by the ceremonial dressing it may have, but by its expressive role vis-à-vis deeply held social and cultural ideals. In this sense, I have been speaking of Tambaran "ritual" all along.[23] Even a task so humble and unpoetic as digging a posthole can become, by the act of signification, a ritual figure embodying cultural meanings which are neither humble nor unpoetical. Indeed, the Tambaran seemingly delights in seeking out mundane objects and activities and insinuating itself into them, steadily enriching itself by converting the base metal of everyday life into the gold of cultural value. In theory, the process is bounded only by the limits of Arapesh imagination; in practice, there is probably a point of saturation beyond which an ideologic insistence on meaningfulness becomes morbidly and dysfunctionally obsessional. Also, the process is reversible, and herein lies an important difference between cultural and biological evolution. Under various circumstances, usually involving the advent of competing needs and symbols, the gold may revert, and digging a posthole may return to being just that.

This raises the crucial matter of how we are to judge the relationship between ideas and actions, about which much more will be said in the following chapters. The preceding paragraph adopted the Arapesh perspective by treating the Tambaran as a sentient, purposive being, one who stands apart from human life and yet presides over it. No tolerance here for the suggestion that the Tambaran is a figment of individual and cultural imagination, its power no more real than the reality ascribed to it. This is as it must be, since objects of religious belief could not last long if the actors perceived them to be contingent on human thought and ac-

---

indicative of this state of affairs. In either case art is potentially a dialect of the language of politics.

23. This approach to ritual is close to the one indicated by Edmund Leach in *Political Systems of Highland Burma* (1954:15).

tion.[24] While it is true that the Tambaran provides structured idioms and occasions for the activities we are discussing, it is also true that without these regular reaffirmations at the level of praxis the idea of the Tambaran could no longer exist, nor could it maintain relevance to the ever changing state of human affairs.

And yet, the ascribed spirituality of art comes close to openly exposing man's creational role in the religious sphere, tempting us to ask: What would become of the Tambaran in the event that its contingent nature were perceived? What happens to religious truth when it is acknowledged to reside in human illusion? As we shall hear, this is a matter about which Nggwal has much to say.

24. When Robert I. Levy (personal communication) asked his Tahitian informants about the seeming absence of previously reported shark gods, they replied that they were no longer around because everyone had stopped believing in them. The subversiveness of this reasoning lies in the ease with which it could be applied to the islanders' currently held Christian beliefs. For the same reason, doctrinal reform within a religious tradition is a very risky business, for it has the potential of undermining the validity of belief itself.

7. Nggwal Bunafunei: The Ritual Climax

KAMBA'WA

Once a woman went down to do some work near the stream, taking her son and some of his young playmates along. While she worked, the boys gamboled about along the stream bank. One of them—the woman's son—took a length of bamboo and put the base of it into the water. When he sang into the other end a great sound arose, startling both himself and the other boys. For, unbeknown to him, he had put the bamboo into a hollow log that lay submerged and hidden under the water. The mother called out in alarm, asking the boys what had caused the sound; but they replied that it was nothing. The boys tried making the sound again, and this time they were pleased with it. But again they lied to the mother when she asked about it. The boys wanted to keep it as a secret for themselves.

That afternoon the boys told the woman to go back to the village; they would follow her there soon afterward. They pulled the log out of the stream —it was actually a large fragment of buttress root—and dragged it into the forest near the village. There, they made a small, rude house in which to hide the bamboo and wood.

Then the boys made a small net and with it trapped a small lizard, which they gave to Nggwal when he sang out, "Bring it to me!" They placed the net again, but this time a large cassowary came and jumped over it. The boys built a bigger net, but again the cassowary jumped over it. Then they made a very big net and succeeded in trapping and killing the cassowary. But they suddenly feared that they had killed a masalai who only looked like a cassowary, and so they fled from the carcass in great terror.

That night the cassowary appeared to them in their dreams, saying she was not a masalai but a woman—Nambweapa'w. They should return and eat her, and in this way the power of her flesh would make them outstanding yam growers and love-magicians. The next day they returned to the forest site and, while Nggwal sang out, ate the cassowary.

The father of the boy who first discovered Nggwal heard the voice of the tambaran and went to the forest house to investigate. Nggwal sang out as he approached, and the man shrank back in fear. Then his son came out of the house, reassured him, and invited him to come inside and see what was there. Eventually all the men found out about this secret. They resolved that the boys' voices were too weak and puny to do justice to Nggwal, and so they devised a plan for killing them all through sorcery. After the boys were dead the men took over Nggwal, built a fine large house for him, and organized themselves into initiation groups. The name of this nggwal was Kamba'wa.

Kataomo I

Long ago it was our custom that initiation partners should give each other their children to eat. In those days they did not exchange pigs, just children. One man had eaten the children of his partner and he was preparing to send his own children in return, but they ran away. They ran until they found a cave in the mountains; their parents, try as they might, could not find them. The parents finally decided that someone else must have caught the children and eaten them.

The children stayed in the cave and saw a pig and a python nearby. These they took back to the cave with them, being careful to draw up their ladder after them.

Meanwhile, their father's partner was becoming very cross at not having received the children. "I gave you my children and you ate them. You promised to return your own, but you lied. Now I have nothing to eat but shit. Before, you cried and cried to eat my two children, and I gave them to you. Now I am hungry."

The children lived hidden in the cave with the pig and the python for a long time. Finally the pig gave birth to three offspring, one male and two females. Afterward the children killed the mother and ate her. The legs of the pig went to the girl child, but the remainder was eaten by the boy child, who was becoming the Tambaran. It was really the Tambaran that was eating the pig.

One day everyone in the village went to the forest, leaving behind only the mother of these children. The boy went to her with some meat. The mother started to cry out, but the boy silenced her, saying that if anyone caught him there he would be killed. He gave her a piece of pork and a piece of snake meat and the woman asked, "What are these things you are giving me?" The son replied, "Never mind, just eat them. When your husband my father returns, tell him to go down near the stream and to rattle his limestick as he comes. When he hears a noise come out of the mountain he must not be afraid. He must stand and listen to it, and only when the sound is finished may he return to the village."

When the woman's husband returned she suggested to him that they cook some greens. When they were cooked she took him to look inside the basket lying there. When the man saw the meat, he asked her what it was and who had brought it, but she would not tell him. So they cooked the meat and ate it along with the greens. When they had finished eating, the woman told her husband that he must go down to the stream and listen to the sound from the mountain. The husband did so, rattling his limestick as he went. As he stood there he heard the sound come from the mountain. It was the voice of the tambaran, and the man was very frightened. He wanted to run away, but he remembered the words of his wife and so stayed until the sound ceased. Then he returned to the village. Sitting down with his wife he remarked, "That's all. That was our children; we have found them." Then his wife told him that they had been hiding in the cave and that they still had three pigs in their possession.

Later the son returned to his parents and told his father to come to the stream the following day. The father did so, and when they met there his son told him, "All right, now you must gather all the men and prepare decorations. One group will make the decorations while the other supplies the food. When everything is ready the tambaran will come to you."

The father carried out these instructions, and when all was prepared he and the other men killed a pig and a snake. The animals were cut in half lengthwise and then cooked. The two halves of meat were put on the platters of the respective initiation classes. Then the tambaran came among them, sat with them, and ate the meat. The name of the tambaran was Kataomo.[1]

⌐⌐⌐⌐⌐⌐⌐⌐⌐⌐⌐⌐⌐⌐⌐⌐⌐⌐⌐⌐⌐⌐⌐⌐⌐

E ARLY in this volume it was suggested that the Tambaran is a cultural concept so varied in its meaning that simple definition is not possible in the usual sense. "Nggwal" is only slightly less troublesome in this respect, which would account for some of the minor obscurities and inconsistencies that the reader may already have noticed. For

1. See Appendix B for an alternative rendition of this myth, along with a brief analysis indicating that an enriched understanding of "Kataomo" can be obtained by thematically "overlaying" one version on the other.

a start, Nggwal is such a paramount figure in the men's cult that one often hears him elevated above his specific grade and made to be synonymous with the Tambaran himself—perpetrating thereby the same order of semantic mischief.

On the other hand synonymy, so to speak, cuts both ways, and the advantage gained by studying Nggwal is that it transmogrifies the abstract concept into a form that is implicated more directly in human action and fantasy. The same, it is true, may be said of the lesser grades-*cum*-spirits, each being a manifestation of the Tambaran. But Nggwal far surpasses these in the extent to which it is identified as *the* Tambaran— a perception which, I suspect, is largely facilitated by the fact that it is more thoroughly and elaborately personified. In brief, Nggwal has three major aspects: a theistic immanent Ideal by which morality is reckoned and human conduct judged; a gargantuan pseudo-incarnation with ferocious habits and a voracious appetite for pork, yams and people, but who also acts as tutelary spirit and champion in all *village* endeavors (especially war and ritual); and, finally, the assembly of these giant spirits, each of which is identified with a particular patriclan of the village, with its own name and set of paraphernalia. All three are Nggwal,[2] each is ideational. But the images in which the ideas are cast occupy a descending order of abstractness—until, at the lowest level of clan spirits, the idea is embodied in, and practically coterminous with, a statue, painting, drum or other physical object. To reduce the chance of ambiguity, I use the lower case ("nggwal") in referring to the individual clan spirits. On balance, the strongly masculine overtones of the personified forms recommend the use of "he"—the pronoun used by the Arapesh themselves when referring to Nggwal.[3]

For reasons that will become obvious, it is necessary to preface my account of Nggwal initiation by describing the

---

2. That is to say, they are *collectively* Nggwal, just as they are individually so. This may seem paradoxical, but the problem dissolves when the unified *ideational* class is conceived separately from the differentiated *imagistic* class.

3. It should be understood, however, that both their usage and mine tends to obscure subtle but important feminine elements possessed by the figure.

cultural and historical factors that lend to this tambaran its exceptional character.

EXTERNAL ORIGINS

Considering the gravity of Nggwal in Arapesh religious culture, it is startling to discover that the concept and its rich ceremonial trappings are importations dating from the not-too-distant past—albeit somewhat naturalized to the Arapesh cultural setting.[4] During the last century groups from the Middle Sepik region, the Kwanga and the Abelam, moved aggressively into the area and, among other things, stimulated the formation of large, defensible villages such as Ilahita. The social and ritual organization that evolved in tandem with settlement expansion drew heavily on elements present within the culture of the invaders (Tuzin 1976:320). Though Arapesh myths tell of Nggwal's local origins (see above), all independent evidence points to his having been adopted under circumstances of culture contact. As we have already glimpsed in the logistics of spirit-house construction, Nggwal is symbolically and organizationally predicated on a dense, stable and reasonably large settlement situation, whereas nothing in the conduct of the first three grades precludes a dispersed population of actors, coming together at intervals to cooperate in various ceremonies. Moreover, the Arapesh themselves, in seeming contradiction of their own mythology, fully recognize that Nggwal is a relatively "new" tambaran compared with the preceding three grades, which are reputedly very ancient. Nggwal's remarkably un-Arapesh character, most notably his taste for human sacrifice, is further evidence that this tambaran was superimposed on a pre-existing tri-layered initiation system. The fact is, however, the Arapesh with whom I discussed the matter were not especially interested in where Nggwal came from or how he got there. What matters to them is that Nggwal now holds a

4. One of the most interesting mechanisms serving this naturalization process involves transliterating foreign symbolic themes into the Arapesh mythic genre. See Appendix B for a discussion relevant to this topic.

central position in the life of their society; he is their own as if he had never been otherwise. And yet, to the anthropological observer the historical aspect remains interesting, for it is a lesson in the rapidity with which—given the proper set of circumstances—a symbolic system can be authentically incorporated by a culture.

To return to Nggwal: the best evidence for external origins comes from the fact that both Kwanga and Abelam apply the term to the highest grade of their own cults; and, at least among the latter, "*nggwalndu*" have also been characterized as "clan spirits" which are ultimately responsible for pigs and long yams (Forge 1966 : 28–29).[5] Either could have given Nggwal to the Arapesh, but local history favors Kwanga as the immediate source.[6] This aside, it is plain that the Abelam/ Kwanga Nggwal has an Iatmul cousin—a cognate which has explicitly ancestral significance. Thus, *nggwail* refers to "father's father, father's father's sister, son's son, son's daughter. This term is also applied [in Iatmul] to the totemic ancestors of a clan" (Bateson 1936 : 310).[7] Among the other societies named, including the Arapesh, the relationship between Nggwal and the ancestors is conceived to be intimate but shadowy, and I never found an informant who would agree that they are one and the same entity. How, then, is Nggwal perceived?

ATTRIBUTES

The myths placed at the start of this chapter agree that Nggwal's nature—at least as epitomized by the individual spirits Kataomo and Kamba'wa—is that of a supernaturally transformed and elevated humanity. In one story, the powerless boy becomes an all-powerful culture hero who is the

---

5. Richard Scaglion informs me (personal communication) that, at least among the Western Abelam, "Nggwalndu" is a generic term referring to the two highest grades (*lu* and *puti*, respectively) in a four-tiered hierarchy.

6. In Ilahita the term does not possess a plural form, suggesting that the language has not yet assimilated it. Similarly, to my ear the word *sounds* typically Abelam/ Kwanga and seems ill fitted to Arapesh speech.

7. In light of what was said at the start of this chapter, note that this kin term abolishes the sex distinction in favor of generation and agnation.

nggwal Kataomo; in the other, the metaphor is located in the *voice* of mortals, which becomes supernaturally enlarged with the aid of the mysterious sound-making device. As part of the same series, we may recall the story of Olafen, in which an artist exalted and personified his own spirit in the act of carving an effigy, creating thereby a figure with knowledge and powers far greater than his own. Likewise, on several occasions I was told, without further explanation, that Nggwal was originally a ghost—of whom, my advisers neither knew nor cared.[8] In all cases man is in some sense, intentionally or otherwise, the creator.

But, as the god of the Hebrews is reported to have observed (Gen. 6:5-6), and any parent can affirm, creations of this sort have a tendency to get out of hand—or at least acquire a degree of autonomy and willfulness which can inflict problems on the relationship. This comes close to describing one aspect of the attitude of cult members toward Nggwal. They know the secret myths, they know that Nggwal depends on them for food and shelter. Metaphors conjure forth an infantile image; a vast baby crying piteously to be fed, its tears the untimely rains that spoil hunting and gardening activities. On the other hand, this is no ordinary toddler. His monumental power and monumental dependency evoke worrisome prospects of what he may do if his needs are not smartly and amply met. And even if they are, this is no guarantee that a moment's whimsy will not move Nggwal to deliver death or discomfiture on those who support and care for him.

Feeding Nggwal not only forstalls his wrath; more positively, it induces him to dispense fertility and general well-being (including war success) to his human clients. Indeed, Nggwal presides over the welfare of all species, especially ensuring the reproductive prosperity of his favorite food—pig. Many assert that without Nggwal's imprimatur garden magic would

8. Lest this appear to contradict my earlier claim that the Arapesh deny ancestral significance to Nggwal, let me note that an unidentified ghost cannot be an "ancestor." Also, there is in this culture a clear and important distinction between ghosts—the dangerous and capricious newly dead—and ancestors, who are more remote in time and whose influence on the living is mostly benign. For more on the subject of Arapesh ghosts and ancestors see Tuzin (1975, 1977).

be ineffectual.[9] In other words, whatever man's creative and care-giving role was and is, the dependency relationship is now largely mutual. In this capacity, Nggwal is portrayed as an adult figure—of superhuman proportions, it is true, but agreeable to sitting among men and sharing with them his songs and feasts. Toward the uninitiated, on the contrary, especially women and children, Nggwal's manner is implacably hostile: he either shuns them entirely or preys upon them as a cannibal ogre.

Men who have "seen" Nggwal know of course that these characterizations are metaphors—imagistic devices for dissimulating Nggwal's nature to the uninitiated and, more fundamentally, for expressing to themselves an actual relationship of quite different order. The "real" Nggwal possesses the attributes mentioned, but—something the women are reckoned incapable of understanding—he is invisible. At feasts he eats the invisible essence of the food; when he "devours" his human victims, he either does so through a human agent—a sorcerer or *laf* executioner—or by striking directly, in which case the physical body displays no outward sign of having been "eaten." The more senior and sophisticated initiates, however, privately betray a distinct cynicism over the status of these so-called metaphors. More than once it was intimated to me that, just as the fiction of a *physical* Nggwal enables men to dominate women, so the fiction of an *invisible* Nggwal enables the senior initiates to dominate their junior colleagues. The lie is itself a lie. On first hearing this, alarmed at seeing the object of my study dissolve before my eyes, I asked what, then, was the *truth* about Nggwal?, to which my

9. Nggwal's relation to horticulture is somewhat ambiguous. His clients claim that he (i.e., *they*) must be given the first fruits of the yam harvest, suggesting that Nggwal is in some sense being credited for the garden produce. And yet, Nggwal's residence in the village is intermittent, and during the long periods when he is incommunicado the garden magicians would not have the benefit of his support. Also, as one man expressed it, yams and other garden products arise from the hand of man, and accordingly it is more appropriate to beseech the ancestors for help in this sphere. "But what control have we over the creatures of the forest? This is where Nggwal helps us." By the same token, without pig meat Nggwal would not have the strength to "come up"—which is to say, the men would supposedly be too weak to undertake the great works associated with Nggwal ceremonialism. If some readers wish to make of this a structuralist recognition of the Nature/Culture dichotomy, I have no objection.

informant replied, with study-saving insight, "Nggwal is what men do."

This statement is epistemologically provocative, for it hints that the system of signs governing this important segment of Arapesh belief and experience is thus cognized by one and probably many more of the actors. It is tantamount to admitting the contingency of one's own belief—by implication undercutting the foundation of belief itself, and in the end producing a theory of existence which renders cultural meaning all but impossible (cf. chap. 6, n. 24). The Arapesh appear to have resolved (if that is the word for it) this dilemma in a manner *resembling* the radical atheism of certain branches of existentialist philosophy: the import of the informant's assertion would seem to be that belief in self replaces belief in Nggwal; the human actor assumes the godlike functions of Nggwal. We saw evidence of such hubris once before, when Kumbwiata arbitrarily invoked the authority of Nggwal to scold some youngsters for annoying him with their ukeleles (chap. 5). And yet, it would be grossly inaccurate to portray either Kumbwiata or the previous informant as radical atheists, since the identity of self and Nggwal is mediated by a third variable. It is not what *I do* but what *men do* which is Nggwal; the individual male identifies proximately with *collective male society*—an idea whose reality has been his constant study since entry into Falanga, and which in countless ways has commanded his loyalty and assimilation. The binding traditions cradling this idea are in turn personified as Nggwal. Thus, Nggwal enables men—both individually and collectively—to glorify and indeed apotheosize themselves. What was discussed in the Introduction as a symbolic property of the Tambaran—namely, the significance of cultural selfhood—becomes most clearly and instructively revealed in the subordinate institution of Nggwal.

To return to specifics. The involuted skein woven by the various images of Nggwal ultimately turns back on itself; for it was not many mornings later that the previously quoted informant came to me disconcerted over a dream he had just experienced: several Nggwal statues had come to life and had chased him with their giant spears! The menacing interpretation, based on the Arapesh notion that dreams are actual or foretold happenings projected on a different phenomenal plane (Tuzin 1975), was that he (the dreamer) was out of favor with Nggwal. More than that, he was a marked man. No longer the free-wheeling agnostic, he had reverted to an anxious literalism that verged on the abject credulity which, in happier moments, he scornfully ascribed to women.

The "truth," then, about Nggwal is that there are several truths. Progression through the cult grades—and, within Nggwal, from young manhood to full social maturity—entails a growth of knowledge and (more profoundly) *understanding*. But this implies only an overlay, not a loss, of the relatively naïve sensibilities of the beginning and intermediate stages. Affect and image merely recede until consciousness summons them for the expression of positive or negative feeling. In Western society there is the stereotype of the devout atheist who begs extreme unction on his deathbed. Similarly, whatever the specific source of our dreamer's anxiety may have been, it is understandable that he should express it according to the horrific fantasies of earliest memory. That they are available to him to perform this function is proof enough that they continue to influence his mental life. In a happier vein, at cult feasts and singsings the senior men seem by all appearances to suspend their disbelief in order to enjoy as full participants the sentiments recommended by the ceremony and its prevailing metaphor.

In sum, Nggwal comprises a spectrum of ideas and images serving a considerable variety of instrumental and expressive functions. From structuring dominance relations to enforcing a truce, from shaping a dream to inspiring great collective works—in these and other ways yet to be described, Nggwal presents itself as a central symbol condensing and, above all, *integrating* key elements of Arapesh social, cultural and psychological identity.[10]

10. The present section emphasizes the cultural and psychological significance of Nggwal to the relative neglect of its social aspect. See Appendix C for a sociological treatment of Nggwal categories formulated in a manner that is relevant to substantive and methodological issues raised in the previous study (Tuzin 1976).

We have been speaking, however, entirely of men. Locating the place of women in this otherwise comprehensive scheme entails practical problems because of the extreme mystery and danger surrounding the subject as seen from the feminine perspective. Women are well aware of Nggwal's hunger, for to them falls much of the gardening, hauling and cooking needed to feed him; they know of his baleful misogyny, because women are his most common victims.[11] The gruesome images reviewed above no doubt claim numerous adherents among the women. At the same time, one can occasionally observe instances of impious skepticism. Especially among the older women, who have been around too long not to have glimpsed signs that things are not always what they seem, there is at least partial recognition that Nggwal is "what men do"; grumblings or even angry defiance over the demands of the Tambaran can sometimes be heard from such women, even though such talk is certain to shock and offend everyone within earshot—men and women alike.

Though I have no positive evidence to support it, I cannot resist the suspicion that women—at least some of them— know more about Nggwal than they are willing to reveal. Repeatedly, my wife, who had established close friendships among the women, tried to lead confidants into discussions that would shed some light on the women's actual perception. Always the result was the same: the moment her companion noticed where the subject was leading, she would make it clear that she did not know anything, did not *want* to know anything and, furthermore, did not want to talk about it![12] Candor is impossibly risky: although the Australian law protects women from being killed outright for "peeking" or for appearing to know too much, there remains the worry that the sorcerer's arm is longer than that of the law. And, even if she successfully guards her suspicions, Nggwal him-

---

11. Chap. 9 will examine the circumstances under which women become victims of Nggwal and the way in which the threat of ritual murder operates as a social-control mechanism.
12. In one such exchange my wife asked if the women did not have secrets of their own. "Oh yes," her informant replied, referring to matters of childbirth, abortion, and the like, "but the men know them all."

self can monitor her thoughts and strike her directly with disease or some other fatal mishap. In conclusion, whatever doubts a woman may have over the publicized nature of Nggwal, contextual factors deter her from sharing them with anyone else—or even, perhaps, admitting them to herself. The sociological effect therefore is nil.

To complete this qualitative opinion survey: the attitudes of children toward Nggwal are both freely given and sociologically provocative in their own right. Not surprisingly, their general feeling is that of undiluted terror. Theirs is the purest image of the giant ogre, the towering monster whose bloody, toothy maw waits hungrily for naughty or unwary children and whose great feet and legs (the latter are likened in girth to six-gallon drums) crush young bodies to a pulp. The Nggwal fantasies of older children are refined through their sleepless amusements at tormenting younger playmates with luridly graphic accounts of what is in store for them.[13] Adults disapprove such cruel play and, if present, will intervene before it goes too far. But children spend much of their time in play groups unsupervised by adults, and there is ample opportunity for unrestrained retailing of these most primitive images of Nggwal. The role of children as "culture bearers" has been largely unattended in anthropological analysis; but in attempting to understand the beliefs and values associated with Nggwal, in accounting for the multilayered adult construction, we cannot fail to appreciate the special and important contribution of the younger generation. Here, as everywhere, the child is father of the man.

Forewarned, then, that "belief in Nggwal" is by no means a uniformly expressed feature of this cultural population, but is subject to wide variation according to factors of sex, age, ritual standing and, indeed, temperament, it is time to examine how all these perspectives are accommodated within the procedures of Nggwal initiation.

---

13. Of course, these little terrorists are themselves still highly susceptible to the same fears, which is probably why they delight so in purveying them to ones *more* susceptible. That they may have seen Falanga or Lefin in no way mitigates—indeed, it may magnify—their dread of Nggwal.

DAY ONE: THE SAHOPWAS DISPLAY

Soon after the yams are harvested, several weeks before the Nggwal initiation is to occur, a number of initiators representing all sub-moieties of the village withdraw from society and live in seclusion in the ceremonial hamlet. They are chosen for their youth and good looks. The flower of Sahopwas manhood, they are segregated with the intention of acquiring maximum purity and potency, incarnating a spiritual power of which their entire group may partake during the forthcoming ritual of initiation. They cover themselves with a special black paint produced by allowing sago leaves to decay under water: when this material is dried and pulverized and mixed with a bit of water, it yields an adhesive, opaque wash which lasts until it is deliberately removed with coconut husks, *sambwingix* stinging nettles, and a type of fuzzy leaf called *tingwangux*. While in this state the men must not be seen by women, lest the female influence undo what they are trying to achieve.

During their seclusion each Sahopwas man also wears a woven, coconut-fiber ring (*numalimb*) on the back of his head. The hair is pulled tightly back from the scalp, and the ring, about five to six centimeters in diameter, is tied firmly into it. Wearing the *numalimb* is calculated to be an ordeal, since it is painfully uncomfortable and interferes with restful sleep. On the other hand, if the wearer is physically robust, has good bones and skin, and has observed all necessary food and sex taboos, the *numalimb* will supposedly have only a minor effect on him.[14]

14. More specifically, the amount of discomfort depends on whether one has a "good" or "cold" hand rather than a "bad" or "hot" hand. A man with a "bad" hand (*atem numbwitimwi*) is one who throws a spear straight and kills his victim instantly. A man with a "good" hand (*atemb bo'omb*) always wounds his prey, which then takes some time to die. It is the man with the "bad" hand who will experience pain wearing the *numalimb*.

"Badness" here is equated with a tendency toward violence and excitability. It is a character type which society finds useful at times but does not particularly admire. Interestingly, the *numalimb*, if properly attached, would presumably inflict discomfort on anyone regardless of character profile. Most or all of the Sahopwas would thus be revealed as "bad" in this sense, by which contrivance they come to see themselves as capable of the ritual murder they must commit on the eve of the initiation.

The soup these men eat during their retreat is laced with beauty magic in anticipation of their glorious reentry to the village. No matter how handsome the man, or how splendid his raiment, without magical assistance the crowd will not perceive him as beautiful. Accordingly, each Sahopwas commissions a beauty magician from within his sub-moiety—one to whom he is attached in some way or whose skills were proven superior at the last initiation. Afterward, the magician is rewarded with gifts of meat.

A word about these adepts. Generally speaking, each clan possesses a secret beauty formula which is handed down in one of the patriline couplets in the context of cult initiation. The same magic governs the hunting of birds of paradise, and each magician lays hereditary claim to one or more trees which are known to be display bowers for the magnificent males of these species.[15] Competition arises between the two or more magicians of a sub-moiety by virtue of an individual's right to choose from among them, even though some pressure naturally exists to use the magic of one's own clan. The more serious rivalry is manifest at the time of the display itself, when it becomes general among all the beauty magicians of the village. Identifiable in their black face-paint,[16] they stand by eagerly watching the amount of praise their clients receive in comparison with the others. Success is measured by the number and placement of lime strokes administered by impartial outside villagers. Various conventional phrases are invoked to honor the decorated figure, such as "See, the hornbill is sitting in a mighty tree!"—referring, that is, to the stature of the man and the hornbill feather which figures in his costume. In return for their encomiums, these visitors are rewarded by the decorated man's senior *ombaf* with a sizable chunk of pork and smaller gifts of tobacco, betelnut, salt, yams and soup.[17] After the display one is likely

---

15. Bird-of-paradise pelts are key elements in body decoration. The magic which controls access to them likewise governs the success of the ornamentation.

16. Thus the magician makes himself ugly in order to enhance, by contrast, the "red" beauty of his charge. There is a popular myth in which the same color contrast is likewise used to metaphorize the difference between beauty and ugliness (Tuzin 1976: 193).

17. Mindful of the reward to come, the visitors—even those from enemy villages—

to hear the magicians bantering over the outcome of the pageant: "Yes, yours truly has lime on his face; but, see, mine has lime on his face, chest and back!" If the magician has excelled, he may be sporting lime strokes on his own body.

As best I could determine, all magic recipes call for a concoction of the same basic range of barks, leaves and other vegetable matter with the addition of some secret ingredient that supposedly distinguishes each man's magic from the rest. As noted, the men who are to be decorated ingest the magic throughout the period they are wearing black body-paint. Their soup is prepared by the prepubescent daughters of their senior *ombif*—girls whom they call "mother" in recognition of their nurturing role. The magic substance—a moist, aromatic compost—is divided into small packets wrapped in cordyline leaves. The girls bring the pot of yam soup to the boil; then they hold one of these packets over the soup, douse it with cold water, and wring its essences into the soup. The packet is then put to one side on a limbum sheet. At the close of the seclusion period, many pots of soup later, a considerable heap of these spent packets has accumulated. On the morning of the men's display the girls perform a final, homeopathic ministration by decorating this heap: covering it over with ashes gathered from regular hearths, they then ornament it with a pretty array of purple cordylines and yellow crotons.[18]

The last of the enchanted soup is eaten two days before the big event. On the eve of the display a special food is prepared. Bark scrapings from a particular tree (species unknown) are mixed with diced tulip leaves and vegetal salt (potassium chloride) and cooked in a bamboo tube. Roasted yams are cut lengthwise and the cooked mixture is rubbed into their flesh. The men eat these in the afternoon and evening, during the breaking-of-the-plank ceremony heralding the end of their seclusion. They also drink a flavorful infu-

---

are unstintingly generous in their praise. When Ilahita men attend the ceremonies of their ally Kamanakor they are careful to ask for their payment in pots, the manufacture of which is that village's specialty.

18. Although ostensibly imitative, this magic is perceived to have a "contagious" element as well. This occurs because the packets are referred to as the quid of the men who are to be decorated, thereby positing a (fictitious) physical connection.

sion of scrapings from red and yellow coconuts (*amboninga* and *angil*), aromatic betel pepper (*nifux*) and aromatic ginger leaves (*amafux*). The following morning they eat yams roasted by close female kinsmen (mother, wife, sister)—though, of course, up to this time neither these women, nor the "mothers" who have fed them all these weeks, may look upon them. After going down to the stream to wash off the body paint and pray to the ancestral dead to grant them irresistible beauty, the men return to eat another meal, this time of *boiled* yams lest they soil their clean hands. Then they sit down for the lengthy business of being made beautiful.

The work is done by fellow Sahopwas, usually men closely related to them, under the supervision of the beauty magicians. Although by now their bodies ought to be thoroughly primed, some final mystic precautions are needed if success is to be guaranteed. The men are fed flesh scraped from either red or yellow coconuts which has been rubbed with magical earth colors (*akwaliwa*) of corresponding hue[19] and also with ashes from a cremated bird of paradise. Mouth and urethra are stoppered to prevent the magic from escaping before it has worked its effect. Thus, a fuzzy *nambai'w* stem smeared with *akwaliwa* paint and bird-of-paradise ashes is inserted in the urethra.[20] It is metaphorically referred to as *wambe'w*—"spear." There is no pain involved here, and after the display when the man steps discreetly into the bush

19. This paint is gotten from stones collected near the Nanu River, on the land of their northern neighbor Balangabandangel. The scrapings are initially yellow, but oxidization through heating turns them into a deep red. This chemical phenomenon provides tidy (albeit unnecessary) "confirmation" of the recurrent Arapesh notion that yellow is "cool" and red is "hot." For a discussion of the magical significance of paint among the neighboring Abelam see Forge (1962).

20. The predominantly yellow blossom of the *nambai'w* plant is, in conjunction with the "masculine" red hibiscus, a standard Tambaran design element. It belongs to a series of symbolically feminine items which include—each in their yellow manifestations—paint, coconuts, feathers and leaves. Indeed, corresponding with this sexual and color opposition, the connotatively yellow term *nambai'w* stands in a complex metathetic relationship with the connotatively red term *waimba*. The same color coding shows up again in the context of gardening excellence: thus, a successful short-yam (*Dioscorea esculenta*) gardener decorates himself with a yellow ensemble, while the proud long-yam (*D. alata*) grower uses the red counterparts. A familiar accolade used for such men is: "They gather ocher every year, but every year the earth restores it anew."

to relieve himself the force of the urine is enough to eject the stem.

His mouth is sealed by a more elaborate procedure. A large, aromatic, ground-dwelling beetle (*timbalen*) is put in the man's mouth. The insect has been cooked (along with others) in a bamboo tube, after which it is split and its body cavity smeared with the magical ashes and paint (see above). The *timbalen* is a recognized food item[21] and may be swallowed or not as the man prefers. To make sure its magical effect is not lost, an ornamental mouthpiece (*saiak'w*) fashioned of pig tusks and shells is quickly placed between his teeth. The same type of device was used traditionally by warriors seeking to add extra ferocity to their appearance.

From now until the end of the display ceremony the operation of the magic depends on these men remaining totally subdued. A sudden movement or a flash of emotion could ruin everything, and therefore they adopt at this time a passive, seemingly stuporous demeanor.

The men to be decorated (I will call them the "dancers") congregate in clan and sub-moiety groupings just outside the ceremonial clearing so that the debris created in the process can be readily discarded into the adjacent bush.[22] The decorators work with painstaking care. Except for his eyelashes, all the dancer's facial hair has been removed, and his hairline has been shaved back to expose the front half of his scalp. A yellow oil (*akwalif*)[23] applied to the face gives his skin a

21. *Timbalemb* are often given to unweaned infants who are proverbially fond of sucking the sweet, milky juices from the body cavity after it is cooked. Recalling the previous inversion wherein young girls are made the "mothers" of these grown men, the notion that the *timbalen* is primarily *baby* food may explain its appropriateness in the context of Sahopwas beauty magic. Cf. earlier discussions regarding the "baby" image in Tambaran ideology.

22. At any rate, this is the reason they give. When girls are being prepared for the ceremony marking their first menses, the decorating activity likewise occurs just behind the houses fronting onto her father's hamlet clearing—the reason, again, being practical. And yet, recalling the peripheral location of the "green rooms" ("menstrual houses") at Wamwinipux (chap. 4), and noting also the rather modest amount of rubbish actually generated, it seems likely that a ritual factor was involved here which was not known to my informants.

23. The oil is prepared as follows. The beauty magician masticates together flesh from a ripe coconut, turmeric, and an aromatic *tambol* leaf. The mixture is spat into a natural cloth formed from the bast tissue of the coconut palm, and the

much-admired golden glow and uniform texture. (This is the first step in decorating any figure, including wooden statues.) At the center of the artificial hairline a spot of magical red paint (noa'w) is applied.[24] Concealed under layers of cosmetic trappings, the noa'w is the final, mystic agent of ritual beauty. Its existence is known only to cult members, but its effects are reputedly felt by all.

Present purposes would be little served by describing in detail the elements or procedures of decoration. Insofar as the parts and their arrangement are dictated by aesthetic rather than iconographic considerations, the accompanying photographs do ample justice to this sartorial extravaganza. Suffice it to say that the decorators exploit virtually every type of pleasing material known to them—feathers, natural fabrics, colorful and/or aromatic leaves, berries, blossoms, shells, and sundry other items—to create a costume so striking that the audience will be spellbound by its transcendent beauty. The pièce de résistance is a tall, pointed headdress rising from its point of attachment at the back of the man's head, that is, from the coconut-fiber ring discussed earlier.[25] The dancer is transformed into a being akin to the Tambaran itself; and, indeed, numerous myths tell of this event permanently changing the mortal protagonist into a spirit entity. The rites of this and the following two days must be judged, then, the climax of Arapesh religious culture. In the truest sense ordained by this cosmology, the Sahopwas re-achieve the Tambaran immediately before they give it away. The aura of myth and magic woven by ritual-aesthetic devices sig-

---

packet is then dried over a fire. The contents are pulverized, producing a yellow, aromatic powder. This again is chewed up, liquified with saliva, and strained through a piece of cloth into a coconut shell. The liquid is poured into a bamboo tube which is placed unsealed into a fire. Just as the contents start to boil, the vessel is removed from the heat and yellow croton leaves are stuffed into the open end. The oil is quite perishable and must be used within a day or so of manufacture. Although the technique just described is neither secret nor taboo to women, men are conventionally the only ones who make this decoration oil.

24. The paint itself is called ambon, since it is made from the ashes of an ambon (red) parrot mixed with red akwaliwa paint (see above).

25. The details of the costume, including the headdress, appear in simplified form in the adornments of long yams and are rendered graphically in the paintings of cult spirits. The costume announces the presence of a spiritual essence which, despite its plural contexts of expression, is ultimately monistic.

23. A young Sahopwas man is being decorated for preinitiation rites later that day. His somber expression reflects his determination not to let the beauty magic escape his body prematurely.

nifies that behind this mundane initiation ceremony, wherein one group transfers ritual knowledge and status to another, there stands a higher reality in terms of which the Tambaran is bestowing itself on the people. What does this bestowal entail? Nothing less than renewal of the grand conditions of existence: human and natural fertility, physical security, so-

24. A Nggwal Bunafunei initiator in full costume.

cial harmony and cultural meaning. The interesting point is that while the connection between these ultimate purposes and the initiation is stated with certainty, informants, by virtue of their participation in this symbolic drama, are unable to rationalize how it comes about. Many details of the initiation have, it is true, explicit iconic significance; but the penetration of this "higher reality" is brought about not by such symbols conceived in isolation but rather by their mutual *arrangement* in combination with other symbols which may

25. Close-up of decorated Nggwal Bunafunei initiator.

not impinge directly on the initiation ceremony. The privilege of the external vantage point derives from its ability to adduce this arrangement analytically, and thereby to *articulate* a relationship between the sacred and the profane which for the actors must remain at the level of *feeling*. The profound significance of ritual ornamentation provides one such analytic opportunity; there will be more as the present discussion advances.

On the occasion witnessed, at Ningalimbi village,[26] eighteen men were decorated. By 1600 the job was nearing completion, while a growing din from the next hamlet gave notice that a crowd of spectators was gathering. Before they were admitted, however, the festooned figures were taken into the ceremonial clearing and paraded before the members of the cult. Finishing touches and minor corrections were applied as the dancers perfected a lilting gait which animates all dangling parts of the ensemble and adds considerably to the overall effect. This was also the opportunity for the mother's brother to rejoice in the beauty of his sister's son, both in verbal praise and in presenting either his outstretched leg or his entire body for the latter to step over (Tuzin 1976:154; cf. Bateson 1936:20).[27] When all was ready the dancers were ushered to the Afa'afa'w side of the spirit house. Undecorated Sahopwas men gathered in the narrow opening between the spirit house and the flanking auxiliary house, obscuring the dancers from view and leaving only the tops of their headdresses visible from the clearing.

26. Fieldwork concluded before the Ilahita initiation was held. Reliable informants from Ilahita confirmed that the Ningalimbi ritual was identical in all important respects to their own, except that the scale of their proceedings would be much larger.
27. Ilahita does not practice this gesture. Instead, the mother's brother merely dances in front of his sister's son, holding high a spray of cordyline leaves or jawbone souvenirs of meat he has been given (Tuzin 1976:154) and singing the manly virtues of his nephew. In reply, his ritual enemies (*nautamana*) proclaim that he is praising only the costume; that the man himself is only a "wild banana"—implying doubt over whether he will ever be a successful yam grower. If visitors from enemy villages are present they may say, for example, that a new *hangamu'w* spirit has arisen who will later chase (and kill?) his own people. Such banter is entirely expected and is carefully dispensed to stay within the bounds of ritual license.

At a signal the women and children began streaming into the clearing. Many wore yellow face-paint, yellow cockatoo feathers, and colorful new netbags. A couple of the women brandished spears and carried their netbags flung over their shoulder in jaunty male fashion. Among them was a slender youth in his early twenties who feigned femininity by wearing yellow decorations, a skirt, and a netbag suspended on his back. The female party consisted of the dancers' wives, who afterward would present the new netbags to the wives of their husband's junior *ombif*. The rather unhappy-looking male transvestite was, I learned later, the younger brother (uninitiated) of a bachelor dancer who had prevailed upon him to perform this role.[28]

As soon as the women and children had entered, a great tumult arose, as into the clearing burst a horde of screaming, spear-wielding men. Some of them also carried long, thick banana or taro stalks with which they beat the ground loudly as they ran. This was a mixed group of outsider males (either Sahopwas or Owapwas) and both junior and senior segments of the local Owapwas class.[29] Racing counterclockwise around the clearing, they displayed their battle prances and lunged threateningly at spectators (mostly women and children, some old men) standing around the periphery. Then they joined in a cluster at the center of the clearing.

This was the signal for the decorated women to arrange themselves in groups of two, three and four. Arms interlocked, displaying their characteristic goose-stepping prance, they began by dancing taunts at the knot of Owapwas men— singing that they would be conquered that day, that they were not manly enough to take over the Tambaran. The

28. It was not explained why a *male* is called upon to perform the role, and why it is the *younger brother*. Notably, the Iatmul regard "wife" and "younger brother" (and also "ritual novice") as interchangeable in some symbolic contexts (Bateson 1936:131). In both places, the metaphor appears to rest on the common property of super/subordination between husband–elder brother–initiator and wife–younger brother–novice.

29. The key members of this group are the Owapwas classmen, who, with the initiation of the junior members the following day, will once again accede to the Tambaran. Visitors are assigned to this group, irrespective of their ritual status, merely to enlarge the impressiveness of the ceremony.

rhythms of their song and dance were accented by a raspy, swishing sound caused by the rattle of myriad small objects (shells, nuts, gravel, broken glass) carried in their netbags.

After about three minutes of this, the men in the cluster began slowly to break ranks. Singing their own cult songs and rattling their spears, they forced the women to retreat toward the Sahopwas men who still concealed the decorated dancers. The roar of singing and whooping became deafening as the women were crowded between the unyielding Sahopwas and the advancing Owapwas. Just as the sound and emotion reached its astonishing peak of intensity, there suddenly arose from behind the Sahopwas an even mightier thunder: the unison roll of a dozen or more large dance drums. Then, something from behind began forcing the standing Sahopwas men forward; prancing with lowered spears, they drove back the women and, in turn, the Owapwas men. The dancers now stood revealed to the assemblage, framed between two lines of drummers.

In point of fact, the dancers had their backs turned to the audience. Two by two, they backed their way toward the clearing. Just as they crossed the threshold, each pair wheeled around and presented their plumage to the crowd. Allowing enough time for the full impact to register—one could almost hear the popping of invisible flash bulbs!—the pair started their parade around the clearing, either holding hands or grasping opposite ends of a short length of sago wood.[30] The dramatic presentation was repeated for each pair until all dancers were moving (counterclockwise) around the clearing.[31]

The parade continued'for about twenty-five minutes, with various persons—men and women, young and old—falling

---

30. Although the rebirth theme of Arapesh initiations is not nearly so prominent as it is in many other cultures, it may be more than coincidental that sago wood, which is prescribed in this context, is also the source of the razor blade uniquely employed in severing umbilical cords, and in lacerating the penes of Falanga and Lefin neophytes.

31. Senior outsiders decide who shall pair up on the basis of costume similarity. They also determine the order of presentation, calculated so that the most gorgeous specimens go first. Accordingly, the decision of these impartial judges —arrived at during the preview showing to cult members—ranks as the most important moment in the beauty contest.

in and out of step with the dignified, profoundly composed
figures. A large number of Sahopwas pranced about with
them as if acting as escorts, thrusting their spears at the surrounding spectators—women, children, and Owapwas classmen. The decorated women were also active. Singly or in
pairs they danced backward, facing the advancing male
dancers. This time it was a gentle movement, a lightly lilting
goose-step with sound effects again coming from the netbag
contents. As they danced before their husbands, each ges-
tured with a large shell ring toward their faces, signifying a
likeness of beauty and purity between the two objects. Quite
apart from the ritually prescribed context, the women
seemed genuinely impressed with the costumes and were
clearly enjoying themselves. After executing four or five
steps in front of one dancer, they would lope off around the
clearing and find another one to praise.[32] This phase lasted
about twenty minutes, and was followed by the dancers discreetly stepping out of the clearing to remove their urethral
inserts. They returned laughing and chatting among themselves and were arranged in a line along the front of the spirit
house. While decorators touched up face paint and made
minor adjustments in the costumes, the crowd milled about
and an *aolaf* peace marker was erected in the middle of the
clearing. Another brief parade featuring only the dancers
ensued, and, with twilight now well advanced, the all-night
singing began. Torches were lit, and the pageant of drumming and dancing took on that supernal quality which torchlight so effectively bestows.

During this, in traditional times, it was expected that one
or more of the younger Sahopwas men would secretly take
a ceremonial cassowary dagger from inside the spirit house
and slip off in search of a sacrificial victim. This was the institution of ritual murder (*laf*), another expression of which

32. As they danced, the women continually chewed a piece of pitpit taken from the
growing sprout (*ilapum*), which caused them to salivate. The frequent spitting
which results serves the important purpose of saving them from swallowing their
saliva—important because their saliva carried the taste and smell of the Tambaran, and for a woman to swallow it would bring sickness upon her. Indeed, all
non-initiates present at the ceremony are forewarned to avoid swallowing,
though the special role of the decorated women places them at special risk.

has been described in connection with *hangahiwa* masks. As in the earlier case, the killer himself remains anonymous; the assumption is that he is driven homicidally mad by the Tambaran, to whom the glory of the deed is therefore assigned. Preferably the victim was an enemy; but because the honor of the entire initiation class depended on at least one life being taken before dawn, the executioners were sometimes forced to resort to a fellow villager, perhaps even a member of their own family. Persons actually present at the singsing were immune to this danger, but woe betide anyone unfortunate enough to be caught alone on that night.

At dawn the women and non-initiates were sent away; costumes were removed, and the men rested for a time before preparing themselves in battle attire for the attack which they knew would soon be launched against them.

THE REGIONAL ASPECT

To set the larger stage of this ritual drama, it must be noted that these initiation-eve activities which were witnessed in Ningalimbi have their counterparts in all the surrounding villages, including, of course, their ally and patron Ilahita. Each village, it is true, sends a delegation to the day's events —the outsider visitors referred to in the preceding section— but the greater number of the inhabitants stay behind to prepare for their role on the following day. This consists mainly of assembling and arranging for display shell treasures which are to be lent to enhance the ceremony. Spears are decorated with cordyline leaves and shell rings tied along the shaft, and anthropomorphic figurines are fashioned out of various types of shells and ornamental materials. Fancy cassowary daggers, their hilts carved as parrots or hornbills, are given fresh paint and bedecked with leaves and feathers. That night, in the presence of these valuables, there is a feast[33] and a breaking-of-the-plank singsing, both of which are

33. Ostensibly, the feast is sponsored by the Owapwas in payment to their partners for assembling the valuables. As we have seen before, however, both classes provide food—though the Owapwas are charged with supplying the pig—and both classes lend shells and other goods for the occasion.

26. While the decorated initiators are parading, their wives dance before them with uplifted shell rings, praising their beauty and manliness.

restricted to cult members. At dawn the men quickly dress for battle and start off—in this case, for Ningalimbi—with their valuables carefully packed in netbags and palm-spathe wrappers.

The journey to Ningalimbi, lasting about one hour, involved one of the most curious of all Tambaran customs. Normally, when men are traveling about on Tambaran business—carrying pigs to the Maolimu seclusion, transporting statues and paintings to ritual centers, et cetera—they warn non-initiates of their coming with Tambaran whistles or other sound-making devices. This time the men move silently, with forward scouts dodging from house to house, or from tree to tree, as if expecting an ambush. The hamlets through which they pass betray no signs of life. Not only are there no humans around, but the usual complement of dogs, pigs and chickens is nowhere to be seen. Even the birds of the forest seem to know something is afoot, doing their part to sustain an eerie, pervasive stillness which strikingly departs from the ambient bustle that usually surrounds a settlement. The reason is known to all: the travelers are ritually obliged to kill any person or animal they encounter en route to the Tambaran ceremony. Hence the precaution of removing all pets and domestic animals from their path.[34] Moreover, the military deployment is necessary because it is equally conventional that the men of the host village ought to attempt an ambush. In this instance no sign of the Ningalimbis appeared until we entered the approaches to the ceremonial hamlet, when a fiercely arrayed band of warriors blocked our way and compelled us to force entry into the precinct.

At issue here is the problem of ritually prescribed aggression. Ilahita and Ningalimbi villages have been staunchest allies ever since the latter settled in the area (Tuzin 1976:63), and thus it is most peculiar that, here in the midst of cooperation, they should adopt even the pretense of mutual hostility. Furthermore, according to informants these battles are only recently a mockery; prior to European control spears were actually thrown, and it was not unusual for someone to be wounded or even killed. Aggression and agonistic display are ubiquitous in Arapesh ceremonialism—we have seen it before and will see it again—and in due course it will be necessary to confront this fact as a central component of cult drama. For now, it is sufficient to call this to the reader's attention, and to allow the pattern to unfold further before hazarding an interpretation.

DAY TWO: THE FIRST REVELATION

The Ningalimbi defenders were, of course, Sahopwas initiators who had just finished their nocturnal singing (see above). Within a short time bands of "attackers" from each cooperating village converged on the ceremonial hamlet, and each was greeted in the same way. After entering the clearing

34. As it happened, the party I accompanied did not encounter any persons or animals, so I can only report without endorsement their solemn claim that they *would* have killed anything they had met. Their knowledge and fear of the Australian law is such that I doubt whether they would have killed a human being; on the other hand, it is also clear that none of their fellow Arapesh was inclined to test their resolve in this matter.

and encircling it triumphantly, the visitors carried their shells and daggers into the spirit house and installed them with the swelling display of such items.[35] During most of the morning, while this and various other preparatory activities were in progress, non-initiates were kept well away from the ceremonial hamlet.

To begin, then, with the events that occurred outside the house. The day was August 14, 1971.[36] By 1330 all the shells

35. Astonishing as it may seem, the volume of paraphernalia—statues, paintings, shells, daggers—was so great that before the morning was over the spirit house was filled to capacity. Only a narrow aisle down the center of the house had been left clear for the novices to pass. A disagreement arose over what should be done with the overflow paraphernalia. The Ningalimbis proposed a rather complicated procedure whereby the objects would be displayed in the clearing and shown there to the novices, who would then be sent away while the paraphernalia were hidden; then the uninitiated audience would be allowed to enter, and the initiation procedure would proceed as usual. The men from Ilahita insisted orthodoxly that the goods should be stuffed into the spirit house, even if it meant piling them on top of one another. Finally, a compromise was reached: the bulk of the overflow would be crammed into the spirit house, while the rest —the over-overflow—would be displayed in the small, auxiliary houses on the clearing.

   Though trivial in itself, the incident reveals how cultural (in this case ritual) understandings are negotiated and communicated between different villages. Ilahita was not the only visitor that expressed its opinion in this matter. In soliciting the aid and cooperation of these villages, the quid pro quo required of Ningalimbi is that these visitors be allowed some say in how the ritual is to be conducted. Moreover, given the vicissitudes of inter-village politics, and the general tendency toward village self-assertiveness, virtually every stage of the operation is pressed into rhetorical service. Here, then, ritual and politics are, so to speak, mutually implicated: the great ceremonial conclaves present groups and individuals with signal opportunities for prestige advancement, while the line between orthodoxy and heterodoxy is constantly shifted this way and that in harmony with changing political realities.

36. This day's events posed certain observational problems, the solution of which ought to be mentioned lest the reader puzzle unnecessarily over how the ethnographer managed to be in two places at once. As has been seen in earlier rites, initiated visitors, apart from adding visually to the occasion, perform important tasks which if left to the men of the place might result in the central illusions being destroyed. In the present instance several men of Ilahita volunteered to serve *inside* the spirit house to operate the actual initiation and to perform certain acts which induced the audience to believe that the house was indeed occupied by gigantic cult-monsters. It was obviously crucial that these interior events be recorded—no less than the activities in the clearing—and yet I could scarcely allow myself to be seen moving blithely in and out of the house. In the end I decided to accompany the early-morning "attackers" to Ningalimbi and, before the non-initiates were admitted to the precinct, to take my place with the Ilahita workers inside the house, there to be closeted for most of the afternoon. Under the pretext that I was ill and bedridden that day, my wife attended to events outside the house, and it is therefore thanks to her observations that a complete record was obtained.

and other paraphernalia brought by visitors had been stowed out of sight, and the men had agreed, not without some acrimony, what the details of the imminent ceremony should be. A group of about sixty Sahopwas, featuring those who were most decorated, arrayed themselves defensively in front of the spirit house with their spears banked. The slit-gong was sounded and immediately a large group of women, some carrying or leading small children, filed in and by prior instruction formed an arc-shaped line on "stage right" of the clearing.[37] They entered not from the main path leading from the next hamlet but from an eccentric access route opening from the adjacent forest. The rest of the men present were standing on the sidelines or were grouped in the center of the clearing.

As soon as the women were in place, the Sahopwas lunged forward and began running counterclockwise around the clearing, whooping and brandishing their spears. Several of the men spat upon the spirit-house door as they passed it, the object being to bespell the threshold and thereby to intensify the forthcoming ordeal.[38] This continued for nearly five minutes, whereupon the motion abruptly ceased and the men turned to ambling aimlessly about the clearing. At this time it was noticed that several men had tucked *su'witip*-tipped sticks between their legs to warn of the *akutum* ("sore")

37. At risk of overdoing the theatrical analogy I find that this descriptive convention is a useful shorthand for my purposes. The audience/reader is conceived facing the spirit house from across the clearing.
38. These men are ritual specialists who are renowned for their personal power—that is to say, artists, sorcerers and garden magicians. At dawn on initiation morning the magician chants a spell over a mixture of tart lemons and wild pit-pit sprouts, which he then wraps in a cordyline leaf. Only then does he urinate, bathe, drink water, eat, smoke, or chew betel. Chewing the enchanted materials just before the ceremony stimulates the quantity of saliva needed to energize the threshold. As mentioned in the previous volume (1976:241n), one of the Ilahita initiators hidden in the house sought to counteract the threshold magic by spitting on it himself. This was because an adoption transaction had resulted in his own son being in the line of novices, and the father was intent on mitigating the ordeal.
   This procedure—called *malangal* ("mouth")—was alleged to have caused three mishaps among the Sahopwas group. Two men accidentally speared themselves (one in the hand, another in the leg), and a third man inexplicably fainted upon arriving at Ningalimbi and could only be revived with stinging nettles. These random casualties were taken as evidence of the aura of power and danger generated by the magic.

that would afflict any novice who broke the taboos prescribed over the next year.[39]

After a few minutes the novices were led running into the clearing by older men—their mother's brothers.[40] As they grouped in the center of the clearing they were encircled by the initiators, who ran shouting, singing and brandishing their spears in the manner already described. Meanwhile, about half the initiating group maintained their bellicose position in front of the spirit house, stomping up and down in unison with their spears. Overhead, the row of *kwongwof* spears along the house façade jerked in time with the general rhythm of the scene. There were, be it understood, many hundreds of persons joining in this tumultuous display. The color, the waves of crowd frenzy, above all the crescendo of collective emotion being transported to levels of almost painful intensity—these are beyond my power of description. But an inkling of the sheer immensity of the event is given by Ilahitans who stayed at home that day and reported—though the distance was several kilometers—that they were able to follow what was happening because so much of it was audible to them.

When the running and shouting and stamping had reached maximum pitch, the inner group of novices and their sponsors broke through the men encircling them and twice approached the Sahopwas guarding the spirit house. Each time they were driven back. Suddenly there appeared Kumbwiata, a prominent Owapwas Senior from Ilahita. He carried a bamboo pole five to six meters long, at the end of which was tied the blackened, smoked liver of a wild pig. Twice he circled the men of the clearing, and each time he passed the house façade he touched the painted area with the pig liver. On the third pass, as the novices and sponsors surged closer, Kumbwiata thrust the pole behind the carved crosspiece. When it was withdrawn an instant later the liver was gone. Kumbwiata turned to the crowd with the empty pole held high, proclaiming that the Tambaran had accepted his offer-

39. This ritual convention has already been described in the context of Maolimu.
40. The ritual status of the mother's brother is immaterial here, since the kinship tie
    is of overriding importance when the actual sister's son is being initiated.

ing, had submitted to being given over to the new group. The novices were once more guided to the center of the clearing, and again were encircled by running, threatening Sahopwas. This time the circle progressively expanded, until the outer crowd of women, children, and old men was forced back to the edges of the clearing. A large space was created in which the Sahopwas now converged to form the chute through which the novices would pass on their way to the now-exposed maw of the Tambaran.

Occasionally, such ceremonies direct the novices to crawl between the legs of the initiators, in the "rebirth" symbolism familiar to anthropologists but apparently uninterpreted as such by the Arapesh. This time the line would have been far too long. Instead, a double line of initiators joined hands and formed a tunnel stretching almost across the clearing and of several ranks' thickness at the end nearest the door.[41] As a desperate keening started from their kinswomen, the young men, visibly fear-stricken, were abandoned by their sponsors at the mouth of the tunnel, shoved into a stooped or crawling position, and shunted roughly on their way.[42] Some of the Sahopwas passed them on with gentle pats and soothing reassurances; others swiped at them with daggers or adzes and gave them assurances of a more menacing kind. As each novice disappeared into the dark doorway a sickening thud was heard from within—the wretch's head being crushed under the heel of the Tambaran. By now many of the women were sobbing uncontrollably.

Once organized, the procession moved quickly, and within five minutes all thirty novices had been swallowed up by the

41. Characteristically, in this and all other initiations requiring a gauntlet of sorts, the line is never perpendicular to the house façade, but rather extends obliquely from the door to stage left. No explanation was given for this, but it may—for practical or ritual reasons—have to do with the women being grouped on the stage-right side of the clearing.

42. As I had only sketchy data on the ritual affiliations of Ningalimbi individuals, the most I can say about the order of the novices is that it reflected the ubiquitous precedence of Afa'afa'w over Ondondof members. As I discussed in the earlier volume, in Ilahita these attributes are assigned to the categories I have termed "sub-moieties." In common with all other Ilahita Arapesh villages, none of which has sub-moieties, the Afa'afa'w-Ondondof distinction is assimilated to the moiety structure. See Tuzin (1976:261) for a discussion of these regional differences and their implications for the analysis of Ilahita social evolution.

house. To be exact, the Balangaisi novices entered in this manner; for, as we have noted in earlier initiations, the older novices are obliged to endure the greatest ordeals. After a few minutes in the house they emerged from the rear portal and, to the extravagant delight of the women, appeared smiling and unscathed in the clearing. At this the Sahopwas assembled the Owangufwisi group and led them to the rear door of the spirit house, where they were admitted without ceremony. They in turn exited through the front door.

When everyone was back in the clearing—except for the ethnographer and the several operators who remained cloistered in the house—the Sahopwas removed the feather ornaments (bird of paradise, cockatoo and hornbill) from the lower façade of the spirit house and, after circling the clearing to display them, presented them to the new initiates. The latter, in turn, reciprocated with gifts of smoked meat (mainly bandicoots) and the ritually ubiquitous sprouted coconuts. In addition, the Owapwas class provided a large quantity of steam-baked yams. Putting some of the food aside for immediate consumption, the Sahopwas distributed generous portions among the foreign visitors in thanks for their general participation and for the use of their paraphernalia. The feast was enjoyed by all in an atmosphere of jovial contentedness, while orators eulogized the greatness of the Ningalimbi Tambaran, congratulated the new initiates, and admonished the assemblage to remember the value of maintaining peace and solidarity among themselves. As darkness advanced, the women and children packed up any remaining food and started for home. The new initiates were asked to leave, while their fathers and senior *ombif* prepared for a private feast of pork and yams and a nighttime of Tambaran singing.[43]

The corresponding events taking place inside the spirit

---

43. The new initiates were excluded, first, because the Nggwal flutes featured here would not be revealed to them until the following day, and, more to the point, because their fathers would be ashamed if they were discovered to be partaking in the pork feast. The pigs were supplied by the new initiates, who ostensibly remained under the impression that the meat was consumed by Tambaran spirits. It would be months or even years before they gradually came to realize that their senior *ombif* and fathers were, in fact, the recipients of these feasts; but, by then, any sense of betrayal would be largely muted by the consolation that they were now the beneficiaries of this ritual dissimulation.

house are easily stated. There were, in all (and excluding
myself), nine operators—eight from Ilahita and one from
Mui village. Three men tugged rhythmically at the rope
which activated the *kwongwalef*. Another man created the
sound effect of the Tambaran's stomping by pounding a
sprouted coconut on the hardened earth. A fifth man, after
cutting loose the pig liver as it was thrust through the façade,
joined two others who were stationed just inside the door.
As the novice crawled in he was cuffed about the head and
shoulders and doused with ashes.⁴⁴ To add verisimilitude,
the first in line was thrust down into a prone position, partly
blocking the doorway, and told to remain there, giving those
who followed (and who had to climb over him) the fearful
impression that he was dead or unconscious. The disoriented
supplicant was then seized by two men who forced soft, over-
ripe bananas into his mouth and propelled him down the
center aisle of the house.⁴⁵ As his fear abated and his eyes
adjusted to the darkness, the novice beheld the lavishly
decked interior: on the right, the gallery wall of spirit paintings running the entire length of the house and festooned
with decorated cassowary daggers, mounted birds of paradise, and a multitude of shell arrangements; on the left, filling the larger portion of the outer sanctum, a towering line
of impassive spirit effigies, and at their feet another line of
sculptures in dignified repose. All the remaining floor area
was crammed with shells, feathers and daggers. The aisle
itself was demarcated with long strands of orange *su'witip*
fruits.

It must be remembered that these novices were adult men
—a couple of them were grandfathers—who were seeing for
the first time the master works of an artistic tradition whose
very existence had been unknown to them. Afterward I
asked several of them what went through their minds as they
first beheld the interior. Their replies—simply that they

44. The pale-colored ashes signify that the novices are entering the years when their
hair will turn white. The four types of plants burned to produce them are noted
for their white flowers or leaves.
45. By this act Nggwal lifts the taboo on bananas which has been in effect since the
novices were young adolescents. Theoretically, women may never resume eating
bananas, but in practice the privilege extends to the wives of initiates.

were surprised by what they found, and that they greatly admired the artistic and decorative fineness—seemed to me gross understatements when measured against the intense emotion their faces showed at the time. Apprehension appeared to be turning to amazement, then to the delighted awe awakened when symbols of supreme importance excite feelings of transcendence that signify and subjectively verify the presence of something preternaturally higher—in this case the Tambaran.

Untold numbers of Arapesh have, because of untimely death or unsuitable gender, never enjoyed these wonders of tradition. This poignant fact presents a problem: By what logic must the majority of the group be excluded from articles of central symbolic importance to the culture, and what are the supporting motivations? Of this we can be sure: something in the life experiences of Arapesh males commits them to a principle which, to borrow a phrase of Theodore Schwartz (1973:157), cannot be relaxed.

DAY THREE:
THE REVELATION OF FLUTES AND DRUMS

On the morning of the third day the initiates and their fathers are sent away while the Sahopwas remove the shells and daggers from the spirit house and place these in clusters in and around the clearing. One display seems to be of special interest to them. It consists of a decorated cassowary dagger stained with generations of red paint, two bamboo spearblades tipped with *su'witix* fruits, and a 13-centimeter length of human femur, incised and stained with age. A stake tied with pitpit leaves is erected in the middle of the clearing.

When these materials are in place a signal is given and the Owapwas (fathers and sons) charge into the clearing, singing and prancing with their spears. After circling the stake, the "attackers" unite in the center and advance in a body toward the special display. They behave as if assaulting it, calling with a vibrato "Wa . . . wa . . . wa" as they jab at it with their weapons. By prior arrangement one of the initiates rushes forward, seizes the cassowary dagger and runs off with it, and two others grab the spear-blades and dash from the clearing in different directions. These are the *laf* weapons which, within the next day or two, must claim at least one human victim in the name of Nggwal.[46] As in all other *laf* situations the human agent remains anonymous, though the assembled cult membership can plainly see the self-nominated group of executioners. Later, at the time the initiates are decorated for their coming-out, those who have thus displayed their mettle will receive unusual praise. As for the one who actually performed the deed, it is said that *his* beauty will shine with a special luster.

The previous night's revelry had left the clearing cluttered with debris—food scraps, banana leaves, hearth and torch ashes, decorative materials, and the like. The Sahopwas began ostentatiously to complain about the untidiness. After a few moments they ordered the initiates, who had by now ceased their singing and stomping, to spread out and sweep the clearing. The young men worked with their bare hands in a squatting position and, amid comically exaggerated instructions from all sides, converged duck-walking to a point about two meters in front of the spirit-house door. Just as they seemed to realize that this was no simple cleanup, they were furiously accosted by two men who dashed out from each side of the spirit house and ran around the crouched initiates, swiping at them with steel-bladed adzes. The attackers were Mangas (see chap. 5) and Watasiwi, two Sahopwas leaders from Ilahita who were relative strangers to the

46. These *laf* devices are ritual heirlooms of Tangumbai, the paramount nggwal of Ningalimbi. They are said to be of great antiquity, and the bone has a vaguely conceived, primordial significance. In Ilahita the privilege of representing the spirit pantheon in this event goes to Kamba'wa of Nangup, who has the distinction of owning both a claw from the mythic cassowary-mother Nambweapa'w and the remains of the hollow log that figured in the Tambaran story of Kamba'wa (see above). In most other contexts, however, the paramount nggwal of Ilahita is Bila of Hengwanif. Noting the Ningalimbi case, and considering also the relative recency of Nangup's establishment in the village, it appears that Kamba'wa is in the process of taking over general supremacy from Bila. This precedence is, I should mention, little more than nominal, though the pride and rhetorical advantage it gives the client group should not be underestimated. As a rule, the importance of any particular nggwal—or paraphernalia—reflects the prestige of living or recently deceased clients. Accordingly, in this, as in many other cult areas, ritual orderings are maintained in rough alignment with political reality.

Ningalimbi initiates comprising the majority of the beleaguered group.[47] To add to the effect, some of the initiates' fathers, who were standing near the crouched group, took flight when the armed intruders appeared.

Just as these two figures exited the clearing, two more men, also Sahopwas from Ilahita, burst from the door of the spirit house and ran around the group sounding hornbill flutes (*timbalen*, pl. *timbalemb*).[48] After three revolutions they joined two other *timbalen* flautists in front of the house and continued their bird song in unison. From inside the spirit house an accompaniment arose: the deep-throated bellowing of the Tambaran itself. In response, all the other men present—Sahopwas and Owapwas alike—produced *kokolalo'w* whistles from their netbags and blew them as a background chorus imitative of the smaller birds of the forest. Smiles and nods appeared among the novices as they recognized sounds they had heard and feared all their lives as harbingers of the Tambaran.

Harbingers still—for no sooner had the flute-and-whistle din commenced than the youths were unceremoniously ordered into the spirit house. Once inside, they were instructed to rap on the gallery wall, which precipitated the removal of one of the painted panels. As they filed past the opening, they could see by torchlight the sixteen giant *bowas* flutes being played by as many Sahopwas initiators; these flutes

47. It is recalled that about ten of the initiates were from Ilahita. Consequent to political developments in their own village, they had been brought to Ningalimbi for induction.

   That the attackers carried adzes is significant in terms of the new context of subordination which the initiates are entering. Carrying an adz tipped with white feathers is the prerogative of the cult's most senior members—a category which, in the Ilahita case, is formalized as Nggwal Walipeine. The present initiation directly foreshadowed the entry of Mangas and Watasiwi into Nggwal Walipeine —an event which was to take place the following year—and the aggressive use of the adzes was a way of impressing on the initiates the new symbols to which they must now submit themselves. Technically, of course, Mangas and Watasiwi were not entitled to carry these adzes until after their own initiation; but this restriction was waived for the present ritual. Moreover, in Ningalimbi, where there is no Nggwal Walipeine grade, men start sporting the badges of senior authority as soon as they have transferred Nggwal Bunafunei to their junior *ombif* and have, so to speak, passed out of the "top" of the cult.

48. These are pipes a little over a meter in length which the player shouts into with a hooting sound. I should mention that both the flautists and the adz-wielding pair circled the initiates in opposite directions.

were the voices of the nggwals taking part in this initiation. All the novices were given a brief chance over the next several minutes to test themselves on the *bowas* flutes. When they emerged, each was given a new name by his senior *ombaf*, who also presented him with a *kokolalo'w* whistle and invited him to practice. By now the mood of the novices was relaxed and playful, as the pride of "knowing" the Tambaran mingled with relief that there would surely be no more ordeals or nasty surprises. After a time the youths left with their fathers to fetch long yams and sprouted coconuts for donation to the Tambaran. Two pigs were also brought forward, and a feast was convened forthwith in the absence of the new initiates. The nggwal spirit Baiwam was said to have devoured it, "washing his mouth" in preparation for the singing that was to follow.[49]

When the feast was over the *bowas* flutes were brought out of the spirit house and the initiates were summoned back to the hamlet. This is their first experience as choristers in a full-scale *bowas* singsing. The giant pipes are lined across the front of the spirit house, with their bases placed in large, open-ended drums. Sago leaves are strewn over the line of drums as a temporary measure: later, they will be replaced with a denser layer of 'kunai' grass (*walal*) which transforms the sound into the eery, muffled resonance of the "voice."[50] The lyrics are extremely simple: the name of the proprietor nggwal is repeated in drawn-out tones embellished by a variety of nonsense syllables—also attenuated—the effect of which is to enhance the aural thrill of the song. To the outsider the various nggwal names are all that distinguish the songs from one another. A song is deemed well sung if the

49. After the revelations of that morning, the new initiates know that such statements are metaphorical to the extent that the spirits allegedly eat only the immaterial essences, while men secretly enjoy the physical portion. What remains hidden from them is the fact that their fathers share in the feast, which is why, as in the previous night's banquet, they must be excluded. Such dissimulation occurs only when the food is being passed from Owapwas to Sahopwas. In the reverse instance the Owapwas Seniors ostentatiously refrain from eating and, instead, apply themselves to recording the number of yams given so as to ensure an equivalence when the return feast is eventually sponsored.

50. There is a trick involved here, similar to the one played on Lefin novices when they are first given the bullroarers. Not only does the use of sago thatch yield a relatively weak sound, the men also claim that without the covering of *walal* the boys' throats will quickly grow sore from the singing.

effort displays proper gusto and choral unison. Compared with the demanding vocal technique and lung power needed to "fill the pipe with sound," the novice flautist has little trouble mastering either tunes or lyrics. Still, even these elementary skills require some practice, and beginners cannot be expected to project the power and unison sufficient to convince women within earshot that they are truly hearing the voice of the Tambaran. Accordingly, veteran cult members crowd themselves behind and among the row of novices and bellow the songs in their ear, both to instruct them and to camouflage their mistakes.[51]

THE VOICE OF NGGWAL

The exceptional importance of the preceding ritual justifies a brief digression on the subject of these flutes. They are, to begin with, not really flutes in the technical sense, since the airflow is not manipulated with stops, valves, or other devices. The Arapesh, however, classify them along with a series of genuine flutes, and on that authority there is reason to do likewise. The object in question is a plain, unadorned bamboo pipe about 3.5 meters long and six to eight centimeters in diameter. No solemn sentiment attaches to them, and they are casually discarded after a sequence of singsings is concluded.[52] Mindful of the myth and heirloom of Kamba'wa, informants emphasize that the "true" Nggwal is the *drum*; the flute is merely a "limestick,"[53] while the two objects together are referred to as *kalangal*—a type of parrot. Each drum is

51. Bateson (1935:163) describes how the Iatmul sent him into the forest to practice playing a flute—out of female earshot.

52. This attitude, which appears to be shared by other nearby Torricelli peoples, is a point of contrast with the Middle Sepik flute complex, where beautifully carved and appliquéd instruments are treasures apparently worth preserving. In Ilahita, smaller flutes are often hidden away between ceremonies; but this is a matter of convenience, not because they are regarded as heirlooms.

53. The Arapesh are quick to associate the image of a rod stuck in a vessel of some kind with the notion of a limestick. Thus, for example, a curious rock formation near the village, consisting of a rodlike fragment of limestone protruding enigmatically from the ground to a height of almost two meters (a "limestick" in the literal sense!), is taken to be the "limestick" of the culture-hero Baingap. Natural or not, I cannot say; but the object is heavily scarred from generations of gardeners taking scrapings for their yam magic. The growth and fertility implications of a coital image are also apparent in the dagger-and-coconut magic presiding over the Maolimu seclusion (see chap. 4).

individually named and associated with a particular nggwal. Each nggwal has at least one drum, and several have two, indicating that the client group either has absorbed an extinct descent line or is ritually preparing itself to segment.

Although each song/flute/drum is owned by a particular nggwal, the entire set of instruments joins in the singing. Corresponding with the reciprocating pattern of the song, the line of seated performers divides itself equally into "head" (right) and "tail" (left).[54] A member of the ritual group immediately associated with the particular nggwal occupies the middle (*la'afen*) and leads "his song" by cuing the respective sections on their entries. When the song is done, shuffling occurs as another man comes forward to lead the next song[55] and those who are tired turn their flutes over to fresher members of their ritual group. The flutes and drums remain stationary.

The symbolic importance of the *bowas* flutes—summarized as the voice of the Tambaran—is indicated in the cosmogonic significance of the ritual wherein they are revealed. The inner sanctum of the spirit house is likened to Nggwal's netbag, which he carries slung over his shoulder.[56] The bag is heavy, for it contains the children of all creatures, crying to be born.

54. The terms *balanga* and *andep* imply comparison with, to use my informant's examples, the head and tail of a snake or yam.
55. Enemy nggwals perform in pairs, but this is said to be a matter of convenience rather than contest. It must be added, however, that this ordering reflects a fundamental and pervasive logic which regards individual nggwals as somehow incomplete in the absence of their *nautamana*. The formulation would seem to be: a nggwal by itself is simply nggwal; with its *nautamana* it is Nggwal. The paradox thus resolved is that Nggwal—like society itself—is more than the sum of its parts.
56. An interesting comparative sidelight: Forge (1966:26) reports that the Abelam spirit house is symbolically feminine, with the dark interior being likened to "her" belly. No such imagery applies in the Arapesh case. However, Kaberry (1941:246n) notes that the Abelam word *mbia* means both "belly" and "womb." This datum, taken in conjunction with the commonplace New Guinea association of "womb" and "netbag"—both of which are termed 'bilum' in Pidgin English—suggests a possible link between the two sets of beliefs. It would not be the first instance in which ritual elements appear to have undergone a translation error when passing from Abelam to Arapesh usages. Thus, "womb" was mistranslated as "netbag," prompting the creation of an exegesis which, by a farfetched but rather charming contrivance, rationalized a fertility significance for this object that was meaningful in local cosmological terms. This is, needless to say, highly conjectural; but it makes sense that linguistic quirks of this sort could be implicated, with possibly creative effect, in the general process of cultural diffusion by which elements are naturalized to their new setting.

But though the burden is very great, Nggwal must eat before he can set it down. By feeding Nggwal with pork and yams, and then ritually opening the inner sanctum (to the novices), the future progeny of all species are liberated, and the natural order is born again.[57] The voice of the Tambaran *speaks* creation, with a mysterious, intrinsic efficacy which both signifies and ordains a fructifying accord among all things; hence the felt appropriateness of summoning Nggwal to rectify matters when crises such as famine, epidemic and social discord plunge them into disarray. We have, then, a classic instance of a magico-religious figure serving at once to formulate widespread public anxiety and to provide measures for its alleviation. And, at least in those areas susceptible to human intervention, the mechanism operates with remarkable effectiveness.

DENOUEMENT

The revelation of the *bowas* flutes ends the climactic phase of the Nggwal Bunafunei initiation; what remains is a protracted decrescendo leading to eventual resolution some two to three years hence. Briefly: after participating in one full song-cycle, the novices are sent away while the older men dine secretly on pork; later, they are brought back to join in an all-night session with the flutes. The following day life returns to normal, permitting the men to catch up on various chores that have accumulated during the preceding period. Then, after some weeks, a two-to-three month period of seclusion begins for the erstwhile novices. A crude shelter of coconut and sago fronds is erected *inside* the spirit house; the youths bring their bed mats, and there they sleep for the duration.[58] They wear black body-paint, rigidly avoid being seen by women, and enjoy their retreat in a convivial atmo-

57. In explicating the meaning of this ritual, informants also point to the exegetical support given by certain spirit-house elements that are reminiscent of fecundity, in particular, the birds' nests and the reproductively suggestive crosspiece.
58. This is the only time when the spirit house serves as a men's residence. That the liminal period is construed as being spent "sleeping" in the internal spirit-house shelter is not irrelevant to the womb symbolism discussed in an earlier footnote. The same figure will appear again, somewhat altered, in the Nggwal Walipeine initiation.

sphere of feasting and flute singing. The women are led to understand that the incarnate Tambaran is chief consumer of the vast quantities of food taken to the precinct—which, as noted before, is "true" only in the spiritual sense. The mundane goal of the gluttony is to fatten the initiates against the day when they will return to society more beautiful than their womenfolk remembered them. The food is provided by the initiating class, whose nubile kinswomen do the actual preparation. During the seclusion, the Sahopwas also assemble sartorial elements for the ceremony of reentry.

As the day approaches, excitement returns to the high level that prevailed a few months earlier—without, however, the same shadow of apprehension. Unlike the last time, Nggwal is not hungry. Having been gorged continuously for three months, there is little chance he will be tempted to snap up up an unwary woman or child. So, even the women welcome the advent of the Tambaran, for it means being reunited with husbands, brothers and sons who have been absent these many weeks serving Nggwal. Once again, hopes are pinned on the success of the body decorations. Starting on the eve of the display, close relatives of the men to be decorated refrain from eating, drinking, smoking and betel chewing; if a child of the family cries, the mother must soothe it without giving it the breast, lest it innocently foul the beauty magic.

The coming-out ceremony is in most important respects a duplication of the one organized earlier on behalf of the initiating class, and it would be redundant to recount it in detail. The main difference is that the affair is divided into two parts: an initial debut, in which the initiates display themselves only to cult members, from their own and other villages, and, two days later, the splendorous, public display in which female relatives formally participate in exalting the beauty of the dancers.[59] During the two nights intervening, the initiates remain hidden in the spirit house while a public breaking-of-the-plank singsing is held in the clearing out-

59. At this time the fathers of the initiates sponsor a massive feast to repay the opposite class for having fed their sons during the period of seclusion. Married initiates, whose gardens would have been tended in their absence, contribute the major portion of these repayment yams.

side. The sequence concludes with a public drum singsing by torchlight on the night following the second display. At about midnight the flaming torches are tossed into a heap in the center of the clearing, and the initiates disport themselves in an athletic display of fire leaping. The fire, it is said euphemistically, heats them against the chill of the night air; more to the point, it kindles the inner flame of their manhood, urging them to the sexual celebration that begins after the lights are out.

AFTERMATH

The preceding ceremony takes place at the very end of the dry season, well into the time for clearing and planting the new yam gardens. The program of frequent feasting over the past two years has badly depleted the yam stores; even the usually well-conserved seed yams have been tapped for the sake of satisfying initiation partners and visitors. Of necessity, the community enters a period of relative austerity lasting two to four years—that is, until there is a sufficient surplus of yams to finance the removal of Nggwal from the village. The amount must be adequate to recompense the initiating class for all the food they supplied while sponsoring the induction rituals. Accordingly, it is the novice class —fathers and sons—which decides on the basis of its yam stocks when the time has come to chase Nggwal back to his watery lair.

This material condition is, as usual, ritualized through the metaphor of Nggwal. Thus, during the interval of subsistence vulnerability, the community perceives itself to be relying on the well-fed, benevolent Tambaran to see it through. Traditionally, it was a time of offensive war-making; for not only had the truces expired,[60] but the men felt themselves maximally supported by their patron cult-spirits. Thus sev-

60. Villages, as I have mentioned before, commonly solicited truces from their regular enemies in anticipation of a major Tambaran initiation—chiefly to remove the security threat, but also to gain their positive assistance in providing food and performing certain ritual roles. Such uneasy agreements did not survive long beyond the active phase of the ritual sequence.

eral factors—the resolution of (mostly inter-class) tensions that led up to and finally precipitated the initiation, the confidence borne of knowing that Nggwal has renewed his covenant with man, the reaffirmation of ritual unions and partnerships, the material condition favoring hard work over petty intrigue, and the aggravation of a common external threat—all conduce to a situation of peace and solidarity within the village. By virtue of the teleology intrinsic to Tambaran ideology, this state of social felicity is taken to be proof-positive of the benign and immanent presence of Nggwal.

Inevitably, however, as more time elapses since the preceding initiation, the instability of post-ritual accord reveals itself. Structural and behavioral forms reassert themselves as life sinks back into the balanced pattern of amity and enmity that characterized the status quo ante. The consensus develops that Nggwal's strength must be waning, his use to the village diminishing; providing the yam stocks are back to surplus levels, there is nothing to be lost by banishing him.[61]

The first step is quietly and secretly to empty the spirit house of its paraphernalia. Paintings, statues, drums, and other sacra are removed and hidden away in their new owners' yam houses—in the rear section where women may not go.[62] As the hunting magicians prepare their occult bundles, the recent initiates are told by their senior *ombif* that they will "chase Nggwal" on the following morning. And yet, when the time comes, they are ordered instead to deploy themselves for a pig hunt. Their fathers explain that "Nggwal" in this instance is a metaphor for "pig"—the true object of the chase. When, during the morning, women in the village hear shouts and whoops coming from different parts of the forest as the pigs are netted, they are told that another nggwal has been cornered and his spear seized: "With only his penis

---

61. And yet, at any other time a hungry Nggwal is seen as dangerous and worthy of being placated with feasts, not weak and contemptible as he is here. Informants could not resolve this contradiction for me.

62. Nowadays, most of the paintings and statues are thrown away in a tabooed and physically inhospitable area of forest that is claimed (mostly as a warning to women) to be infested with snakes. This is the sad result of the fact that European art hounds occasionally pass through the village, and the men would rather remove the commercial temptation than risk having the pieces revealed to the uninitiated.

remaining, he will now return to the water." Actually, the older men had earlier removed the *kwongwof* spears from the spirit house and secretly taken them to the forest site of Wamwinipux (chap. 4).

At about noon the hunting parties bring their catch to Wamwinipux, where the older men have already started preparing the feast. In addition to the generally shared pork and yams, the initiates are given two special foods by their senior *ombif*: a baked pudding of mashed banana, coconut and salt which is a delicacy reserved for this occasion, and a quantity of roasted, chestnut-like breadfruit seeds which may only be eaten by men who have reached this ritual stage and by women past menopause.

The long season of Nggwal began years before when the men fetched Nggwal from the water and restored to him his giant spear. Now the initiates, accompanied by their fathers and ritual preceptors, parade triumphantly into the village, brandishing the spears before the women as proof that they have subdued the Tambaran, driven him back to the water, and taken custodial possession of his power. Henceforth, until the next such initiation a half-generation away, they are the chief defenders of Nggwal's worldly estate; they speak with his authority; they are Sahopwas.

It is late afternoon. In the remaining daylight the massive yam payment is made to the initiating class, followed by a public feast and an all-night singsing—which is, at last, the finale. Anyone would think that these people have had enough ritual to last, well, indefinitely. Not so: plans for the next initiation are already under way.

8. Nggwal Walipeine:
The Consolation of Old Age

BAINGAP, PART TWO

(This is a sequel to the story of Baingap, a culture-hero who originated in Ilahita. As a result of his wife's bumbling inquisitiveness, Baingap is swept away far to the south by a raging flood [cf. Tuzin 1977]. As he is carried along he calls out to the peoples he passes [Arapesh, Kwanga, Abelam and others unnamed] the foods they will henceforth eat as their staple diet. What follows are the adventures of his younger brother Imoina, now grown old.)

When Baingap departed Ilahita, he left behind his younger brother Imoina. Having no longer any family, he lived alone. As he grew old he never gave thought to women or to marriage; his mind dwelt entirely on his long-lost brother.

One day Imoina saw a young and beautiful woman pass by, and, lusting after her, the thought occurred to him that he would marry this girl. At this time the girl's parents were harvesting their yams, and it was the girl's job to carry baskets of yams back to the village. At night she returned to the garden to sleep with her parents.

The old man saw this and fetched some magical water from his house. Then he went to the forest and found an ants' nest and brought it back to the village. He soaked some grass in the water and then put a large number of ants on the grass. They ate the water and grass, which caused their urine to smell very bad and rotten. Then Imoina put the ants on the path where the girl was sure to pass.

The next time the girl came down the path the ants crawled on her and began biting her on the legs and vulva. She tried in vain to brush them away. As the ants bit her vulva their urine mingled with her vaginal fluids and so found its way up inside of her. Later she went to the village.

After she emptied her yam load she started back toward the garden, but just then her thoughts went with overwhelming desire to Imoina, the old man. She ran to the garden and asked her parents if she could sleep that night in the village with her friends. The next day, she promised, she would bring them along to help carry the yams. Her parents agreed that this was a good idea.

Now, when the old man prepared his love magic he did not realize that he was being observed by two young men who had lately been courting the young girl. They had brought her coconut hearts and arm-bands and to-bacco in an effort to win her affection. So they watched and they knew, but of course they could not work the magic because they did not have the magic water.

The girl left her parents and rushed back to the village with a basket of yams. She put the yams in her father's storehouse. Then she gathered some bamboo vessels and coconut-shell cups from her mother's house and went straight to the old man's house. Putting these utensils in his house, she hur-ried to the stream to fetch water so that she could cook his food. When she returned, she went in and took hold of the old man, trying to bring him out-side to bathe him. Imoina pretended that he did not know what was happen-ing, saying, "Hey, you must not hold me so tightly. I am an old man; you will tear my skin. What are you doing?" The girl replied that she was trying to clean the ashes off his body—to which he agreed, providing she handled him gently. While she was washing him, the girl tried to scrape some of the grime with her fingernail, but Imoina protested that she would draw blood that way. (You see, Imoina was the brother of Baingap, and he had the power of shedding his skin and emerging as a strong young man. He did not want the girl to see the underlying skin.)

After she had washed the old man she placed him in the sun and then swept and cleaned his house. Later in the evening, when she started to make yam soup, the old man feigned concern. "Say, woman, what do you think you are doing? You can't stay with me. All the men will be angry with me if you do; they will beat me. You should marry a young man." The girl an-swered that she loved him and had to look after him. Her parents would not be angry with Imoina.

When the two had eaten they slept. In the night the girl became aroused and held the old man's penis. Imoina woke with a start. "Woman, what is this you are doing? I am old. My penis is no longer strong enough to have intercourse with you." But the girl answered that he could at least try. He did, and the girl felt him strong inside her and was amazed that such an old man could do this. But, remember, Imoina was tricking her, and he had the power to transform himself into a young man.

The next morning the girl started back to her parents in the garden. They had already heard from her friends that she had slept with the old man and that they were therefore married. The parents said they would confront her with this news when she arrived. But, back in the village, after the girl had left, Imoina sang a magic song that quelled the anger of everyone in the place toward him on account of his having taken the young girl. So, when the girl admitted to her parents what she had done, they were not angry with her or the old man. They all returned to the village, and the girl moved in permanently with Imoina.

Several years passed, during which the couple had two children. After the birth of the second child, Imoina began playing tricks on his wife. One day he said he was going down to the stream to wash. Putting aside a bunch of betelnuts, he instructed his wife, "If while I am gone a friend of mine comes, you must give him these betelnuts and also something to eat. Tell him to wait for me; if he cannot, that's all right too."

As soon as he was out of sight, Imoina quickly took off his old skin and put it into a bamboo container. He was a young man again. He took three spears and circled around the village so as to reenter it on the main path.

As he walked Imoina carried a rattle in his netbag. This was made from a sea shell in which he had put some cassowary teeth [?]. The woman heard him coming and knew that it was her husband's "friend." When he arrived he asked after Imoina, and the woman replied that he had just gone down to the water to bathe. She gave him the betelnut and suggested he wait for her husband. But, after a long time, the handsome young man said he could wait no longer. When he was out of sight he dashed into the forest, retrieved the bamboo container, resumed his old skin, and hobbled up to his house. His wife was angry with him for taking so long and for missing his nice young friend, but the old man protested that, at his age, he could not walk quickly.

This happened many times. Also, whenever a singsing was being held in another village, Imoina would tell his wife to go to it and take with her some betelnut "for his friend." Then, when she had left he would take off his old skin, decorate himself, and go to the singsing, pretending to be the young man. This, too, was repeated often.

Finally, Imoina's wife began to suspect that something was amiss. The next time a singsing was being held, she told her oldest son to stay behind and secretly watch what his father did. She would go ahead with the infant and wait for him up the path. So the boy did this. He hid in a coconut palm and observed his father remove his old skin and adorn himself for the sing-sing. Then the boy ran ahead and told his mother what he had seen.

Later in the evening, when the wife was joined at the singsing by her husband's "friend," she pretended that she was still deceived. As they were

sitting there, the infant defecated, and the wife asked the young man to
hold the child while she went to throw away the feces. But the man replied
that he must not hold the child, lest his friend be angry with him. Only the
father of the child should hold him. At this the wife lost her temper and
cried: "Who do you think is the father of this child! You alone are the father!
All the time you are tricking me by changing your skin; you lie to me about
this friend of yours. Now, hold the child while I throw away the feces!"

This talk made her husband very angry, and he threw his limestick, strik-
ing her on the breast. She screamed, but instead of a human voice it was
the scream of a parrot. The blow had turned her into a parrot, and she flew
crying to the tree tops. Imoina returned to his house and changed himself
back into an old man. From then on he lived alone, for he had ruined his
wife. . . .

(From here the story line abruptly shifts to a time many years
later. Imoina recruits all the young boys of the village to carry him
south to rejoin Baingap. Along the way they are provisioned with
food which Imoina magically vomits forth. After the party has settled down with Baingap near the Sepik river, and the boys have
grown up and married the local women, the two young suitors
from early in the story appear and demand that Imoina give them
some of his magical water, which he does. They return home, attempt a grand seduction of all the women of their village, and are
speared to death by the irate husbands. The story ends with the
lament that the secret of the water magic died with them.)

F OR the reader who has remained attentive thus far,
despite the detailed and sometimes protracted nature
of the descriptions, I have the good news that the ritual
specifics of Nggwal Walipeine can be dealt with fairly swiftly.
Several major elements of belief and action are nearly identical to their counterparts in the preceding grade, and it is
possible to do justice to this tambaran without having to repeat much that is already familiar. Instead, the object is to
present the general character of Nggwal Walipeine, reporting only those particulars that contribute to its distinctiveness. At the same time, in dealing with this, the culminating
grade of the cult, it is appropriate to retrospect certain fea-

tures of the entire sequence, and to gather our thoughts in preparation for later discussions on the nature and influence of Tambaran ethics.

Nggwal Walipeine is the tambaran of old men; hence the relevance of Imoina's mythic exploits to the substance of this chapter. Pending analysis of the story at a more opportune moment in the discussion, I ask the reader to note that Imoina's agedness is totally deceptive, a skin-deep mask to conceal the miraculous powers within. Such is the mythic construction of old age; such, also, is the central illusion of Nggwal Walipeine.

What is perhaps most remarkable about this tambaran is that it exists at all. In a survey of all Arapesh villages conducted near the close of fieldwork, it was confirmed that Ilahita is the only place which represents this segment of the population with a distinct ritual category.[1] The reason is partly historical. Among the groups that found refuge in Ilahita late in the last century were several bands of mutually unrelated Kwanga that had been dislocated by pressures created by Abelam predatory migrations. They were assimilated to Ilahita village by being organized into a new ward—Nangup (Tuzin 1976:64). One widely held story is that these Kwanga brought with them their own Nggwal, and after much negotiation, the details of which are lost to us, it was decided between hosts and strangers that effective integration of the latter would best be achieved by reciprocal assimilation. Accordingly, Nangup was absorbed into Ilahita's Nggwal (Bunafunei) and Ilahita was absorbed into Nangup's Nggwal (Walipeine)—in both cases the mechanism being to extend initiation partnerships (*ombif*) and enemy partnerships (*nautamana*) to members of the other group.[2]

---

1. My own and others' data on surrounding cultures further verify Ilahita's singularity in this respect.
2. Refugees comprising the other "new" ward (Ilifalemb) also brought their own Nggwal. However, perhaps because they arrived in a group (from the Bumbita Arapesh area to the west), there was a greater urge on their part to maintain their collective identity. To this day Ilifalemb has remained ritually independent of the other five wards, although the recent imposition of a vehicular road through their ward, and their consequent inability to seclude their ceremonial hamlet for long periods, is pushing them toward joining the main cult of the village.

We cannot say with certainty what inspired these planners to introduce the new Nggwal into the cult hierarchy at a position *above* that of the aboriginal Nggwal. Knowing the subsequent sociopolitical effectiveness of that arrangement, one is tempted to embrace the functionalist fallacy (see Spiro 1963) and retrodict past and irrecoverable motivations from present-day utilities. However, logical considerations and my strongly felt sense of how the Arapesh deal with such situations suggest to me the following probabilities.

First, prior to Nangup's formation the Ilahita cult was already, so to speak, filled up; an alternative to the solution adopted is not easy to visualize. From early childhood to middle age, the male's ritual standing developed through an unbroken sequence which sensibly paralleled stages of social and physical maturation. Leaving aside females and pre-Falanga infants, the only remaining segment left unaccounted for was the old men. Under the traditional system —as it can be seen today in other villages—men retire from the cult after transmitting Nggwal (Bunafunei) to their junior *ombif*. As senior advisers to their sons and younger initiation partners, their authority remains real, and those with the right combination of personal traits continue to be powerful figures in the community. But, in cult terms their status is informal. They have no tambaran. They occupy the unhappy limbus between social manliness and final oblivion. Judging from what we have seen of the cult's implications for social and personal identity, and the boastful pride which the men take in lionizing "their" tambaran, one can easily imagine that superimposing the new Nggwal on the preexisting cult would have been welcomed as a marvelous remedy for what amounts to the Arapesh mid-life crisis, that is, as a way of *formalizing* elderhood and rendering it psychoculturally meaningful.

One may ask, if this need for identity is as compelling as I claim it to be, why Nggwal Walipeine has not spread to other villages—where, presumably, the need is equally great. The answer, I suggest, has to do with Ilahita's singularly large size: even with natural attrition taking its heavy toll, there would still be enough men in this category to implement ceremonies on a scale commensurate with the importance of this grade's members. Other villages simply lack the manpower to make this a viable or credible cult grade.[3]

Another question arises. If men glory so in the might of their tambaran, what would induce them to place a foreign spirit above their own in the hierarchy or, indeed, to admit it in the first place? Taking the latter part first, introducing a foreign Nggwal to their village is no more or less weighty than introducing the foreigners themselves. To regard the refugees as worthy additions is, ipso facto, to evaluate their Nggwal in equivalent terms. Such acceptance would also be consistent with the general Arapesh tendency (cf. Mead 1938) to esteem imported ritual items for their novelty, mystery and presumed power. On the matter of hierarchy, it is a curious fact that Nggwal Walipeine's supremacy is markedly qualified. True, it is the "highest" tambaran in the temporal sequence, and its members are unsurpassed in the authority they wield. And yet, in every other respect Ngwal Bunafunei is more important and is recognized as such. He commands the greatest ceremonial investment; his wrath is dreaded more, his gifts valued more; when men speak of Nggwal out of context, it is invariably Nggwal Bunafunei that is intended. The ambiguities of precedence between these two Nggwals may or may not be traceable to the historical circumstance which we are discussing. But the persistence of this faintly paradoxical relationship is, I propose, attributable to the expression it gives to a perennial problem in social relations, namely, whether the guiding ethic is to be predicated on considerations of *power* or on considerations of *authority*. Walipeine can wheedle, bribe, threaten, pontificate and intrigue to get his way in the public arena; but in the end he is powerless. The best he can do is to employ stratagems to convince Bunafunei that the latter's awesome power—the power to create yams, babies and enemy dead—is ultimately answerable to Walipeine's moral authority. The old men back their authority by claiming special ritual knowledge and special

---

3. That men take account of such limitations is supported by abundant evidence. Recall, for instance, from the previous volume the remark of one Hengwanif man who explained the absence of *olawa* partnerships in his ward by noting that there would not be enough men to sustain them (Tuzin 1976:232).

intimacy with both these cult spirits;[4] at the same time they are too sophisticated not to recognize, and in private moments to admit, that their position is based on a good deal of sham. The real power rests with Bunafunei—men in their prime who plant the gardens, inseminate the women and fight the battles—and this is why it is the greatest tambaran. Placing Walipeine above it in the hierarchy has formalized and enhanced the elders' authority, the eufunctional effects of which will be examined in the next chapter. However, the continuing political supremacy of Nggwal Bunafunei confirms symbolically that power relations are only indirectly altered by the innovation.

Granted, we cannot appeal to these post-facto functions to illuminate precipitating motivational factors. But the preceding material does support the inference that attitudes (especially those of the old men) would have favored accepting Walipeine, and as best we can tell there would have been no good reasons for not doing so.

There is an entirely different body of local lore surrounding this event which is worth reporting if only because it instances the diversity of opinion that encrusts nearly every subject that has political implications and is open to debate or interpretation. This version has it that Kamba'wa, the nggwal whose story is told in the myth introducing the preceding chapter, is the true "papa" of all Nggwal tambarans. It was brought by the forebears of present-day Nangup residents when they arrived from the area of Ingamblis, Ilahita's neighbor to the south (cf. above). Soon afterward, the men of Ilahita became envious of Kamba'wa and accordingly set about creating nggwals of their own. From there Nggwal spread to all the surrounding cultures, some of whom claim —erroneously, say the Ilahitans—to be the true origin place of the spirit. Nggwal Walipeine thus exists in recognition of the historical and ritual precedence of Kamba'wa and of the descendants of the men who brought him to Ilahita.

4. The generational problem symbolized here in religious ideology is manifest also in the domestic sphere. Adult sons seem on the whole to be respectful and attentive toward their aged fathers. Nevertheless, it often happens that a man will withhold some of his personal magic until the very end, lest his sons be inclined to waver in their piety toward him. See Tuzin (1976:99).

Despite the fact that this history was given to me by clients of Kamba'wa,[5] and must on that account be treated warily, it is not at all incredible. The precedence of Kamba'wa is generally acknowledged by cult members, who respect the cassowary claw and log fragment as authentic material evidence for the veracity of the story. As to whether Nangup's ancestors came from Ingamblis or the Kwanga area, there is no real contradiction since migrants from the latter would have passed through and perhaps abided for a time in the region of Ingamblis. (Nangup residents themselves aver that their forefathers arrived in Ilahita speaking a different language.) The most attractive aspect of this version is that it confirms the advent of Nggwal from a southerly direction at a time and under circumstances that are compatible with independently based reconstructions. Indeed, the only part that is plainly dubious is the incidental claim that Kwanga and Abelam peoples obtained Nggwal from the Arapesh; such notions may gratify the cultural ego, but they do not bear up under comparative cultural and linguistic evidence to the contrary (see chap. 7). In rendering Kamba'wa the prototype for *all* of Ilahita's nggwals, this history does stand the earlier one on its head. However, I am disinclined to take sides, since in this study the issue is subordinate to the problem of power and authority, which remains alive today and is no longer contingent on the question of Nggwal's historical origins.

PERSONAL AND SOCIOLOGICAL ATTRIBUTES

Nggwal Walipeine is the "old tambaran." This description has a double meaning. First, there is the unhidden metaphor (portrayed to the women as true) which personifies this spirit as an old man—frail, unsteady, his skin white with age and with the coat of ashes he has acquired by spending most of his time lying near warming fires. He neglects to bathe. For

5. My informants were Ililip men, who explained their involvement with Kamba'wa by recalling that their forefathers had been among those that welcomed the arrivals and provided them with land and sago groves. In appreciation for this hospitality, they were offered a share in the ritual estate of Kamba'wa.

additional warmth and protection he takes the broad leaves of the wild taro (*bondaf*), bleaches them in the sun, and covers himself with them. He is a figure both wretched and faintly comical—in tone (and with his white leaf covering) not unlike the image in our own society of the derelict with his comically pathetic newspaper blanket.[6] His appetite is not what it used to be: he no longer swallows sacrificial animals whole, but eats only parts of them and, like his human coeval, especially favors male pork genitals. Wild boars are therefore de rigueur, since their gelded village cousins lack the necessary delicacies. Also, having passed his prime, Nggwal Walipeine is unthreatened by the dangerous *maulas* spirit that inhabits pythons,[7] so these too become part of the ceremonial repast. The old Nggwal's taste for human blood has also diminished, and it is rare that a death is attributed to him.

The other connotation of "old tambaran" is maintained as a private joke among members of this grade. Quite simply, there is nothing new about this grade; it is, in our terms, "old hat." Prospective initiates—that is, men who have seen Nggwal Bunafunei—are sophisticated enough not to fear the entry ordeal; but they are led to believe that Nggwal Walipeine holds knowledge and powers of a quite distinctive sort. What they find are variations of themes and devices that are already known to them. On piercing the innermost core of the cult, they find that it is hollow; the secret is that there is no secret. Lest this hoax be construed as a moral or logical flaw in the character of the Tambaran, it is worth pausing to remind ourselves what the existence of a secret entails.

In considering the politics of ritual secrecy among the Ara-

---

6. Many Arapesh seem to find deformities and infirmities vastly amusing—unless, of course, they are the ones afflicted.

7. *Maulas* also inhabit large shell rings. Interestingly, the same word is applied to the collective ancestral dead. Informants were inclined to regard the latter *maulas* as homonymic with the former. Nevertheless, ancestral spirits are strongly associated with supernatural pythons of immense size, which also figure prominently in totemically significant myths. Large shell-ring heirlooms have a phallic significance (cf. Tuzin 1972:245) and are closely identified with the spiritual purity and continuity of the proprietor clan. Much more could be said about pythons and shell rings in these terms, but this is enough to warrant that the lexical coincidence has a symbolic aspect which my informants did not recognize, or at least could not interpret.

pesh, it is necessary to distinguish between the *content* of a secret and the fact of there being a secret "something," whatever the content. Thus, the content of a secret is less important sociologically than the fact of it being secret—providing, of course, that the secret is publicly known to exist. The "voices" of the Tambaran—flutes, trumpets, bullroarers, whistles—are secret. However, their importance in social life lies in convincing the women and non-initiates that the spirits may assume material form. Since this is a fiction, this most vital secret has, in fact, no content at all; or, rather, its content shifts from substance to metaphor. By the time the seeker has advanced to Nggwal Walipeine, the metaphor itself has been considerably eroded by the realization that the Tambaran is "what men do" (see chap. 7). The main thing is that outsiders think there is a content, and this gives those "in the know" power over them. One consequence is that cult beliefs and paraphernalia do not lend themselves to secularization or popularization.

For example, a few years prior to fieldwork members of the British Royal Family visited the local subdistrict headquarters at Maprik, and villagers from all around assembled to entertain them with traditional dances. Among the performers were men wearing *hangahiwa*, the full-body costumes which occur as common cult regalia throughout Abelam and Arapesh territory (chap. 2). When the performances ended, the Ilahitans were shocked to see men from other villages remove the costumes in full view of the women in the crowd. Nothing more was said or done about the *hangahiwa* until, during my stay in Ilahita, some youths wanted to refurbish them to wear around the village. Most of the older men said this was out of the question: the secret was now known to the women; wearing the *hangahiwa* would only bring shame and ridicule. In the end the young men had their way, for they were of the class that currently owned and controlled the masks. Though the women were probably undeceived, for reasons reviewed in chapter 7 they did not express their cynicism openly. Thus, rather than bring the women into the circle and enjoy the *hangahiwa* for what they really are, the deception was maintained, and today everyone acts as though the revelation had never occurred. There can be little doubt, however, that on that day in Maprik some of the glitter was permanently shed from the men's authority.

A NOTE ON SIGNS AND BELIEFS

The preceding remarks on ritual secrecy evoke the much larger issue of native epistemology in relation to Tambaran beliefs.[8] Probably more than once the reader has wondered whether and to what extent the non-initiates "actually believe" the lies and dissimulations fed to them by cult insiders. The subject received some attention in chapter 7, when I discussed the "multiple truths" surrounding Nggwal. A broader treatment is now required, for we are approaching, in this chapter and the next, an area of Tambaran custom in which the nuances of belief acceptance have major implications for the political life of the society. As an approach to the issue, consider the following vignettes:

1. One night, a few weeks after arriving in the village, I was up late talking with Kwamwi, a middle-aged healer who is highly respected for his occult skills and for his immense charm and friendliness. As the sky was wonderfully starry, the conversation naturally turned to the area of Arapesh sidereal lore. After several minutes of Kwamwi telling me the local wisdom regarding various celestial phenomena, I casually remarked that Europeans believe that if you wish on a shooting star, your wish will come true. My companion thought hard for a few moments, and then asked, "In that case, how does anyone ever get any sleep?"

2. Several months after the incident just related, I watched while Kwamwi treated a sick child. As the family stood worriedly around, the beplumed doctor went through his examination. Muttering spells, he soothed and patted, thumped and probed, blew in one ear, then the other, and splattered the boy with magical sputum. Then, using banana-leaf holders to prevent "contaminating" himself, Kwamwi began "pulling" bits of debris—bones, pebbles, twigs —out of the boy's midsection. After pronouncing the treatment a success, he accepted a smoke from the patient's father, collected his fee, and motioned to me that it was time to leave.

Not only had Kwamwi used sleight of hand in pretending to

---

8. See Needham (1972) for a characteristically incisive examination of the problem of belief from the anthropological perspective.

extract the offending objects, he had had the audacity to use one of the same objects twice! As soon as we were out of earshot, I challenged his fraud with feigned shock and indignation. "You took their shilling, but you only tricked them! You pretended to pull objects out of the boy's body, while all the time you had them hidden between the banana leaves!" At first, Kwamwi was very amused that I should be upset over such trifles; but then he went on patiently, in a tone not unmixed with condescension, to explain how it is that things are sometimes not what they appear to be.

In a conversational setting we tend at first to approach each other's beliefs warily—and rightly so, for even in a relatively familiar situation one cannot be sure how ardently another holds to an expressed belief, whether the attachment is of an intellectual, emotional, or aesthetic kind, or whether, in fact, the idea is more akin to a fairytale fantasy and should not be dignified as a "belief" at all. The problem is compounded when the conversation occurs between representatives of different cultures, for then the very parameters of belief are thrown into question, and even the standards governing what is credible must be negotiated. While in some cases we may have the background to suspect a figurative meaning, our desire to avoid giving offense, added to the tactical dictates of interviewing, probably inclines us to err on the side of taking these avowals too literally, and to assume that statements which prescribe or even merely imply action will automatically impel such action most of the time. The preceding cases illustrate how understandings can go awry in these circumstances. And, while trivial in themselves, they disclose a conceptual distinction that is crucial in evaluating how Tambaran ideology relates to behavior.

As he later described it, Kwamwi's reaction to the shooting-star "belief" was good practical anthropology. After dismissing the intriguing possibility that there might be something in it, he went on to consider whether Europeans actually believe such a preposterous thing. If so, they would behave accordingly by sitting up all night watching the sky. When I explained that it was merely a "play" belief which no one took seriously, he immediately understood, adding that many of their beliefs are of the same type. We then speculated for a time on why people espouse beliefs and tell tales which they know to be untrue, concluding, first, that they are harmless amusements and, second, that we would *like* them to be true. The point is that probably all cultures possess acknowledged superstitions which command assent not because of any assumed relationship to empirical causation, but solely because they belong to and signify a cultural tradition which has intrinsic value and appeal.

The second case reversed our roles, but its lesson was fairly similar. Far from exhibiting the contrite or excusatory reaction I would have expected, Kwamwi was convulsed at the prospect of my believing that such a performance could be anything *but* an illusion! Many healers, he confided, claim to be able to pull objects out of their patients' bodies, but they are simply lying: "I know because I taught most of them!" I asked whether people in general knew of the trickery. Kwamwi replied that he did not know; probably many of them did. Then he added, in a more serious tone, that the deceptive element did not affect the authenticity of the treatment. Even the best healers have to use tricks—because, "if people did not see something happening, they would not believe that the magic was working." In short, a *sign* is needed, something to guide attention to what is "really" happening. Only someone who is naïve or crazy would confuse the sign with the reality.

So it is with many of the beliefs and practices surrounding the Tambaran. Signs in the form of tricks and illusions are contrived to make it *appear* to the naïve uninitiated that supernal beings do, as the men claim, assume material shape and participate in the secret rites. And yet, the inevitable question arises: Are the women truly as hoodwinked as the men think they are, or are they diplomatically concealing their skepticism? As discussed in the preceding chapter, the fear that they will be killed for their doubts prevents women from responding candidly to such a question. Thus, we may say with certainty only that if any scepticism exists its social consequences are negligible, and there is nothing approaching a conspiracy of acquiescence among the women.

Against all this evidence of religious and moral corruption, not to mention violent coercion, there is a redeeming factor in the men's favor. It is based on the same distinction between appearance and reality that acquitted Kwamwi of my malpractice charge. The fact is, informants gleefully admit that the Tambaran is redolent with sham and trickery; but, they insist, this pretense on the material plane mirrors, and in some obscure way precipitates, the magical and invisible essence of the proceedings. So, for example, the men pretend that the spirits materialize and eat the food prepared (mostly by the women) for the secret feast. In "reality," the spirits are *invisibly* present, feeding on the spiritual essence of the food, while the men merely finish off the material remains. Why do they exclude the women? This, informants aver, is regrettable, but necessary. Human welfare depends on the Tambaran being regularly fed. If the women realized that the men were sharing in the feast they would demand an equal participation. The trouble is that the Tambaran is known to despise women and to be intolerant of their company. "Now, we know our women, and we know that they would be angry at being left out of the feast; in fact, if we told them the *truth* about why they cannot attend, they would probably think we were lying!" Therefore, the only way to keep the Tambaran fed and the women unrebellious is to preserve the fiction that the Tambaran is appearing in the flesh and is eating *all* aspects of the food brought to the feast.

The flaw in this tidy scheme is guilt, the problem of which is exacerbated by the realization of some of the men, some of the time, that the will of the Tambaran is subject to human manipulation (chap. 9). All rationales aside, in a place where food is so conspicuously important, and where meat is especially rare and coveted, a man would have to be gravely deficient in the social virtues of compassion and familial tenderness to escape feelings of remorse over his inherited role in such an unjust arrangement. The subject of ritually induced guilt will be touched on later in the study; we have already seen signs of its companion emotion—fear. It is clear by now that the brutality of the Tambaran is in part defensive. The men cling nervously to a precarious sovereignty, the meaning and necessity of which are shrouded in artifice and illusion going all the way back to Falanga. To this we may trace

the chief dread of Arapesh male culture, as it recurs in figures of myth, ritual and, indeed, conversation: the prospect
of female reprisal. Thus, the story of Nambweapa'w projects
with particular vividness the interwoven themes of deception and retribution as they apply to the symbolism of male-
female relations in Arapesh culture. Moreover, many of the
subsequent cult myths reveal that the men acquired the Tambaran through trickery or usurpation, leaving as a future
"mythic" possibility the bloody resolution foretold by Nambweapa'w's revenge.[9]

The anthropology of belief would be aided immeasurably
by a technique that would enable us to read other people's
minds. As it is, we may not even take at face value what others *say* they believe, for this would presuppose agreement on
the nature of belief itself; and, as noted earlier, this problem
is most intense when we are speaking cross-culturally. And
yet, these obstacles are constantly overridden by the practi-
calities of cultural life, by the fact that we must take precisely
these liberties in order to communicate meaningfully in the
human mode. Verification proceeds without positive knowledge, in that we infer the presence of belief by observing the
appropriate response of others (and ourselves) to the conventional *signs* of that belief. In the process, a kind of metaphysical truth is generated: gestures of belief are taken to be
evidence of a reality that is created by those very gestures;
the sign marks the intersection of appearance and reality.
The Tambaran offers an unusually good example of this
mechanism in operation: the selective spread of ritual knowledge has produced a situation in which different segments
of the community apprehend the sign in distinct, socially
prescribed ways, and yet the affective contents of Tambaran
belief remain surprisingly uniform.

We ask, Do the women actually believe what the men tell
them about the Tambaran? Are they so utterly taken in by
appearances? In the absence of any evidence to the contrary,

9. Elsewhere, I have analyzed the symbolism of Arapesh flood myths in terms of
this primordial fear of female retribution—a fear that is exercised simultaneously on social, cultural and psychological planes; see Tuzin (1977).

we assume that they are. However, it is also true that the mystical authority of the Tambaran is wedded so closely to the worldly authority of the men that we cannot be sure which to assign as the actual object of female subservience. Even granting a measure of agnosticism to individual women, an overt challenge to the Tambaran is unthinkable because it would signify a challenge to tradition in its most condensed form. At any rate, if the Tambaran is a sign spanning the two poles of appearance and reality, it would seem that the apprehension of women (and children) rests almost entirely on the pole of appearance.

For most men achievement of the two highest grades occurs at about the ages of twenty-five and fifty, respectively. The three lower grades are entered in the years of childhood and early adolescence. This means that, in addition to the entire teen-age male population, there are a substantial number of socially competent men who are familiar with the trickery of the inferior grades and who, unlike the women, have reason to be sceptical about the secrets from which they are still excluded. Being part of the company of men, they have over the years heard and seen things which tempt them privately to question the candor of the older men when they claim comradeship with the incarnate Tambaran. This element of doubt, which the elders certainly know to exist, contributes a political flavor to contests of will between groups on different rungs of the ritual ladder. In principle, the youths accept the traditional authority of their elders, especially in magical and religious matters. Wisely, the older group avoids showing itself divided on any issue directly involving Tambaran ideology. But, as we have seen on numerous occasions, cult leaders are inclined to generalize their authority in the name of the Tambaran. Whether or not they meet resistance depends on the issue at hand and on the various interests aligned on each side—interests which, in strictly secular contexts, may undercut the solidarity of ritual groups. Not surprisingly, with their years of experience in political gamesmanship, the elders are skilled at knowing when and how far to impose themselves; and in rare instances of miscalculation, they invariably extricate themselves through some diversionary tactic.

It would seem, then, that the younger generation of males lies somewhere between apprehending the Tambaran as appearance and as reality, with the degrees of sophistication varying widely within the group. The years spent in the lower ranks witness a movement toward greater enlightenment. Hints and previews, usually accidental but sometimes deliberate, prepare them for the eventual discovery that the Tambaran, when finally confronted face to face, is not what it has always appeared to be. Meanwhile, as these men advance to their social majority and assume greater responsibility and assertiveness, their submission or defiance in reaction to the dictates of cult leaders becomes more overtly a *political* act, though the religious idiom is rigorously maintained. Such affairs must be conducted with extreme delicacy; for, with wisdom on one side and muscle on the other, the two groups are well aware that they need one another.

In some ways the position of the senior males is the most interesting and complex of the three. Masters of the illusion, they scoff at the credulity of the uninitiated and affect the sophistication of knowing the "true" significance of the Tambaran ceremonies. And yet, the case of the man whose urbanity was undone by a dream (chap. 7) reminds us that, ironically, the men are prey to their own devices. The situation is reminiscent of the American parent who has long since ceased to "believe" in the myth of the Nativity, but who, for the sake of the children and in the name of tradition, re-creates the domestic ceremonies of Christmastide—only to find himself captured by their magic. In effect, he has replaced a childish attachment to appearances with an adult reverence for significances. And, to a greater extent than he would probably care to admit, the *signs* of the occasion—the stories, paraphernalia and procedures—are what excite his religious experience. The sentiment, overlaid with adult rationality, is grounded in the early years, when magical thinking presided over the growth of the imagination as a tool of emotional expression.

For the Arapesh male, the years of religious ignorance and peonage condition the emotions to withstand the shock of discovering that the entire cult, in its material aspect, is an elaborate falsehood. Apostasy is unlikely, since half a lifetime of beholding in terror the signs of the *mysterium* cannot be undone by the mere revelation that these signs are human contrivances; the mystery and magic survive, thereafter rationalized according to the ideology of spiritual significances. Further, as a major compensation, the very act of revelation admits the novice to the rank of the elect. The system that had exploited him is now his benefactor. The older men need not fear retaliation, for the resentment of the new initiate has an institutional outlet: the systematic cruelty and subjection required against women and junior males. Soothing to his guilt are the demands of the *real* Tambaran as he now understands it. And so the system perpetuates itself. Do the senior males really "believe" in the Tambaran? Yes and no. But one thing is sure: even the most sceptical among them would warmly embrace the Sophist dictum that, whether or not the gods exist, they certainly ought to be worshiped.

THE OLD AND YOUNG NGGWALS

Nggwal Walipeine belongs to men over the age of approximately fifty, few of whom will survive long enough to pass this tambaran on to their junior *ombif*. Two problems arise from this situation. First, the transmission of knowledge is jeopardized by placing this grade in the keeping of a group certain to experience high attrition during the twenty years (or more) until the next initiation. Second, the men of this cohort are few and feeble enough to be limited in their capacity to undertake the demanding tasks involved in producing the initiation ceremony. The spirit house, though somewhat smaller than that of Nggwal Bunafunei, is built on the same plan and is still a major construction effort; and, in addition, there is a considerable amount of artistic paraphernalia that has to be fashioned. Both these problems are solved by the mechanism of mass ritual promotion which I described in the previous study (Tuzin 1976:284–285). To review briefly:

at the time the *kwongwof* spears are installed in the newly built spirit house of Nggwal Bunafunei the senior age-set (Owangufwisi) of the Sahopwas group are informally advanced to the ranks of their senior *ombif*.[10] It will be remembered that the group promoted corresponds in age of members with the junior age-set (Owangufwisi) of the group to which they are now aligning themselves.[11] The effect is to double the size of the senior group[12] just at the time they are most in need of reinforcements. The enlarged group builds the spirit house without difficulty, and the chances are substantially increased that the secret knowledge involved in preparing this tambaran will survive until the next initiation. Furthermore, reconstituting the action groups in this way rotates an opposition based heretofore on ritual criteria to one based on the criterion of chronological age; the principle of age seniority, which has quietly informed the cult all along, is now the sole determinant of effective ritual-group composition.

This radical replacement of one governing principle by another is deeply implicated in the problem of power and authority discussed earlier. Members of the Balangaisi age-set are the elder brothers of their respective sibling groups. Having dominated their younger brothers all their lives, they are now entering a final phase of waning vitality; literally and figuratively, their power is largely spent, and the prospect they face is to suffer disadvantage at the hands of their younger, still active brothers.[13] The redefinition of status engineered by Nggwal Walipeine in effect recognizes the

10. This is a de facto promotion from Sahopwas to Owapwas class membership—something that is theoretically impossible in cult ideology. It occurs nonetheless and maintains ideological respectability by the arrangement being kept informal: the promotees do not relinquish nominal membership in the Sahopwas initiation class.

11. A further refinement of this mechanism is the simultaneous promotion of two or three members of the junior age-set of Sahopwas. Termed Umbaisi, these youths are upgraded for the explicit reason of ensuring the future transmission of ritual knowledge in the event that some disaster decimates the older cult stratum. See Tuzin (1976: 282) for a full discussion of this and related practices.

12. The size is doubled rather than increased by 50 percent because the Owapwas would have already lost half its members through natural attrition.

13. This development must be viewed against the generally problematic nature of the fraternal relationship in this society, about which I had a good deal to say in the previous volume (Tuzin 1976: 177ff.).

plight of the aging older brother and remedies it to the extent of conferring on him an authority equal to that of his senior *ombaf*, thereby reaffirming the subordinate status of his younger brother(s). It is the old Nggwal coming to the rescue of the men with whom he most closely identifies.[14]

Of the forty-three individual nggwal spirits in Ilahita, only ten participate in Nggwal Walipeine.[15] These are from Nangup itself (four nggwals) and the three other wards which originally welcomed Nangup's forefathers (see above) and established exchange relationships with them—Ililip (three), Balanga (two) and Bwi'ingili (one). Although Hengwanif and Ilifalemb, as well as men associated with nonparticipating nggwals from the other four wards, are technically unconnected with Nggwal Walipeine, the fact is that all men of appropriate age and ritual standing convene in Nangup's ceremonial hamlet and consider themselves members of the grade. The difference is that they do not undergo the initiation procedure, but are admitted to the secrets afterward and informally. In all practical respects their participation in the ceremonial activities is indistinguishable from that of the "official" members. The absence of their nggwals is no disability; indeed, fewer nggwals implies smaller-scaled proceedings—which, in addition to reflecting the relatively mod-

14.As indicated by the preceding footnote, the scenario of fraternal discord and its eventual resolution in the ritual segregation of power and authority domains conforms well with the empirical situation as disclosed through statistical tests, case studies and direct observation (Tuzin 1976). But it is important to emphasize that the validity of the present analysis does not immediately depend upon more or less conformance at the empirical level. In this context Nggwal Walipeine is an expressive form, and the "problem" for which it provides resolution is of a similar order. In principle, the problem could be purely imaginary and bear no relation whatever to things as they are. It is a template available to cultural actors who seek understanding of, and perhaps a solution to, homologous problems in their own life.
   This is where the question of empirical "fit" enters in. For, without something to express, without the presence of these homologies at some (unknown) level of frequency, it is difficult (if not impossible) to account for the expressive form itself. As it happens, in the present case the symbolic figure is strongly concordant with a widely recurring problem affecting fraternal relationships, from which it (the symbol) constantly draws ideological nourishment. This I take to be a sign of "health" and functional efficiency in the ritual process.
15.See Tuzin (1976:355–356) for a full listing of Ilahita nggwals, their client populations and wards of residence. In gross terms the number of nggwals in each ward are: Balanga, 6; Bwi'ingili, 2; Hengwanif, 6; Ililip, 9; Ilifalemb, 12; Nangup, 8. There are 43, all told.

est character of this tambaran, is a welcome relief in the midst of Nggwal Bunafunei obligations.

It should be evident by now that Nggwal Walipeine is a rather odd tambaran in comparison with the others that precede him in the cult hierarchy. It is even arguable that his niche ought not to be described as an independent "grade" at all, but rather as a ritual afterthought, an epilogue tacked on to Nggwal Bunafunei. The evidence for this view is quite compelling. First, the initiation into Nggwal Walipeine must be timed to come in the year *preceding* that of Nggwal Bunafunei. That is, not only is the sequence inviolable, which is more or less the case at all levels of the cult, but there is an unusually restricted temporal dimension to the relationship between the two Nggwals. Accession to Walipeine is achieved by the Sahopwas class while it is still in possession of Bunafunei, thus creating a ritual imbalance which the actors perceive to be rectified by the transfer of Bunafunei to the Owapwas class. This suggests that the two are subphases of a single ritual transaction.[16] Secondly, the two "grades" share the same spirit entities, both at the specific level of individual nggwals and in the summary concept applied to them. Thus, the two Nggwals are the same "person" viewed at different life stages; hence is repeated the familiar youth/age dichotomy which characterizes subphases of earlier grades.

Against these arguments, we must admit two overriding reasons for treating them as separate grades. First, notwithstanding the shuffling of age-sets (see above), the fact remains that except for one year in the twenty-five-year half-cycle the two tambarans are held by different initiation classes; to regard them as subphases would therefore be to confound a ritual distinction that is central to cult ideology and practice. The second reason has already been discussed: the role implications of belonging to one grade or the other

---

16. The men themselves are not much help on this issue. In the abstract, as when being questioned by an anthropologist, they usually maintain that Walipeine is an independent grade; yet at other times they use the subphase terminology of *ambalinei* and *wafitanei* in characterizing younger and older Nggwals, respectively. In practice, e.g., when ceremonies are being planned, they often imply that they are subphases. In general, it must be said that the men are indifferent to the academic niceties of the case.

may be different in kind from those obtaining at lower cult levels, but they are every bit as weighty. The remaining ambiguity does not permit great confidence in classifying these as "grades"; however, it may point to other, more interesting possibilities: that the relationship between the two Nggwals is in a state of major transition, and/or that the uncertainties are inherent to the extent the relationship expresses the equally ambiguous division between power and authority (see above).

THE INITIATION

The activities surrounding Nggwal Walipeine—*bowas* flute singsings, feasts and the initiation itself—occur exclusively at Kaunaweli, the ceremonial hamlet of Nangup. In form and external décor the spirit house is identical to that of Bunafunei, and its construction involves the same secret techniques and accompanying magic. However, its smaller size means that it can be erected with greater dispatch and less fanfare, and the entire task is manageable within the post-planting lull preceding the onset of the ritual season in which the initiation is to occur.[17] The house's chief distinction lies in its interior appointments. Rather than being divided longitudinally into outer and inner sancta by a gallery wall, the house's inner sanctum is contained within a large, free-standing structure (*bondafip*) in the middle of the floor. Shaped like an inverted tub or ark, the *bondafip* consists of a wooden frame covered entirely with painted panels.[18] The designs are strikingly unlike the motifs of Nggwal Bunafunei. In addition to some amount of anthropomorphic treatment,

17. Also, the men who build this spirit house are generally past the age and station in life when, for reasons of prestige or a large and hungry family, they are driven to maximize the size and number of their gardens. The older men allow themselves more leisure time, which in this year they spend building and equipping the spirit house. As noted earlier, the "official" clients of Nggwal Walipeine are assisted by the senior age-set of the group to be initiated; however, only the former are ritually eligible to work on the interior of the house once it is built.
   I should mention that the feasting done in conjunction with this project is modest and informal. Since all involved are veteran spirit-house builders, none of the techniques is revelationary, and accordingly no payment feast is called for.
18. The structure is approximately six meters long, three meters wide, and three meters tall. The sides slope inward toward the top.

we find an abundance of graceful free-form patterns of leaves—wild taro leaves (*bondaf*) from which the structure derives its name. And, in keeping with the notion that Nggwal Walipeine bleaches the leaves before covering himself with them, the paintings show a predominance of white coloration. The leaves are outlined in white, and are divided by a white spine from which are drawn a multitude of closely spaced fine-line white ribs. Enormous patience goes into producing even one of these leaves, but the final effect is to create a remarkable impression of textured relief over the surface of the paintings. The upper parts of the structure's front and rear are each hung with a painted wooden mask decorated with a feather-and-dog's-teeth headdress, shells, and birds of paradise. Each mask is surmounted by a hornbill effigy. The top of the structure rises at its center to a peak covered with plaited-fiber fabric and crowned with a carved black cockatoo finial. Auxiliary decorations placed on the *bondafip* and on the ground next to it include shell rings, bird-of-paradise pelts and orange *su'witip* berries. Access to the interior is achieved through a hidden door at the rear of the structure.[19]

The induction ceremony is a simplified, abbreviated version of that already described for Nggwal Bunafunei. Leaving aside the *bowas* singsings that herald the advent of Walipeine and continue nightly for a month after the initiation, the entire business is discharged in only two days. There is no preliminary display of the initiators (Owapwas); no obligation is imposed on either party to commit *laf* murder; the new initiates (Sahopwas) are not enjoined to spend a period in ritual seclusion, and accordingly there is no ceremonial reentry into society. In positive terms we may compare the general organization of the event: entry into the house on the first day and revelation of the flutes on the second, and also various details, such as the occurrence of mock aggression and the ritual feeding of the pork liver to Nggwal as a precondition of the novices' accession. What remains are a

19. The *bondafip* is the only part of the spirit-house interior that is decorated. Except for a statue of Kamba'wa laid on the floor to one side and one or two items needed during the initiation rite, the remainder of the house is empty and bare.

few differences occurring at the level of detail, to which we should now give attention.

First, the "combat and feeding" sequence leading to the novices' entry into the spirit house is preceded by a carnival parade conducted by the "sons" of the initiators in playful abuse of the novices.[20] As the novices cluster in the center of the clearing, the parade enters opposite the spirit house, circles them once, and exits stage right. The procession begins with two running *hangahiwa* led by their youthful Sahopwas proprietors, who are in turn escorted by their senior *ombif*, that is, men from the group conducting the parade.[21] Next to appear are two men carrying a log, followed by several comrades with pangal shovels. The log is dropped in the clearing and the men go through the motions of shoveling "water" from in front of it. This is to simulate the local fishing technique, thereby signifying the notorious meat hunger of the novices and predicting their feckless inability to observe the taboos that are about to be levied upon them.[22]

After these mimes have left, a number of men move through the hamlet pretending a calculatedly comical variety of physical and characterological deformities, all of which are intended either as commentaries on the novices or as warnings to them of what will happen if they violate the forthcoming taboos. One man distorts his nose with a string passed through the septum and tied tightly behind his head, thus representing a leprous, wasting disease. Some of the men hobble with the unsteady gait of premature old age,

20. Note that these "sons" comprise the sub-class that is to be initiated into Nggwal Bunafunei the following year, at which time they (and their "fathers") are renamed Sahopwas. The present novices are their senior *ombif*, who, having not yet relinquished Nggwal Bunafunei, are still Sahopwas.

21. In other words, all four sub-classes have a role in these proceedings. Thus: (1) as chief initiators, the Owapwas Seniors are arrayed in front of the spirit house to "defend" the Tambaran; (2) the Owapwas Juniors conduct the parade; (3) the Sahopwas Seniors perform passively as novices; and (4) the Sahopwas Juniors are recruited by the Owapwas Juniors as incidental participants in the parade. The "grand finale" feature is quite intentional.

22. The technique consists crudely of damming a stream and shoveling out a pool below the dam until the fish can be caught by hand. The additional insult implied here is that these adult men would have a taste for fish, which is generally regarded as a disgusting food fit only for women and children.

while one even scoots along on his buttocks. Another wag holds a *su'witip*-tipped stick between his legs—the *akutum* sore we saw in earlier initiations—and makes lewd advances on some of the ladies in the front row of the audience, who react with shrieks of laughter and exaggerated alarm. Still others pair up in hilarious imitation of sexual intercourse, suggesting that the novices' gluttony in this domain is also unrestrained.[23]

The audience's attention is then directed to two men who enter carrying a pole, from which are suspended a banana stalk and an ants' nest trimmed to resemble a pig. Two attendants hold burning torches below the objects. This reiterates the ban on pork and extends it to plantains and sweet bananas. Immediately thereafter comes a litter on which is borne a female figurine (*walufwin*) decorated with green cordyline leaves. This is the "mother" of all leafy foods—edible greens, banana, sugar cane, pumpkin, bamboo shoots, papaya, sago, tulip—which are thereby added to the list of tabooed foods. Blemished pitpit and taro of the type with linear-spreading rather than encircling rhizomes are likewise to be avoided. Finally, although they are not represented in the parade, it is understood that the proscription includes coconut water and flesh and, at least until the vines of the new yam plantings have grown up and covered the support poles, cold water and bathing. This leaves the Walipeine initiates with a Spartan regime of sexual abstinence, yams, certain taros, unblemished pitpit and warm water.

When the parade is finished, the mood of the participants noticeably sobers. A mock attack is staged against the initiators guarding the spirits, the pork liver is received by the Tambaran, and the novices are arranged in a line for entry

---

23. The only stock figure missing from this parade was, according to informants, one who inserted a hibiscus blossom in the urethra of his erect penis and, with appropriate gestures, indicated that a sore as big and as red would result from sexual contact during the subsequent period of taboo. The latter extends from this, the preplanting season, until after the yam harvest, an interval of seven to nine months. In the event that a taboo is violated, the punishing agent is said to be *dombaf*—a portion of undercooked wild taro which prospective entrants are tricked into eating and which putatively remains in their stomachs during the interdictory period.

27. The *walufwin* carving is painted and decorated prior to the Nggwal Walipeine initiation.

28. At the moment of highest intensity during the Nggwal Walipeine initiation, a man from the novice class reaches a pole over the heads of the initiators and inserts a pig liver into an aperture on the left side of the spirit-house façade.

into the spirit house.[24] After all the supplicants have crawled out of sight, the doorway is sealed with a woven mat decorated with yellow croton leaves as a sign that "something beautiful" dwells within. A *bondaf* (taro) leaf is laid in front of the door to verify that a pig has been given to the Tambaran in payment for this initiation. This ends the public phase of the ceremony: the crowd of non-initiates is dismissed to allow the old and new men of Walipeine to prepare their private feast and *bowas* singsing.

Upon entering the spirit house the novices are subjected to an ordeal similar to, but somewhat milder than, that which marked entry to Bunafunei. Thus, the individual is cuffed gently about the head and shoulders and doused with ashes, while nearby someone simulates the stomp of the tambaran by thumping a sprouted coconut on the ground. As the novice is shunted forward, other initiators splash liquid on his back with leaf sponges. This is a putrid concoction produced by steeping aromatic leaves in a tub of pond water for one month. Nggwal has "anointed" him, the alleged effect being to hasten skin degeneration and promote general decrepitude—in short, to become like Walipeine himself. The novices spend some minutes examining the *bondafip* structure and then depart through the rear of the house. Thereupon, anyone else of sufficient ritual maturity is permitted to enter through the rear door and view the secrets of the house.

Next day, the novices are unceremoniously returned to the house, where they hear the voice of the tambaran emanating from the *bondafip*. In answer to their rapping the rear aperture is uncovered, and they are invited to behold the sacred *bowas* flutes associated with this tambaran. Standing inconspicuously against one of the dimly lit inner walls is a small figurine for which informants can give little exegetical

---

24. First to enter are the pig magicians from among the novice group, after which no particular order is maintained. Since there are only a few nggwals associated with this tambaran (see above), the number of novices is much smaller than at the Nggwal Bunafunei initiation. It should also be noted that, for the first time in the entire series of Tambaran grades, it is the *junior* age-set—the Owangufwisi—that is made to suffer the primary ordeal of initiation. Their older brothers (Balangaisi), having been previously promoted, are casually admitted to the secrets a few minutes later, after the women and children have left the hamlet.

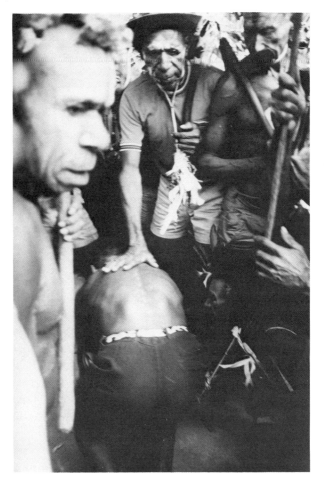

29. A Nggwal Walipeine neophyte stoops to enter the spirit-house portal. Note the adzes over the initiators' shoulders, signifying their membership in Nggwal Walipeine.

accounting, saying only that it represents Nambweapa'w, the mythic Cassowary-Mother, and that they are certain "she" belongs there.

Even without their elderly appearance, most initiates of Nggwal Walipeine are easily recognized as such, since entry into this grade entitles them to exclusive use of a variety of ornamental status markers. The main emblem is the stone-

or steel-bladed adz, which these men are permitted to decorate with white chicken feathers. Other insignia similarly carry forward the theme of whiteness which links Walipeine
with the physical facts of old age. Thus, initiates may wear
a bailer shell on their chest and, as a forehead ornament, a
shell disc produced when a shell ring is cut. They carry a
netbag of fibers in the natural light beige color with the fancy
touch of small shells woven into the fabric.[25] They commonly
adorn their hair with black and white feathers mounted in a
comb carved from bone. On special occasions members may
be seen wearing a distinctive neck ornament consisting of a
stiff collar made from a strip of lawyer-vine skin, which protrudes some distance out from the throat. In sum, the men
of Walipeine tend to be the most beplumed and bedecked
members of the community and are rivaled only by Nggwal
himself, whose effigies are decorated in the same way.

CONCLUSION

In attempting to draw specific conclusions about Nggwal
Walipeine the difficulty faced is that this grade is unintelligi-
ble except in relation to its ritual antecedents. A commentary
on this tambaran is necessarily a commentary on the entire
cult. Contrarily, the preceding grades, although parts of a
series and therefore finally meaningful only in this broader
context, display a relatively greater degree of thematic autonomy. To this extent it is possible to epitomize them individually with minimal distortion of the complexities which,
by now, the reader may know as well as he cares to. Thus,
sparing few words: Falanga has to do with sundering the
nurturant and affectual bonds that unite a young boy with
his mother and, by extension, others of her sex; Lefin certi-
fies a boy's membership in male society by bringing him into
intimate contact with beings of another order, who inhabit
a world which men regard as their spiritual homeland;
Maolimu celebrates the youth's dawning sexuality and immi-

25. This privilege extends to members' wives. Babies must never be carried in netbags of the uncolored natural fiber, lest their youth endanger the elderly owner
and hasten her death.

nent majority, signifying the gravity of this transformation with the radical image of species metamorphosis; Nggwal Bunafunei toasts the achievement of full social and biological prowess while gloating over the raw dominance enjoyed by men in relation to women. Then comes Nggwal Walipeine, with its inherently antireflexive theme of "old age."

The point is that Walipeine shifts the individual into a wholly different ontogenetic register. The preceding grades have monitored an unbroken sequence of growth and maturation, a steady accumulation of physical and social competence that is marked at each major step by the acquisition of additional ritual knowledge and experience. The sham of Walipeine is that this process continues into old age; the truth is that the knowledge acquired is "old hat," and the physical condition personified is the undoing of all that has gone before. Here, as in many if not all societies, the difference between growing up and growing old is, to say the least, profoundly important. For this reason, it is no mere coincidence that the English phrase "growing old" is oxymoronic in a sense that precisely applies to the expressive character of Walipeine: in both cases the inherent contradiction has the effect of euphemizing the phase of *decline*, the unconcealed facts of which are painfully repellent to conscious thought.

The construction may seem bleak, but it does accord with Arapesh perceptions insofar as I was able to infer them. The evidence is that these people possess an anxiety about old age and enfeeblement that would excite an insurance salesman. Witness the custom whereby fathers strategically withhold magic to ensure that their sons will protect and care for them in old age; or the preference shown daughters because it is hoped they will cook food and fetch water and firewood when the eventually aged parents can no longer fend for themselves (Tuzin 1976:95); or the cathartic laughter often provoked by the sight of some crone hobbling past. Childless couples or individuals are unknown, since one of the express purposes of Ilahita's liberally constituted adoption practices is to provide heirs and prospective care-givers wherever the need exists in the clan or wider kinship community. The problem of physical disability is compounded by the ramified notion that essential productive activities such as gardening and hunting are dependent on a modicum of ritual and sexual power. In sum, the hypothetical image of an old man without family, sexual vitality or ritual affiliation is devoid of any redeeming features whatever; and yet, it is an image—however hypothetical—that is well within the tendencies of Arapesh imagination.

Anyone doubting this has only to cast back to the opening story of this chapter, which was reported less for its specific or immediate connection with the Tambaran than for its penetrating insight on the subject of Arapesh old age. Imoina, the protagonist, is the hypothetical man just described. The storyteller begins by dwelling upon Imoina's social isolation and physical decrepitude. We are told that the old man has been without family since his older brother departed; he has never given thought to women (presumably as sexual objects) or to marriage; he is dirty and unkempt, his skin so fragile it cannot withstand gentle scraping with a finger nail. From the absence of any indication to the contrary we must assume that his ritual and political standing in local male society is equally moribund.

The image drawn in the story's opening paragraph is uncompromisingly negative. But quickly we discover two extraordinarily redeeming elements in Imoina's situation: first, he controls a unique love magic powerful enough to attract a lustful interest from one of the village belles; second, he rises to her seduction with unwrinkled vigor thanks to the amazing fact that beneath his frail exterior is the skin and body of a virile young man.[26] The two potencies unite with the previous image in an oxymoronic wedding of youth and age. The idea that a pretty, sought-after young girl would lust after the wizened Imoina is presented as a paradox which, the storyteller notes, is sure to be socially disapproved; however, magical devices secure both the girl's favor and the community's approbation. For this unlikely union to produce

26. The figure of an old man who is able to become young by doffing his skin is common in Arapesh mythology, as is the closely related image of an old man who dies and is magically reborn as a handsome Lothario. Cf. similar qualities of Nambweapa'w as recounted in the myth at the beginning of this volume.

children stretches belief even further and, like the tardy fertility of Abraham and Sarah (Gen. 18:11–14), requires nothing less than miraculous intervention. The corresponding miracle in our story is that, outward appearances notwithstanding, Imoina—the codger par excellence—is in reality a young man.

Placed in the light of Arapesh feelings about "growing old," the adventures of Imoina gleam with all the appeal of a wish-fulfilling fantasy—which may go far toward explaining the popularity of the old-yet-young theme as it occurs and reoccurs throughout this culture's myth repertoire. In the case of Nggwal Walipeine we see the same oxymoronic symbol extended to the mythic component of ritual. This Nggwal is personified as an old man. Now, however, we are alert to the cryptic significance of agedness when it appears in a mythic setting. Walipeine's evident frailty is only skindeep, his "true" character is youthful and powerful. In the logic of the system this is a truism requiring no demonstration, for it is fully implicit—both to initiates and non-initiates alike—in the mythically derived definition of old age.

Actually, Imoina's relevance to our understanding of Walipeine may be specified further through reflection on the enigmatic presence of Nambweapa'w inside the *bondafip*. The role of this omnibus symbol in relation to Nggwal is, as we have seen in several mythic and ritual contexts, something akin to an Arapesh "conscience," a figure that appears unexpectedly to remind everyone that this alien spirit holds meaning only by virtue of its assimilation to the ancient core of Arapesh tradition. In the chronicle of man's genesis Nambweapa'w is presented as the ultimate image of female power. Her unnamed human husband creates her vagina and fathers her children, but in the end is no match for her. Her *real* counterpart, as revealed in the iconography of the spirit-house crosspiece, is none other than the culture-hero Baingap, whose miraculous powers are comparable to her own. The union of male and female principles in their purest forms yields the wonder of continuing creation which is construed as Nggwal Bunafunei's gift to humanity. Nambweapa'w's appearance inside the *bondafip* confirms the implicit understanding that a creative prepotency carries over into old age.[27] As a mythic partner at this stage of life, Baingap is unsuitable, for the records of his exploits always portray him as young or in his prime. However, it requires little imagination to recognize in his younger brother Imoina the missing image of Baingap as an old man.[28] It would be convenient for my interpretation if Imoina were overtly represented in the iconography of Walipeine, but in a larger sense it does not matter: Imoina establishes the complementary, masculine principle within the Arapesh mythic scheme, but this scheme embraces *within a single symbolic set* the cryptic (and often not so cryptic) elements of both sacred tales and ritual practices. The logic of the system therefore demands that Imoina's *significance* be incorporated into these proceedings, whether he himself is or not.

Briefly put, the apocalyptic significance of Nggwal Walipeine is precisely the opposite of what he appears to be on the surface. By the time men have reached this grade they are masters of the technique of manipulating—unconsciously or by design—truth and illusion to their own advantage. Insofar as they actively identify with this tambaran, and yield thereby to a benign self-deception, the fantasy in which they indulge serves as a comforting denial of their powerless condition. In the end, however, the truth in this instance is precisely what it *appears* to be and the wish that it were otherwise must compete with the knowledge that the "old hat" aspect of Walipeine exists as a secret indictment of the old men's claim to ritual and worldly power. Their authority over the authentically powerful and ritually sophisticated men of Bunafunei rests insecurely on the latters' belief that Walipeine holds secrets of ultimate value and importance. It is no wonder that the men of Walipeine have a penchant for ritual insignia: power has no need of trappings; authority can scarcely survive without them.

27. Recall that although Nambweapa'w is first introduced as a lovely young woman, her full magical, creative and aggressive powers are not revealed until later in the story, after she has borne and raised many children—when, in other words, she is old.

28. Consistent with the oxymoron we are discussing, Baingap the older brother is *young*, while Imoina the younger brother is *old*.

9. Toward a Religious Ethic

THE Tambaran is a master of illusion and disguise. We have seen it perform with dazzling virtuosity: as a young man and an old man, a young woman and an old woman, a towering monster and a swaggering dwarf, a crying baby and a creator god; a pig, a ghost, a bird, a bat; and more. These are the fragments of Arapesh religious consciousness, interlocking pieces in a mosaic mirror which the Arapesh hold up to themselves and their worldly condition. "Man," says Feuerbach, "is nothing without the objects that express his being" (1972:100). Through the images and workings of its cult, the Tambaran aligns this multitude of expressive objects with existential themes such as identity, sexuality and power. The symbolic organization thus effected has a unitary character, signified by the Tambaran transcending its objects and assuming its ultimate guise as an *abstract religious ideal*. My purpose in this chapter is to examine the way in which this particular aspect of the Tambaran presides over the conduct of individuals and groups in the village and rationalizes their fortunes according to its ethical doctrine.

The proposed plan frees us from further consideration of two sorts of Tambaran-related activities that have already been treated at some length: (1) ritual actions specifically ordained by the Tambaran; and (2) nonritual actions directly entailed by the Tambaran. The latter, residual category is potentially very large, consisting of all social phenomena arising in some measure from ritual necessity. The urgent resolution of local discord during the ritual season, the negotiation of truces between enemy villages in accordance with

Tambaran scheduling, the production of economic surpluses and other matériel required for the ceremonies—the list of such matters touched by the Tambaran could go on and on. Both types of activity, taken together, form the substance of the cult, and it would be possible to conclude the ethnography at this point without leaving an impression of gross incompleteness. However, turning from the complexities of the cult aspect to the unitary idea by which it is often represented, we discover two additional areas in which the Tambaran's influence is systematic and pervasive: one is the domain of social organization, the other is that of religious ethics.

In the earlier volume of this study, the dual organization of Ilahita society was heuristically detached from its ritual predicates and analyzed as an historically derived mechanism of social process and integration, one capable of sustaining a community very large by New Guinea standards. With little reference to the Tambaran, attention was given to the dynamics of the dual organization both in its internal aspects and in its relationship to elements of marriage, residence and kinship. We now see that the dual organization is (appropriately!) Janus-faced, uniting in its complex gaze the vicissitudes of everyday life and the sacred meanings of the ritual system, both of which operate through the same structural scheme.

The ethical implications of Tambaran doctrine function similarly in the sense that questions pertaining to the secular field are regularly brought within the orbit of values specifically promulgated by the cult. The existence of an authentic, albeit rudimentary "religious ethic" is rarely reported in the New Guinea literature;[1] accordingly, the Ilahita case offers

1. Although not analyzed in precisely these terms, the data presented in Reo Fortune's masterful study of Manus religion (1935) clearly point to an ethical component in the Sir Ghost system of beliefs. More recently, there has been a growing interest in the nature and productivity of New Guinea epistemological systems, especially as they are embodied in religious and quasi-religious ideas. Thus, for example, Burridge (1969) studies the way in which traditional narratives are used by the Tangu to rationalize experience and augment self-awareness in the context of changing circumstances; Wagner (1972) shows how the Daribi are able to generate new cultural meanings through the creative manipulation of traditional metaphors; Barth (1975) analyzes Baktaman ritual

an unusual opportunity to examine the social and ideological conditions under which a magically bound religious system may, so to speak, transcend itself, arriving at a more abstract and encompassing metaphysical account of the world. As we will see, this elaboration is intimately connected with the continuing solidarity of Ilahita village and with the form of cultural self-identity which these people have developed since discovering the world outside their borders.

THE INTERPRETATION OF MISFORTUNE

The discussion in this chapter will revolve around a series of cases featuring death and divination in Ilahita.[2] The ethical system exemplified by these cases operates in a most interesting manner. Death, the supreme misfortune, is subject to construal as a justified punishment for offenses committed against the Tambaran, either on the part of the victim or on the part of someone emotionally close to the victim. In order to appreciate the social and epistemological significance of this theory of causation, it is worth pausing to contrast its effects with those of the available (and traditionally exclusive) alternative: death by malicious sorcery.

Here, as in many societies, the social and emotional upsets triggered by a death in the community are radically intensified by the prevalence of sorcery beliefs. In Ilahita, nearly all deaths are in principle ascribed to willful sorcery. The only exceptions are those in which death has struck someone so old and unimportant as to be a social nonentity, or when the deceased is a very young child whose parents are divined as having neither personal enemies nor a history of socioreligious misconduct (see below). Most divination techniques are designed to solicit the advice of ancestral shades as to the identity of the sorcerer. In more than half the observed cases, however, the ancestors revealed that the sorcery had

---

as a repository of intuited knowledge. See also Gell (1975) and Schieffelin (1976). In the next chapter I will have more to say about the general epistemological significance of Tambaran ideology.

2. Much of the ethnographic material in this chapter has appeared elsewhere (Tuzin 1974), analyzed more exclusively in terms of its implications for law and social control in Ilahita, and without explicit regard to religious ethics as such.

been enacted on behalf of the Tambaran, usually in the form of a particular nggwal spirit. Either this, or it was divined that Nggwal (or, again, a particular nggwal spirit) had destroyed the victim directly. The automatic interpretation in such cases is that the death was a divinely sponsored execution, and therefore morally righteous. Any reprisals sought against a suspected human agent would, it is believed, be punished in their own right by Nggwal. The victim's history is searched until some reason is found for the mystical attack, and there the matter ends.

The alternative diagnosis, which lays blame on a sorcerer acting for his personal interests, throws the community into a potentially unmanageable crisis situation. Whether or not an actual accusation is uttered, tension between the group of the deceased and their current enemies is greatly augmented in an oppressive climate of suspicion and fear of violent or mystical retaliation. The problem is worsened by the fact that, although there are professional sorcerers in the community, most men are thought to have techniques of lethal magic, and thus the field of suspects is practically unlimited. Furthermore, even if the sorcery is divined to have originated in an enemy village, someone close to the deceased must have betrayed him by stealing personal leavings and sending them to the foreign sorcerer.[3] This brings women into the list of suspects, even though they are presumed to be unable to perform sorcery magic themselves. The "enemy within" (Winter 1963) is a source of profound distress; and, according to informants, sorcery attacks and accusations were traditionally the most frequent cause of village fission in the region. Ilahita appears to have largely escaped this fate, thanks to the uncommonly acute awareness of generations of leaders that security lay in numbers, and that exter-

---

3. Recall, for example, the case reported in chap. 5, in which Mangas was accused of such a deed in connection with the death of Silembin. Furthermore, Mangas's alleged conduct was largely excused—indeed it was accorded a degree of legitimacy—because he was perceived to have acted in defense of Tambaran values. A potentially disruptive confrontation was thus averted, much to the relief of those whose main interest was to restore harmony and get on with the spirit-house project. By virtue of such Tambaran-related features, the example properly belongs to the category of cases illustrating the theme of this chapter.

nal enemies would surely descend upon any segments which detached themselves from the main village (Tuzin 1976: chap. 3).

The cessation of warfare in the early 1950s tamed this hostile environment and created a situation in which sorcery disputes could play ungoverned havoc with village unity. And yet, this did not happen: although the modern period has witnessed some dismantling of the village's nucleated structure, individuals who removed themselves to bush camps in the hinterland rarely did so as a reaction to sorcery entanglements (Tuzin 1976:199ff.). Sorcery beliefs continued unabated, but their socially deleterious effects were now moderated in a new and different way. For, according to informants, it was during the first decade of pacification that Nggwal, his supply of enemy dead no longer forthcoming, began feasting in earnest on his own people.

This unpleasant turn of events was nonetheless highly adaptive for village solidarity, especially when judged against the otherwise unrestrained action of sorcery beliefs. The reason is that the invocation of Tambaran ethics on the occasion of death transforms a putatively man-made calamity into one governed by superhuman responsibility. What was first seen as an act of unmitigated wickedness is recast as an act consistent with the divined motives of the Tambaran. In the process something resembling—in its social and psychological effects—the naturalistic explanation for death emerges: the mood of the crisis shifts from revenge to resignation on the part of the aggrieved, and the potential for community disruption is removed. Consider, then, the following cases.

1. Leitipen, a woman of about fifty, was the wife of an important man and the mother of five sons, three of whom were married at the time of her death. Approximately a month before Leitipen died, two of her daughters-in-law fell ill with identical symptoms, an understandable coincidence in the opinion of this observer since the women were neighbors and spent much time together. As the younger women started to recover, Leitipen began displaying the same symptoms. Within a fortnight she was dead.

On the evening of her burial one of the neighborhood diviners, Wangi, went into a spirit-possession trance. During it, he was heard to sing the song of Wanimbea, the nggwal spirit of Leitipen's husband's clan. Afterward a number of senior cult leaders belonging to various clans met to ponder the meaning of the song's occurrence during the trance. Their eventual interpretation was accepted by everyone, including, most importantly, the dead woman's bereaved husband and sons. The interpretation was as follows.

Three years before Leitipen's death, a Tambaran feast had been held in the village. As we know from earlier chapters, such events may continue intermittently for weeks, and the women's task is to prepare soup and other foods which, they are told, the men will feed to Nggwal. Leitipen's sons commanded their wives to make soup "for Nggwal." The women angrily retorted that they were weary of working so hard for Nggwal, and that if Nggwal was hungry he could eat feces. This was a serious blasphemy, much publicized, and the women were soundly beaten by their husbands.

In the opinion of the cult leaders, Leitipen's death was a consequence of this offense. The daughters-in-law were being punished and would surely have died, had not Leitipen by some mysterious altruistic means caused the sickness to be transferred to herself. Leitipen was fondly hailed as a great and good woman, but there was no attempt to avenge her death.

2. Songwanda'a was a youth of sixteen when he died of what local medical missionaries diagnosed as cerebral malaria. He left his middle-aged parents, a younger brother, and two older married sisters. The divination involved viewing the body of Songwanda'a some hours after it had been placed in an open grave. When this was done it was noticed that pale gray markings on the corpse's skin resembled the body designs used during Nggwal ceremonies. This observation yielded the following interpretation.

Some years earlier, preparations had been under way for a Nggwal ceremony in the hamlet of Songwanda'a's father, Gaiapo. Just before the festivities were to begin, Gaiapo got into a fearful row with his wife, Kowala. In the heated exchange Kowala was heard to say, "You are an old man, weak and with white hair. How can you hope to satisfy me [sexually]?" The insult against her husband's virility was made much worse—sacrilegious even—by the imminence of Nggwal. Kowala's final punishment was the loss of her son.

A sorcery bundle, said to have been found concealed in the nearby forest, was produced at the deathbed of Songwanda'a. This was evidence enough for people to believe sorcery was killing the boy, and Gaiapo had the option of performing retaliatory sorcery through the agency of the dead boy's ghost. Having been apprised, however, that Nggwal was implicated in the affair, he abandoned whatever plans he may have had for revenge. Vague rumors circulated that the husband of one of Songwanda'a's sisters had performed the sorcery, but these evaporated quickly without, apparently, affecting Gaiapo or his relations with his son-in-law.

3. Galasala was an old widower who had taken to living alone in the nearby forest to spare himself the shame of being seen doing womanly chores for himself. Though considered somewhat of a crank who had alienated his adult children, he did keep a hand in village affairs, and his older and younger brothers were both important men. When he died and his body was inspected in the grave, the pale designs were clearly those of Nggwal. And, later, the local diviner, in trance, confirmed the diagnosis by singing the song of Sowambon, the nggwal of Galasala's clan.

The interpretation was not difficult, for Galasala's fatal blunder had occurred only a few months previously. At that time another ward of the village was preparing a Nggwal ceremony, at which there was to be much feasting and flute playing. For historical and structural reasons detailed in the earlier volume (Tuzin 1976:293–294), Galasala's ward, Ilifalemb, is the only one of the village's six wards that is not part of the main Tambaran Cult. Traditionally, Ilifalemb men held ceremonies by themselves, and attended functions elsewhere in Ilahita as spectators rather than as full participants. Then, some years ago, a road was built through Ilifalemb, preventing the local men from sealing off various ritual hamlets at necessary intervals during the Tambaran calendar. Under encouragement from the other wards they were becoming increasingly drawn into the main cult—knowing, however, that it was somehow improper and fearing that their own Nggwal might well disapprove.

The men of Ilifalemb held a meeting to decide whether they should participate in the others' ceremony. Most of them favored the idea, arguing that their membership in the main cult was an accomplished fact anyway. Galasala protested passionately that if they wanted to feast Nggwal, they should do so in the rightful place, in Ilifalemb—even if it meant barricading the road. For too long, he complained, Ilifalemb had contributed glory to the cult of the other wards, while their own Nggwal was being neglected. In this he was supported by only one other, a young man named Binas.

Galasala was decisively overruled. As the meeting closed, Galasala and Binas swore that if the others insisted on participating in the ceremony, they would feed their own Nggwal with feces. This is a picturesque way of saying that feces is what the men would be eating in humiliating themselves in this way. For this Galasala was killed, with the complicity of Sowambon. At the conclusion of my fieldwork some months later, Binas was still worried that his might be a similar fate.

4. Nahiana was a childless man of about thirty-eight years, long afflicted with nonvirulent leprosy. When he died after a three-day illness, all the signs were that he had been sorcerized. His wife, Seingin, on being questioned at the funeral by village leaders, told the following tale. The day before Nahiana had fallen sick, he and Seingin had been at work in their garden. Nahiana retired to the garden house for a brief nap. While dozing he heard something strike the side of the house near his head, as if someone had thrown a handful of dirt against the thatch. Thinking it was merely Seingin working outside, he resumed his nap. Later, when he mentioned the incident to Seingin, Nahiana was disturbed to hear that she had not been in the garden at the time. That night he saw his dead father in a dream, and the apparition informed him that he, Nahiana, was dead, that his soul had already been taken. In the morning he found a thin sago spine stuck in the ground beneath the stilted house in which he had slept. Tied to the spine were the burnt remains of a type of vine known to be a common ingredient in sorcery magic. As he slept he would certainly have inhaled some of the smoke rising from the burning vine. Hours later Nahiana began to feel ill; in two days he was dead.

A case as obvious as this could have led to an immediate oracular consultation to learn the name of the villain. Even at the funeral, names were whispered—suspicions which could easily have been tested. Instead, the elders of the community insisted that, before this was done, there should be a viewing of Nahiana's body. Late that night the people gathered in the cemetery and saw indistinct markings on the corpse, faintly reminiscent of the designs of Falanga, the most junior tambaran.

The following morning the elders met to interpret the markings. They soon decided that the culprit was Doapapa, who was present at the meeting. Although Doapapa was from a different ward of the village, he was the initiation partner of Nahiana with particular reference to Falanga; together they were clients of the Falanga spirit Bwisahim.[4] Doapapa vigorously denied this, reminding the men that he was a Christian and had long since lost interest in sorcery or in Bwisahim. Why, he demanded, would he bother to sor-

---

4. As a matter of interest, the two wards involved were Ilifalemb (Nahiana) and Hengwanif (Doapapa). The two men came to share the clientage of Bwisahim as a consequence of Ilifalemb's progressive absorption into the cult of the main village.

I should explain that the individuation of tambaran spirits, which has been discussed only in the case of Nggwal, is a characteristic of all grades of the cult. The reason it was omitted in my description of Falanga, Lefin and Maolimu is that, in contrast with the elaborate personification of nggwal spirits, the shared spirits of the lower grades are strictly nominal; they are idioms by which initiation partners are able to specify their relationship vis-à-vis a particular grade.

30. Nahiana lies dead in his grave. Here, at the midnight inspection, the lantern lowered into the grave reveals blotchy, pale discolorations on the chest and upper arms of the corpse—a sure sign that the Tambaran was implicated in the death.

cerize a man for the sake of a spirit he no longer cared about? The elders did not seem impressed with this reasoning, and before long Doapapa stormed out of the meeting in angry defiance.

Certain aspects of this case were puzzling, and when Doapapa had gone I questioned the man who had informally presided over the meeting. First, why was such a firm accusation produced from evidence which everyone agreed was extremely ambiguous? The man dissembled, but after some persistence on my part, he exclaimed: "It *had* to be Doapapa. No one else could have done it." And then he added, somewhat parenthetically, "Besides, it is in the nature of initiation partners that they sorcerize one another." That is, Nahiana must have said or done something which Doapapa took to be disparaging to Bwisahim. It fell to him to punish Nahiana, and the markings on the body showed that Bwisahim approved.

I then asked whether any action would be taken against Doapapa. The man replied that the matter was now closed. If Doapapa realized there would be no recrimination, then why was he so intent on arguing his innocence? The elder considered this for a moment, and then answered with a shrug, "Perhaps he does not want the other Christians to think he is still following the old ways."

The following year the widow Seingin married a man who was a close classifactory "son" of Doapapa's son-in-law. This aroused some talk, and thoughts returned briefly to the previous accusation. The talk, however, led nowhere.

5. Ku'umbwili and Imul were initiation partners, both clients of the nggwal spirit Nimbea. They died within a week of one another, and this alone suggested that their deaths were linked. The grave inspection and trance divination left no doubt of it. Indeed, the hideous sore in Imul's throat which caused him to die of starvation lent itself to the community interpretation of their deaths. Their joint offense was to have confounded the strict separation between the initiation classes.

It has been noted in earlier contexts that the system of Tambaran succession contains mechanisms for promotion. Under certain circumstances (Tuzin 1976;242ff.) it would be possible for Ku'umbwili, the junior *ombaf* of Imul, to be upgraded to the ritual status of his (Ku'umbwili's) father. Under no circumstances may a person be promoted across the initiation class line. But this is exactly what happened to Ku'umbwili. Over a decade ago, he was brought by Imul to a ceremony which he was forbidden to attend. Because such a deed cannot be undone, Ku'umbwili became in effect identical in status to Imul. There was much public consternation over this, for the action disrupted the orderly succession of their descendants. At the time, Imul had no explanation for his mischief. Years later Imul's death signified the fact that it was his voice, in telling Ku'umbwili to come to the forbidden ceremony, that had, in a manner of speaking, caused the transfer of their partnership from this world to the next.

6. Lango had a six-year-old son who died, and there was no question that Lango himself was to blame. Nggwal's complicity in

the death was so apparent that a divination procedure was considered unnecessary.[5]

The trouble began when Lango behaved in a way ill befitting his important position as pig magician. There are eleven such posts in the village, hereditary within a select few of the initiation couplets; that is to say, Lango had inherited the magic from his senior *ombaf* in conjunction with Tambaran initiations (Tuzin 1976:272). The office brings its encumbent considerable prestige, but it also exacts certain sacrifices. To these magicians falls the prodigious task of keeping Nggwal gorged with wild pork. For long periods they must observe taboos on bodily hygiene, various foods and sexual contact. Failure to do so means the magic will not work, and Nggwal will go hungry—with potentially dire consequences for the entire community.

During the prolonged Tambaran feast alluded to in the case of Galasala (above), Lango's magic repeatedly failed to attract a pig to the net. Lango quickly became discouraged and fell back on the expediency of raising money among his followers to buy village pigs for Nggwal. Because, however, Nggwal is known to despise the fatty flesh of village pigs, Lango's fund-raising efforts were condemned as an inadequate substitute for hunting success. He reacted to the criticism with sullen defiance. A few weeks later the death of his son yielded the obvious interpretation that sorcery directed at the unworthy Lango had gone astray and killed the boy. Community opinion was vindicated a short time later when Lango's wife began showing signs of pregnancy, confirming the suspicion that he had been lax in his ritual avoidances.

Additional cases could be cited, but these illustrate sufficiently the sociological and epistemological points being developed. Their common features are fairly evident. In each instance, the complicity of tambaran spirits, revealed by oracular means, indicated that the deceased (or someone close to him/her) had committed some act offensive to Tambaran doctrine, broadly defined, and punishable by death. Close kinsmen are denied redress under sanctions of public opprobrium and Tambaran vengeance. Thus death, which in a climate heavy with sorcery beliefs might have led to se-

5. It was a measure of the consensus arrayed against Lango, and of the relatively low "social value" of the deceased, that the divination procedure was dispensed with in this instance. Still, it is remarkable that the male community *presumed*, purely on the basis of its own construction of Tambaran ethics, to pass judgment on the case. In the development of religious ideology, shortcuts such as this are potential pathways in the passage from magic to systematic ethics.

vere and prolonged social unrest, is forestalled in its effects by the action of a countervailing set of beliefs. The contingencies surrounding these beliefs, as regards both the kind of adherence they command and the manner in which they are applied, must await treatment for the present while certain operating assumptions are brought to light.

The procedure is legitimated on three grounds. First, the sorcery killing is deemed legitimate by virtue of its association with Tambaran images, relationships or practices. Second, it is presumed that the ancestral spirits are omniscient with respect to divine will and human action, and that they will not confound the living with false signs. Finally, oracular signs are thought to be authentic messages from the dead, messages subject to interpretation by qualified mortals. Let us consider this nexus of assumptions more closely.

ANCESTORS AND MEN

Two forms of divination were mentioned in the above cases.[6] Although there are several other varieties, these are the only ones designed to detect involvement by Tambaran spirits.[7] Accordingly, the mere fact of the selection of one or both of these in preference to any other (e.g., the case of Nahiana) points to a prejudging of the case by those conducting the proceedings.

Ilahita has only a handful of accomplished spirit mediums. Women are automatically disqualified from this role, for it is known that the ancestral dead, like the Tambaran, abhor them and shun their presence. Moreover, ancestors choose only to communicate with men who have achieved at least Nggwal Bunafunei, and indeed their preference inclines toward elders who occupy the highest grade of Nggwal Wali-

6. In this and the following sections I am limiting myself to a small province in the realm of Arapesh eschatology. For more on the subject of Arapesh ancestor beliefs, see Tuzin (1975, 1977).

7. It would not serve present purposes to describe other forms of divination, which I hope to do in a future study. Suffice it to say that all are designed to elicit ancestral messages which identify the culprit. Unlike the two techniques associated with the Tambaran, the others do not require mystic or otherwise esoteric skills.

peine. In preparation for a trance the medium avoids contact with women for at least one day. On the morning of the funeral he goes to a part of a nearby stream wherein the dead of his clan are thought to dwell. A few water insects are caught and fastened, together with various edible greens collected near the water, in the leaf of a wild banana plant called *wambeta*.[8] The medium returns to the village, puts the *wambeta* packet to one side, and then tucks several tobacco leaves under an armpit of the corpse. These are removed just before burial and are also put to one side.

In the evening the medium chews up the *wambeta* packet and, lying on his back, blows a fine spray of spittle into the air and over his face. It is thought that if he swallows any of the spittle, the strength in it will drive him permanently mad. Then he takes the tainted tobacco leaves infused with the "smell" of the corpse and passes them around another bunch of tobacco leaves, which he rolls in a *wambeta* leaf and smokes. The leaves that had been in contact with the corpse are thrown away, their essence having been transferred to the second bunch. The medium falls into a deep sleep in which he experiences a tickling sensation that starts in his toe and moves up his body, finally plunging into his heart. He springs awake, fully possessed by a long-dead clan ancestor.[9]

The trance itself consists of much garbled shouting and screaming, rapid thumping of feet, and heavy breathing alternating with panting. The medium remains aware of things going on around him, and is able to converse with men listening close at hand.[10] Then comes the climax. If Nggwal is involved, his song is bellowed with mad passion,

---

8. *Wambetangw* (pl.) are associated with the dead partly because their stalks have a high moisture content. It is believed that the dead live in and require a watery medium. And, along with another banana called *ha'awin*, the *wambeta* is the "door" of the dead when they pass between this world and the next. For more on the subject of Arapesh water symbolism see Tuzin (1977).

9. Spirit mediums are self-selected Nggwal initiates who have tried and succeeded in going into trance. On any given occasion several local mediums may volunteer their services, but during the session spectator attention focuses on the one first showing signs of possession. To my knowledge, spirit mediums do not serve outside their own village.

10. The seance is carried out in total darkness, since it is thought that shades of the dead will not come near a light. However, and perhaps ironically, their peregri-

accompanied by initiated spectators. If illegitimate sorcery is the putative cause of death, the medium whispers the criminal's name in barely audible tones. In either case, the medium then slips back into sleep and is later revived with stinging nettles, reputedly unmindful of what he said while in trance.[11] In all of this, there seems to be nothing to prevent the medium from passing any messages he likes, especially through autosuggestion aided by a knowledge of community expectations.

The grave-inspection divination employs rather more subtle manipulation. After the corpse is placed in the open grave, four or five small bamboo tubes of water are emptied over its face and trunk. The man pouring the water must be of high (preferably Nggwal Walipeine) ritual standing and should not belong to the clan of the deceased. Palm fronds and banana leaves are laid over the mouth of the grave and the crowd withdraws, leaving a few men to guard against anyone's tampering with the body. When the men observe fireflies hover near and descend into the grave they know that the ancestors are delivering their message.

The spirits are attracted by the water on the corpse, which is believed to be supernaturally charged, and is collected from ground-crab holes located in the ancestral hamlet of the recent deceased. These crab holes, ubiquitous in the village, are supposedly alternative abodes of the dead. The reason for this is consistent with general eschatological notions. That is, the crab (*wala'anga*) digs a deep hole and locates its nest on a shelf it cuts into the wall of the shaft. Rainwater flows into the lower chamber, leaving the nest dry. Even during severe droughts one can always expect to find water in the bottom of these holes, which is why the spirits depend on

nations are visible in the form of meandering fireflies—the only natural light in the dead night of the forest.

11. As evidence of their cognitively ordered state, I recall an instance in which the medium, hearing my noisy tape-recorder switch, shifted position and began speaking more consistently in the direction of the microphone. On another occasion, the medium had been troubled recently with a painful eruption of scabies. As a man approached with stinging nettles at the end of the seance, the medium stirred from his "deep sleep" and said quietly that they would not be necessary this time.

them when away from their watery homes in the stream shrines.[12]

Getting at the water requires enlarging the crab holes, which cannot be done without muddying the water. After the water is poured on the corpse, the liquid evaporates, leaving the suspended particles on the skin in dessicated rivulets: the divinatory sign. The manipulative opportunities arise, therefore, when the water is actually administered, and also when the interpretation is made.[13] And on both occasions the matter is in the hands of cult members who are not clansmen of the deceased, and who are ostensibly "impartial" judges.

THE PRAGMATICS OF BELIEF

From the preceding there emerges a curious pattern in which senior cult members bestow upon themselves the privileged responsibility of investigating and resolving crises of public concern—nearly always with the result that Tambaran values are reaffirmed and shown to be applicable to varied and particular cases. Now, it might be argued, based on evidence from elsewhere in Melanesia, that death by sorcery is not a "public concern" but an affair between the deceased's revenge group and the individual (or group) judged guilty. To be sure, my notes contain cases in which this view appears to have been taken; before the advent of Pax Australiana, blood vengeance occasionally occurred within the village. But, according to informants who had reached adulthood before peace was imposed, this sort of thing happened much

12. It may be recalled that in the story of Nambweapa'w the young son located his fugitive cassowary-mother by throwing a blade of grass which landed in a ground-crab hole near where she was hiding. The significance of this detail rests in the complex symbolism of the "water-filled hole" as it figures in Arapesh images of birth, death and eschatology. See Tuzin (1977) for a more complete discussion of this topic in the context of Arapesh water symbolism.

13. I do not enter into the tangled problem of whether the man consciously reproduces Tambaran designs when he pours the water. Certainly, all whom I asked *denied* doing so. But even if some amount of positive intent is involved, this need not undermine the operator's confidence in the authenticity of the divination. As with many magically based ideologies, notions of natural and supernatural causation, which might to a Western observer appear contradictory on rational grounds, are here easily embraced simultaneously. Recall, for example, Kwamwi's delectation over my naïve criticism of his curing techniques (chap. 8).

less frequently in Ilahita than in other Arapesh villages. Why? Because, say these informants, people elsewhere do not know how to live together; because, also, Ilahita understood better than they the advantages of keeping the village unified; because, finally, the Tambaran of Ilahita was strong and vigilant. Two additional points can be made in this connection. First, the knowledge that a sorcerer is active alarms most people, particularly those who suspect—as most men do—that they have enemies. By the modern device of identifying the sorcery as Tambaran-inspired, considerable tension is relieved by revealing that the victim got only what he or she deserved, and that the innocent are safe. There is, on the other hand, a residual anxiety to which I shall return later.

The second aspect of public concern is much more serious. This is the general worry that the close kin of the deceased, rather than taking physical action against the suspect, will enact *ngwamngwam* retaliatory sorcery. The magic stimulates the ghost of the victim to become its own avenger. This is a very dangerous expedient because the ghost of someone recently deceased does not behave like the mature, long-dead ancestors who assist and counsel men in various ways. A newly liberated soul is in a state of high agitation and distress. It is likely to be vindictive and has now the supranormal insight to ferret out the deeply concealed sentiments of the living. The ghost may strike the person who performed the lethal sorcery, but it may also attack anyone who has ever harbored a private enmity toward him in life—and in this very few are innocent (Tuzin 1975). A regime of terror randomly directed is immensely threatening to everyone, and the divination does the community a great service by convincing the revenge group that *ngwamngwam* is neither appropriate nor in their best interests.

Implicit in the discussion thus far is the assumption that people accept the judgment of the diviner and the elders unquestioningly. This must be qualified in the light of evidence that senior men occasionally look askance at the way their colleagues manage a case. To a close informant I once casually referred to the death of a woman from another ward, remarking that everyone was saying the Tambaran had killed her. The man's reaction was more forceful than expected, for I had not been aware that he and the woman had for years been conducting a secret affair. After explaining his relationship with the woman, he said bitterly, "They are all lying. Her own [affinal] kinsmen killed her, and they blame Nggwal to cover their guilt." I asked if he intended to denounce their fraud. His response: "No, everyone wants to see the trouble ended. If I said anything they [the community at large] would not believe me and would be angry. Also, I would show my special interest in her. People would suspect that I had been sleeping with her, and they might even claim I killed her." In other words, recalling from previous chapters the distributive nature of belief, for these divinations and their supportive ideology to have political effect, it is not necessary that everyone believe in them all the time. The important point is that, on any given occasion, the majority of persons do accept the authenticity of the divination, which they use as justification for imposing a settlement on those more closely involved with the case. It is also apparent that members of the victim's group may sometimes privately welcome the verdict, as an excuse for not initiating dangerous revenge actions.

ANCESTORS, MEN AND THE TAMBARAN: AN IDENTITY MATRIX

The notion that the ancestral spirits can authoritatively report on the will of the Tambaran is one which the Arapesh find difficult to explain. For them, it is enough to assert that the two are in league, and nowhere in the Arapesh metaphysical system do we find an explicit recognition that the range of meanings subsuming ancestors and tambarans are, at least in large part, identical. And yet, we do have many clues that such an identification exists at some implicit level, if only because the two are lodged together in so many areas of cultural imagination. Nggwal, especially, is closely involved with descent ideology, and, in the invisible world, nggwal and *hangahiwa* spirits reside in the water shrines in and among the dead of the clan with which they are associated. The intermingling of ancestral and cult essences in the watery medium is exampled also in the fact that initiation into the junior grades of Falanga and Lefin takes place at a stream site, during which the youths are introduced to all the ethereal beings inhabiting the supernatural place. Ancestors and tambarans appear at each other's ceremonies: the former are magically invoked to lend assistance at the building of the Tambaran spirit house; the latter attend funerals—the event of supreme interest to ancestral shades—in the guise of a mock attack staged on the mourners by the *nautamana* of the deceased (Tuzin 1976:256). Similarly, magical formulas that depend proximately on the patronage of the ancestors ultimately rest on the favor of the Tambaran, and supplementary appeals can be made to Nggwal directly by rubbing the magic bundle on his statues and painting. Nor should we forget the intimate involvement of Nambweapa'w and Baingap—the ancestral figures par excellence—with the Tambaran. My point is that, whether or not one wishes to argue a latent identity on such grounds, the welter of ritual juxtapositions unquestionably enriches by a kind of symbolic cross-referencing the already profound cultural significance of each entity in its own right.

That men stand as the third party to this relationship is demonstrated empirically, especially by material covered in the four chapters concerning Nggwal, and also logically, in the sense that images of ancestors and tambarans are, when all is said and done, projections by men of qualities belonging to themselves. Deferring general consideration of this matter until the next chapter, I will say here that the identity exercised between senior cult members and the Tambaran is at once the source of their power and of their vulnerability. The dogma that an act of sorcery is legitimized by the complicity of the Tambaran is sanctioned by the weight of tradition combined with the continuing authority of senior cult leaders, who are the self-styled interpreters of custom. Their claim to authority is based on the belief that ancestral spirits communicate with them and no one else, combined with the belief that they enjoy a modus vivendi with the monstrous, devouring Nggwal. They are able to enter unharmed into his presence and, on certain occasions, may even exercise a tenuous control over him.

We have reviewed in previous chapters the multitude of tricks and illusions devised to sustain this fiction and the systematic deception that goes with it. The cost exacted by an authority thus predicated is reckoned by agitated emotions of guilt and a corresponding fear that the men's pretense will be discovered, both of which have far-reaching effects on the ideological provisions and structure of relationships in this society. The dilemma of the men, who are after all both benefactors and victims of a tradition handed down to them, was succinctly stated by one of the cult elders. When asked why he and the other men did not open the cult to women and invite them to share the feast, he had this to say: "It is true that sometimes men feel ashamed and guilty over eating good food while their wives go hungry. But, if we told them now that for all these generations they had been deceived, they would make life unbearable for us. There is nothing we can do." The dogma, then, cannot be relaxed (Schwartz 1973), but must be ever renewed.

THE LESSONS OF RETRIBUTION

The informant's admission confirms, as a recognized "article of faith" in Tambaran ideology, that masculine domination, and indeed the way of life traditionally pursued by the Arapesh, depend on the preservation of cult secrets. The prospect that circumstances could be reversed in some awful way is imagined in the secret Tambaran myths recited in this volume—tales which recount the origins of the several grades and the discovery of important paraphernalia. In all cases, except in "The Dogs and the Maolimu Tambaran" (chap. 4), the discovery is made either by children or by women. The men, having learned of the new wonder, steal it from the owners and kill them so that the secret will always remain with the men. The implication is that there persists a danger (and worry) that the rightful owners might learn of the primal theft and claim back their privileges—just as

Nambweapa'w did in the story that began it all. On that day the dominion of the men will cease, and in the ensuing chaos society will crumble. For this reason, any woman appearing to deviate from unqualified respect for the Tambaran is brutally punished. Traditionally, a woman who "peeked"— by accident or design—was killed outright.[14] Neither was she saved by escaping unseen, for she had been taught that Nggwal can monitor her thoughts and punish her directly. Alternatively, an agnostic or irreverent woman can depend on being sorcerized. By reminding the community of this, the divinations pronounced over the deaths of Leitipen and Songwanda'a (above) upheld the sanctity of the Tambaran. In both cases men also suffered loss (the husband and sons of Leitipen, and the father of Songwanda'a), but as a lesson to others the crucial thing was that blame was attached to women who had challenged ritual authority. The deaths were indisputable "proof" that female miscreance will be punished, even if indirectly.

The Tambaran's vigilance is by no means limited to the conventions of male-female relations. Four of the victims in the cases were themselves Nggwal initiates. Their mistakes were to commit some act which inhibited the smooth and orderly sequence of Tambaran activities. Thus, the joint demise of Imul and Ku'umbwili, as signified by divination, emphasized the rules of succession to cult grades and the need to maintain distinct ritual boundaries. The offences of Lango, Nahiana and Galasala violated Tambaran morality in other ways. Lango's laxity in pursuing his craft was a dangerous precedent which, if left unpunished, was liable to set an example for other pig magicians. Nahiana's crime was not discovered, but the accusation against Doapapa was significant for other reasons. First, Doapapa was an initiation partner of the deceased, and was therefore entitled to punish Nahiana for deeds perhaps known only to the two of them. Second, Doapapa was from another ward. His nomination diverted blame from Nahiana's ward where the logical suspects—Nahiana's kinsmen, neighbors and Nggwal partners

14. There was no provision for such women to be inducted themselves into the cult, as was the case among the Iatmul (Bateson 1935: 169; cf. Mead 1938: 169).

—lived. This may explain the unusual fact that the accused was related to the deceased through a minor grade rather than through Nggwal. Finally, Doapapa was a Christian, by reason of which many persons would remain in doubt over his genuine guilt. The resolution of the case thus contained a minimum of disruptive potential.

Galasala's angry outburst amounted to a curse on the Nggwal ceremonial. We know from earlier contexts that, in Tambaran ideology, if ill will exists among the men of the village on such an occasion, Nggwal will detect it and deliver hardships rather than blessings. More fundamentally (but what amounts to the same thing), Galasala would not yield to consensus opinion; to Nggwal this is the greatest crime of all, even if committed with noble intent. The case reveals with particular clarity the strict Durkheimian sense in which Nggwal is the symbolic epitome of social cohesion: "the idea of society is the soul of religion" (Durkheim 1965:466). From another point of view, it might be said that the case exposes Nggwal as a corrupt deity: rather than standing above the ethical system he created, he is a part of it, subject to manipulation by the very men who proclaim his sacrosanctity, a judge suborned by the prosecution. And yet, it could not be otherwise: Galasala's fatal error was to forget (or never to have known) that Nggwal is "what men do," and that the "eternal" principles governing the religious system are ever answerable to their human creators. Galasala stood virtually alone in his defense of the Tambaran, thus committing, in the eyes of that same Tambaran, the unforgivable and capital offense of religious arrogance. It is, from all we have seen, a system that cannot tolerate prophets.

POWER AND AUTHORITY REVISITED

Taking the cases as a whole, the mode of resolution to the recurring crisis of death serves and interrelates various social, political and religious ends. By its intervention the Tambaran reminds the community of its abiding immanence: alive, vigilant, jealous of the cult it fosters. Given the wide range of acts construable as offenses against the cult, this presence is definitely a mixed blessing. Few persons are without blemish, and the promise of retribution aggravates an underlying or residual anxiety in individuals by reminding them of their constant vulnerability. If such a mechanism does not engender brotherly love among villagers, it does enforce a kind of harmony in which the interests of the individual are subordinated to those of the collective.

For guidance in times of public distress the community turns to the cult leaders, who alone hold converse with the ancestors and secret access to the Tambaran. To protect their privilege and authority the elders demonstrate these mystical prerogatives as often as possible. This entails a reaffirmation of Tambaran ideology, through which patterns of dominance are validated in the society. We have, then, an instance of what Firth (1951:247–248) has formulated in general terms:

the claims of the protagonists of religion to a special kind of knowledge of reality, to a revelation, a mystical experience, a traditional authority, take their place among the justificatory acts which seek to preserve the peculiar quality of that in which they have an interest. . . . the assumption of a unique source of authority is precisely the kind of sanction which religion needs in order to carry on.

At the same time, discord arising out of death by presumed sorcery is averted, not because everyone accepts the judgment without qualification, but because on any single occasion the great majority wish to see the matter carried no further—and in this, above all, they express the will of the Tambaran. Hence, the control mechanism may be viewed as a convention whose importance lies in promoting the high level of social cohesion implied by an enduring village as large as Ilahita.

The question arises, What of the cases in which Tambaran intervention is not invoked as an explanation for death? Material presented earlier indicates that the selection of the particular divination to be used prejudges the case for or against a Tambaran-related interpretation. This decision is reached in the moot of elders convened immediately after the death. The opinions expressed and the shape of the final consensus are the outcome of each participant's understanding of, and interest in, current political circumstances. Granted, if leaders are at the time in raw contention over some matter, and if a death occurs in the group of one of them, it will be difficult to avoid a political crisis. Significantly, however, to men in this senior position the strategy of splitting their group off from the main village is not advisable. They lack the physical vitality for this, and they also have the wisdom to see that their long-term advantage lies in remaining where their position is well established. As discussed in the previous volume, in former times segmentation also meant reduction of military security and possible annihilation for the small group separating itself from Ilahita. These factors combine to make the Tambaran diagnosis an extremely attractive way of managing a crisis and ensuring solidarity into the future. In rare instances where this expedient fails to be adopted, the conflict ensuing from the death takes the form of a dominance struggle between the principals and their immediate supporters, while the rest of the village maintains, as best it can, a steady neutrality until the smoke clears.

For the most part, however, benign relations tend to prevail within the group of village elders, especially among the initiates of Nggwal Walipeine. After a lifetime of political intrigue they know each other extremely well; they have stood together many times in battle and in ritual; prestige nuances among them are highly stable, enabling them to behave as amiable colleagues. Their interest lies not in advancing their position in the peer group, but in protecting their authority against the more vigorous and hotly competitive younger men, those of Nggwal Bunafunei. The danger of severe public disturbance centers on these younger men, who are impetuous and optimistic enough to think that splitting off from the main village can advance their careers— either as an independent settlement, or as a worthy addition to another, possibly enemy, village. The merit of the social-control mechanism described in the foregoing is that the authority behind it lies not in the hands of those whose political shenanigans constantly threaten village harmony and unity, but rather is exercised by prudent old men who recognize that their personal and collective self-interest coincides completely with the welfare of the village. Their agent is the Tambaran—the idealization of themselves—a human invention applied to extremely human problems.

THE GROWTH AND DEVELOPMENT
OF RELIGIOUS IDEOLOGY

Most of this chapter has been spent describing how the Tambaran neutralizes the disaffecting influence of sorcery beliefs by appropriating them to its own ideological purposes. Capitalizing on the mystery and implied violence of death, the Tambaran has made the sorcerer its own henchman and has firmly established itself in an area of experience that was formerly outside its sphere of interest. Strikingly homologous are the customs of official and judicial sorcery reported, for example, among the Trobrianders (Malinowski 1926:88ff.) and the Mekeo (Hau'ofa 1971). In those societies the legitimating authority is that of the chief, whose personal and institutional interests are served through the operation of sorcery beliefs. In Ilahita the homologous custom, while having far-reaching political implications, must also be understood as a creature of religious ideology. In this respect, the question is: What are the *theological* implications of the ethical system which was exemplified by the cases of Tambaran-sanctioned sorcery? The answer, I suggest, is that the functioning of this system has helped to resolve a theodicy in traditional Arapesh religious life, one brought about by the former indifference of the Tambaran to the problem of death in the community. Let me explain.

According to Obeyesekere (1968:11–12) "when a religion fails logically to explain human suffering or fortune in terms of its system of beliefs, we can say that a theodicy exists." It follows, therefore, that "in order to achieve a resolution the idea or ideas that fail to explain suffering or that pose logically untenable contradictions would have to be excised from the system of religious beliefs, or new ideas would have to be invented to counter the contradiction." In the Judaeo-Christian tradition, the problem of theodicy classically arises from the coexistence of a benevolent and omnipotent God with the logically contrary fact of unjust suffering in the world; resolution is effected through such notions as sin, salvation and divine inscrutability, which variously render the suffering meaningful in relation to religious truths.

In Ilahita, the problem of theodicy existed traditionally not because of a contradiction of the Judaeo-Christian type, but simply because Tambaran ideology did not formerly account for death due to disease, accident or other natural causes. By extending its jurisdiction into this area of experience in the post-pacification period, by generalizing the notion of *laf* ritual murder to include these sorts of deaths, the Tambaran did more than rescue the community from its own sorcery beliefs; it gave death meaning in relation to the ultimate sacred propositions of the society. Superimposing an ethical frame of reference on the amoral magicality of sorcery was a crucial step in the rationalization of Tambaran ideology. Death—life's greatest mystery—had become an object of moral discourse at the most public level, providing the community with frequent occasions on which to reaffirm their central and unifying values.

In closing this section, I can do no better than to quote Fredrik Barth's unsentimental account of the socially and morally debilitating effects of sorcery beliefs among the Baktaman (1975:134–135). It offers a vivid contrast to the rationalized form which has emerged in Ilahita.

Finally, the way in which a 'Sorcery Theory of Man' affects moral debate may be noted. The way we in the West conceive of morality is very closely tied to the notion of impartial judgement: my action may be right even though all others believe it to be wrong. The simplest, and perhaps commonest, way to conceptualize this idea of impartiality is by means of an almighty and all-knowing god. Our moral discourse obliquely refers to this: what were the objective circumstances, what ought a person to do in such a situation regardless of the particular pressures that might have been exerted on him. The Baktaman, on the other hand, have only their ancestral spirits, which are entirely human in their capriciousness and

subjectivity. And when the ultimate sanctions on a social relationship depend on the anger or pleasure of a sorcerous neighbour,
the exploration of the objective circumstances becomes irrelevant
at best. Moral discourse will concentrate on discovering the basis
for *affect* and the easiest way to rectify it, and secondarily to generate public opinion to frighten and make him step carefully. Once
relationships deteriorate from their everyday praxis of tact there
is nothing incongruous in turning to a grotesque theory: e.g. that
your neighbour's wife, because the piece of pork you gave her was
smaller than she had hoped, is angry enough to perform cannibal-
istic sorcery-murder.

CONCLUSION

It is a commonplace in anthropological methodology that
social conventions are best examined in the breach. To be
sure, Arapesh leaders use community disorder as occasions
for vociferous pronouncements on the rules of proper conduct. In the heat of the moment, these pronouncements are
often without effect, especially when the leaders are themselves among those causing the disturbance. The opportunity
for effective moral injunctions may come years later when,
with casuistic ingenuity, a second, unrelated event is made to
intersect causally with the first. The second event must be
a death—a common-enough occurrence in a village as large
as Ilahita—for only then may the cult leaders receive com-
munications from the ancestors. Evans-Pritchard's classic
example of fatal accidents among the Azande (1937:69–70)
showed how such casuistry is used to "explain" coincidences
that we would dismiss as the imponderable workings of Fate
or, perhaps, Providence. Arapesh sorcery beliefs are founded
on assumptions similar to those of the Azande. In Ilahita,
however, a new and transcendent form of explanation has
emerged. Sorcery remains the immediate cause, but it now
tends to be rationalized according to a Final Cause, which is
the Tambaran. Natural death has been effectively retrieved
from human hands and is taken to be a sign of divine dis-
approval and punishment. The ideology operates both to
confirm the efficacy of sorcery and to palliate its social and

psychological effects. Moreover, the existence of this mechanism, designed as it is out of indigenous parts, suggests that social, cultural and historical forces are converging in such a way as to fracture the chrysalis of magical causation and allow an entirely new form to begin unfolding. The nature and broader significance of this process will be the subject of my next chapter, to which we now turn.

10. The Voice of the Tambaran

THE anthropological study of another people's religion is a formidable undertaking, one demanding more than the usual degree of ethnographic humility. While the Voice of the Tambaran speaks with consummate clarity and eloquence to Arapesh auditors, to the outsider these utterances are often cryptic and must be deciphered, using the guide of Arapesh cultural principles combined with our own expectations about the way humans think and behave. The hermeneutic approach is most effective when the expressive form it addresses is limited enough to be "thickly" described (Geertz 1973). When, however, the object of interpretation is something so encompassing as the Tambaran, compromises are necessary. In the preceding chapters some aspects, most notably the economics of the cult, have been omitted; some ritual elements have been taken more or less at face value, included for the sake of descriptive completeness, while others have been wrung more vigorously for the meaning they bear. Throughout, my guiding objective has been to account for the Tambaran *as such*: the parts which compose it, the sources of its instrumental and expressive power, and, above all, the significance of the Tambaran's cultural and ideological wholeness. Leaving the basic ethnography to stand as its own summary, this chapter will review and expand upon some of the Tambaran's more abstract qualities, in particular those which argue in relation to broader issues in the study of religion. "And if perchance these arguments separately fail to convince you, nevertheless in combination their collective weight will be bound to do so" (Cicero, *De natura deorum*).

ETHICS AND RELIGIOUS EVOLUTION

The evidence culminating in chapter 9 suggests that the anthropology of the Tambaran bears on problems of traditional interest to the historian of religion. A critical moment in the development of religious ideology occurs if and when the transition is made from an epistemological system locked within the teleologies of magical thinking to one that is, so to speak, liberated by the emergence of a rationalized religious ethic. Because this is also the moment when the chronicles of so-called historical religions *begin*, it happens that scholars concerned with these great traditions usually lack the information necessary to reconstruct, with any degree of probity or precision, the sociocultural conditions governing the transition itself. In the absence of contemporary ethnographic materials, surviving texts such as the Gilgamesh epic are painstakingly scrutinized for distant glimmerings of the forces in ancient Mesopotamian society which produced a new religious consciousness. Such efforts, however ingenious, can achieve very little, and often they produce truistic, anthropologically vapid recitals of the sort given by the philosopher Whitehead in his *Religion in the Making* (1960: 33).

Rational religion emerged as a gradual transformation of the pre-existing religious forms. Finally, the old forms could no longer contain the new ideas, and the modern religions of civilization are traceable to definite crises of this process of development.

The form and function of Tambaran ideology suggests that the Arapesh have been recently undergoing such a moment of transition in their history. Moreover, the relevant sociocultural conditions are still reasonably accessible.

In positing this, I do not for an instant mean that an examination of Ilahita village will tell us what transpired in ancient Mesopotamia, or anywhere else for that matter. Beyond elucidating the dynamics of Tambaran ideology, my aim is to understand something of the general process through which religious ideas evolve in their particular historical settings. Furthermore, I propose that the Ilahita case is instructive of the errors of three general assumptions which have retarded the scientific study of religious change and evolution. The first of these, implied in Whitehead's remark, is the Hegelian notion that "ideas cause other ideas." While this assumption carries some weight when applied to a literate tradition, as a general proposition it fails by not recognizing the behavioral filter through which all culturally salient ideas, especially religious ideas, constantly circulate. A major theme of my study has been the mutuality between religious ideas and their social and cultural environment.

The second assumption embodies what might be called the "uniformitarian fallacy." This is the tendency to regard the community as essentially undifferentiated with respect to religious knowledge and commitment. Here, admittedly, the Arapesh are an extreme case: men, women and children belong to distinct religious subuniverses. And yet, this extremism highlights two additional features of more general significance. First, religious process operates to a large extent on the very basis of these category differences. Where, we might ask, would the men's cult be without the ostracized women? Even the children have a crucial role in the propagation of cult images. It is clear that, just as these distinctions and oppositions lend themselves to the Tambaran as it now exists, so they will figure prominently in the dynamics of future change in this system. Second, the gross distribution of religious knowledge should not obscure the clear differentiation of awareness *within* ritual categories. Whether for reasons of temperament or circumstance, adherence to Tambaran doctrine in word, thought and deed is a constantly fluctuating commodity in the society.[1] And, indeed, with-

1. In 1927 Paul Radin, provoked by what he construed as a defamatory bias in Lévy-Bruhl's studies of primitive mentality, published a book whose object was to prove that religious philosophers and sceptics are to be found in *all* societies (Radin 1957). While this recognition of intellectual diversity brought Radin to the verge of an improved theory of cultural evolution, his exclusive focus on temperamental determinants and on distinguished individual philosophers led him, instead, in the nugatory direction of "great man" theories of history. Intent on refuting Lévy-Bruhl, Radin ignored the full range of diversity within a society, and the conditions temperamental and situational under which it is manifest. Ironically, by highlighting the exception Radin was, if anything, proving the rule which Lévy-Bruhl was supposedly promulgating.

out such variation it is difficult to conceive how religious change of an authentically evolutionary sort could occur at all.

The third assumption in need of correction is the hoary idea that religious and intellectual evolution advances by definable stages. Late in the last century, when anthropologists began to investigate primitive societies in search of clues to the origins of civilization, their commitment to an orthogenetic evolutionary view blinded them to the more complex and subtle features of evolutionary *process*. Regrettably, the reaction of succeeding decades was not to repair the defects of this paradigm, but to discredit the evolutionary perspective altogether, leaving us with no satisfactory way of dealing with processes of change in epistemological traditions. Considering, for example, the amount of anthropological ink that has been spilled on the subject of magical belief systems, the following passage from Keith Thomas's *Religion and the Decline of Magic* (1971:643) must be read as a sad and poignant indictment of our discipline. After noting that such systems of thought cannot by virtue of their logical closure be undermined from within, Thomas writes:

> The most difficult problem in the study of magical beliefs is thus to explain how it was that men were able to break out of them. This is a topic on which social anthropologists have as yet thrown little light, and it is one which the historian of Tudor and Stuart England must also find peculiarly intractable. The period abounded in sceptics, but it is rarely that one comes upon documented instances of an individual's loss of faith. Contemporary literature was written by men who occupied well-defined positions; it throws little light on how people come to change their minds. Nevertheless, we must try to determine the circumstances which made traditional modes of magical thought appear increasingly out-dated.

In a footnote to the same passage Thomas corroborates this assessment by citing Jarvie and Agassi (1967:71): "The really urgent sociological problem posed by magic" is "can people with inefficient magical beliefs come to be critical of them, under what conditions and to what extent?"[2]

---

2. LeVine (1973:269) has answered this challenge with an intriguing, albeit somewhat speculative, analysis which interprets the precipitous decline of English

These authors appear to assume that societies jettison their magical beliefs with relative suddenness; that social and intellectual forces converge on a point of ideological breakthrough; that at one moment people are thinking magically, at the next they are not. Such was also the implication of my earlier reference to Ilahita's "moment of transition" from a magically based to an ethically based religious system. But if our interest is in the circumstances leading up to such a change, then this kind of intellectual catastrophism will not do, for it fails to take account of the less visible processes of change proceeding in the population of believers before and after the moment which an outsider perceives to be transitional.[3] The abrupt expression of new forms of thought at some point in time, such as occurred during the epoch described by Thomas, in no way testifies to the absence of those forms during the preceding period. On the contrary, the likelihood is that they were present but that various social or other factors prevented their free and open expression. In Ilahita, skepticism is often evinced about Tambaran beliefs, and there is no reason to suppose that these reservations are not as ancient as the beliefs themselves. Until now, sociocultural conditions have militated in favor of such doubts remaining private and to some extent unformulated; by the same token, it is easy to imagine that a change in these conditions could suffice to permit or encourage their open expres-

---

witchcraft beliefs as resulting in part from a marked change in child-rearing practices during the generation preceding this decline.

3. In his Gifford Lectures, Edwyn Bevan (1938) mentions only one of the many difficulties facing the student of historic religions when he tries to discern, from a distance of thousands of years, these more diffuse aspects of religious change. Speaking of the history of Judaism, he writes: "It is impossible to say exactly when the grosser anthropomorphic ideas [about Jehovah] gave place to more spiritual ones, because the old language continued in general use long after the ideas it covered had undergone essential change. Even to-day we commonly speak of the eyes of God or the hand of God. The ideas changed by a subtle and gradual process under the uniform language, and it is often impossible to say in regard to the documents of a particular time how far expressions relating to God or the unseen world were understood literally by those who used them, how far only as symbols." [P. 253]

All the more reason why ethnographers should take advantage of whatever opportunity presents itself to understand the movement from literal to figurative systems of meaning.

sion. For the actors, the ensuing revelation would be that others have unknowingly shared their private thoughts *all along*. When this happens, there is nothing to prevent the establishment of the new mode with nearly explosive rapidity. Only one whose access to this process is limited to the gleanings of public documents or other records of the achieved event would find the suddenness of the changeover mysterious or perplexing.

For the Arapesh the transition from magic to ethics is, needless to say, far from complete.[4] The ideas and practices centered on the Tambaran are redolent with magical elements, enabling the Arapesh to continue to satisfy the urge to participate in the cosmic and theistic forces which rule their lives. The important point is that the Tambaran has come to symbolize Arapesh tradition as conceived by the actors to be an autonomous idea, an almost palpable entity. As such, the Tambaran stands as the ultimate value to which social thought and action can be referred. In its most abstract aspect the Tambaran transcends its magical origins and becomes the focus of an ethical system whose relevance reaches far beyond religious matters per se to embrace the very way of life from which it springs.

4. It is questionable whether the transition is *ever* complete. Consider the following statement by Max Weber (1963:143–144): "Belief in providence is the consistent rationalization of magical divination, to which it is related, and which for that very reason it seeks to devaluate as completely as possible, as a matter of principle. No other view of the religious relationship could possibly be as radically opposed to all magic, both in theory and in practice, as this belief in providence which was dominant in the great theistic religions of Asia Minor and the Occident."

Weber's distinction is certainly valid, and his comments focus the evolutionary import of the divination procedures described in chap. 9 of this study. Still, he appears in this passage too willing to ignore the fact that even these "great theistic religions" display—in the practice of laymen, if not in the practice of priestly theorists—varying commitments to a magically colored view of the world. Prayer for the attainment of personal advantage is the obvious example. Weber's overdrawn position may be part of his reaction to the excesses, in the years just prior to 1913, of psychological approaches to religious phenomena and ideas (1946: 286). For, to admit that magic is present in (or inevitably attendant on) even the most rationalized faiths would instantly suggest that emotion is a factor in the individual's adherence to religious doctrine, and that, in accounting for the genesis and operation of religious ideas, the sociological determinist is on no firmer ground than is his psychological counterpart.

A rationalization of this magnitude both feeds upon and nurtures a corresponding transformation in the social sphere. Emerging from a fragmented society in which various residence and descent groups pursue distinct and often contradictory interests in the name of their unique tambarans, the Tambaran, as a kind of super-tambaran, crystallizes the spiritual significance common to all these lower-level entities, thereby morally unifying the community and providing a compelling idiom through which an ever shifting majority is able to rationalize its will in an endless variety of situations. Conversely, Tambaran doctrine is itself contingent on majority and/or dominant interests in the society. In the end, therefore, the ultimate revelation is that the Voice of the Tambaran is the voice of men raised to a power.

Weber (1946:286) reached similar conclusions in his analysis of the "rational religious pragmatism of salvation"—a doctrine which, "flowing from the nature of the images of God and of the world, [has] under certain conditions had far-reaching results for the fashioning of a practical way of life." Religious values and social structure are mutually determinative:

the nature of the desired sacred values has been strongly influenced by the nature of the external interest-situation and the corresponding way of life of the ruling strata and thus by the social stratification itself. But the reverse also holds: *wherever the direction of the whole way of life has been methodically rationalized*, it has been profoundly determined by the ultimate values toward which this rationalization has been directed. These values and positions were thus religiously determined. Certainly they have not always, or exclusively, been decisive; however, they have been decisive in so far as an *ethical* rationalization held sway, at least so far as its influence reached. [Pp. 286–287, first emphasis added]

Likewise, this study has shown that the sacred values epitomized by the Tambaran are dictated largely by the interests of the adult males. Conversely, dominance relations are expressed and legitimated by ritual distinctions—between males and females, and between males of different age and ritual standing. Insofar as these categories also form the prime differentiae of social life, the religious values informing them are decisive in their influence over conduct. And, since the ethical rationalization illustrated in the previous chapter connects great public concerns with the most intimate problems of social actors, the nature of this influence is, at least potentially, absolute (Weber 1946:287).

The limitation of this line of analysis is that it *presupposes* the sweeping rationalization with which it begins. Given that the Tambaran epitomizes the Ilahita Arapesh way of life, it is a simple tautology to conclude that that way of life is suffused with religious meaning. The prior task is to establish that the Tambaran does in fact possess the symbolic grandeur attributed to it, and to ascertain, if possible, the psychocultural and historical factors underlying its ascendency. In short, the rationalization itself must be accounted for, if we are to understand how the corresponding set of values exerts its influence. In the remaining pages, let us consider the Tambaran with this object in mind.

DIMENSIONS OF A NEW IDENTITY

We have seen that the Tambaran Cult in Ilahita achieved its present form at a time when the Arapesh were under stress from Middle Sepik tribes invading their territory from the south. Collective security was at a premium; previously scattered bands gathered together into large, defensible villages (Tuzin 1976); new social forms developed in response to the altered settlement patterns; and, as a parallel development, clan-specific tambarans united under the patronage of a *village*-specific spirit entity—the Tambaran. Ironically, many of these organizational and religious innovations are traceable to the cultural traditions of the invaders, having been imported and naturalized to the Arapesh system of meanings. Most importantly, the establishment of large, stable villages (especially Ilahita) radically expanded "the range of persons to whom moral rules are held to be applicable" (Ginsberg 1953:119), thus setting the precedent and the predisposition for subsequent historical events—in particular, contact with white foreigners—to stimulate further symbolic growth in the shape of a rationalized religious ethic centered on a fully cognized notion of the Tambaran as an expression of cultural identity. I will return to this point in a few moments.

In cultural terms the symbolic supremacy of the Tambaran is grounded in an ideology which systematically imbues experience and existence with religious meaning. Growth and maturation are ritually ordained as the individual advances through culturally salient life-stages. And, while Tambaran doctrine formally excludes females from this benefice, their participation is none the less elaborately entailed: first, because the ritual differentiation of masculinity defines femininity as a residual type; second, as wives, mothers, sisters and daughters of ritual actors, women have a part in Tambaran proceedings, and indeed a good deal of the necessary work depends on them; finally, the entire thrust of Tambaran ideology is predicated on the existence of a class of cult outsiders. The Tambaran also bestows fertility on all species and regulates the natural order. As champion of village wars, it is the provider of physical security and dictates the pattern of truce and hostility according to its ritual schedule. In a broader sense the Tambaran, president of a cult of war, virtually monopolizes violence: since the cessation of warfare and ritual homicide, its sanguinary appetite has been appeased by natural deaths in the community, many of which are construed to have been caused by or on behalf of the Tambaran. Furthermore, violence is an essential component of nearly all cult activities: in the brutal hazing of lower-grade novices; in the mock (but not always bloodless) attacks staged between ritually interdependent groups; and in the unceasing threats aimed at females and junior males. A loving, punishing parent, the Tambaran demands steady devotion in return for its spiritual patronage.

The exercise of such devotion, though costly in human and material resources, is profoundly meaningful. Quite apart from the alleged advantages to be gained from the magic of the ritual, the exaltation of the Tambaran is at once the celebration of personal and collective identity, reaching ultimately to a level of significance at which the metaphysics of self merge with, and are indistinguishable from, the highest values of the culture. This quality of sublime expressiveness is most evident in the symbolism of cult art, architecture, and mythology; but, it is equally present in the many areas of ritual action. When personal motivation is brought into such close accord with collective interests and ideological prescriptions, the necessary conditions are met for the formation of a rationalized ethic. Conduct and morality are now referrable to a monotheistic figure which is compellingly "real" because it projects the qualities and concerns of humans both alone and in society. Its transcendence renders the Tambaran a useful agent of social control, while its autonomy equips it as a vehicle for the creation of new metaphors. Both features are, of course, illusory; but their functional consequences are real and important as mediators between the sociocultural as against the strictly religious significances of the Tambaran. We have witnessed numerous examples of the Tambaran operating in social-control contexts. As regards its metaphoric utility, a few more examples may help to clarify the *meaning* of the Tambaran in terms of this analysis.

One lazy, sunny afternoon a circle of middle-aged men sat lounging in front of the spirit house, wistfully speculating on the private merits of a local beauty. During a lull in the conversation one of them—a notorious wag who usually instigated such topics—took a deep drag on his cigarette, exhaled soulfully over his shoulder, peered for a long moment at the structure looming behind him, and then said with an exaggerated sigh: "Let me open my trousers. *Then* she'll see the Tambaran!" The others were highly amused.

A trivial incident, it nevertheless illustrates how certain elements of Tambaran ideology (in this case masculinity and secrecy) may be used as a symbolic link between a situation in need of immediate expression and the higher values of the culture. As a more telling example, one hears the mysteries of menstruation and childbirth referred to as "the Tambaran of the women." And again, when asked what the children played at all day in the forest, one man—who, after all, had once played in the forest himself—testily replied, "How do I know? That is *their* Tambaran." Such figures of speech are indicative of the symbolic productivity of the Tambaran. That is to say, the concept has evolved semantically to such a point that it is no longer bound to initial or primary meanings and is, correspondingly, easily recruited to the creation of new metaphors and other symbolic forms. Some of these may be trivial or quaint, as in the preceding examples. Others, as the current discussion is intended to show, may have grand consequences for the developing character and expressive potential of Arapesh culture.[5]

Leaving aside these figurative possibilities, the profusion of primary meanings surrounding the Tambaran is already considerable. The concept refers simultaneously to things and to the categories subsuming these things. This plurality points to a criterion of pure abstractness: the Tambaran possesses an implied significance which transcends ad hoc manifestations while also imbuing them with a quality loosely describable as "sacredness." This is the symbolic foundation for the Tambaran's versatility and influence in social life and ideology; for, as anticipated above, once the concept is established at this abstract level, it becomes available for further semantic elaboration and for manipulation in the service of expressive or instrumental ends. Of course, the same potential exists for all components of culture; only, in the case of the Tambaran, by virtue of its involvement with central existential concerns (fertility, sexuality, dominance, death, etc.), this tendency is carried to a remarkable extreme. Moreover, with its essential character defined so abstractly, the Tambaran is able to gather new elements to itself easily and without, for the most part, violating doctrinal consistency. In view of the fact that such additions are proclaimed by human agents (the cult leaders) whose authority is thereby enhanced, it is not surprising that the Tambaran tends to have imperial-

5. The most famous parallel case concerns the influence of Calvinist doctrine over the course of economic development in the pre-industrial West as analyzed in Weber's classic study (1958). Both instances have to do with the symbolic productivity, under particular circumstances, of religious themes, images, and prescriptions. Cf. the opening discussion of this chapter.

istic appetites and is eager to extend its influence into new and uncharted cultural areas.[6]

The intellectual and political manipulation of the Tambaran, observed many times during this study, verifies that its nature includes a quality of profound abstractness. However much everyday conversation tends to label a given thing (or lower-level concept) as "the Tambaran," its abiding significance is that of a constructed reality, a Gestalt which unites a complex of ideas and experiences into a symbol of broad metaphysical stature. Only by stressing this aspect can we interpret the fact (hitherto ignored in the analysis) that the Arapesh language contains no word meaning "Tambaran." To be sure, there is a host of terms—both common and proper nouns—denoting the many manifestations of the Tambaran, but with regard to its abstract aspect the Arapesh speaker is silent. Like the well-worn case of the Eskimo having no general term for "snow," the concept is of such central importance to the culture, so much *the* context for life itself, that it surpasses the need for conscious reflection or concern. Certainly for the traditional Arapesh the concept of the Tambaran was profoundly implicit.

Then, during the two decades following 1935, changes occurred which prompted the creation of a new level of Arapesh self-awareness. As a chronicle for these years is provided elsewhere (Tuzin 1976), let me say only that it was a period of unprecedented contact between the Arapesh and other societies. The suppression of warfare by the Australians permitted wider local travel, introducing the Arapesh to neighbors near and far in the Sepik region. Also, growing numbers of young men contracted to work on the coastal and island plantations, bringing them into contact with New Guineans of diverse cultural character. Then, of course,

6. After some initial hesitation, cult leaders granted me permission to photograph Nggwal novices as they crawled through the spirit-house portal. Accordingly, the first thing the frightened suppliants beheld on entering the house was the blinding flash of my camera attachment. The senior initiates instantly seized on this as a splendid addition to the repertoire of Tambaran devices and besought me to supply them with a flash unit for use in future initiations. If the Arapesh are "an importing culture" (Mead 1938), then the Tambaran must surely be the Grand Acquisitor!

there were encounters with missionaries, administrators, employers, even Japanese occupation troops. Westerners, who have pondered the fact of cultural differences since the time of Herodotus, are poorly equipped to appreciate the impact of these revelations on a complacent, nondefined Arapesh identity which had previously supposed that the world ends at the horizon.[7] Imagining, if we can, the rearrangements that would be forced upon our own philosophy if contact were to be made with extraterrestrial intelligence, we may well understand that the Arapesh experience was, in a sense, a discovery of themselves. Other Melanesian groups have reacted to this situation in ways too various to summarize, though cargo cultism is perhaps the most widespread (and extreme) means for signifying cultural entities and relationships in a world of suddenly unfamiliar proportions. The people of Ilahita, however, applying an age-old strategy, incorporated the White Man into their epic myth of creation ("Nambweapa'w"), and then elevated their own cultural selfhood by formulating the supreme, but previously transparent, values governing their lives.[8] And because the inter-

---

7. One might suppose that contact with adjacent groups would have familiarized the traditional Arapesh with the relativity of cultures. Other circumstances, however, prevented such an awareness from developing very far. Between the Arapesh and their neighbors there was a good deal of social (including marital) interaction; their customs overlapped considerably; and, though the Arapesh regarded the others as rather odd in some ways, including the languages they spoke, there was apparently no systematic reflection on cultural differences per se. Furthermore, adjacent traditions were seen to intermingle with those of the Arapesh. So, for instance, the story of Nambweapa'w tells of a common origin for the Arapesh and all other groups known to them. Even the culture-hero Baingap (chap. 8) spent his retirement years among foreigners.

   Perhaps the clearest indication of cultural "innocence" is that the Arapesh, like many other ethnographic subjects, have no name for themselves—even though they and their neighbors have names for each other. The latter fact suggests, paradoxically, the existence of a "self-consciousness de facto" on the part of traditional cultural groups. The self-contradiction of the marked phrase is no problem if we allow that the culturally expressive value currently assigned to the Tambaran must have existed previously in some latent or intuited form.

8. There is a striking parallel in the rise of prophets among the Sudanic Nuer and Dinka. These are men claiming inspiration from the supreme being who presides over the lesser spirits involved in more limited social spheres. For the Dinka, "any marked increase in the importance of the wider world must be associated with a marked increase in emphasis on the supreme being" (Finnegan and Horton 1973:47). Furthermore, in their convergence with the formal properties of Islam and Christianity, such moves "open up fascinating possibilities

cultural exchanges prompting this development were spoken through the Melanesian lingua franca, it is fitting that the name given to this congeries of values be taken from Pidgin English: Tambaran. Thus rationalized, Arapesh culture entered a new phase of self-knowledge and ethical coherence.

In conclusion, the Tambaran is more than the sum of ideas and artifacts associated with the men's cult; it is the very sign and symbol of Arapesh culture, the personified mystique of a total way of life. When children play in the forest, when women menstruate or give birth, they are engaged in uniquely self-defining acts; it is their natural custom to do these things, it is their Tambaran. As for the men, while ritual may bestow on them the potencies of play, menstruation and fecundity, in the end these are nothing more than illusions. The true nature of men—their custom, their Tambaran—is to exercise grave stewardship of that wondrous legacy which sustains a world of meaning and order. In this, they are nobly fulfilled.

---

for an understanding of the so-called 'conversion' of pagan peoples to these two great monotheistic religions. 'Conversion' has long been a puzzle for historians, for anthropologists, and, most of all, for missiologists. In the light of the analyses by Evans-Pritchard and his associates and of the instances of movement toward the supreme being before direct influence by Islam and Christianity, it becomes less mysterious. The move toward a more monotheistic religion can be seen as an inherent possibility of the pre-existing system, actualizable in specific social and political circumstances. Islam and Christianity are catalysts, hastening reactions all of whose necessary ingredients were already 'in the air.'" (Ibid.)

Similarly, Christianity has been a catalyst (one among several) in the process of religious change in Ilahita, and it would be simplistic to infer that the monotheistic tendencies of the Tambaran are merely imitations of the foreign creed. As an intimate and utterly faithful exponent of Arapesh cultural identity, nothing could be more indigenous than the Tambaran.

11. Epilogue

THE flowering of Tambaran ethics in Ilahita village was stimulated by a crisis of cultural identity. That crisis has now largely passed, and the society has entered a post-transitional phase in which the future of the Tambaran is very much in doubt. Today's generation of young adults grew up with an easy awareness of the outside world, and it is impossible for them to share the bewilderment and suspicion of their elders in the face of radically alien cultural forms. Increasingly, their concerns and activities lie where the Voice of the Tambaran cannot reach them. The older people view this trend with sad resignation; for they know that the Tambaran will not sing if it is not heard, and that when its song stops, the world—*their* world—will end forever.

Appendix A.
Selected Glossary
of Technical, Vernacular
and Pidgin English Terms

Afa'afa'w: Senior sub-moiety status, meaning "those who go first"; cf. Ondondof

age-set: Age-based subdivision of the initiation sub-class consisting of the senior brothers (Balangaisi) and the junior brothers (Owangufwisi)

Balanga: Residential ward of Ilahita village; population, 309

Balangaisi: Senior age-set, signifying "senior brothers"; cf. Owangufwisi

Bandangel: Totemic moiety of Ilahita village, subsuming the wards of Ililip, Bwi'ingili and half of Nangup; totemic moiety of Ilifalemb ward; cf. Laongol

Bunafunei: Junior grade of Nggwal, entered between the ages of fifteen and fifty

Bwi'ingili: Residential ward of Ilahita village; population, 172

Falanga: Lowest grade in the Tambaran Cult, entry into which marks separation from the mother and the advent of childhood; sago variety (pl. *falangax*)

***hangamu'w*:** Known in Pidgin English as 'tumbuan,' a full-body costume with wickerwork helmet mask representing a spirit of the Falanga Tambaran grade (pl. *hangahiwa*)

Hengwanif: Residential ward of Ilahita village; population, 148

Ilifalemb: Residential ward of Ilahita village; population, 213

Ililip: Residential ward of Ilahita village; population, 487

initiation class: Village-based dual structure, localized in the patriclan, and subsuming cyclically alternating statuses of Sahopwas (elder brothers) and Owapwas (younger brothers); actualized through individual or patriline partnerships whose parties refer to one another as *ombaf*

initiation sub-class: Dual generation division within the initiation class, subsuming Senior (father) and Junior (son) statuses

kwongwof: Large ceremonial spear which is part of the Nggwal paraphernalia (pl. *kwongwalef*)

laf: Pig- or cassowary-bone dagger; licensed ritual homicide or sorcery executed in the name of the Tambaran spirits

Laongol: Name of an Ilahita patriclan; totemic moiety of Ilahita village, subsuming Balanga and Hengwanif wards and half of Nangup ward; totemic moiety of Ilifalemb ward; cf. Bandangel

Lefin: Second grade in the Tambaran Cult, entered in middle childhood; also, *lefin*—general term for edible sago (pl. *lefis*)

'limbum':   A palm (*Kentiopsis archontophoenix*) whose wood is used for spears, floors, walls and other purposes; its tough, fibrous spathe (flower sheath) is fashioned into baskets and is used as wrapping material

Maolimu: Third grade in the Tambaran Cult, signifying the advent of social adolescence and sexual maturity; also, *maolimu*—the growing point of a sago palm (pl. *maolihiwa*)

maolinimuna: Known in Pidgin English as 'masalai,' one of a diverse array of nonhuman sentient beings who are usually mischievous or moderately dangerous in their dealings with humans: nature spirits (anthropo- or zoomorphic), demons, sprites, imps and ogres (pl. *maolinipunemb*)

'masalai':   See *maolinimuna*

moiety: Totemic, nonexogamous dual structure obtaining at the village level and dividing Balanga and Hengwanif wards and half of Nangup ward (Laongol moiety) from the wards Ililip, Bwi'ingili and the other half of Nangup (Bandangel moiety); the division has significance in ritual and in conventional competition

'mumu':   A process of steam cooking with hot stones and leaves, usually in a pit oven or an above-ground bundle oven

Nangup: Residential ward of Ilahita village; population, 161

nautamana: Ritual competitive partner belonging to the opposite moiety; a partnership also said to obtain between individual Nggwal spirits belonging to opposite moieties

Nggwal: Highest level in the Tambaran Cult, divided into junior and senior grades (see "Bunafunei" and "Walipeine")

ola'w: Secondary food-exchange partner belonging to the opposite initiation class (pl. *olawa*)

ombaf: Primary and hereditary food-exchange and initiation partner belonging to the opposite initiation class and (ideally) the opposite sub-clan of Ego's clan (pl. *ombif*)

Ondondof: Junior sub-moiety status, meaning "those who come behind"; cf. Afa'afa'w

owaloman: Kinship term of reference, "younger brother"; cf. *sahaloman*

Owangufwisi: Junior age-set, signifying "junior brothers"; cf. Balangaisi

Owapwas: Metaphorically, "younger brothers"; name applied to the junior initiation class, those currently not in possession of Nggwal Bunafunei; cf. Sahopwas

Owapwasinguf: Junior sub-clan, "younger brothers' line"; cf. Sahopwasinguf

'pangal': The woody midrib of the sago-palm frond; its narrow end is suitable as light planking material, while its splayed base is used for sitting and sleeping mats and as flats for painting

'pitpit': A cultivated grass (*Saccharum edule*) whose tasty inflorescence is eaten either roasted or as an ingredient in sago soup

sahaloman: Kinship term of reference, "elder brother"; cf. *owaloman*

Sahopwas: Metaphorically, "elder brothers"; name applied to the senior initiation class, those currently in possession of Nggwal Bunafunei; cf. Owapwas

Sahopwasinguf: Senior sub-clan, "elder brothers' line"; cf. Owapwasinguf

'singsing': As used in this work, a festival (usually nocturnal) involving singing, dancing and feasting

sub-moiety: Dual structure localized at the ward level, like elements of which combine to crosscut the moiety structure at the village level; subsumes Afa'afa'w (senior) and Ondondof (junior) ritual categories

su'witip: A bright orange, inedible shrub fruit, with semiglossy skin and spongy consistency, which is a popular decoration item for masks and ritual structures (pl. *su'witix*)

'tambaran': Among the Arapesh, the religious ideology, practice and technology centering on the men's secret cult; also, one of the many spirits of this cult

'tulip': A medium-sized tree (*Gnetum gnemon*), grown in the village, whose leaves are a common ingredient of sago soup or are cooked along with meat and other greens, either in a 'mumu' oven or in a bamboo tube placed in the open fire

Walipeine: Senior grade of Nggwal, entered after approximately the age of fifty

Appendix B.
Mythic Variation
and the Naturalization of Meaning

To illustrate the degree and kind of variance typically encountered between alternative versions of the same story, I have recorded below the myth of Kataomo as it was recited to me by another storyteller (chap. 7). Beyond certain noncontradictory differences at the level of detail it is noteworthy that the second storyteller is concerned less with the Tambaran component than with the *quality of relationships* portrayed among the actors—in particular, the mother's anguish over her children being given to the initiation partner for cannibal consumption. Note also that the second version—perhaps in keeping with its more pronounced affective tone—juxtaposes two images of monstrous sexuality: the explicit coupling of pig and snake, issuing in the several pigs primordially acquired by mankind, and the brother-sister incest implied by the fruitful marriage of these siblings during their life in the cave. Although the inclusion of parents, initiation partners and others would seem to rule out the suggestion that the brother-sister pair were ancestral in any ultimate sense, a primordial significance is strongly suggested by the "precultural" overtones of such items as innocent sibling incest, a radical disregard of species boundaries, an image of men as benighted cannibals who in effect prey upon their own children, and—not at all least in Arapesh male eyes—the idea of a civilized existence devoid of pork.

These remarks confirm that the proper analysis of a myth should take account of all extant versions. For, what we see is that the two renditions function together to link the Tambaran firmly with Arapesh mythic ideas having ontological significance. The rather contrived cameo appearance of Nambweapa'w in the myth of Kamba'wa (also chap. 7) is another instance of an Arapesh cast being applied to a story that is probably new to their repertoire. By means such as this, religious elements originating in foreign cultures—whether expressed mythically or otherwise in their indigenous setting—have been naturalized to the Arapesh system of meaning.

KATAOMO II

Long ago there were no pigs and our ancestors ate human flesh instead. If a man had four children, he kept the eldest and the youngest. But the two middle children—a son and a daughter—he killed and gave to his initiation partner to eat. Later, his initiation partner returned two of his own children to be eaten.

One time there was a man with four children, and he was ready to offer the two middle ones to his partner. His wife was very upset and cried to the daughter that she and her brother were about to be killed and eaten. The girl told this to her brother. They were frightened and wondered where they could hide. Then the boy took the spine of a sago leaf and went to a mountain called Tata Maninda, near Utamup village. With the sharpened spine he dug a hole in the mountain. He cleared well: part of the inside of the hole he made into a place for sleeping, another a place for cooking, another a place for defecating.

When he returned to the village, his mother cut his and his sister's hair in preparation for their being killed. The mother cried to her daughter that the men were readying everything for cooking and eating the children. That night, the two children pretended to sleep in their house, and when everything was quiet they broke through the rear of the house and ran away to hide in the cave in the mountain Tata Maninda.

One day, the brother and sister saw a baby pig emerge out of a wild ginger plant. At the same time a big python came into the cave. The children looked after both of the animals. When the pig was grown it copulated with the snake and produced many piglets. Then the children killed the mother pig and ate it, finding the flesh very delicious. For many years they stayed in the cave, killing and eating pigs from time to time.

Meanwhile, their parents had searched everywhere, and had finally decided that the children must have run away and that something had killed them. But they were still hiding in the cave, and when they were grown the son married his sister. They had many children. One day they killed and cooked a pig. The husband decided he would sneak back to their village to see if their mother was still alive. He found his mother alone in front of her house, and when he approached her she was very happy to see him and amazed at how much he had grown. The son asked her what part of the house she slept in, adding that he would return that night to give her something. When she had shown him he returned to Tata Maninda and fetched a leg of pork. He returned to the village that night and aroused his mother by pushing a stick through the thatch of her house. She let him in through the front door, and the son gave her the meat, saying that it was bad to eat human flesh and that she must cook this meat and try it.

The mother cooked the pig next morning and found it very delicious. The next time her son brought her some pork he told her to cook it and give part of the meat to her husband, his father, to taste. As she gave her husband the cooked meat, he was suspicious, and he asked who it was he was eating. She replied that this was not human flesh, but it was something else which their eldest son had given her. The husband tasted it and liked it very much. He went to his eldest son and asked where he had gotten the meat, but the son denied having given his mother anything. The man went back to his wife and asked her again. This time she said her sister's husband had given it to her, but on being asked about this the man too denied having given anything to the woman. After that, the wife admitted that it was their second son who had given her the meat. The husband was angry, because the woman had not told him of his son's visit so that he might see and talk with him. The wife told him not to sleep that night, but to lie awake and wait until the son visited her. He could hear him as they talked.

And so it was as she said. The son returned that night with a leg of pork, and when the father heard his adult voice he realized how long his children had been gone, and he wondered where they lived. He listened to what his son said to his wife. "Tomorrow you and my father must gather all the villagers together. They must bring yams and sprouted coconuts. The yams they must leave in the village. Then they should carry their coconuts and gather at the waterfall at the foot of the mountain Tata Maninda. When they are all gathered they must (ceremonially) break the coconuts and call out. If they hear anything respond to this, they must not be frightened. If they want to run away, my father must stop them and order them to remain so that they can see what will happen."

Early the next morning the old couple did what they had been told. When the villagers broke the coconuts at Tata Maninda they were alarmed to hear an enormous voice, the voice of the tambaran, answer them: "Who are you?" Everyone was frightened but the old man told them to stay. A figure appeared at the top of the mountain, followed by two pigs. The figure was the decorated son, who was now the tambaran named Kataomo. They all went to the village where a feast was held and the two pigs were given to

Kataomo to eat. Then the son returned to Tata Maninda, where he and his wife/sister gathered up all their pigs and put them into netbags. They carried them back to the village and gave one pig to each man. That is how we came to have pigs. Some of the pigs ran away and they are the wild pigs of the forest. Before, when we did not have pigs, we had to eat human flesh.

Appendix C.
Nggwal and
Population Flux

In presenting the following brief sociology of Nggwal within a demographic context, my intention is to relate the subject of Arapesh ritual to certain issues developed in the previous study (Tuzin 1976). I refer in particular to the central thesis that the complex dual organization of Ilahita village is to be understood largely as a structural accommodation to population pressures brought on by the influx of refugees displaced by Kwanga and Abelam as they encroached from the south. The methodological plan was to show that the elaboration and maintenance of the organization is traceable to the cumulative effects of individual actions conditioned by the press of broadly shared circumstances amid the constraints of equally shared cultural understandings. The emergent structures, it was seen, serve well to foster village solidarity by neutralizing latent and overt aggression—or, indeed, redirecting it into socially positive channels. Omitted from that analysis was virtually the entire ritual side of these structures, without which their motivational underpinnings (in both instrumental and *expressive* aspects) cannot be fully comprehended. Descriptions of lower-grade initiations have noted in passing that the ceremonies are organized around dual structures—initiation classes, age-sets, sub-moieties and the like—but Nggwal is the proper context in which to address the topic directly and in proper detail.

In what follows, the relevant aspect of Nggwal is that which consists of a multiplicity of named spirits, each associated with a particular clan. This suggests a simple distribution of nggwals in the population. Each clan, it is recalled, contains two sub-clans— Sahopwasinguf and Owapwasinguf—relating to each other as ritual partners (Sahopwas-Owapwas). The system provides for one nggwal per clan, which at any given time is in the possession of one of the sub-clans; until the next Nggwal initiation, that sub-clan holds the senior title of Sahopwas. Additionally, each spirit is paired with another nggwal in the enemy ward of the opposite moiety, with whom it competes in feasts and other ceremonial activities. These two nggwals (or, if you like, the two groups associated with them) refer to each other as *nautamana*, "enemy."

In formal terms the connection between social structure and Tambaran classification is obvious enough. However, the situation that has developed in Ilahita through the demographic turbulence of the last century recalls Lévi-Strauss's resigned remark that, "whenever social groups are named, the conceptual system formed by these names is, as it were, a prey to the whims of demographic change which follows its own law but is related to it only contingently" (1966:66). All the more so when the names in question are predicated on the notion of dual symmetry.[1] It is therefore incumbent on me to show how the tidy scheme of nggwals and groups outlined above has managed to survive the "whims of demographic change." It is advisable to begin by examining comparable structures in a village whose demographic history has been relatively quiescent.

Utamup is a small village (pop. 180) near the Kwanga border. The population is bilingual, and current residents are hard pressed to decide which language (Arapesh or Kwanga) is indigenous and which acquired. Local informants explain that the population is too small to warrant subdivision into residential wards, and accordingly the village occupies a single contiguous settlement. There are only six clans, unevenly distributed between the opposed moieties (table 1). Utamup's nggwals, their client clans and *nautamana*, are shown in table 2. A comparison of these data with those of table 1 discloses the nature of the relationship between ritual structures and demographic change—the short answer being that the former has modified in response to the latter.

In all likelihood the asymmetry between Utamup moieties arose historically from the expansion and segmentation of Moiety-B clans. But the clan level has been rectified in the ritual field by the creation of new nggwal spirits. Hence, Afanim and Utamup clans possess two nggwals apiece and are therefore able to interact ritually with all four opposite clans. Nangup's second nggwal, Elimif, by

---

1. Mechanisms for the maintenance of symmetry among the groups themselves were examined in the previous volume (Tuzin 1976:242).

TABLE 1: *Utamup Clans and Moieties*

	Moiety A	Moiety B
	Afanim	Nangup
	Utamup	Bawakem
		Tatemba
		Balanga

TABLE 2: *Utamup's Nggwal Tambarans*

Nggwal	Proprietor clan	nautamana
Saonei (A)[a]	Utamup	Gandi (B)
Bila'wamwi (A)	Utamup	Windu (B)
Mangieli (A)	Afanim	Nggwas (B)
Gwawi (A)	Afanim	Konowau (B)
Konowau (B)	Nangup	Gwawi (A)
Elimif (B)	Nangup	—
Gandi (B)	Bawakem	Saonei (A)
Nggwas (B)	Balanga	Mangieli (A)
Windu (B)	Tatemba	Bila'wamwi (A)

[a] Refers to moiety affiliation.

not having a *nautamana* reveals two things about itself: first, it exists in name only and does not have a set of ritual paraphernalia; second, it is probably of recent origin or introduction. Men of Nangup clan are not subdivided vis-à-vis their two nggwals (as are the men of Utamup and Afanim clans), but rather they simply maintain the name of Elimif and attend to it only cursorily. And, significantly, a nggwal such as Elimif would not with its present status be credited with a *laf* killing or any supernatural power whatever. Its future depends almost entirely on demographic trends: should the membership of either Utamup or Afanim increase relative to the other clans, another nggwal could perhaps be established in the expanding clan to act as Elimif's *nautamana*. Or, if Nangup clan declines in membership, interest in Elimif may dwindle or expire altogether.

Given the requirement of structural symmetry in the ritual system, and the troublesome instability of natural populations, the creation or adoption of additional nggwals disguises the fact that numbers are out of synchrony with structurally balanced categories. There is probably a limit beyond which continued uneven growth would compel a major redefinition of moiety affiliations if any semblance of numerical symmetry was to be preserved. In the meanwhile, however, the generating of new nggwals deals with the problem less traumatically than, say, relocating clans residentially to accord with new moiety alignments, or effecting the segmentation of small clans. The nggwal system is thus a painless fiction for redressing demographically related imbalances in structural domains of greater everyday importance, namely, in matters of residence and descent affiliation.

Turning to Ilahita village—but keeping in mind the Utamup case—the situation is found to be more complex. As before, clarity is best served by focusing on a representative part of the whole. The example of Balanga ward adequately illustrates the structural effects of demographic change in a large village containing multiple wards in ritual communication with one another (table 3).

Omitting Galawei from consideration by virtue of its nominality, it can be seen in table 3 that each of the three major clans of Balanga possesses two nggwals. Bundahimbil clan, with only seven adult male members, is at present too small to support even one nggwal.

TABLE 3: *Nggwals of Balanga*

Nggwal	Proprietor clan	nautamana	
		Ililip	*Nangup*
Elimif	Laongol	Nimbea	
Galawei[a]	Laongol		
Nggwas	Laongol	Windu	
		Nimbea	
Gwawi	Owapwi	Sao	Kamba'wa
Nanganenga	Owapwi	Ko'ombale	
	Bundahimbil	Daondamba	
Sowambon	Sahopwi	Wanimbea	
	Owapwi[b]		
Tantagafum	Sahopwi	Wanimbea	
	Hengwanif[b]		

[a] Refers to a nominal nggwal without power or full cult paraphernalia.
[b] Clans of Hengwanif ward.

They have accordingly paired with the other clan in their sub-moiety, Owapwi, in joint association with Nanganenga. Indeed, the merger occurred with only one sub-clan of Owapwi, thereby accentuating the ritual cleavage within that descent group. Sahopwi clan is in partnership with two clans of Hengwanif ward (Owapwi and Hengwanif), both of which belong to the Afa'afa'w sub-moiety. This anomaly is explained by a Sahopwi clan legend which traces one line of their ancestry to that ward.

Nggwal alignments generally parallel descent groupings—though they do so more clearly in Utamup than in Ilahita—and they also reflect moiety and sub-moiety oppositions. Thus, Balanga is of the Laongol moiety, while Ililip and the Nangup clan controlling Kamba'wa are of the Bandangel moiety. Moreover, within this larger opposition the division occurs *within* the cross-cutting sub-moieties. The clans controlling Elimif and Nimbea, respectively, are both Afa'afa'w, just as Gwawi and Sao are both Ondondof. Consequently, for all levels of village organization—moieties, wards, sub-moieties, clans, initiation classes—the concept of Nggwal provides a ritual expression.

When the composition of nggwal distributions is analyzed further, it is found that table 3 glosses over an internal complexity. What emerges is not an exact fit of clan with nggwal spirit, but rather a strong statistical tendency in that direction (table 4). Despite the irregularities of nggwal affiliations as shown among Balanga clans, note, first, that in cases of multiple ownership of a particular nggwal, one of the clans clearly predominates numerically. For instance, in the first three listed, Laongol clan outnumbers Owapwi and Sahopwi. This tendency allows us to accept (in a statistical sense) the claims by informants that, for example, Nggwas "belongs" to Laongol, even though it is shared with Owapwi and Sahopwi.[2]

Second, with the exception of Gwawi the number of clans (and sometimes persons as well) is greater for the Sahopwas class than for the Owapwas. The reason is bound up with the political behavior surrounding these ritual affiliations—a subject that was touched on in the previous volume (Tuzin 1976:285). In preparing the large Nggwal initiation, the Sahopwas class is interested in attract-

2. The anomaly of men from opposite sub-moieties sharing the same nggwal—a theoretical impossibility—results from informal ritual "friendships" contracted between men for a short time, often for a single ceremony. I do not deal here with this complication, except to say that a man tied informally to a nggwal not his own does not pass the status on to his heir(s).

TABLE 4: *Internal Compositions of Balanga Nggwals*

Nggwal	Sahopwas initiation class	Owapwas initiation class
Elimif	Laongol (7)	Laongol (10)
	Owapwi (3)	
Galawei	Laongol (5)	Laongol (5)
	Owapwi (2)	
	Sahopwi (1)	
Nggwas	Laongol (4)	Laongol (4)
	Owapwi (1)	
	Sahopwi (1)	
Gwawi	Owapwi (10)	Owapwi (11)
		Laongol (2)
		Balangapwi (1) [a]
Nanganenga	Owapwi (6)	Bundahimbil (4)
Sowambon	Owapwi (3) [b]	Sahopwi (5)
	Hengwanif (1) [b]	Laongol (1)
	Laongol (1)	
	Balangapwi (1) [a]	
Tatangafum	Hengwanif (2) [b]	Sahopwi (5)
	Tata (1) [c]	

[a] Belongs to Bwi'ingili ward.
[b] Belongs to Hengwanif ward.
[c] Belongs to Ililip ward.

ing Owapwas Seniors to bolster their work strength. This leads to a number of men taking the prestigious "middle position" vis-à-vis the two initiation classes; that is, they assume as an additional responsibility an unoccupied status in the opposite initiation class and operate the exchange system in both directions at once (ibid., p. 239). The younger and more ambitious Owapwas accept such invitations, gaining the prestige of possessing, if only for a time, another nggwal spirit. Indeed the invitation is itself a mark of honor, signifying that the other group regards his industry and yam excellence as an asset. In the great majority of cases, however, this arrangement is short lived: few men can perennially produce enough yams to carry the burden of a double partnership indefinitely. Nevertheless, the situation I have just described does give men with promise an opportunity to sample and test themselves in a position of potentially great renown.

Bibliography

ARNOLD, JENNIFER M.
1972   "Part III. Climate of the Wewak–Lower Sepik Area." In *Lands of the Wewak-Lower Sepik Area, Territory of Papua and New Guinea*, compiled by H. A. Haantjens, pp. 49–60. Melbourne: Commonwealth Scientific and Industrial Research Organization.

BARTH, FREDRIK
1975   *Ritual and Knowledge among the Baktaman of New Guinea*. New Haven: Yale University Press.

BATESON, GREGORY
1935   Music in New Guinea. *The Eagle: St. John's College Magazine* 48:158–170.
1936   *Naven*. London: Cambridge University Press.

BETTELHEIM, BRUNO
1953   Individual and Mass Behavior in Extreme Situations. *Journal of Abnormal and Social Psychology* 38:417–452.
1954   *Symbolic Wounds: Puberty Rites and the Envious Male*. Glencoe, Ill.: Free Press.

BEVAN, EDWYN
1938   *Symbolism and Belief*. London: George Allen & Unwin.

BOAS, FRANZ
1911   Review of *Methode der Ethnologie* (by Fritz Graebner). *Science*, N.S., 34:804–810.

BURRIDGE, KENELM
1969   *Tangu Traditions*. London: Oxford University Press.

CHURCHILL, WILLIAM
1890   The Duk-Duk Ceremonies. *The Popular Science Monthly* 38:236–243.

DURKHEIM, EMILE
1965   *The Elementary Forms of the Religious Life* (first published in 1912). New York: Free Press.

EPSTEIN, A. L.

1969   *Matupit: Land, Politics, and Change among the Tolai of New Britain*. Canberra: Australian National University Press.

EVANS-PRITCHARD, E. E.

1937   *Witchcraft, Oracles and Magic among the Azande*. Oxford: Clarendon Press.

FEUERBACH, LUDWIG

1972   *The Fiery Brook: Selected Writings of Ludwig Feuerbach*. Translated by Zawar Hanfi. Garden City, N.Y.: Anchor Books.

FINNEGAN, RUTH, AND ROBIN HORTON

1973   "Introduction," In *Modes of Thought: Essays on Thinking in Western and Non-Western Societies*, edited by Ruth Finnegan and Robin Horton, pp. 13–62. London: Faber & Faber.

FIRTH, RAYMOND

1936   *Art and Life in New Guinea*. London: The Studio Ltd.

1951   *Elements of Social Organization*. London: Watts.

FORGE, ANTHONY

1962   Paint—A Magical Substance. *Palette* 9:9–16.

1966   Art and Environment in the Sepik. *Proceedings of the Royal Anthropological Institute, 1965*, pp. 23–31.

1973   "Style and Meaning in Sepik Art." In *Primitive Art and Society*, edited by Anthony Forge, pp. 169–192. London: Oxford University Press.

FORTUNE, R. F.

1935   *Manus Religion: An Ethnological Study of the Manus Natives of the Admiralty Islands*. Lincoln: University of Nebraska Press.

1942   *Arapesh*. New York: J. J. Augustin.

GEERTZ, CLIFFORD

1973   *The Interpretation of Cultures*. New York: Basic Books.

GELL, ALFRED

1975   *Metamorphosis of the Cassowaries: Umeda Society, Language and Ritual*. London: Athlone Press.

GINSBERG, MORRIS

1953   On the Diversity of Morals. *Journal of the Royal Anthropological Institute* 83 (pt. 2): 117–135.

GIRARD, RENÉ

1977   *Violence and the Sacred*. Baltimore: Johns Hopkins Press.

HALLOWELL, A. IRVING

1955   *Culture and Experience*. Philadelphia: University of Pennsylvania Press.

HAU'OFA, EPELI

1971   Mekeo Chieftainship. *Journal of the Polynesian Society* 80(2):152–169.

HERSKOVITS, MELVILLE J.

1948   *Man and His Works: The Science of Cultural Anthropology.* New York: Knopf.

HIATT, L. R.

1971   "Secret Pseudo-Procreation Rites among the Australian Aborigines." In *Anthropology in Oceania: Essays Presented to Ian Hogbin*, edited by L. R. Hiatt and C. Jayawardene, pp. 77–88. Sydney: Angus and Robertson.

HOGBIN, IAN

1970   *The Island of Menstruating Men: Religion in Wogeo, New Guinea.* Scranton, Pa.: Chandler.

JARVIE, I. C. AND J. AGASSI

1967   The Problem of the Rationality of Magic. *British Journal of Sociology* 18(1):55–74.

KABERRY, PHYLLIS M.

1941   The Abelam Tribe, Sepik District, New Guinea: A Preliminary Report. *Oceania* 11:233–258, 345–367.

KEESING, ROGER M.

n.d.   Review of *Culture and Practical Reason* (by Marshall Sahlins). *American Anthropologist* (forthcoming).

LANGER, SUSANNE K.

1953   *Feeling and Form.* New York: Scribner.

LAYCOCK, DONALD C.

1973   Sepik Languages: Checklist and Preliminary Classification. *Pacific Linguistics*, ser. B, no. 25.

LEACH, EDMUND

1954   *Political Systems of Highland Burma.* Boston: Beacon Press.

1976   *Culture and Communication: The Logic by Which Symbols Are Connected.* Cambridge: Cambridge University Press.

LEVINE, ROBERT A.

1973   *Culture, Behavior, and Personality.* Chicago: Aldine.

LÉVI-STRAUSS, CLAUDE

1963   "Do Dual Organizations Exist?" In *Structural Anthropology*, by C. Lévi-Strauss, pp. 132–163. New York: Basic Books.

1966   *The Savage Mind.* Chicago: University of Chicago Press.

LÉVY-BRUHL, LUCIEN

1935   *Primitives and the Supernatural.* New York: Dutton.

LEWIS, GILBERT
1975   *Knowledge of Illness in a Sepik Society: A Study of the Gnau, New Guinea*. London: Athlone Press.

LIFTON, ROBERT JAY
1961   *Thought Reform and the Psychology of Totalism*. New York: Norton.

MALINOWSKI, BRONISLAW
1926   *Crime and Custom in Savage Society*. London: Routledge & Kegan Paul.

1961   *Argonauts of the Western Pacific* (first published in 1922). New York: Dutton.

MEAD, MARGARET
1934   Tamberans and Tumbuans in New Guinea. *Natural History* 34(3):234–246.

1938   The Mountain Arapesh: An Importing Culture. American Museum of Natural History, *Anthropological Papers* 36(3):139–349.

1940   The Mountain Arapesh: Supernaturalism. American Museum of Natural History, *Anthropological Papers* 37(3):319–451.

MIHALIC, FRANCIS
1971   *The Jacaranda Dictionary and Grammar of Melanesian Pidgin*. Brisbane: Jacaranda Press.

MUNN, NANCY
1977   The Spatiotemporal Transformations of Gawa Canoes. *Journal de la Société des Océanistes* 33(54–55):39–53.

NEEDHAM, RODNEY
1972   *Belief, Language, and Experience*. Oxford: Blackwell.

NEWTON, DOUGLAS
1971   *Crocodile and Cassowary: Religious Art of the Upper Sepik River, New Guinea*. New York: Museum of Primitive Art.

OBEYESEKERE, GANANATH
1968   "Theodicy, Sin and Salvation in a Sociology of Buddhism." In *Dialectic in Practical Religion*, edited by E. R. Leach, pp. 7–40. London: Cambridge University Press.

POPPER, KARL R.
1957   *The Poverty of Historicism*. London: Routledge and Kegan Paul.

POWDERMAKER, HORTENSE
1933   *Life in Lesu: The Study of a Melanesian Society in New Ireland*. London: Williams & Norgate.

POWELL, WILFRED
1884   *Wanderings in a Wild Country; or, Three Years amongst the*

Cannibals of New Britain. London: Sampson Low, Marston, Searle, and Rivington.

RADIN, PAUL

1957   *Primitive Man as Philosopher* (first published in 1927). New York: Dover.

SAHLINS, MARSHALL

1976   *Culture and Practical Reason.* Chicago: University of Chicago Press.

SAPIR, EDWARD

1917   Do We Need a "Superorganic"? *American Anthropologist* 19:441–447.

SCHIEFFELIN, EDWARD L.

1976   *The Sorrow of the Lonely and the Burning of the Dancers.* New York: St. Martin's Press.

SCHWARTZ, THEODORE

1963   Systems of Areal Integration: Some Considerations Based on the Admiralty Islands of Northern Melanesia. *Anthropological Forum* 1:56–97.

1973   Cult and Context: The Paranoid Ethos in Melanesia. *Ethos* 153–174.

SPIRO, MELFORD E.

1951   Culture and Personality: The Natural History of a False Dichotomy. *Psychiatry* 14:19–46.

1963   Causes, Functions, and Cross-Cousin Marriage: An Essay in Anthropological Explanation. *Journal of the Royal Anthropological Institute* 94:30–43.

THOMAS, KEITH

1971   *Religion and the Decline of Magic.* New York: Scribner.

THURNWALD, RICHARD

1916   Banaro Society: Social Organization and Kinship System of a Tribe in the Interior of New Guinea. American Anthropological Association, *Memoirs* 3:253–391.

TURNER, VICTOR W.

1967   *The Forest of Symbols: Aspects of Ndembu Ritual.* Ithaca: Cornell University Press.

TUZIN, DONALD F.

1972   Yam Symbolism in the Sepik: An Interpretative Account. *Southwestern Journal of Anthropology* 28(3):230–254.

1974   "Social Control and the Tambaran in the Sepik." In *Contention and Dispute: Aspects of Law and Social Control in Melanesia,* edited by A. L. Epstein, pp. 317–344. Canberra: Australian National University Press.

346 / BIBLIOGRAPHY

1975 The Breath of a Ghost: Dreams and the Fear of the Dead. *Ethos* 3:555–578.

1976 *The Ilahita Arapesh: Dimensions of Unity.* Berkeley and Los Angeles: University of California Press.

1977 Reflections of Being in Arapesh Water Symbolism. *Ethos* 5:195–223.

1978a Politics, Power and Divine Artistry in Ilahita. *Anthropological Quarterly* 51(1):60–67.

1978b Sex and Meat-Eating in Ilahita: A Symbolic Study. *Canberra Anthropology* 1(3):82–93.

VALENTINE, C. A.

1961 *Masks and Men in a Melanesian Society: The* Valuku *or* Tubuan *of the Lakalai of New Britain.* Lawrence: University of Kansas Publications.

VAN GENNEP, A.

1909 *Les rites de passage.* Paris: Emile Nourry.

WAGNER, ROY

1972 *Habu: The Innovation of Meaning in Daribi Religion.* Chicago: University of Chicago Press.

WEBER, MAX

1946 *From Max Weber: Essays in Sociology.* New York: Oxford University Press.

1958 *The Protestant Ethic and the Spirit of Capitalism.* New York: Scribner.

1963 *The Sociology of Religion.* Translated by Ephraim Fischoff. Boston: Beacon Press.

WEBSTER, HUTTON

1968 *Primitive Secret Societies: A Study in Early Politics and Religion* (first published in 1907). New York: Octagon Books.

WEDGWOOD, CAMILLA H.

1933/34 Report on Research Work on Manam Island. *Oceania* 4(4):373–403.

WHITEHEAD, A. N.

1960 *Religion in the Making* (first published in 1926). New York: Macmillan.

WINTER, E. H.

1963 "The Enemy Within: Amba Witchcraft and Sociological Theory." In *Witchcraft and Sorcery in East Africa*, edited by J. Middleton and E. H. Winter, pp. 277–299. London: Routledge and Kegan Paul.

Index

Malinowski, B., 35, 122n, 307, 344

Manam, 50n

Manus, 285n

Maolimu tambaran, 26, 31–32, 40n, 79–115 *passim*, 130, 231, 235n, 279, 291n, 328

Maolinimuna. See Masalai

Maprik sub-district headquarters, 11, 143, 260, 261

Marriage, xvi, 16, 21–22, 23, 66n, 99n, 113, 172; in mythology, 5, 168–169, 331, 332

Masalai, 42, 72, 88–89, 134n, 147, 205, 328

Masculinity, 32, 37, 56, 57, 72, 73, 76–78, 81, 139, 169, 182, 231, 301, 302–303, 320, 324; acquisition of, 80, 104–106, 117

Mask, 34, 40, 48, 51n, 177. *See also* Costume; *Hangamu'w*

Master artist. *See* Artist

Masturbation, 71, 75–76

Maternal bond, 46, 72, 80, 104, 106n, 113n, 279

Maulas, 45, 189n, 259. *See also* Ancestral spirits

Mead, M., xiv, 11, 39n, 49, 100n, 109n, 120n, 256, 303n, 322n, 344

Mekeo, 307

Menstrual house, 4, 34, 35, 92, 153, 221

Menstruation, 2, 19, 85, 113, 139, 221n; male envy of, 77; as ritual idiom, 84, 86, 320, 324

Mesopotamia, 312

Metamorphosis, 5, 7, 280; of cassowaries, 1–3; of dancers, 222; of flying foxes, 88–89, 94, 103, 109, 114, 115; of houses, 4, 158; of Imoina, 251, 253, 281n; of Imoina's wife, 253

Metaphor, xiii, 57, 84n, 146, 154, 157n, 211, 260, 290, 320–321, 324, 325; in art, 177–178; in Falanga, 38n, 39, 40, 43; in Lefin, 58; in Maolimu, 84, 85, 86, 87–88, 95, 100, 103; in Nggwal Bunafunei, 212, 219, 220, 221n, 226n, 227n, 229, 236, 242, 248–249; in Nggwal Walipeine, 258–259; in spirit-house construction, 132, 137, 160, 161n, 163n. *See also* Expressiveness; Sign; Symbol

Metaphysics, 72–73, 117, 140–141, 169, 177–178, 180, 186–192, 210, 222, 223–226, 268, 295, 300–302, 304, 309–310, 322–324, 325. *See also* Sign

Methodology, xiv, xv, 23, 127–128, 154, 202–203, 224, 226, 255, 262–263, 265–266, 270n, 309, 311, 312–315. *See also* Ontology

Mihalic, F., xvii, 344

Mimi'unemb, story of. *See* Mythology

Mitchell, W., 158n

Mock attacks, 61–65, 95, 98, 110n, 194, 227–229, 232, 234–236, 239, 240–241, 274, 275, 301, 319. *See also* Violence

Moiety, 29, 87, 91–92, 110, 111, 216n, 328, 337, 338, 339. *See also* Dual organization

Morality, 22, 208, 263, 308. *See also* Tambaran ethics

Mountain Arapesh, xvii, 109n. *See also* Mead, M.

Mui village, 238

Mundugumor, 120n

Munn, N., 122n, 344

Murder. *See* Homicide

Mythology, xv, 35–36, 127n, 155, 173, 189–193, 207n, 209, 218, 222, 254, 265, 320, 331–332; Ambupwiel, 61n, 88–89, 91n, 99; Baingap, 250–253, 280–283; The Dogs and the Maolimu Tambaran, 79, 302; Kamba'wa, 134, 205–206, 210, 240n, 257, 258, 273n; Kataomo, 206–207, 210, 211, 331, 332–334; Mimi'unemb, 55, 57; Nambweapa'w, 1–8; Ngwangwa'um, 116–117, 157, 169; Olafen, 106n, 134n, 168–169, 178n, 211; The Woman and the Falanga Tambaran, 34–35

Nahiana, case of, 291–293, 303–304

Nambweapa'w, xv, 8–11, 19, 134, 240n, 282; myth of, 1–8, 61n, 81, 283n, 298n, 303, 323n; relation to Tambaran, 9–10, 189, 190, 192–193, 205, 265, 278, 281n, 301. *See also* Iconography; Symbol

Naturalization of meaning. *See* Diffusion

Nautamana. See Ritual enemy

Needham, R., 261n, 344

New Britain, 50n

New Ireland, 50n

Newton, D., 119, 120n, 344

Nggwal, 83, 109, 111n, 113, 117, 134, 140, 148–149, 166, 254–258, 329, 336–340; attributes of, 129, 191–192, 301–302; and death, 142–146. *See also* Tambaran

Designer:	Jim Mennick
Compositor:	G&S Typesetters, Inc.
Printer:	Thomson-Shore, Inc.
Binder:	Thomson-Shore, Inc.
Text:	VIP Baskerville
Cloth:	Joanna Arrestox B 51000
Paper:	55 lb. P&S Offset Regular